Birds of Botswana

Princeton Field Guides

Rooted in field experience and scientific study, Princeton's guides to animals and plants are the authority for professional scientists and amateur naturalists alike. **Princeton Field Guides** present this information in a compact format carefully designed for easy use in the field. The guides illustrate every species in color and provide detailed information on identification, distribution, and biology.

Birds of Aruba, Curaçao, and Bonaire, by Bart de Boer, Eric Newton, and Robin Restall
Birds of Australia, Eighth Edition, by Ken Simpson and Nicolas Day
Birds of Borneo: Brunei, Sabah, Sarawak, and Kalimantan, by Susan Myers
Birds of Botswana, by Peter Hancock and Ingrid Weiersbye
Birds of Central Asia, by Raffael Ayé, Manuel Schweizer, and Tobias Roth
Birds of Chile, by Alvaro Jaramillo
Birds of East Africa: Kenya, Tanzania, Uganda, Rwanda, and Burundi, by Terry Stevenson and John Fanshawe
Birds of East Asia: China, Taiwan, Korea, Japan, and Russia by Mark Brazil
Birds of Europe, Second Edition, by Lars Svensson, Dan Zetterstrom, and Killian Mullarney
Birds of the Horn of Africa, by Nigel Redman, Terry Stevenson, and John Fanshawe
Birds of India, Pakistan, Nepal, Bangladesh, Bhutan, Sri Lanka, and the Maldives, by Richard Grimmett, Carol Inskipp, and Tim Inskipp
Birds of Kenya and Northern Tanzania: Field Guide Edition, by Dale A. Zimmerman, Donald A. Turner, and David J. Pearson
Birds of Melanesia: Bismarcks, Solomons, Vanuatu, and New Caledonia, by Guy Dutson
Birds of the Middle East, by R. F. Porter, S. Christensen, and P. Schiermacker-Hansen
Birds of New Guinea, by Thane K. Pratt and Bruce M. Beehler
Birds of Peru, by Thomas S. Schulenberg, Douglas F. Stotz, Daniel F. Lane, John P. O'Neill, and Theodore A. Parker III
Birds of Southeast Asia, by Craig Robson
Birds of Southern Africa, Fourth Edition, by Ian Sinclair, Phil Hockey, Warwick Tarboton, and Peter Ryan
Birds of Thailand, by Craig Robson
Birds of the West Indies, by Herbert Raffaele, James Wiley, Orlando Garrido, Allan Keith, and Janis Raffaele
Birds of Western Africa, by Nik Borrow and Ron Demey
Parrots of the World, by Joseph M. Forshaw
Raptors of the World, by James Ferguson-Lees and David A. Christie

Birds
of Botswana

Peter Hancock and Ingrid Weiersbye

Dr. Stephanie J. Tyler, Scientific Editor

PRINCETON UNIVERSITY PRESS
PRINCETON AND OXFORD

"Unpublished information benefits no one."
—Kenneth Newman, ornithologist, artist, and author

Text and range maps copyright © 2016 by Peter Hancock
Illustrations copyright © 2016 by Ingrid Weiersbye

Requests for permission to reproduce material from this work
should be sent to Permissions, Princeton University Press

Published by Princeton University Press, 41 William Street,
Princeton, New Jersey 08540
In the United Kingdom: Princeton University Press, 6 Oxford Street,
Woodstock, Oxfordshire OX20 1TW

press.princeton.edu

Cover art of Kori Bustard and Southern Carmine Bee-eater by Ingrid
Weiersbye

ISBN 978-0-691-15717-7

Library of Congress Control Number: 2015939781
British Library Cataloging-in-Publication Data is available

This book was produced by Zona Tropical Press (project manager:
Robin Kazmier; designer: Gabriela Wattson; editor: Amy Hughes)
This book has been composed in Myriad Pro
Printed on acid-free paper. ∞
Printed in China

10 9 8 7 6 5 4 3 2 1

Contents

Foreword

As avitourism gains popularity around the world, Botswana is host to increasing numbers of bird-watchers who come to observe our beautiful and abundant birdlife. These visitors travel from near and far with good reason. There is no better place in the world to see the Slaty Egret or Wattled Crane than the Okavango Delta, for example, and the magnificent Kori Bustard, the national bird of Botswana, that roams our Kalahari grasslands is truly a stunning sight to behold. But these exceptional birds are just a few of the nearly 600 species found in Botswana's varied habitats. With several internationally recognized Important Bird Areas, Botswana is of crucial importance to scores of species.

Now more than ever, ecological tourism and the conservation of our avifauna are important to Botswana's future. Peter Hancock and Ingrid Weiersbye's outstanding new field guide will undoubtedly make an important contribution in these areas. This comprehensive volume—meticulously researched and exquisitely illustrated—reflects the most up-to-date information available on the birds of Botswana, and will certainly be an invaluable tool for bird-watchers, scientists, and local naturalist guides for years to come. Adding to its immense value is the fact that it's truly a homegrown product—by including species names in Setswana as well as interesting local information, Hancock has made the book relevant and accessible to all Batswana. Additionally, Weiersbye has made a monumental effort to accurately illustrate the specific subspecies found in Botswana, creating a vast collection of illustrations that is truly representative of the birds found within the country.

I am confident that this work will succeed not only in engaging the international community of bird-watchers, but also in nurturing the interest of citizens and advancing their knowledge of the birdlife that is such an important part of our heritage. I congratulate the authors on their extraordinary efforts, which are reflected in each and every page of this field guide.

Lieutenant General Seretse Khama Ian Khama
President, Republic of Botswana

Acknowledgments

One does not simply sit down and write a field guide of this nature based on personal field observations (even if they do span a 25-year period); it is necessary to consult all available literature to verify and supplement these original data. In this respect, Wendy and Remigio Borello's *Birds of Botswana: An Annotated Working Bibliography, 1835 - 1995* was a huge kick-start, and my only regret is that it didn't cover the intervening 20 years up to the present! The regional bird journals, particularly *Babbler* (Botswana), but also *Honeyguide* (Zimbabwe), *Lanioturdus* (Namibia) and *Ostrich* (South Africa) were also invaluable sources of information. *Gabar* and *Vulture News* provided items of interest related to raptors in Botswana. The recently established Maun Bird Forum has also been useful. I owe an enormous debt of gratitude to Margaret Koopman at the Niven Library of the Percy FitzPatrick Institute of African Ornithology, for tracing obscure references with unabating good humor.

The *Bird Atlas of Botswana* (1994), compiled by the late Huw Penry, informed the species range maps, although many required considerable updating thanks to huge advances in our knowledge of certain species since the atlas was published. In that regard I must thank Chris Brewster for sharing his detailed knowledge of bird distribution in Botswana. Taryn McCann and John Mendelsohn both assisted with technical aspects of map drawing, and I greatly appreciate their patience and support. In compiling the breeding bars, I drew greatly from Ken Oake's "Observations of Birds Breeding in Botswana" (2014); it contains almost 3,000 records of 220-plus species. In addition, he has been unstinting in sharing his knack for finding birds' nests! Neville Skinner's summary of bird breeding seasons in Botswana (1995, 1996, and 1997), published in *Babbler*, was also useful in this regard. Desmond Cole's *Setswana—Animals and Plants* (1995) remains the "bible" for local bird names, although Sekgowa Motsumi and many local professional guides graciously contributed information on vernacular names. I am also indebted to Johan van Jaarsveld for generously sharing a lifetime of knowledge on raptors and providing detailed information on raptor identification in Botswana. Thanks, too, to Drs. Glyn Maude and James Bradley of Raptors Botswana for their support throughout the project.

Most of all, I'd like to pay tribute to the "Big Four" Botswana birders who have the definitive information on our birds at their fingertips, and who have shared much of it over the years. They are (in alphabetical order): Chris Brewster, Mark Muller, Richard Randall, and Stephanie Tyler. I thank each of them for enriching my understanding of Botswana's avifauna, and thereby contributing to this field guide. Additional thanks are due to Stephanie Tyler for undertaking the onerous and exacting role of Scientific Editor. I am also doubly indebted to Richard Randall for checking through several drafts of the manuscript.

This book has benefitted tremendously from the professional input of John McCuen and Robin Kazmier at Zona Tropical Press and Robert Kirk at Princeton University Press. I also wish to thank designer Gabriela Wattson and editor Amy Hughes, whose hard work is evident in the quality of the final product.

Last but not least, Ingrid Weiersbye's massive contribution to this guide in the form of over a thousand precise, meticulously executed, original illustrations is obvious, and I am grateful to have had an artist of her caliber on this project. However, she has gone much further than that, and provided detailed information from her own field observations of Botswana's birds, thereby effectively co-authoring this guide. Even a hippo sinking our boat at Lake Ngami could not put a damper on her commitment to documenting firsthand the riches of Botswana's avifauna! I look forward to our next book together.

Peter Hancock

It was a privilege to be approached by Peter Hancock to illustrate a field guide to one of my favorite birding destinations, the country of Botswana.

I must first thank John McCuen of Zona Tropical Press, who took a giant leap of faith in initiating this first field guide dedicated to the birds of Botswana—an area he had never been to—with strangers he had never met. I also thank Robin Kazmier of Zona Tropical for her work managing the project, and designer Gabriela Wattson for her meticulous work in putting together a beautiful book.

The best part of such a project is always the research, and I owe a huge debt of gratitude to Dr. Hugh Chittenden, Chairman of the John Voelcker Bird Book Fund, for access to his library of superb digital photo references, and his awesome field skills that have so extended my own. I am also grateful to Bill Howells for sharing his raptor expertise, Dr. Robert Payne for his learned contribution in helping me with the Viduidae (Whydahs and Indigobirds), and Dr. David Johnson for his invaluable help with the Euplectes (Bishops and Widows).

I must also thank my son Sean, who sorted out my computer issues and kept me online and connected. And finally, I extend my deepest gratitude to my ecologist husband, Roger Porter. He has been my birding companion in the field, and although sorely neglected for the long hours I shut myself away in the studio, remains generously supportive of every project I tackle.

Ingrid Weiersbye

Introduction

The objective of this book is to provide a comprehensive, user-friendly guide to the birds of Botswana for the layperson, including both citizens and residents of Botswana, and visitors to the country. The species accounts treat the 595 species known to occur in Botswana as of November 2014; new species that appeared during the production of the book are covered in the appendix on page 384. Botswana's bird species come from 92 families. Particularly well represented are diurnal and nocturnal raptors, cuckoos, francolins and spurfowls, larks, cisticolas, and, perhaps surprisingly for a semiarid country, ducks, geese, herons and egrets, and waders. Seabirds, by contrast, are virtually absent.

Botswana at a glance

Botswana is a landlocked country in the center of the southern African plateau, covering a total area of 581,730 sq km (224,607 sq mi). It has a semiarid climate with annual rainfall ranging between 25 cm (10 in) in the southwest and 65 cm (26 in) in the northeast. Botswana has two main seasons: a hot summer from November to April (during which rain falls) and a dry winter from May to October. The overall dryness is intensified by the fact that most of the country is overlain by deep sands that soak up any rain that falls. These conditions make the area a semidesert, with

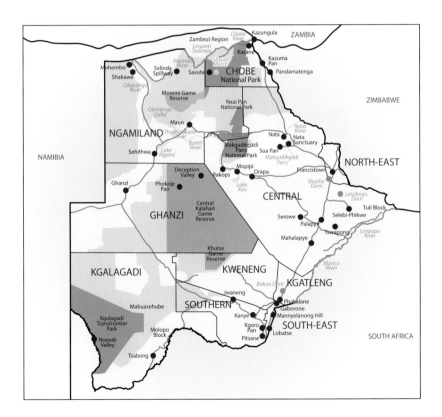

sufficient rainfall for plants to grow but an almost complete absence of surface water. As a result, Botswana's vegetation mainly comprises deciduous Kalahari woodlands and shrublands as well as extensive grasslands. A further consequence of the sandy terrain is that the topography is very flat—the windblown sands form an essentially level surface ranging from 1,000 to 1,150 m (3,280 to 3,770 ft) in elevation.

A few large tropical rivers are found along sections of the eastern and northern borders. What is referred to as the Kwando-Linyanti-Chobe river system is a single river that forms part of the northern border with Namibia and changes names over the course of its eastward path; the Kwando River becomes the Linyanti where it turns northeastward along the Linyanti fault line, and later becomes the Chobe, a tributary of the Zambezi River. The Okavango River flows into the Kalahari basin and ends in a unique alluvial fan sometimes referred to as an inland delta. A notable feature of the Okavango Delta is that it floods during the dry winter season when there is little or no rainfall. This unseasonal flooding—which triggers "unseasonal" breeding of water-fowl—happens because it takes up to six months for rain that falls in the catchment in Angola to reach Botswana. Evidence of previous wetter times include fossil river beds (e.g., Nossob Valley), and the Makgadikgadi Pans—the salty remnants of a huge inland lake that once covered a considerable part of northern Botswana.

Botswana has a relatively small population of just over 2 million people, with over 60% living in urban areas—mainly along the eastern hardveld between the capital, Gaborone, and the city of Francistown 450 km (280 mi) to the northeast. The country is divided into ten administrative districts, each with its own district center, and these are linked by a network of good paved roads. The major district centers are also linked by air.

Botswana has an outstanding system of protected areas, comprising national parks, game reserves, and wildlife management areas. Together these cover approximately 40% of the country's territory and protect a wide range of bird habitats. Most of the remaining area is communal grazing land administered by land boards on behalf of the nation.

Biogeographic context

To understand patterns of bird distribution in Botswana, it helps to first look at the country's location in relation to larger biogeographic regions known as biomes. Botswana straddles the interface of two biomes—the Zambezian to the north, and the Kalahari-Highveld to the south—with a large transition zone between the two. Each of these supports a different suite of endemic birds. However, both biomes extend well beyond Botswana's borders, which partly explains why Botswana doesn't have a single endemic bird species.

The moist, tropical Zambezian biome covers a small section of northern Botswana and stretches northward almost to the equator. Botswana's Zambezian endemics tend to occur only in the northern part of the country. This group includes

Biomes of Botswana

Dickinson's Kestrel, Racket-tailed Roller, Collared Palm Thrush, Miombo Rock Thrush, Arnot's Chat, Rufous-bellied Tit, Shelley's Sunbird, Souza's Shrike and Meves's Starling, among others. The temperate Kalahari-Highveld biome, with its fluctuating climate, covers most of the southern part of the country and extends westward into Namibia and south into South Africa. Botswana's Kalahari-Highveld endemics include Burchell's Sandgrouse, Short-clawed Lark, Kalahari Scrub Robin, Burchell's Starling and Sociable Weaver.

Vegetation and habitat types

Vegetation and habitat types are one of the primary factors influencing local bird distribution. Some birds are habitat generalists and are consequently widespread throughout the country, while others are habitat specialists and may be restricted to specific areas. To understand bird distribution in Botswana, it is useful to recognize nine major vegetation and habitat types and the bird species typical of each, keeping in mind that habitat generalists may frequent many habitats.

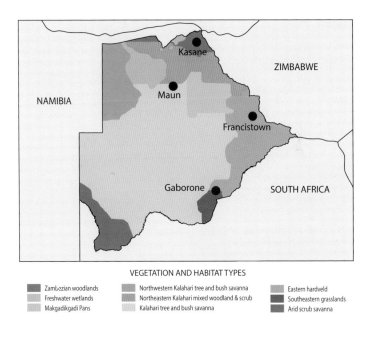

VEGETATION AND HABITAT TYPES

▮ Zambezian woodlands	▨ Northwestern Kalahari tree and bush savanna	▨ Eastern hardveld
▨ Freshwater wetlands	▨ Northeastern Kalahari mixed woodland & scrub	▮ Southeastern grasslands
▨ Makgadikgadi Pans	▨ Kalahari tree and bush savanna	▮ Arid scrub savanna

Zambezian woodlands. Broad-leaved, deciduous woodlands of the Chobe District and the area north of the Okavango Delta. Chobe has the highest rainfall in Botswana, and although soils are sandy, the vegetation comprises large deciduous trees, often with an understory of shrubs. This vegetation type is characterized by species such as Zambezi Teak (*Baikiaea plurijuga*), Kiaat (*Pterocarpus angolensis*), Camel's Foot (*Piliostigma thonningii*), Mopane (*Colophospermum*

Kiaat (*Pterocarpus angolensis*).

Zambezi Teak (*Baikiaea plurijuga*) and understory shrubs. Photo: L. Francey.

11

mopane), Baobab (*Adansonia digitata*) and Manketti-tree (*Schinziophyton rautanenii*). Most of these species have simple, broad leaves, as opposed to the feathery bipinnate leaves of the acacias that are dominant in other habitats. This is the habitat for a number of birds typical of the Chobe District area such as the Racket-tailed Roller, Stierling's Wren-Warbler, Common Whitethroat, Miombo Rock Thrush, and Orange-winged Pytilia and its brood parasite, the Broad-tailed Paradise Whydah.

Northeastern Kalahari mixed woodland and scrub. Mixed woodland characterized by vast stretches of broad-leaved Mopane (*Colophospermum mopane*), interspersed with patches of acacia species, particularly along drainage lines. Mopane often occurs in shrub form. Another conspicuous broad-leaved tree is Leadwood (*Combretum imberbe*), while the fine-leaved acacias are represented by Umbrella Thorn (*Acacia tortilis*) and Camel Thorn (*Acacia erioloba*). Birds typically found in this habitat are Arnot's Chat, Meves's Starling, and Southern Red-billed and Bradfield's Hornbills along with a few species that extend their normal range by moving along warm, moist river valleys into this region, such as Red-capped Robin-Chat, Tropical Boubou, Eastern Nicator, and Bearded Scrub Robin. Acacia patches attract Acacia Pied Barbet, Burnt-necked Eremomela, and Barred Wren-Warbler.

Mopane (*Colophospermum mopane*).

Acacia species amid "endless Mopane."

Freshwater wetlands. The Okavango, Linyanti, and Chobe wetland systems are quite varied, encompassing open and vegetated bodies of water (and floodplains) as well as mature riparian woodland and adjacent savanna areas. Plant species include Common Reed (*Phragmites australis*), Bulrush (*Typha capensis*), sedges (*Cyperus* spp. including Papyrus), water lilies (*Nymphaea* spp.), and woody species such as Northern Lala Palm (*Hyphaene petersiana*), Wild

Permanent lagoon in the Okavango Delta.

Open channel along the Okavango River, fringed by overhanging riparian trees.

Date Palm (*Phoenix reclinata*), wild figs (*Ficus* spp.), Jackal-berry (*Diospyros mespiliformis*), African Mangosteen (*Garcinia livingstonei*), Sausage Tree (*Kigelia africana*), Apple-leaf (*Philenoptera violacea*), Fever-berry (*Croton megalobotrys*), and Knob Thorn (*Acacia nigrescens*). The avifauna of this biome includes many ducks, geese, and other waterbirds such as the near-endemic Slaty Egret, Rufous-bellied and other herons, Wattled Crane, Marabou and Saddle-billed Storks, Long-toed Lapwing, and Coppery-tailed Coucal. In addition, the associated woodlands support species including Swamp Boubou, Holub's Golden Weaver, Brown Firefinch, Hartlaub's Babbler, Pel's Fishing Owl and Western Banded Snake Eagle.

Aerial view of Lake Ngami just after flooding in 2004. This is arguably Botswana's most important wetland for birds and is home to globally significant numbers of ducks and geese, as well as several globally threatened waterbirds. Photo: H. Oake.

Northwestern Kalahari tree and bush savanna. Mixed, woody vegetation on sandy soils with relatively high rainfall. Prominent trees are Silver Cluster-leaf (*Terminalia sericea*) and Purple-pod Cluster-leaf (*T. prunioides*), Mopane (*Colophospermum mopane*), Camel Thorn (*Acacia erioloba*), Kalahari-sand Acacia (*A. luederitzii*), and Albizias (*Albizia* spp.). Trees are interspersed with shrubs of Black Thorn (*Acacia mellifera*), Blue Thorn (*A. erubescens*), Blade Thorn (*A. fleckii*), Kalahari

Kalahari Apple-leaf (*Philenoptera nelsii*) is a common species of the "bush" component of this habitat type, particularly in areas of deep sand.

Camel Thorn (*Acacia erioloba*).

13

Apple-leaf (*Philenoptera nelsii*), and Sickle-bush (*Dichrostachys cinerea*). Birds typical of this habitat are Black-faced Babbler, Bradfield's Hornbill, Chestnut Weaver, Black-bellied Bustard, Sharp-tailed Starling, and Retz's Helmetshrike.

Makgadikgadi Pans. This unique habitat comprises open alkaline flats known as pans. When flooded after rain, the open pan surface attracts a multitude of breeding waders. Surrounding the pans are short, halophytic grasslands covered by Salt Grass (*Sporobolus spicatus*), which are home to Northern Black Korhaan, Pallid and Montagu's Harriers, Ant-eating Chat, Eastern Clapper Lark, and a variety of other larks and sparrow-larks.

 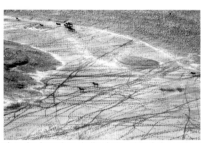

Bare, open pan surfaces are unproductive (for birding) when dry, but when shallowly inundated, they attract large numbers of inland waders.

Eastern hardveld. A vegetation type characterized by rolling hills, rocky outcrops, and loamy soils, which extends in a relatively narrow strip from Southern District to the North-East District. The vegetation is a mixture of broad-leaved and acacia woodland, with trees such as bush-willows (*Combretum* spp.), Knob Thorn (*Acacia nigrescens*), White Kirkia (*Kirkia acuminata*) and African-wattle (*Peltophorum africanum*). Characteristic birds of this habitat are Red-winged Starling, Boulder Chat, Mocking Cliff-Chat, Freckled Nightjar, African Black Swift and Short-toed Rock Thrush. Two important features are the Tswapong Hills and Mannyelanong Hill (see p. 19), which provide breeding cliffs for various raptors, notably the Cape Vulture, Verreaux's Eagle, Rock Kestrel and probably Peregrine and Lanner Falcons.

Mannyelanong Hill, an important breeding site and habitat for many eastern hardveld species. The fallow field in the foreground is habitat for the near-endemic Short-clawed Lark.

North of Francistown, the flat monotony of most of Botswana is broken by occasional kopjes.

Riparian vegetation along "sand rivers" in the eastern hardveld. Water moves through the sand, but does not pool at the surface.

Southeastern grasslands. A relatively small, but important vegetation type characterized by short grasslands, but with open Camel Thorn (*Acacia erioloba*) savanna and patches of Candle-pod Thorn (*Acacia hebeclada*) and Black Thorn (*Acacia mellifera*). Part of the area has been cultivated, and fallow, partly bush-encroached fields form a key habitat for the near-endemic Short-clawed Lark. Other typical bird species include Melodious Lark, Bokmakierie, Cape Longclaw, Long-tailed Widowbird, Sociable Weaver, Fiscal Flycatcher, Long-billed Pipit, White-bellied Bustard, Pallid Harrier, Lesser Kestrel and Secretarybird.

Open areas of short grasses lightly interspersed with low, thorny shrubs.

Kalahari tree and bush savanna. A very extensive vegetation type, covering most of central and southwestern Botswana. The vegetation comprises open savanna with tree species such as Camel Thorn (*Acacia erioloba*), Kalahari-sand Acacia (*A. luederitzii*), and Shepherd's Tree (*Boscia albitrunca*), interspersed with shrubs of Velvet Raisin (*Grewia flava*), Black Thorn (*Acacia mellifera*), and Candle-pod Thorn (*A. hebeclada*). Long-dry fossil riverbeds and pans are fringed with Trumpet-thorn (*Catophractes alexandri*), Black Thorn (*Acacia mellifera*) and Water Thorn (*A. nebrownii*). Five species typical of Kalahari habitats are found here: Marico Flycatcher, Crimson-breasted Shrike, Kalahari Scrub Robin, Great Sparrow, and Southern Pied Babbler. This area is also known for Pale Chanting Goshawk, Greater Kestrel, Swallow-tailed Bee-eater, Kori Bustard, Black-chested Prinia, Rufous-eared Warbler, and migrants such as the Red-backed Shrike. The Ghanzi hardveld (in northwestern Ghanzi District) is a subset of this vegetation type, and is overall similar to the fossil riverbeds and pans found in the Kalahari tree and bush savanna, with calcareous soils favored by Purple-pod Cluster-leaf (*Terminalia prunioides*), Leadwood (*Combretum imberbe*), Trumpet-thorn (*Catophractes alexandri*), and Worm-cure Albizia (*Albizia anthelmintica*). Burchell's Sandgrouse, Red-capped Lark, Double-banded Courser, Capped Wheatear and Ant-eating Chat are typical species.

Most of the Kalahari tree and bush savanna comprises open scrubland.

Nutrient-rich soils of fossil riverbeds and pans bring variety to the Kalahari tree and bush savanna.

Arid scrub savanna. The extreme southwestern part of Botswana (including the Kgalagadi Transfrontier Park) has the lowest rainfall in the country and supports a sparse scrub savanna, except along fossil riverbeds such as the Molopo and Nossob Valleys. The sandy dune vegetation comprises scattered trees and shrubs of Camel Thorn (*Acacia erioloba*), Kalahari-sand Acacia (*A. luederitzii*), Grey Camel Thorn (*A. haematoxylon*) and Shepherd's Tree (*Boscia albitrunca*). The fossil riverbeds are open with occasional large specimens of Camel Thorn (*Acacia erioloba*); there is a dense dwarf shrub layer consisting of Three-thorn Rhigozum (*Rhigozum trichotomum*) and Velvet Raisin (*Grewia flava*). This arid region appears to be a harsh environment, but supports healthy raptor populations and a variety of seed-eaters that thrive by being nomadic and opportunistic. It is also the only place in Botswana to see the Rosy-faced Lovebird, Black-eared Sparrow-Lark, and Black-headed Canary; additionally, it is favored by the Common Ostrich, Kori and Ludwig's bustards, Cape Crow, Namaqua Sandgrouse, Sociable Weaver, and Pygmy Falcon.

The Mabuasehube area comprises part of Kgalagadi Transfrontier Park and is characterized by red sands and numerous pans.

Large Camel Thorn (Acacia erioloba) trees in the Nossob Valley provide suitable sites for Sociable Weavers to build their huge communal nests.

Overview of Botswana's Birds

Botswana currently has 595 bird species on record, 415 of which are residents present year-round. During the wet summer months, the bird population is boosted significantly by the arrival of numerous migrants. Additionally, many birds breed during this time and are conspicuous in their nuptial finery (and can be seen actively displaying), making this a particularly interesting time for birders.

The migrants include 71 Palearctic migrants and 67 intra-African migrants (just two vagrant Nearctic migrants have been recorded). They are mostly present between August and April, although there are some interesting exceptions to this pattern. For example, the Fairy Flycatcher breeds in South Africa during summer and then disperses northward into Botswana during winter. Likewise, the resident Lanner Falcon and Knob-billed Duck populations are joined by migrant populations that come to Botswana to breed, and the Booted Eagle is represented by various migrant populations that arrive at different times of the year. Migrants generally traverse a variety of habitats.

Botswana has many "visitors," which are southern African resident species that occur in Botswana at the edge of their normal range, or having wandered a short distance outside of their normal range. Vagrants, on the other hand, are unexpected species that only arrive in Botswana having wandered well outside of their normal range. Some have only been recorded once, probably blown off course by unusual weather conditions, so there is no predictability to their occurrence (e.g., Long-tailed Jaeger). Other vagrants include long-distance migrants that "overshoot" their normal destination (e.g. Isabelline Wheatear), while a third group includes nomadic species like the Red-headed Quelea, which are highly mobile and opportunistic—they may even breed in Botswana when conditions are right, and then disappear, not to be seen again for years.

Although Botswana does not have a single endemic species, its two near-endemics, the Slaty Egret and Short-clawed Lark, are best seen in Botswana. The Slaty Egret is a floodplain specialist whose very small range is centered on the Okavango Delta, where 85% of the global population of approximately 4,000 birds can be found. The Short-clawed Lark also has the bulk of its global population in Botswana, in the southeastern grasslands (a habitat that extends slightly into South Africa), where it is currently thriving. Of the southern African endemics—birds that only occur south of the Cunene, Kavango and Zambezi Rivers—23% occur in Botswana and are easily seen here, as are 72% of the southern African near-endemics.

According to the International Union for Conservation of Nature (IUCN), the vast majority of Botswana's bird species fall into the category of "Least Concern" in terms of conservation status. However, there are 17 Near Threatened species, 10 Vulnerable species, and 6 Endangered species. Many bird species are protected by law in Botswana, and all species have protected status when in the country's national parks and game reserves. These extensive parks and reserves, which cover some 17% of the country's terrain (note that this does not include wildlife management areas), also protect important bird habitats, which are crucial to the long-term survival of bird populations. Indeed, Botswana is a stronghold for many globally threatened species, such as the Lappet-faced Vulture, which have declined significantly in other parts of their range. Unfortunately, there is a steep gradient in numbers of (mainly) large birds within and outside of protected areas. This is a common pattern in places where the intact habitats have become fragmented into isolated ecological islands.

Where to see birds in Botswana

Botswana is a huge country with an almost bewildering variety of birds and birding opportunities. Although identifying the "best" birding sites is a subjective exercise, the 12 Important Bird and Biodiversity Areas (IBAs) identified by BirdLife Botswana are an excellent guide. These sites are among Botswana's most productive birding destinations, and also meet BirdLife International's criteria for IBAs, meaning that they regularly hold at least one of the following: significant numbers of globally threatened species, species with a restricted range, or large congregations of birds exceeding 1% of the global or regional population of the species. Botswana's 12 IBAs are:

Chobe National Park. The northern Chobe District has the highest bird species richness in the country, with 468 species recorded to date. This is explained by the fact that it lies at the junction of two major biomes as well as several habitat types—Kalahari savanna meets broad-leaved and acacia woodlands as well as Zambezi Teak (*Baikiaea plurijuga*) woodlands, and the area is bisected by the Chobe River, with its riparian forest and extensive floodplains. Highlights of this area (particularly for southern African birders) include Olive Woodpecker, Orange-winged Pytilia, Broad-tailed Paradise Whydah, Black-eared Seedeater, Racket-tailed Roller, Brown-necked Parrot, and Copper Sunbird; additionally, Collared Palm Thrush and Dickinson's Kestrel are virtually guaranteed sightings. The riparian forests of the Chobe River are home to several tropical species that travel up the Zambezi Valley, and occur nowhere else in Botswana: Schalow's and Purple-crested Turacos, Trumpeter and Crowned Hornbills, and Crested Guineafowl. As if that weren't enough, in late winter thousands of waterbirds are concentrated in the drying floodplains of the Chobe River, an absolutely spectacular event!

Okavango Delta. The world-famous Okavango Delta, recently inscribed as a World Heritage Site, is one of the most beautiful and unspoiled wetlands in existence. It is home to 22 globally threatened species, including the near-endemic Slaty Egret as well as the Wattled Crane, for which it is the global stronghold. The Okavango Panhandle, where the Okavango River enters Botswana before spreading into the fan-like delta, is the best place to see many of the Okavango "specials" that characterize this IBA. These include Pel's Fishing Owl, African Skimmer, Greater Swamp Warbler, Coppery-tailed Coucal, White-backed Night Heron, Southern Brown-throated Weaver, Brown Firefinch and Western Banded Snake Eagle. The other must-visit area in the Okavango is the mixed heronries at Gadikwe Lagoon in Moremi Game Reserve, and the nearby "Lediba la dinonyane," which together form the largest breeding site for Marabou and Yellow-billed Storks in southern Africa. A variety of other waterbirds, including increasing numbers of Pink-backed Pelicans, nest at the latter site, with activity peaking during September.

Lake Ngami. Although Lake Ngami is an appendage of the Okavango Delta, it is considered its own IBA. It is most famous for its large congregations of waterbirds, as tens of thousands of ducks and other waterfowl flock here from all over the world when the lake has water; since it is a nutrient sink, the mere presence of water is enough to activate rich food chains that can draw birds almost overnight and fuel the breeding of dozens of species immediately upon arrival. The lake's water level is erratic because it depends on outflow from the Okavango Delta; it was dry for decades before flooding in 2004, and has since transformed into a huge wetland and is recognized as a major breeding ground for waterbirds. There are 18 bird species whose numbers at the lake regularly exceed 0.5% of the global or regional population, including Little Grebe, Great White Pelican, Whiskered Tern, Great Egret, Black-crowned Night Heron, and Hottentot and Red-billed Teals.

Linyanti Swamps/Chobe River. A relatively remote area bordering the Zambezi Region of Namibia, this IBA hosts a mixture of wetland and woodland birds, but is renowned for its raptor populations. These include Lappet-faced, White-backed, Hooded, and White-headed Vultures as well as Martial Eagle and the ubiquitous Bateleur (all of which are globally threatened). A special attraction during summer is the Southern Carmine Bee-eater nesting colonies, many of which are on flat ground. When breeding is in full swing, the flashing colors and melodious, bell-like calls of large groups of these flying jewels create a vibrant scene.

Makgadikgadi Pans. This area, comprising Sua and Ntwetwe Pans, is a well-known birding destination. Sua Pan in the east is home to one of only four breeding sites in Africa for the globally threatened Lesser Flamingo. Its breeding colonies are in the southern basin of the pan (together with those of the Greater Flamingo) inside the recently created Flamingo Sanctuary, which is off limits to birders. However, it is possible to see 100,000 flamingos from a single vantage point in the Nata Sanctuary if one is there at the right time. The key is to remember that the pan dries from south to north so that by late winter the birds are heavily concentrated in the Nata Sanctuary in the northern basin, where they feed in the last remaining shallows. This is when the other Makgadikgadi "special," the globally threatened Chestnut-banded Plover is also most concentrated and easily seen. Nata Sanctuary is not just a crucial feeding ground for flamingos; when conditions are right after heavy rains, Great White and Pink-backed Pelicans also come here to nest. This is one of the few breeding sites of the Great White Pelican in Botswana (and, in fact, all of southern Africa); thousands of individuals nest on the ground on islands in the area. This area is so inaccessible that Goliath Herons nest on the ground here too, although not in association with the pelicans! The isolated acacias dotting the fringes of the pans are favored nesting sites for Lappet-faced Vultures, while the attractive Camel Thorn (*Acacia erioloba*) woodlands support large breeding colonies of White-backed Vultures.

Central Kalahari Game Reserve. This is the largest IBA in Botswana and, apart from being the best place to see the Kalahari "specials", is probably the global stronghold for the massive Kori Bustard. During summer, bird numbers are boosted by the presence of numerous migrants; Lesser Kestrels and Red-footed and Amur Falcons pass through the area following the fossil riverbeds (and rain fronts), and it is suspected that these landmarks are also used by other migratory birds. Pallid and Montagu's Harriers are present at this time too, coursing over the short, open grasslands, and Caspian Plovers are abundant. Many species display during summer when breeding—the fluttering and falling display of the Eastern Clapper Lark, accompanied by a descending whistle, is a characteristic Kalahari experience, as is the raucous clattering of Northern Black Korhaans as the males vie for the attention of females.

Gemsbok National Park. This IBA in southwestern Botswana, together with the contiguous Kalahari Gemsbok National Park in South Africa, now forms part of the Kgalagadi Transfrontier Park (KTP). This is another enormous, semi-arid area that draws birders time and time again for the thrill of seeing highly adapted desert species in a harsh but pristine environment. The dry Nossob Valley, with its large, ancient Camel Thorns (*Acacia erioloba*) adorned with enormous Sociable Weaver nests, is the focus for birding and game viewing. This is a paradise for raptors of all varieties. The numerous waterholes along the fossil riverbed are renowned for spectacular sightings of Red-necked and Lanner Falcons hunting queleas or doves, not to mention the continuous traffic of other smaller denizens of the area, such as Black-headed Canary, Black-eared Sparrow-Lark, Rosy-faced Lovebird and Namaqua Sandgrouse. Kori Bustards also abound here, and lucky birders may also see the southern African endemic Ludwig's Bustard, or the Black Harrier, an occasional visitor to the area.

The remaining IBAs are much smaller than those described above, and are mostly dedicated to the protection of single species:

Mannyelanong Hill and the **Tswapong Hills,** in southern and eastern Botswana respectively, are the only breeding areas in the country for the (Vulnerable) Cape Vulture, but have other attractions for birders as well. Verreaux's Eagles and Black Storks nest on the cliffs with the vultures, as do smaller species such as Mocking Cliff-Chat and Boulder Chat (the latter at Tswapong only). Moremi Gorge in the Tswapong Hills is a true "oasis in the desert" with permanent streams and waterfalls, and is home to the Mountain Wagtail.

Southeast Botswana. This IBA occupies an area along the border with South Africa, near Ramatlabama. It comprises a unique area of open grasslands with a special suite of birds, including the near-endemic Short-clawed Lark. This IBA is not currently protected, but a recent study conducted by BirdLife Botswana showed that the Short-clawed Lark population is thriving. This is due largely to its compatibility with traditional farming practices, which allow fields to lie fallow for some years, creating suitable habitat for this large lark. Also present in this area are Cape Longclaw, Bokmakierie, Melodious Lark, and Cloud Cisticola.

The final two IBAs, **Bokaa Dam** and **Phakalane Sewage Lagoons** are somewhat anomalous in that they are man-made bodies of water. They are home to significant numbers of Southern Pochard, Maccoa Duck, and Great Crested Grebe. Phakalane Sewage Lagoons has turned up some other interesting birds over the years, including African Yellow Warbler, Basra Reed Warbler, and numerous Eurasian Reed Warblers.

How to use this book

The species covered in this book are grouped by family; each family is introduced by a general description in a blue box, which is followed by individual species accounts and illustrations on the facing page. For reasons of design and user friendliness, the order of families does not strictly follow the true taxonomic order, nor does the order of species within the families. Instead, both have been adjusted in an effort to keep similar families near each other, and, within the families, to put the most similar-looking species on the same page for easy comparison. Each species account contains the following elements:

Species names. The scientific and common species names align with the International Ornithological Congress's World Bird List (v 4.3), in an effort to move toward global standardization (as initiated by recent regional field guides). Where it is relevant to bird identification, subspecies are also described, in accordance with *Roberts Geographic Variation of Southern African Birds* (2012), which provides the most up-to-date and detailed analysis of southern African subspecies. Both scientific and common names appear in the Species Index (p. 386). Setswana names, where known, follow Cole (1995). The names given cover some or all of the following dialects: Hurutshe, Kgatla, Kwena, Lete, Ngwaketse, Ngwato, Rolong, Tlokwa, Tlharo, Tswapong, and Tawana. Since Setswana is a tone language in which tones identify the word along with consonants and vowels, the dialectal differences are often reflected in only slight spelling differences. Batswana who can contribute any Setswana names to fill the gaps are invited to contact Pete Hancock at birdlifemaun@gmail.com.

Measurement. At the beginning of each species account, a length measurement is given in both centimeters and inches. This represents the length of the bird from tip of the bill to the tip of the tail; where elongate tail streamers are included in the measurement, that is indicated.

Identification. The text complements the illustration(s) of each species by highlighting key identification features, describing any aspects not depicted (e.g., additional color morphs), and explaining how the species differs from similar species. The descriptions are written based on the sexes being alike unless otherwise indicated. Where applicable and relevant to identification, the text also describes subspecies.

Call. The call is described where it is useful for identifying the bird. For example, call is particularly important for identification of cisticolas, larks, and nightjars, but is emphasized less for seldom-heard species such as Egyptian Vulture and Secretarybird.

Status (migratory and breeding). Each bird's migratory status is described by one or more of the following terms (which are also represented by the colors of the range maps):

- **Resident:** A species that is present year-round.
- **Intra-African migrant:** A species that spends the austral summer in Botswana and the remainder of year elsewhere in Africa.
- **Palearctic migrant:** A species that spends the austral summer in Botswana and the remainder of the year in the Palearctic region.
- **Visitor:** A species resident in southern Africa, which occurs in Botswana when just outside of its normal range. Visitors' status is generally poorly known; some may be resident in certain years or seasons.
- **Vagrant:** A species that has occurred in Botswana when well outside its normal range.

In addition to migratory status, this section describes the species's breeding status in these terms:

- **Breeding:** Nests containing eggs or young, or juveniles out of the nest under parental care have been recorded, or birds in breeding condition collected.
- **Nonbreeding:** Does not breed in Botswana.
- **No breeding records from Botswana:** Breeding is likely but not proven in Botswana.

Abundance. Each species's abundance is described in the following terms:

- **Rare:** Less than 10 records in Botswana in the past 25 years (Category A Rarity according to BirdLife Botswana's Records Subcommittee).
- **Scarce:** More than 10 records in Botswana in the past 25 years, but irregularly and infrequently seen in suitable habitat (most of BirdLife Botswana's Category B Rarities are in this category).
- **Uncommon:** Encountered regularly but infrequently in suitable habitat.
- **Common:** Likely to be encountered at least once in four or five visits to suitable habitat.
- **Abundant:** Encountered frequently and often in large numbers in suitable habitat. Note that some "abundant" species will never be as numerous as others (e.g., Ring-necked Doves will always be more numerous than Pale Chanting Goshawk)

This section also describes where the bird occurs in Botswana, including the various subspecies.

Habitat. The species's typical habitats are described, often in terms of the vegetation and habitat types outlined on pp. 11-16.

Habits. Habits and behaviors that are useful in identifying the species are described; these may be related to sociality, courtship, feeding, or simply characteristic body movements (e.g., the frequent fanning and flicking of the tail by the Grey Tit-Flycatcher).

Conservation. Conservation status according to the IUCN Red List of Threatened Species. Botswana's birds currently fall into four IUCN categories:

- **Least Concern**: species does not qualify for any threat category on the IUCN Red List (most species in Botswana fall into this category)
- **Near Threatened:** species does not qualify for Vulnerable category, but is close to qualifying in the near future.
- **Vulnerable**: species faces high risk of extinction in the wild.
- **Endangered**: species faces very high risk of extinction in the wild.

Also noted are species that are protected by national legislation or designated as game birds and may be hunted, according to the Fourth Schedule of the Hunting and Licensing Regulations (2001).

General. Varied information of interest that is not necessarily related to species identification (e.g., cultural details, endemism, behaviors such as brood parasitism, etc.).

Illustrations. Each species is depicted in one or more illustration(s). Some species show significant differences in plumage pattern and coloration in different regions, and the illustrations provided in this field guide represent coloration specific to Botswana. Likewise, where there are subspecies in Botswana that are obvious and discernible from those that occur elsewhere, these are described in the text. In general, Botswana's most common and widespread subspecies is illustrated (this may not necessarily be the nominate). When all illustrations are of a specific subspecies, the subspecies name appears under the species common name. Alternately, where multiple subspecies are illustrated, the individual illustrations are labeled accordingly. The user should assume that the illustrated birds are adults unless otherwise indicated. Species that have multiple adult plumages, or for which multiple plumages are illustrated, are labeled accordingly. Species on the same page are shown at the same scale. Birds in flight are generally shown at a smaller scale than perched/standing birds, but are still proportional among themselves.

Range maps. Each species account is accompanied by a range map that represents the bird's distribution and, through colors, it's migratory status and relative abundance throughout Botswana. (To orient the user, each map shows an outline of the Okavango Delta and Makgadikgadi Pans, and dots that represent the urban centers Maun, Kasane, Francistown, and Gaborone.) The colors and markings on the range maps represent the following:

- **Green:** Resident, present year-round. Dark green indicates where the species is more common; pale green shows where it is less common.
- **Blue:** Intra-African migrant. Dark blue indicates where the species is more common; pale blue shows where it is less common.
- **Red:** Palearctic (or Nearctic) migrant. Dark red indicates where the species is more common; pale red shows where it is less common.
- **Red X:** An accepted record of a bird outside of its normal range, mostly visitors and vagrants.

Where the maps employ more than one color, they represent two different populations; where the map shows a range "striped" with different colors, that indicates that the range is shared by both resident and migrant populations. The distribution of individual subspecies in Botswana is poorly known and therefore is not depicted on the maps. For a more comprehensive analysis, please refer to "Roberts Geographic Variation of Southern African Birds" (2012).

Breeding bars. Species accounts for residents and migrants include a "breeding bar," a graphic that represents both the species's seasonal presence and breeding patterns in Botswana (breeding bars are excluded for visitors and vagrants). Within the bar, each block represents a month of the year, indicated by the first letter of the month. The species's relative abundance or sightability is indicated by the color of the block, as specified below. Breeding status is represented by dots, as specified below. The dots actually represent egg-laying data for the species, which is based on the number of clutches started in each month. For species with insufficient breeding data in Botswana, the breeding season has been depicted based on published information from elsewhere in the southern African region. Breeding information from Botswana is based on Oake (2014), Skinner (1995, 1996, and 1997), and the author's personal observations over an extended period; breeding information from outside Botswana is based largely on Tarboton (2011).

White: absent
Light blue: present in reduced numbers
Dark blue: present in increased numbers

No dot: no egg-laying
Small dot: normal egg-laying
Large dot: peak egg-laying

BirdLife Botswana

BirdLife Botswana is a professional bird conservation agency that aims to conserve birds and bird habitats by raising awareness, conducting research and bird counts, and promoting ecological sustainability and beneficial relationships between birds and people. It is the Partner Designate of BirdLife International in Botswana.

BirdLife Botswana's Records Subcommittee is the custodian of the official Botswana Bird List and solicits information on new birds and rarities. Birders are invited to submit records of such species as well as breeding records of any species, as the Nest Record Card Scheme is a valuable source of information on birds breeding in Botswana. For more information, visit www.birdlifebotswana.org.bw.

Glossary

accipiter – member of the genus *Accipiter*.
aigrette – long filamentous breeding plume of egrets.
alate – winged, reproductive termite.
alien – introduced from another part of the world.
allopatric – having non-overlapping ranges.
altricial – describes a chick that is born naked and helpless, and requires prolonged parental care.
alula –small, stiff feathers at the wrist, which can be flared to prevent stalling.
antiphonal – describes a duet where two birds call alternately.
aquatic – living in or on freshwater.
arboreal – tree dwelling.
ardeid – member of the family Ardeidae (i.e., a heron, bittern, or egret).
barbule – small hook on the feather barb, which functions to maintain the feather structure.
biome-restricted species – a species confined to a particular biome or biogeographic region.
broad-leaved woodlands – a vegetation type dominated by trees that have simple or compound leaves with large leaflets.
brood parasite – a bird that lays its eggs in another bird's nest, leaving that bird to raise its chicks.
Cainism – refers to when older, first-hatched chick kills its younger sibling.
carnivorous – meat eating.
carpal patch – marking on the underside of the wing at the carpal joint (wrist).
carpal spur – rudimentary "thumb" on the carpal joint of the wing, usually used for fighting.
casque – horny ridge on the upper mandible of hornbills (particularly males), or bony projection on the head of guineafowl.
cere – fleshy covering at the base of the upper mandible of some birds, notably raptors, but also parrots and pigeons.
CITES – Convention on International Trade in Endangered Species of fauna and flora.
cock's nest – nest-like structure added to the top of a ball-shaped nest; it may serve as a decoy, or it may simply be a roosting site for the male.
conspecific – member of the same species.
congener – member of the same genus.

congeneric – of the same genus.
cooperative breeding – breeding system in which the breeding pair is assisted during the nesting cycle by one or more "helpers."
cooperative polyandry – breeding system in which the female has more than one male partner undertaking the parental duties.
corvid – member of the family Corvidae.
crèche – nursery flock of juveniles.
crepuscular – active at dawn and dusk.
crop – distensible part of a bird's oesophagus, for storing food.
cursorial – runs on ground.
coverts – small contour feathers that protect sensitive parts of the body (e.g., ear coverts) or streamline parts of the body (e.g., wing coverts).
covey – collective noun for francolins and spurfowls (i.e., a flock).
culmen – ridge along upper mandible, from tip to forehead.
eclipse plumage – post-nuptial plumage stage (of shorter duration than winter or nonbreeding plumage) in species that show marked seasonal change, mainly some male sunbirds and ducks.
ecotone – transitional habitat between two adjacent vegetation types.
endemic – a species confined to a specific region.
eucalypt – tall, alien tree of the genus *Eucalyptus*, planted in small woodlots in Botswana.
eye stripe – pale or dark line running through the eye from the lores to above the ear coverts.
flapper – bird that has molted all its flight feathers and is temporarily flightless (e.g., ducks, geese).
fossil riverbed – long-dry riverbed; these form important habitat for birds that prefer open, short-grassed areas.
frugivorous – fruit eating.
gallinaceous – belonging to the order Galliformes (includes guineafowls, quails, spurfowls and francolins, as well as domestic fowl)
gape – skin at the base of a bird's beak, where upper and lower mandibles join. Often white and rubbery in appearance in juvenile birds.
gape flange – accentuated, colourful, fleshy outline to gape of young bird.
globally threatened – collective term that describes species in any of the IUCN Red List

categories for species threatened with extinction, including Near Threatened, Vulnerable, and Endangered.

gorget – area of brightly colored feathers on the throat.

graduated tail – tail in which central tail feathers are longest and each adjacent feather is shorter.

granivorous – seed eating.

gregarious – occurs in flocks.

heronry – site where herons and egrets breed colonially (term also applied to sites where storks, cormorants and darters breed colonially).

Holarctic – biogeographic region that includes both the Palearctic and Nearctic regions.

immature – pre-adult bird that is not specifically a juvenile; in most cases describes birds that have molted from juvenile plumage, but have not acquired adult plumage.

insectivorous – insect eating.

intra-African migrant – species that spends the austral summer in Botswana, and the remainder of the year elsewhere in Africa.

irruptive – refers to a species that makes irregular movements into a new area, usually temporarily and in significant numbers.

juvenile – young, recently fledged bird in its first fully feathered plumage.

kleptoparasitism – stealing of food from another individual, not necessarily of the same species.

kopje – small rocky outcrop.

lamellae – thin plates or comb-like projections on the tongue or along the edge of the bill, used for filter-feeding.

lanceolate – spear shaped, tapering at each end.

lek – a breeding display arena where males congregate to which females are attracted for mating. May be a large, expanded area of several hundred square meters with males spread out, as in the case of bustards.

leucistic – having reduced pigmentation, which makes the bird appear whitish.

lores – part of bird between eye and base of upper mandible, often concave to permit binocular vision.

malar stripe – a line extending from the lower mandible down the side of the throat

mandible – upper or lower part of the bill.

mantle – the middle to upper back of a bird, including the scapulars.

melanistic – having an excess of the pigment melanin, which makes the bird appear black.

monogamous – having a single breeding partner.

monogeneric – having only one genus.

morph – distinctive plumage colors or states within a species.

Motswana (pl. Batswana) – a citizen of Botswana.

moustachial stripe – a line extending from the gape across the cheek.

near endemic – a species that is largely restricted to a region, but extends slightly outside the region's boundaries.

Nearctic – biogeographic region that includes temperate and Arctic North America, Canada and Greenland.

nectarivorous – nectar feeding.

nomadic – changing home range frequently, often with a restless or erratic pattern.

notch – small tooth-like projection on both sides of upper mandible, behind the tip of the bill (present in some falcons and barbets).

onomatopoeic – derived from sound associated with the object; in the case of birds, typically refers to a name derived from the bird's call.

ortstreue – fidelity to a nonbreeding site in subsequent years.

Palearctic – biogeographic region that includes Europe, north Africa and northern Asia, east to eastern Siberia.

Palearctic migrant – a species that spends the austral summer in Botswana, and the remainder of the year in the Palearctic region.

passage migrant – a bird that travels through an area while on migration.

passerine – a perching songbird; a member of the largest order of birds (Passeriformes).

passive fratricide – when the older, larger chick monopolises the food supply, resulting in the death of the smaller chick(s).

pied – black and white.

piscivorous – fish eating.

polyandrous – belonging to a breeding system where one female mates with more than one male; males usually undertake all parental care.

polygamous – belonging to a mating system in which one bird mates with more than one partner (see polyandrous and polygynous).

polygynous – belonging to a breeding system in which one male mates with more than one female; females usually undertake all parental care.

polymorphic – having two or more different plumage forms/colors.

precocial – describes a chick that hatches in an advanced stage of development and requires minimal parental care.

primary feathers – the outermost flight feathers (usually 10 in number) on a bird's wing.

primary projection – describes how far the primary wing feathers project relative to the tertials (not the tail) when the wing is folded.

rallid – member of the family Rallidae.

raptor – bird of prey (includes vultures and owls in addition to other diurnal birds of prey).

rectrix (pl. retrices) – tail feather.

remex (pl. remiges) – flight feather.

resident – sedentary (non-migratory) species present year-round.

reverse sexual dimorphism – where the female is larger and/or more brightly colored than the male.

rictal bristles – hair-like structures at the base of bird's bill that aid it in catching insects.

ringtail – nickname of female and immature Pallid and Montagu's harriers, which have white rumps.

saddle – flat, brightly colored frontal shield at base of upper mandible.

secondary feathers – intermediate flight feathers between primaries and tertials.

Setswana – the national language of Botswana.

sexual dimorphism – when the male and female of a species differ markedly in color or size and thereby occur as two distinct forms.

sibling species – species that are very closely related to one another.

spatulate – having a broad, rounded end; spoon-shaped.

speculum – panel of white or iridescent feathers in the wing of a duck (speculum is Latin for mirror).

sternum – breastbone.

subadult – bird intermediate in age and plumage between immature and adult.

supercilium – eyebrow

sympatric – having overlapping ranges.

tarsal spur – claw on back of tarsus, usually of male bird, used for fighting.

tarsus – lower part of leg of bird, between tibia and foot.

terrestrial – ground dwelling.

territorial – species that defends an area against conspecifics.

tertial feathers – innermost flight feathers, at the proximal end of the wing.

tibiotarsal joint – where the tibia and the fused foot bones (tarsus) on a bird's leg join (the equivalent of the ankle in a human, but often erroneously referred to as the knee in birds).

type specimen – the first specimen collected, from which the species is described to science.

vagrant – a species well outside of its normal range.

vent – area under tail of bird, around cloaca, covered by undertail coverts.

viduine – member of the family Viduidae.

visitor – species resident in southern Africa, which occurs in Botswana when at the edge of or just outside its normal range.

wader – describes a collection of birds belonging to the related families Jacanidae, Rostratulidae, Haematopodidae, Charadriidae, Scolopacidae, Recurvirostridae, Phalaropidae, Dromadidae, Burhinidae and Glareolidae. They are distinct from other long-legged waterbirds which are called "wading birds."

warbler – describes a collection of birds belonging to the related families Macrospheniidae, Phylloscopidae, Acrocephalidae, Megaluridae, Cisticolidae, and Sylviidae.

wattle – bare fleshy skin around eye, base of bill, throat or elsewhere on a bird's head.

wing formula – mathematical representation of the relative lengths of the primary feathers.

wing loading – ratio between body weight and wing area.

zygodactyl – describes a foot structure in which toes two and three point forward and toes one and four point backward.

BIRD TOPOGRAPHY

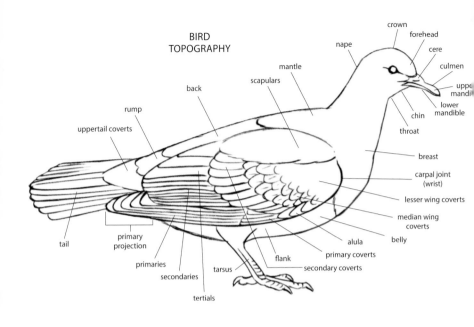

crown
forehead
cere
culmen
upper mandible
lower mandible
chin
throat
nape
mantle
scapulars
back
rump
uppertail coverts
breast
carpal joint (wrist)
lesser wing coverts
median wing coverts
belly
alula
primary coverts
secondary coverts
flank
tertials
secondaries
tarsus
primaries
primary projection
tail

HEAD FEATURES

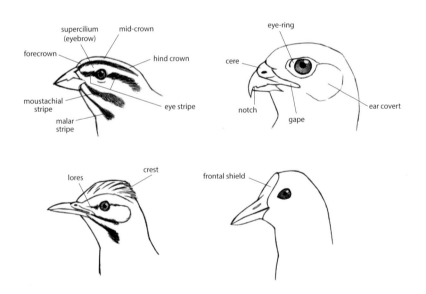

supercilium (eyebrow)
mid-crown
forecrown
hind crown
eye stripe
moustachial stripe
malar stripe

eye-ring
cere
notch
gape
ear covert

lores
crest

frontal shield

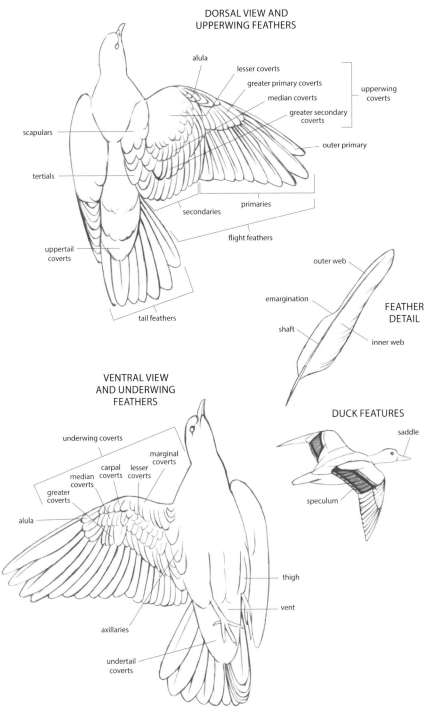

DORSAL VIEW AND
UPPERWING FEATHERS

alula

lesser coverts

greater primary coverts

median coverts

greater secondary
coverts

upperwing
coverts

scapulars

outer primary

tertials

secondaries

primaries

uppertail
coverts

flight feathers

tail feathers

FEATHER
DETAIL

outer web

emargination

shaft

inner web

VENTRAL VIEW
AND UNDERWING
FEATHERS

DUCK FEATURES

underwing coverts

marginal
coverts

saddle

carpal   lesser
coverts   coverts

median
coverts

greater
coverts

speculum

alula

thigh

vent

axillaries

undertail
coverts

OSTRICHES Struthionidae
Large, flightless, cursorial birds that lack a keeled sternum for attachment of flight muscles. The wings are vestigial, and the feathers lack barbules. Ostriches have evolved powerful, elongate legs (with two toes on each foot) that enable them to attain running speeds of 70 km/h (43 mi/h) and make them the fastest animal on two legs. Their eyes are the largest of any vertebrate (five times the size of a human eye) and endow them with superb eyesight. This is a monogeneric family represented in Botswana by the southern African subspecies *S. c. australis*.

COMMON OSTRICH *Struthio camelus*

Setswana: mpshe, mmampshe, ntshwe, mmantshwe, ntŝhe, mmantshwê

200 cm (78 ¾ in). **Identification:** Male has predominantly black plumage but white wings and white or buffy tail; breeding male has red on bill and red scales on lower leg (tarsus). Female and immature are uniform gray-brown. Juvenile is covered in prickly, camouflaging down. **Call:** Low-frequency, trisyllabic, booming *hoom hoom hooooo*. Suggestive of a distant lion's roar. **Status:** Resident, breeding. Egg-laying peaks from August to December, but the species breeds opportunistically throughout year. **Abundance:** Uncommon over most of its range but common in Central Kalahari Game Reserve, around Makgadikgadi Pans, and throughout Kgalagadi District. **Habitat:** Occurs in open, short-grass plains and arid savannas. **Habits:** The species is herbivorous. Breeding is polygynous; alpha male and female start nest on ground, but other females also lay in same nest. Male incubates at night, alpha female during day. **Conservation:** Least Concern.

GUINEAFOWLS Numididae
A family of terrestrial gallinaceous birds that have white-spotted gray plumage and are virtually devoid of feathers on the head and neck. Sexes are alike. Guineafowls nest on the ground; the young (called "keets") are precocial and join the large flocks of adults soon after hatching. The birds roost in trees at night; they have a well-developed hind claw that enables perching (but they lack the spurs of game birds of family Phasianidae, p. 30). The family is endemic to Africa; two genera and two species are resident in Botswana, although the range of one extends only marginally into Botswana.

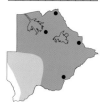

HELMETED GUINEAFOWL *Numida meleagris*

Setswana: kgaka

56 cm (22 in). **Identification:** Terrestrial game bird. Plumage is charcoal gray with white spots. Combination of bare blue head with bony casque and red-tipped wattles distinguishes this species from Crested Guineafowl. The three subspecies (*N. m. mitratus, N. m. papillosus, N. m. coronatus*) differ subtly in casque shape and size and in the shade of blue on the face. **Call:** Raucous, staccato alarm rattle; during breeding season produces a more musical, though repetitive, bisyllabic whistle, similar in cadence to *buck-wheat, buck-wheat*. **Status:** Resident, breeding. In years of good rainfall, breeding may continue past the summer peak until May. **Abundance:** Common in northern Botswana, parts of central Botswana, and in the eastern hardveld. All three southern African subspecies occur: *N. m. mitratus* in the eastern part of the country, *N. m. papillosus* in the northwest, and *N. m. coronatus* in the southwest (the first two are common, the last is uncommon). **Habitat:** Occurs in a variety of woodland types, both broad-leaved and acacia-dominated, in areas with dense grass cover and access to water. **Habits:** Occurs in pairs during breeding season, in large flocks (100-plus) during remainder of year. **Conservation:** Least Concern. Classified as a game bird; may be hunted from April to September.

CRESTED GUINEAFOWL *Guttera pucherani*

Setswana: kgaka

50 cm (19 ¾ in). **Identification:** Terrestrial game bird. Plumage is charcoal gray with pale blue spots. Red eyes. Tuft of black feathers on crown is diagnostic. **Call:** Noisy *chick-chock, chick-chock, chick-chock churrrr*. **Status:** Visitor; no breeding records from Botswana. **Abundance:** Rare. The bulk of the population occurs beyond the borders of Botswana; its range extends up the Zambezi Valley, entering Botswana in the vicinity of the Chobe River. **Habitat:** A forest species, found in riparian woodlands in Botswana. **Habits:** Gregarious, forages on ground but roosts in trees at night. **Conservation:** Least Concern.

juv.

chick detail

juv.

imm.

COMMON OSTRICH

adult male

adult female

subadult

adult
N. m. mitratus

juv.

HELMETED GUINEAFOWL

CRESTED GUINEAFOWL

FRANCOLINS, SPURFOWLS, QUAILS Phasianidae

Cryptically colored, ground-dwelling game birds, the males of which are endowed with tarsal spurs (claws on the backs of the legs) for intraspecific fighting. All are ground-nesting species that have precocial young, which join the covey soon after hatching. The three resident francolin species, belonging to three separate genera, have rudimentary spurs. The three spurfowls, also resident, have pronounced spurs and belong to the genus *Pternistis*, the name of which means "one who trips with the heel," in reference to the tarsal spurs. The remaining two family members found in Botswana are from the quail genus, *Coturnix*; one is resident and the other an intra-African migrant. The Setswana *le.sogo*, given for many species, is a generic name for francolins and spurfowls.

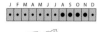

ORANGE RIVER FRANCOLIN *Scleroptila gutturalis*

Setswana: kedikilê, kedikilwê, kelekilê, kebetilwê, le.sogo

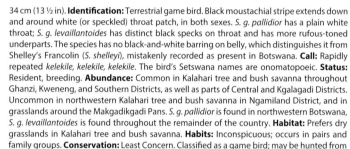

34 cm (13 ½ in). **Identification:** Terrestrial game bird. Black moustachial stripe extends down and around white (or speckled) throat patch, in both sexes. *S. g. pallidior* has a plain white throat; *S. g. levaillantoides* has distinct black specks on throat and has more rufous-toned underparts. The species has no black-and-white barring on belly, which distinguishes it from Shelley's Francolin (*S. shelleyi*), mistakenly recorded as present in Botswana. **Call:** Rapidly repeated *kelekile, kelekile, kelekile*. The bird's Setswana names are onomatopoeic. **Status:** Resident, breeding. **Abundance:** Common in Kalahari tree and bush savanna throughout Ghanzi, Kweneng, and Southern Districts, as well as parts of Central and Kgalagadi Districts. Uncommon in northwestern Kalahari tree and bush savanna in Ngamiland District, and in grasslands around the Makgadikgadi Pans. *S. g. pallidior* is found in northwestern Botswana, *S. g. levaillantoides* is found throughout the remainder of the country. **Habitat:** Prefers dry grasslands in Kalahari tree and bush savanna. **Habits:** Inconspicuous; occurs in pairs and family groups. **Conservation:** Least Concern. Classified as a game bird; may be hunted from April to September.

CRESTED FRANCOLIN *Dendroperdix sephaena*

Setswana: le.tsiêkwane, mo.tsiêkwane, le.kwêêkwane, le.tšaakgarale, le.tsâkarane, le.tšankgarane

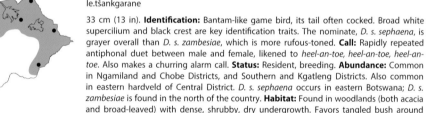

33 cm (13 in). **Identification:** Bantam-like game bird, its tail often cocked. Broad white supercilium and black crest are key identification traits. The nominate, *D. s. sephaena*, is grayer overall than *D. s. zambesiae*, which is more rufous-toned. **Call:** Rapidly repeated antiphonal duet between male and female, likened to *heel-an-toe, heel-an-toe, heel-an-toe*. Also makes a churring alarm call. **Status:** Resident, breeding. **Abundance:** Common in Ngamiland and Chobe Districts, and Southern and Kgatleng Districts. Also common in eastern hardveld of Central District. *D. s. sephaena* occurs in eastern Botswana; *D. s. zambesiae* is found in the north of the country. **Habitat:** Found in woodlands (both acacia and broad-leaved) with dense, shrubby, dry undergrowth. Favors tangled bush around rocky kopjes. **Habits:** Occurs in pairs and family parties. Roosts in trees at night; otherwise it is strictly terrestrial. **Conservation:** Least Concern.

COQUI FRANCOLIN *Peliperdix coqui*

Setswana: le.tsiêkwane, le.twênti, le.tsiakarana, le.tseakarana

M: 26 cm (10 ¼ in), F: 24 cm (9 ½ in). **Identification:** Small sexually dimorphic francolin. Male has pale, buffy head. Female has buffy crown with white supercilium and a black moustachial stripe that continues along and around white throat. **Call:** Shrill, repeated *swem-pie* or *co-qui*. During summer, when breeding, also a loud *jit, jit, jit-jit, jit-jit-jit-jitjerr*. **Status:** Resident, breeding. **Abundance:** Uncommon (slightly more abundant in protected areas, which are less subject to overgrazing). The type specimen for *P. c. vernayi* (the only subspecies to occur in Botswana) was collected by Austin Roberts in 1930 at Tsotsoroga Pan in what is now Chobe National Park. **Habitat:** Found in broad-leaved woodlands, especially Zambezi Teak (*Baikiaea plurijuga*) woodlands with understory of relatively long grass. **Habits:** Occurs in pairs or small family groups. Secretive and easily overlooked, it walks slowly and flushes reluctantly. **Conservation:** Least Concern.

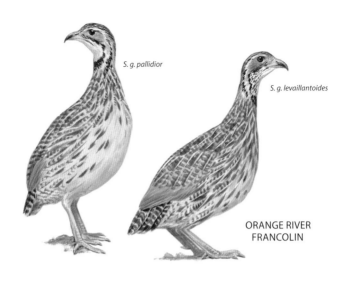

S. g. pallidior

S. g. levaillantoides

ORANGE RIVER
FRANCOLIN

D. s. sephaena

CRESTED
FRANCOLIN

male

female

COQUI
FRANCOLIN

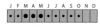

RED-BILLED SPURFOWL *Pternistis adspersus*

Setswana: le.sogo, le.tšankgarane

M: 38 cm (15 in), F: 35 cm (13 ¾ in). **Identification:** Robust terrestrial game bird. The combination of red bill and yellow eye-ring is diagnostic (Natal Spurfowl, lacks the latter feature). Underparts are finely barred. Only male has spurs, and male is generally more robust than female. **Call:** Duet, mostly at dawn; one bird produces loud *chock, chock, chock churrr*, while other simultaneously utters several shrieking notes. **Status:** Resident, breeding. Breeds only after rain; egg-laying may occur through the winter following adequate rainfall. **Abundance:** Common in western and central Botswana. Abundant in the north, especially in the Okavango Delta and adjacent northwestern Kalahari tree and bush savanna; these regions are its stronghold in southern Africa. In eastern hardveld, it is replaced by Natal Spurfowl. **Habitat:** Prefers dry floodplains and adjacent riparian woodlands. **Habits:** Occurs in pairs (when breeding) or small coveys (nonbreeding). Hybridizes with the very similar Natal Spurfowl in Chobe District, where the two species' ranges overlap. **Conservation:** Least Concern. Classified as a game bird; may be hunted from April to September.

NATAL SPURFOWL *Pternistis natalensis*

Setswana: se.gwêba

M: 38 cm (15 in), F: 30 cm (11 ¾ in). **Identification:** Robust terrestrial game bird. Very similar to Red-billed Spurfowl but lacks yellow eye-ring. Underparts have scalloped pattern. Only male has spurs. **Call:** Similar to call of Red-billed Spurfowl. **Status:** Resident, breeding. **Abundance:** Common. **Habitat:** Occurs in a range of woodland types but prefers dry riparian woodlands and woodlands on hills in eastern Botswana. Absent from all types of Kalahari woodlands. **Habits:** Occurs in pairs when breeding and in small coveys after breeding. Hybridizes with Red-billed Spurfowl in Chobe District, where the two birds' ranges overlap. **Conservation:** Least Concern. Classified as a game bird; may be hunted from April to September.

SWAINSON'S SPURFOWL *Pternistis swainsonii*

Setswana: kgwadi, kuku, le.sogokgwalê, le.sogo, kgwalê, rakôdu-khibidu

M: 38 cm (15 in), F: 33 cm (13 in). **Identification:** Robust terrestrial game bird. Bare red skin on face and throat; upper mandible black (lower mandible red). Legs black; spurs in male only. Two subspecies occur: the nominate, *P. s. swainsonii*, is slightly darker-plumaged than *P. s. damarensis*. **Call:** Harsh, repeated, crowing *kraaik … kraaik … kraaik*, given by male from prominent position, especially at dawn. **Status:** Resident, breeding. **Abundance:** Both subspecies are common to abundant. *P. s. swainsonii* is found in eastern and southern Botswana; *P. s. damarensis* occurs in the north of the country. **Habitat:** Found in tall grasses in both woodlands and grasslands. **Habits:** Occurs in pairs and small family parties. **Conservation:** Least Concern. Classified as a game bird; may be hunted from April to September.

RED-BILLED
SPURFOWL

NATAL
SPURFOWL

adult

juv.

SWAINSON'S
SPURFOWL

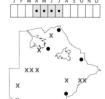

COMMON QUAIL *Coturnix coturnix*

Setswana: le.phurrwana, le.phurulwane, mmalephurrwane, se.khwiri

17 cm (6 ¾ in). **Identification:** Small, ground-dwelling game bird. Male has distinctive dark brown to black throat. Female has buffy throat not differentiated from breast; similar female Harlequin Quail, has more rufous underparts and white throat with black necklace. **Call:** Quick *whit-whit-whit*, similar to that of Harlequin Quail. This species is more often heard than seen. **Status:** Intra-African migrant, breeding. Egg-laying commences after late summer rains. **Abundance:** Sparse to uncommon. The few substantiated records are between April and July. This is a highly nomadic and irruptive species; its movements and appearances in Botswana are tied to rainfall. **Habitat:** Occurs in grasslands. **Habits:** Runs through grass in hunched posture to avoid detection. Rarely seen unless flushed, when it flies strongly, with quick beats of its remarkably long wings, before dropping back into the grass. **Conservation:** Least Concern. Classified as a game bird; may be hunted throughout the year.

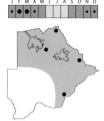

HARLEQUIN QUAIL *Coturnix delegorguei*

Setswana: se.khwiri, mmalephurrwane, le.phurrwana, le.phurulwane

18 cm (7 in). **Identification:** Small, ground-dwelling game bird. Male has rich chestnut flanks, visible even in flight. Female is similar to female Common Quail but has more rufous underparts and a black necklace below whitish throat. **Call:** *Whit-whit-whit*, similar to that of Common Quail. Calls frequently during summer. **Status:** Resident and intra-African migrant, breeding. Present mainly from spring to autumn, but some birds (especially those found in Makgadikgadi Pans) overwinter in Botswana. **Abundance:** Uncommon to common. This is a highly nomadic and irruptive species, its movements and appearances tied to quantity of rainfall. **Habitat:** Found in grassy clearings in Zambezian woodlands, northeastern Kalahari mixed woodland and scrub, and eastern hardveld. **Habits:** Feeds on seeds on the ground in grassy areas. Seldom seen unless flushed. **Conservation:** Least Concern.

BUTTONQUAILS Turnicidae

A family of diminutive, cryptically colored terrestrial birds. They resemble quails but unlike them have no hind toe (and therefore cannot perch) and are polyandrous, and females are larger and more attractively colored than the males. Only one species is found in Botswana. The Setswana name *le.phurrwana* is used for buttonquails and quails.

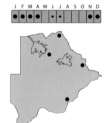

COMMON BUTTONQUAIL *Turnix sylvaticus*

Setswana: le.phurrwana, le.phurulwane, mmalephurrwana, se.khwiri

M: 14 cm (5 ½ in), F: 16 cm (6 ¼ in). **Identification:** Small, quail-like ground dweller. Combination of whitish sides to face, pale eye, orange-brown patch on breast, and black spots on sides of neck and breast is diagnostic. Female has richer markings than male. The species lacks black rump and rufous face of Black-rumped Buttonquail, which has not been recorded in Botswana but should be looked out for in the Kazuma Pan area in Chobe District. **Call:** Female has a booming advertising call, given at night. More often heard than seen. **Status:** Resident, breeding. Egg-laying takes place mainly in summer, but there are single records from June and July. **Abundance:** Common, particularly in Central, Ghanzi and South-East Districts. The species is nomadic, probably in response to rain, as it irrupts in some areas in certain years and is absent in others. **Habitat:** Found in open grassy clearings in Kalahari tree and bush savanna. **Habits:** May be solitary or in pairs or small family groups. Difficult to flush more than once. It has weaker flight than a quail. **Conservation:** Least Concern. Classified as a game bird; may be hunted throughout the year.

male

female

COMMON
QUAIL

male

HARLEQUIN
QUAIL

female

male

COMMON
BUTTONQUAIL

female

35

DUCKS, GEESE Anatidae

Aquatic birds with webbed feet and waterproof plumage. Their flattened, spatulate bills are suited to a varied, omnivorous diet. Most species show varying degrees of sexual dimorphism and are monogamous; some pair for life. In species in which the female undertakes incubation and parental duties alone, she plucks down from her body to line the nest. All species undergo a molt, usually after breeding, that includes the flight feathers and leaves the birds unable to fly for a short period. Of the Palearctic species, the males are present in Botswana in eclipse plumage (transitional plumage after breeding). In many ducks the speculum, a panel of colorful (usually iridescent) feathers on the wing, is a useful identification feature. Botswana is host to an assortment of ducks—16 resident species (all of which are nomadic and move in response to rainfall, while at least one resident has its population supplemented by regular intra-African migrants) and two Palearctic vagrants—but no true geese. Five exotic duck species have been recorded in Botswana (Mallard, Wood Duck, Mandarin Duck, Rosy-billed Pochard, and Red-crested Pochard); these are probably escapees from captivity except for the Mallard, which has a feral population in neighboring South Africa. These species are not covered in the species accounts. The Setswana name *se.hudi* applies to most members of this family.

FULVOUS WHISTLING DUCK *Dendrocygna bicolor*

Setswana: se.hudi, se.fudi

46 cm (18 in). **Identification:** Long-legged, long-necked waterfowl. It has golden-brown underparts and distinctive white plumes on its flanks. In flight, the tail coverts show as a white crescent; this distinguishes the species from White-faced Whistling Duck and smaller White-backed Duck (p. 38), which has white extending up the back. **Call:** Soft whistle, less musical than that of White-faced Whistling Duck. **Status:** Resident, breeding. In the Okavango Delta egg-laying starts in midwinter, as floodwaters from the summer rains in Angola finally reach the distal ends of the delta and Lake Ngami, and peaks in September and October, coinciding with the floods but before the rains have commenced later. In other parts of the country, egg-laying occurs from November to March, following rain. **Abundance:** Abundant along the Okavango River and throughout the Okavango Delta (including the Thamalakane and Boteti Rivers), Lake Ngami, Linyanti Swamps, and the Chobe River; scarce elsewhere in Botswana. The Okavango Delta is the species's stronghold in southern Africa and supports a regionally important population. Large flocks are occasionally seen at Lake Ngami. **Habitat:** Occurs in shallow freshwater wetlands, including lakes, ephemeral pans, and floodplains. **Habits:** This is a diving duck; it spends much of the day resting and preening in small flocks. **Conservation:** Least Concern.

WHITE-FACED WHISTLING DUCK *Dendrocygna viduata*

Setswana: le.wewe, le.wiiwii

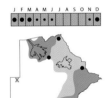

47 cm (18 ½ in). **Identification:** Long-legged, long-necked waterfowl. Appears dark brown nearly overall, except white face, which is diagnostic. When breeding, both sexes have a rusty-brown tinge to the facial feathers—this is not a muddy discoloration but nuptial plumage. **Call:** Whistled *le-wewe* (the Setswana name is onomatopoeic) or *sip-sip-sieu*. **Status:** Resident, breeding. **Abundance:** Common in the eastern hardveld; abundant in northern wetlands of the Okavango River and Delta, Lake Ngami, Linyanti Swamps, and the Chobe River (these wetlands are especially important in the dry season). The Chobe River occasionally supports more than 5,000 birds (over 0.5% of the southern African population) and is a regionally important area for the species. **Habitat:** Occurs in shallow freshwater, especially lagoons, backwaters of large rivers, floodplains, and lakes. **Habits:** Gregarious. Has an upright stance when alarmed. **Conservation:** Least Concern. Classified as a game bird; may be hunted from April to September.

AFRICAN PYGMY GOOSE *Nettapus auritus*

Setswana: se.hudi, se.hutsana

33 cm (13 in). **Identification:** Botswana's smallest duck. This tiny, colorful species has orange underparts and greenish upperparts. Male has green patch on neck; female and immature lack patch. White wing patches, in both sexes and all ages, are visible in flight. **Call:** Squeaking whistle. **Status:** Resident, breeding. **Abundance:** Abundant in the Okavango Delta and Linyanti Swamps; uncommon along the Chobe River; rare elsewhere. The Okavango is the species's stronghold in Africa, supporting its largest population. **Habitat:** Favors still waters of lagoons and quiet backwaters of large rivers with surface vegetation, particularly water lilies (*Nymphaea*) and pondweed (*Potamogeton*). **Habits:** Occurs in pairs or small family parties. Solitary male seen during summer signifies that its mate is incubating nearby. Nests in natural tree cavities near water. It is a perching duck but also upends for unopened water-lily buds in the fashion of a dabbling duck. **Conservation:** Least Concern. **General:** A contender for Africa's smallest duck (as is Hottentot Teal, p. 42).

FULVOUS
WHISTLING DUCK

breeding
adult

nonbreeding
adult

nonbreeding
adult

juv.

WHITE-FACED
WHISTLING DUCK

female

male

AFRICAN PYGMY
GOOSE

male

female

WHITE-BACKED DUCK *Thalassornis leuconotus*

Setswana: se.hudi, se.fudi

43 cm (17 in). **Identification:** Small, low-slung duck. Its relatively large head, mottled black-and-ocher plumage, and white patch on gape of bill are key field marks. In flight, a white triangle extending up the back is visible, and the feet project well beyond the tail. **Call:** Weak whistle, *whit-wee, whit-wee* (it is a whistling duck). **Status:** Resident, breeding. The distal end of the Okavango Delta, including Lake Ngami, provides important breeding sites for this species, and egg-laying peaks from August to October before rains have commenced but coincident with flooding of these areas. This is quite unlike its behavior in the rest of Botswana, where breeding is dependent on summer rains. **Abundance:** Abundant in the Okavango Delta, particularly along the Thamalakane and Boteti Rivers and at Lake Ngami; these are its strongholds in southern Africa and support internationally important populations. Scarce elsewhere in Botswana. **Habitat:** Found in quiet, lily-covered backwaters, lakes, and ephemeral pans. **Habits:** A diving duck, it spends much time foraging underwater. It is an unobtrusive species and sits low in the water. When flushed, it runs along water surface and flies off with a harsh whistle, legs dangling. **Conservation:** Least Concern.

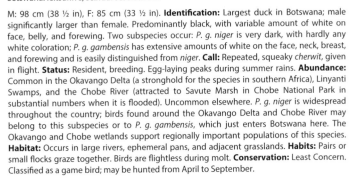

SPUR-WINGED GOOSE *Plectropterus gambensis*

Setswana: le.tsukwê, se.hudi sêsefatshwa

M: 98 cm (38 ½ in), F: 85 cm (33 ½ in). **Identification:** Largest duck in Botswana; male significantly larger than female. Predominantly black, with variable amount of white on face, belly, and forewing. Two subspecies occur: *P. g. niger* is very dark, with hardly any white coloration; *P. g. gambensis* has extensive amounts of white on the face, neck, breast, and forewing and is easily distinguished from *niger*. **Call:** Repeated, squeaky *cherwit*, given in flight. **Status:** Resident, breeding. Egg-laying peaks during summer rains. **Abundance:** Common in the Okavango Delta (a stronghold for the species in southern Africa), Linyanti Swamps, and the Chobe River (attracted to Savute Marsh in Chobe National Park in substantial numbers when it is flooded). Uncommon elsewhere. *P. g. niger* is widespread throughout the country; birds found around the Okavango Delta and Chobe River may belong to this subspecies or to *P. g. gambensis*, which just enters Botswana here. The Okavango and Chobe wetlands support regionally important populations of this species. **Habitat:** Occurs in large rivers, ephemeral pans, and adjacent grasslands. **Habits:** Pairs or small flocks graze together. Birds are flightless during molt. **Conservation:** Least Concern. Classified as a game bird; may be hunted from April to September.

KNOB-BILLED DUCK *Sarkidiornis melanotos*

Setswana: rankô

M: 70 cm (27 ½ in), F: 55 cm (21 ¾ in). **Identification:** Distinctive duck with black upperparts, including all-black wings (iridescent in the right light), and white underparts. Male is almost twice size of female; during breeding season (summer) male has enlarged, fleshy black protuberance on upper mandible and acquires a slight yellowish-buff tinge to head. **Call:** Generally silent. **Status:** Resident, plus summer influx of intra-African migrants; both breeding. Peak egg-laying occurs following rains, on small pans and other wetlands; only rarely breeds in south-east Botswana. **Abundance:** Common at Lake Ngami and outside the breeding season along the Chobe River (both areas support regionally important populations); uncommon elsewhere. Ducks resident in Botswana are nomadic and move to wetland areas where rainfall has been substantial. **Habitat:** Frequents major river systems, lakes, lagoons, dams, sewage ponds, and ephemeral pans. **Habits:** A grazing duck, it strips seeds from grasses, particularly at ephemeral pans during summer. Also dabbles in shallow water for aquatic insects and water-lily seeds. **Conservation:** Least Concern. Classified as a game bird; may be hunted from April to September. **General:** The Setswana name refers to the nose—that is, the large knob on the bill.

WHITE-BACKED
DUCK

SPUR-WINGED
GOOSE

adult male
nonbreeding
P. g. niger

adult female
P. g. niger

adult male
breeding
P. g. gambensis

imm.

nonbreeding
adult male

breeding
adult male

adult
female

juv.

adult
female

KNOB-BILLED
DUCK

EGYPTIAN GOOSE *Alopochen aegyptiaca*

Setswana: le.harathata

M: 75 cm (29 ½ in), F: 60 cm (23 ½ in). **Identification:** Large duck with buffy-brown coloration and a dark brown breast patch. In flight, large white wing panels (upperwing coverts) are visible. Similar South African Shelduck, with which it overlaps in southeastern Botswana, differs in having a gray head (male) or gray-and-white head (female). **Call:** Harsh honking by female, accompanied by hissing from male. However, both will honk when alarmed or taking flight. **Status:** Resident, breeding. Breeds throughout the year, but egg-laying takes place mainly between July and December at perennial bodies of water. **Abundance:** Abundant in the Okavango wetland system, Linyanti Swamps, Chobe River, and at Lake Ngami; common elsewhere. **Habitat:** Found in a variety of wetlands, both perennial and ephemeral. **Habits:** Primarily a grazer; occurs in pairs or small groups. Usually nests on the ground or in holes in cliffs, but also favors old raptor nests as safe breeding sites. It has used nests of Yellow-billed Kite, African Fish Eagle and Secretarybird, and has been recorded appropriating an active nest from a Black Sparrowhawk. Regularly uses Hamerkop nests. Undertakes local annual migration to areas of safe refuge for molting; it molts all flight feathers simultaneously, and flightless "flappers" are often seen at Lake Ngami. **Conservation:** Least Concern. Classified as a game bird; may be hunted from April to September.

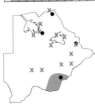

SOUTH AFRICAN SHELDUCK *Tadorna cana*

Setswana: se.hudi, se.fudi

63 cm (24 ¾ in). **Identification:** Waterfowl with rufous-brown body. Male has gray head, female has gray-and-white head. Female may be mistaken for White-faced Whistling Duck (p. 36) but is much larger and has white upperwing coverts, visible in flight. **Call:** Musical trumpeting. **Status:** Resident, breeding. **Abundance:** Uncommon. The South African population just extends into southeastern Botswana; the species's range has expanded in southeastern Botswana since the last century, and it is very occasionally seen as far north as Lake Ngami and the Thamalakane River. It is a southern African endemic. **Habitat:** Prefers shallow, nutrient-rich bodies of water, including dams and sewage ponds. **Habits:** Nests in burrows of Aardvark and other animals. **Conservation:** Least Concern.

CAPE TEAL *Anas capensis*

Setswana: se.hudi, se.fudi

46 cm (18 in). **Identification:** Pale-plumaged waterfowl. Combination of uniformly light-colored head, pink bill, and red eye is diagnostic. In flight, the white trailing edge to the wing is conspicuous. **Call:** Male issues a high-pitched whistle, female a harsh *quark*. **Status:** Resident, breeding. Breeds opportunistically throughout the year, but peak egg-laying occurs in winter. **Abundance:** Common in Makgadikgadi Pans and at sewage ponds in the southeastern part of the country and in Maun. Nata River delta in northern Sua Pan occasionally supports regionally important numbers (several hundred birds). **Habitat:** Found in brackish or saline pans and nutrient-rich freshwater bodies such as sewage ponds. **Habits:** Occurs in small flocks. It is a filter feeder that subsists on aquatic invertebrates and thus is often found with Greater Flamingos. Feeds by dabbling or upending, occasionally by diving. **Conservation:** Least Concern. Classified as a game bird; may be hunted from April to September.

RED-BILLED TEAL *Anas erythrorhyncha*

Setswana: se.hudi, se.fudi

46 cm (18 in). **Identification:** Buff-colored duck with dark cap and red bill. White secondaries show clearly in the upperwing in flight. Larger than Hottentot Teal (p. 42), which has blue bill. **Call:** Male makes wheezy whistle; female gives *quack, quack, quack*. **Status:** Resident plus influx of intra-African migrants; both breeding. **Abundance:** Abundant in the Okavango Delta and at Lake Ngami; common elsewhere in the northern and eastern parts of the country. Lake Ngami supports globally significant numbers at times; in October 1954 500,000 individuals were reported there, but such numbers do not exist today. **Habitat:** Prefers shallow, open, perennial or temporary nutrient-rich waters such as lakes and rivers. **Habits:** A dabbling species, it is highly gregarious. The species is nomadic. **Conservation:** Least Concern. Classified as a game bird; may be hunted from April to September.

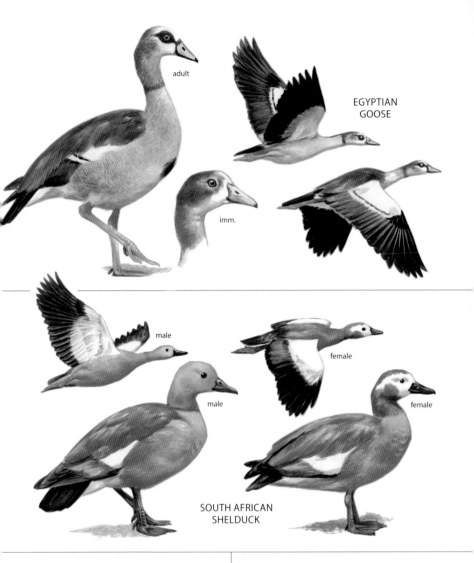

adult

imm.

EGYPTIAN
GOOSE

male

female

male

female

SOUTH AFRICAN
SHELDUCK

CAPE
TEAL

RED-BILLED
TEAL

41

HOTTENTOT TEAL *Anas hottentota*

Setswana: se.hudi, se.fudi

35 cm (13 ¾ in). **Identification:** Very small duck. Blue bill, dark cap, and dark smudge on creamy cheek are diagnostic. **Call:** Soft quacking; not a useful identification feature. **Status:** Resident, breeding. **Abundance:** Common at Lake Ngami and Linyanti Swamps, and in the Okavango Delta and Makgadikgadi Pans. The Boteti River sometimes has regionally important numbers. Occurs in eastern and southeastern Botswana. **Habitat:** Found in permanent and ephemeral bodies of water, including pans, lakes, rivers, and floodplains, with emergent vegetation (particularly bulrushes, *Typha* spp.). **Habits:** Occurs in pairs, or in flocks where food is abundant. A dabbling duck, it is often overlooked among emergent vegetation. **Conservation:** Least Concern. **General:** This species and African Pygmy Goose (p. 36) are Africa's smallest ducks.

YELLOW-BILLED DUCK *Anas undulata*

Setswana: se.hudi, se.fudi

57 cm (22 ½ in). **Identification:** Dark brown duck with a distinctive yellow bill. The green speculum with white edges is visible in flight. **Call:** Typical *quack*. **Status:** Resident, breeding. Egg-laying takes place during the rainy season. **Abundance:** Uncommon in the Okavango Delta, Linyanti Swamps, common in the South-East District. **Habitat:** Found in a variety of bodies of water; prefers standing water, including dams. **Habits:** Occurs in pairs or small groups (fewer than five) but sometimes in flocks of 200-plus as at Bokaa Dam and at Bathoen Dam near Kanye. Feeds by dabbling or upending. **Conservation:** Least Concern. Classified as a game bird; may be hunted from April to September.

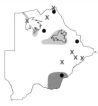

CAPE SHOVELER *Anas smithii*

Setswana: se.hudi, se.fudi

53 cm (20 ¾ in). **Identification:** Large duck with pronounced spatulate bill. Overall plumage color gray-brown. Yellow eye, black bill, and bright orange legs and feet distinguish the male from the drabber female, which has a dark eye and dull grayish-yellow legs. In flight, grayish-blue forewing (upperwing coverts) is a key field mark. **Call:** Female quacks; male has rasping call. **Status:** Resident, breeding. Breeds throughout the year on perennial bodies of water, though egg-laying peaks in winter. **Abundance:** Common in South-East District, mainly on sewage ponds associated with urban centers; uncommon elsewhere. It has become more abundant in southeastern Botswana in recent decades. **Habitat:** Prefers shallow nutrient-rich pans, sewage ponds. **Habits:** Occurs in pairs and small flocks. It uses its large spatulate bill to filter aquatic invertebrates from water. **Conservation:** Least Concern. Classified as a game bird; may be hunted from April to September.

GARGANEY *Anas querquedula*

39 cm (15 ¼ in). **Identification:** Occurs in mottled brown eclipse plumage in Botswana and may be mistaken for a female teal (pp. 40-42), Southern Pochard (p. 44), or Maccoa Duck (p. 44). Key distinguishing features are pale supercilium and dark eye stripe, and straighter, all-gray bill. **Call:** Mostly silent. **Status:** Vagrant from the Palearctic. The few sightings in Botswana, less than 10 to date, have been during summer months. **Abundance:** Rare. **Habitat:** Prefers bodies of nutrient-rich water. **Habits:** Single birds may be seen amid other duck species, notably Red-billed Teal. Dabbles and dips the head but seldom upends when feeding. **Conservation:** Least Concern.

HOTTENTOT
TEAL

male

female

YELLOW-BILLED
DUCK

male

female

CAPE
SHOVELER

male

female

GARGANEY

breeding
male

nonbreeding male
eclipse plumage

female

breeding
male

nonbreeding male
eclipse plumage

female

SOUTHERN POCHARD *Netta erythrophthalma*

Setswana: se.hudi, se.fudi

50 cm (19 ¾ in). **Identification:** Dark brown duck. Male has a black head and red eye. Female has a browner head, red-brown eye, and white facial markings. In flight, both sexes show a distinctive white bar along the flight feathers, and their wings lack a speculum. **Call:** Soft purring, whirring call, not useful for identification. **Status:** Resident, breeding. Breeds opportunistically throughout the year, but peak egg-laying follows rains. Numbers counted during summer are often lower than winter counts; there is apparently no summer influx of intra-African migrants (as is the case with some other duck species). **Abundance:** Abundant at Lake Ngami and Shashe Dam, and in South-East District, particularly at Bokaa Dam, and Phakalane and Tsholofelo sewage ponds, where globally significant numbers sometimes occur. Globally significant numbers also occur along the Thamalakane and Boteti Rivers, although the species is very sparse in the Okavango Delta. **Habitat:** Prefers deep, nutrient-rich, permanent water of lakes, dams, and sewage ponds. **Habits:** A diving duck, it feeds while swimming underwater; also feeds by dabbling. **Conservation:** Least Concern. Classified as a game bird; may be hunted from April to September.

MACCOA DUCK *Oxyura maccoa*

Setswana: se.hudi, se.fudi

50 cm (19 ¾ in). **Identification:** Squat, stiff-tailed diving duck with a low profile in water. Breeding male is rich chestnut, with a black head and bright blue bill. Female (and nonbreeding male) is gray-brown, with a white stripe below eye and whitish neck and throat. **Call:** Harsh, nasal trill. **Status:** Resident, breeding. Breeds opportunistically throughout the year on small pans, but peak egg-laying follows rains. **Abundance:** Common in South-East District (the South African population just extends into southeastern Botswana); Phakalane Sewage Lagoons used to regularly support regionally important numbers, but in recent years, Mahalapye sewage ponds and Jwaneng sewage ponds (in Southern District) have emerged as the best places to see this species in Botswana; uncommon elsewhere in the southeast; rare in Makgadikgadi Pans. **Habitat:** Prefers nutrient-rich waters with emergent vegetation, such as sewage ponds and ephemeral pans. **Habits:** Occurs in small flocks, usually one male and several females, when breeding; flocks of 40-50, and occasionally more than 100 birds, may occur outside the breeding season. Dives for invertebrates and plant material. The stiff tail is often raised. **Conservation:** Near Threatened.

AFRICAN BLACK DUCK *Anas sparsa*

Setswana: se.hudi, se.fudi

55 cm (21 ¾ in). **Identification:** Dark dabbling duck. It has conspicuous white patches on its back, a blackish bill, and orange legs and feet. These features and its habitat preference distinguish it from Yellow-billed Duck (p. 42). In flight, the purple-blue speculum is clearly visible; it is bordered by a white line in front and has a white trailing edge. **Call:** Female has a typical quack; male makes a high-pitched whistle. **Status:** Resident, breeding. **Abundance:** Scarce. Most sightings are from the Limpopo, Marico, and Notwane Rivers. Absent from the Okavango Delta (including the Boteti River) and the Chobe River. **Habitat:** A river specialist, occupies territories along wooded, flowing rivers. Occasionally found on dams and sewage ponds. **Habits:** A secretive species, it occurs in pairs or small groups (fewer than six). Feeds by dabbling or upending. **Conservation:** Least Concern.

NORTHERN PINTAIL *Anas acuta*

58 cm (22 ¾ in). **Identification:** Slender duck with pointed tail. Breeding male striking, with dark brown head, white breast, long lanceolate back feathers, and long, slender tail with central feathers extended to a point. Female and eclipse male speckled dark brown. In all plumages, the pointed central tail feathers are a key field mark. **Call:** Female quacks; male has a *pooop* call. **Status:** Vagrant from the Palearctic. **Abundance:** Rare. Only one Botswana record, a specimen from Lake Ngami, June 1980. **Habitat:** May occur at inland bodies of water. **Habits:** May be found in company with other ducks. **Conservation:** Least Concern. **General:** The specimen collected at Lake Ngami is in the National Museum, Gaborone.

male

female

SOUTHERN
POCHARD

male

female

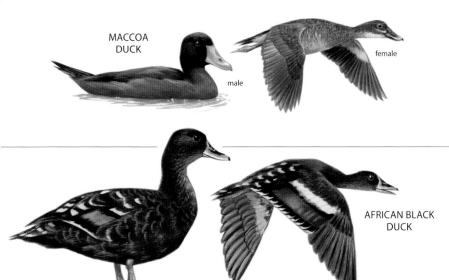

MACCOA
DUCK

male

female

AFRICAN BLACK
DUCK

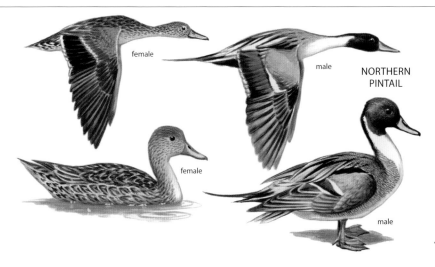

female

male

NORTHERN
PINTAIL

female

male

45

GREBES Podicipedidae

Superficially duck-like waterbirds, grebes have legs positioned far back on the body, lobed toes, and pointed bills. These features enable them to catch prey—aquatic invertebrates, amphibians, and small fish—by underwater pursuit, using the legs for propulsion. They have the peculiar habit of swallowing their own feathers, thought to facilitate regurgitation of fish bones. They appear weak in flight and fly low over the water. The Botswana species breed opportunistically; all construct floating nests of plant material, and some cover their eggs when disturbed. The precocial juveniles leave the nest soon after hatching, but return to it periodically for the first few days; they have black-and-white-striped heads and are frequently carried on the parents' backs. All three Botswana species are nomadic in response to rain.

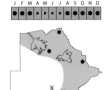

LITTLE GREBE *Tachybaptus ruficollis*

Setswana: se.nwêdi

20 cm (7 ¾ in). **Identification:** Small waterbird, superficially resembling a duck, with a dumpy body and a short, fluffy tail. The bill is short and has a white spot at the gape. The face and neck are rufous in breeding male, pale brown in nonbreeding male and female. **Call:** Descending trill. **Status:** Resident, breeding. Breeds opportunistically throughout the year. Around the Okavango Delta, egg-laying peaks from August to November, before the rains but when the delta's distal areas and Lake Ngami are flooding (i.e., floods provide the stimulus for breeding); in the rest of the country, egg-laying coincides with rainfall (December to March), when ephemeral bodies of water are available for breeding. **Abundance:** Abundant at Lake Ngami (which sometimes supports regionally important numbers), and in the South-East District; common in the Okavango Delta, Linyanti Swamps, along the Chobe River, and in Makgadikgadi Pans. This is the most abundant and widespread grebe in Botswana. It makes local movements in response to rain. **Habitat:** Prefers standing water, such as lakes, lagoons, sewage ponds and ephemeral pans, with emergent vegetation. **Habits:** Usually nests solitarily, but floating nests at Lake Ngami may be spaced only 10–20 m apart. Makes nest of aquatic weeds, and regularly covers eggs with vegetation when leaving nest. Adults often swim with young on their backs. Skitters over water, giving impression of weak flight. Dives readily. **Conservation:** Least Concern.

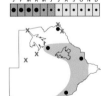

BLACK-NECKED GREBE *Podiceps nigricollis*

28 cm (11 in). **Identification:** Waterbird with tailless appearance. It has a slender, upturned bill, red eyes, and black head and neck. In breeding plumage it has yellow-gold ear tufts and rufous flanks. **Call:** Mostly silent. **Status:** Resident, breeding. Breeds opportunistically throughout the year, but peak egg-laying coincides with rains. Breeding concentrations occur in Makgadikgadi Pans during years of high rainfall. **Abundance:** Scarce. Most frequently found in South-East District, but the species is irruptive and nomadic and may be seen outside its normal range, especially in northern and eastern Botswana, during high rainfall years. **Habitat:** Found in perennial and ephemeral bodies of water (including brackish water) and sewage ponds. **Habits:** Has habit of preening side while floating, thereby exposing the white underparts. This grebe does not cover eggs with vegetation when leaving nest. Dives readily. **Conservation:** Least Concern.

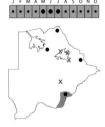

GREAT CRESTED GREBE *Podiceps cristatus*

50 cm (19 ¾ in). **Identification:** Botswana's largest grebe. It has a long, slender neck and a large head, accentuated in the adult by dark lateral crests and a rufous ruff. Immature bird has extensive white on head and foreneck. **Call:** Musical purring *krruuk* followed by lower-pitched *raaa*. **Status:** Resident, breeding. It breeds throughout the year but mainly in winter. **Abundance:** Uncommon in South-East District (the South African population just extends into southeastern Botswana). Bokaa Dam is the only site in Botswana that regularly supports regionally important numbers (occasionally globally important numbers). **Habitat:** Prefers permanent standing water, such as dams, with emergent vegetation; occasionally at sewage ponds. **Habits:** May be solitary, in pairs, or in small family parties. During courtship, pair conducts elaborate, coordinated dance, both birds rising up in the water breast to breast. It usually nests solitarily, constructing floating nest of aquatic weeds, and covers eggs with vegetation when it leaves nest. Young up to three weeks of age are sometimes carried on backs of swimming adults. Dives readily. **Conservation:** Least Concern.

juv.

LITTLE
GREBE

breeding
adult

nonbreeding
adult

breeding
adullt

BLACK-NECKED
GREBE

breeding

nonbreeding

GREAT CRESTED
GREBE

juv.

imm.

adult

47

FLAMINGOS Phoenicopteridae

Highly specialized waterbirds, flamingos have exceptionally long legs, partially webbed toes, long necks, and unique bills with comb-like projections (lamellae) along edges. Bills are dipped upside down in shallow nutrient-rich water, from which the lamellae filter cyanobacteria, diatoms, and brine shrimps. Highly gregarious, flamingos breed opportunistically in southern Sua Pan in colonies of thousands. They make mud-turret nests as repositories for their single-egg clutches. Young are well developed on hatching and vacate the nest within a few days and form huge crèches. Genetically the flamingos' closest relatives are ibises and spoonbills (p. 56). Two flamingo species occur in Botswana, one of which is listed as globally Near Threatened.

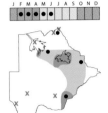

GREATER FLAMINGO *Phoenicopterus roseus*

Setswana: mo.gôlôri, nônyane yatladi

M: 165 cm (65 in), F: 145 cm (57 in). **Identification:** Large waterbird with very long neck and legs. Pale pink plumage; pink bill tipped with black. Juvenile has gray-brown plumage and a gray bill with black tip. **Call:** Goose-like honking. **Status:** Resident, breeding. The species has few breeding sites in southern Africa, although there are more than 20 sites elsewhere on the continent. It breeds on Sua Pan only during years of high rainfall, when precipitation exceeds 50 cm, and there is a reasonable chance of success; egg-laying takes place only in late summer when sufficient rain has fallen. The population has only about four major breeding events per decade. **Abundance:** Abundant in Makgadikgadi Pans, where more than 35,000 pairs bred in the summer of 2008–9; Sua Pan supports globally important numbers. Periodically common at Lake Ngami, which is an important feeding area and regularly supports significant numbers. Flocks of 100 to 1,000 or more occur briefly at many wetlands in eastern and southeastern Botswana, especially the Broadhurst sewage ponds and Bokaa Dam. Birds from Sua Pan are known to move to the Namibian coast and suitable wetlands in South Africa; they are suspected to move farther afield to central and East Africa. **Habitat:** Occurs in shallow saline bodies of water with abundant invertebrate prey; also nutrient-rich freshwater lakes. **Habits:** Highly gregarious. Feeds with head down and bill upturned. Constant foot-stirring gives impression birds are pedaling in the shallows. **Conservation:** Least Concern.

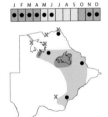

LESSER FLAMINGO *Phoeniconaias minor*

Setswana: mo.gôlôri, nônyane yatladi

M: 122 cm (48 in), F: 115 cm (45 ¼ in). **Identification:** Much smaller than Greater Flamingo, Lesser has pinker plumage and an all-dark bill. Juvenile bird is dirty grayish white; attains a pinkish tinge in second year. **Call:** Guttural, unmusical croaking. **Status:** Resident, breeding. Sua Pan is one of only four breeding sites worldwide for this species. It breeds early every year in anticipation of rainfall; egg-laying can take place from November through June. This strategy differs from the more "conservative" approach of the Greater Flamingo and is less productive (only about three major breeding events per decade). **Abundance:** Abundant in Makgadikgadi Pans when water is present; more than 43,000 pairs bred in Sua Pan in the summer of 2000–1. Scarce visitor at Lake Ngami and other bodies of water such as Shashe and Letsibogo Dams and most wetlands in the southeast. Birds from Sua Pan are known to move to the Namibian coast and suitable wetlands in South Africa; they are suspected to move farther afield to central and East Africa. **Habitat:** Occurs in shallow, highly saline bodies of water where blue-green algae and diatoms are abundant; also nutrient-rich freshwater lakes. **Habits:** Highly gregarious. Flies at night to favored feeding locations. In Sua Pan, the birds move progressively northward as the pan dries until they reach its sump, at Nata Sanctuary, in late winter. **Conservation:** Near Threatened.

GREATER
FLAMINGO

adult

imm.

adult

imm.

juv.

adult

adult

juv.

LESSER
FLAMINGO

49

STORKS Ciconiidae

Storks are long-legged, long-necked birds with long, dagger-like bills. Most fly with the long neck and legs extended (the Marabou Stork folds its neck). Many species occupy aquatic habitats. Most urinate on their legs for cooling purposes, and the legs of these species may be streaked with white. They have a reduced syrinx (vocal organ) and are voiceless. Storks are monogamous and breed solitarily or colonially. Sexes are alike in all species except the Saddle-billed Stork. Five genera and eight species occur in Botswana, a mixture of breeding residents and nonbreeding intra-African and Palearctic migrants.

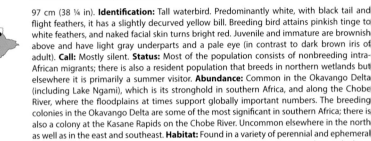

YELLOW-BILLED STORK *Mycteria ibis*

Setswana: le.kôllwane, le.kôlôlwane

97 cm (38 ¼ in). **Identification:** Tall waterbird. Predominantly white, with black tail and flight feathers, it has a slightly decurved yellow bill. Breeding bird attains pinkish tinge to white feathers, and naked facial skin turns bright red. Juvenile and immature are brownish above and have light gray underparts and a pale eye (in contrast to dark brown iris of adult). **Call:** Mostly silent. **Status:** Most of the population consists of nonbreeding intra-African migrants; there is also a resident population that breeds in northern wetlands but elsewhere it is primarily a summer visitor. **Abundance:** Common in the Okavango Delta (including Lake Ngami), which is its stronghold in southern Africa, and along the Chobe River, where the floodplains at times support globally important numbers. The breeding colonies in the Okavango Delta are some of the most significant in southern Africa; there is also a colony at the Kasane Rapids on the Chobe River. Uncommon elsewhere in the north as well as in the east and southeast. **Habitat:** Found in a variety of perennial and ephemeral wetlands. **Habits:** Gregarious, occurs in small parties. Hunts for aquatic prey by touch alone, immersing tactile bill in water and stirring with one foot to disturb fish and frogs, which it snaps up when they touch the sensitive beak. Often leans to one side when feeding, counterbalancing with one extended wing. **Conservation:** Least Concern.

WHITE STORK *Ciconia ciconia*

Setswana: le.kôlôlwane lêlesweu

113 cm (44 ½ in). **Identification:** Tall stork. Mostly white, it has black flight feathers and a red bill and legs (legs frequently streaked with white from dried urine). In flight, wings show contrasting black flight feathers and white coverts, on both upper- and underwing, and neck and feet are extended. Tail feathers are white; Yellow-billed Stork has black tail feathers. **Call:** Silent. **Status:** Palearctic migrant, nonbreeding. Greatest numbers are present in Botswana in summer. Occasional low numbers of birds seen during winter are presumed to be migrants from the small South African breeding population. **Abundance:** Common. **Habitat:** Prefers open grasslands, fallow fields. Avoids large permanent wetlands. **Habits:** Flocks, sometimes numbering hundreds, follow rain fronts and the insects they produce; the birds are particularly partial to Corn Cricket and caterpillar outbreaks. Large numbers also congregate at ephemeral pans when in transit. Flocks soar in disorderly fashion when migrating. **Conservation:** Least Concern.

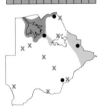

SADDLE-BILLED STORK *Ephippiorhynchus senegalensis*

Setswana: mo.lômbwê, xômbadi.

150 cm (59 in). **Identification:** Tall black-and-white stork. The bill is red and black with a yellow "saddle" at base of upper mandible (hence name). Legs are black with red ankles and feet. Male has dark brown eye and two small, pendent yellow wattles on either side of base of bill. Female has yellow eye and lacks wattles. Immature has dark eyes, brown rather than black plumage, and orange saddle. **Call:** Silent **Status:** Resident, breeding. **Abundance:** Common in the Okavango Delta, which is the southern African stronghold and an internationally important site for this species; the population there is estimated to be between 800 and 1,100 birds. Also common in Linyanti Swamps and along the Chobe River. Scarce outside the northern wetlands. **Habitat:** Primarily found in permanent wetlands but also in ephemeral pans. **Habits:** May be solitary or in pairs; sometimes forms small congregations where food is abundant. **Conservation:** Least Concern.

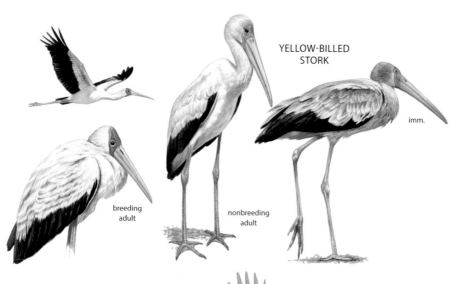

YELLOW-BILLED
STORK

breeding
adult

nonbreeding
adult

imm.

WHITE
STORK

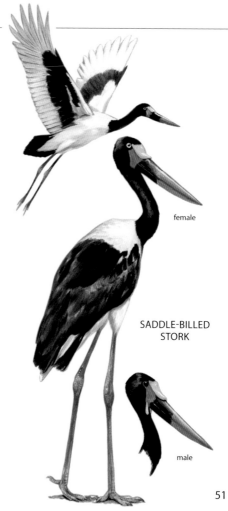

female

SADDLE-BILLED
STORK

male

51

J F M A M J J A S O N D

MARABOU STORK *Leptoptilos crumenifer*

Setswana: ghubê

152 cm (59 ¾ in). **Identification:** Large, distinctive stork with black legs (usually whitewashed with dried urine). It has a bald head and a pendulous pale pink air sac at the throat; there is also an orange air sac at the base of the hind neck. In breeding adult, wing and back feathers are smooth and slate gray with a green sheen; gray secondary wing coverts are conspicuously edged in white (visible in the folded wing and on upperside when bird is in flight); underparts, in particular the undertail coverts, are white with a powder-puff texture; and the hind neck is pale blue. Sides of head stained orange from the hind-neck sac's secretions. Nonbreeding bird is gray above and white below; lacks white edges to wing coverts. Juvenile has a fluffy feathered head, a noticeably shorter bill, and duller plumage. **Call:** Bill clattering plus various grunting and mooing sounds during breeding. **Status:** Resident, breeding. Populations are probably supplemented by trans-equatorial intra-African migrants, although there is no conclusive evidence for this. **Abundance:** Abundant in the Okavango Delta (the bird's southern African stronghold), Linyanti Swamps, Chobe National Park, and Lake Ngami. Less common in east and southeast, where occasional aggregations of up to 1000 occur at garbage dumps. Largest breeding site (300 pairs) in southern Africa currently is in the Okavango Delta at Lediba la Dinonyane. Nesting attempts have been made at Lake Ngami, which is also of regional importance for this species. During summer, several thousand congregate on open dry pans in the Kalahari (these are birds that have dispersed post-breeding, plus possible influx of visitors from farther north). **Habitat:** Found in freshwater wetlands and a variety of Kalahari woodlands; also scavenges at municipal waste dumps. Visits pans in Kalahari woodlands during summer months. **Habits:** Gregarious; aggregations of over 3,000 birds regularly recorded during summer. Flocks are seen foraging on the ground or riding thermal air currents, by which they travel vast distances. Associated with Corn Cricket and bullfrog outbreaks and quelea roosting and breeding sites. **Conservation:** Least Concern. **General:** The air sac on this stork's throat is apparently part of an air-cooling mechanism, but the function of the sac on the back of the neck is unknown.

J F M A M J J A S O N D

AFRICAN OPENBILL *Anastomus lamelligerus*

Setswana: le.kôlôlwane, le.kôllwane

82 cm (32 ¼ in). **Identification:** Relatively short, dark stork. The bill is unique in having a gap between the closed mandibles. Adult plumage is black mixed with iridescent bronze, purple, and brown feathers; these colors are absent in juvenile and immature birds, which are overall duller. **Call:** Silent. **Status:** Resident, breeding. Intra-African migrants possibly supplement resident populations during summer. **Abundance:** Abundant in the Okavango Delta, Linyanti Swamps, and the Chobe River floodplains. Rare in the southeast and scarce in eastern Botswana but has bred at Letsibogo Dam and at Nata Delta. The Okavango Delta is the stronghold for this species in southern Africa, and it and the Chobe floodplains support regionally, and sometimes globally, important populations. It is the most abundant stork in northern Botswana; flocks of up to 5,000 birds have been recorded. In 2010–11, during high flood levels in the Zambezi and Chobe Rivers and the Okavango wetland system, openbills bred prolifically in single-species colonies in reeds and in trees (e.g., at Kasane Rapids); the offspring dispersed throughout southern Africa. **Habitat:** Found in freshwater wetlands; it is a floodplain specialist. **Habits:** Aquatic; feeds on freshwater mussels and snails, which it locates by touch in shallow water. It uses its specialized bill to extract the mollusk from its shell. **Conservation:** Least Concern.

adult

MARABOU
STORK

adult

imm.

adult

AFRICAN
OPENBILL

adult

53

WOOLLY-NECKED STORK *Ciconia episcopus*

Setswana: le.kôllwane, le.kôlôlwane

84 cm (33 in). **Identification:** Medium-size stork. Wings and most of body black; white, woolly neck and head. **Call:** Silent. **Status:** Intra-African migrant, nonbreeding; usually seen only between October and May. (At present there is no resident breeding population in Botswana, but the species has started overwintering, and breeding, elsewhere in southern Africa.) **Abundance:** Abundant in Chobe National Park and in Ngamiland District in grasslands around the periphery of the Okavango Delta, which support regionally, and occasionally globally, important numbers. Uncommon elsewhere, including within the Okavango Delta. **Habitat:** Prefers short grasslands near water. **Habits:** Gregarious, regularly numbering in the hundreds, sometimes exceeding a thousand, in northern Botswana. **Conservation:** Least Concern.

ABDIM'S STORK *Ciconia abdimii*

Setswana: le.kôlôlwane, mo.kôtatsiê

76 cm (30 in). **Identification:** Small black stork with white belly and greenish-gray bill. Legs are pale olive with red tibiotarsal joints (ankles) and feet. Legs often heavily streaked with white from dried urine. **Call:** Silent. **Status:** Intra-African migrant, nonbreeding. A few birds are recorded during winter months. **Abundance:** Uncommon to common throughout the country. **Habitat:** Prefers open grasslands and fallow fields but visits wetlands to drink and bathe. **Habits:** Gregarious. Large flocks of thousands follow rain fronts in search of termite alates; they also feed on caterpillars, Corn Crickets, and locusts. Urinates on legs to keep cool. **Conservation:** Least Concern.

BLACK STORK *Ciconia nigra*

Setswana: le.kôlôlwane, lêlentsho

103 cm (40 ½ in). **Identification:** Large stork. Predominantly black with iridescent sheen, it has white underparts and red bill and legs. Larger size and bill and leg color distinguish it from Abdim's Stork. A partially leucistic individual has been recorded. **Call:** Silent. **Status:** Resident, breeding. **Abundance:** Uncommon in eastern and southeastern Botswana, rare elsewhere. **Habitat:** Prefers mountainous areas in eastern Botswana (nesting in cliffs in the dry season), but occasionally seen along rivers. **Habits:** It is solitary or occurs in pairs. Individual pairs do not breed every year. **Conservation:** Least Concern.

HAMERKOP Scopidae

A monotypic family with one representative, the Hamerkop, endemic to Africa and Madagascar. Though superficially stork-like, it is singular in appearance, structure, and habits.

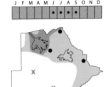

HAMERKOP *Scopus umbretta*

Setswana: mmamasiloanoka, mmamasilaanoka, mmamasêlanoka, masilaanoka

56 cm (22 in). **Identification:** Waterbird with uniformly drab brown plumage but a distinctive hammer shape to the head formed by the large bill and heavy crest. Immature has crest and pale eye when it fledges (in contrast with dark brown eye of adult). **Call:** Peculiar squeaky, whistling call. **Status:** Resident, breeding. **Abundance:** Common in the Okavango wetland system, Linyanti Swamps, and the Chobe and Limpopo Rivers. Less common along waterways and at dams and sewage ponds in the east and southeast. **Habitat:** Found in a variety of perennial and ephemeral freshwater habitats, including man-made dams. **Habits:** May be solitary or in pairs, sometimes in small groups, foraging in shallow water. Monogamous; performs a bizarre courtship ritual that includes repeated false mountings with the male standing on the female's back and vice versa. Huge, oven-like nest takes pair about six weeks to construct. The entrance tunnel and nest chamber are plastered with mud and the nest is often adorned with bits of plastic, papers, and such. The nest is about 2 m (7 ft) in height and 1.5 m (5 ft) from front to back and weighs between 25 and 50 kg (55 and 110 lb). **Conservation:** Least Concern. **General:** This bird is the subject of the Setswana proverb *Bopelonomi bo bolayile mmamasiloanoka* ("kindness killed the Hamerkop"), a reference to the fact that after it works so hard to build its large nest, other birds (such as Western Barn Owl, Egyptian Goose, or Verreaux's Eagle-Owl) then appropriate it.

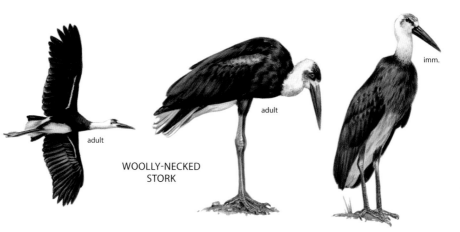

adult

**WOOLLY-NECKED
STORK**

adult

imm.

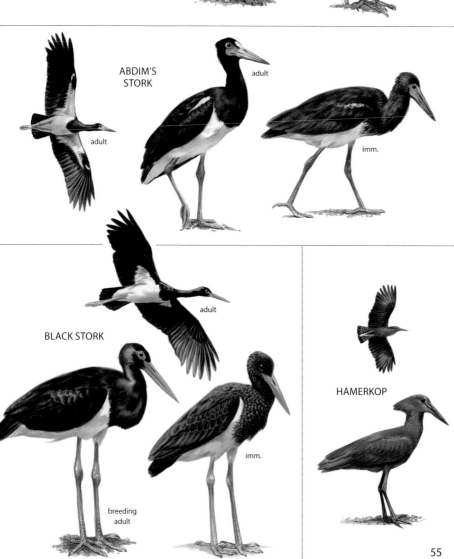

**ABDIM'S
STORK**

adult

adult

imm.

BLACK STORK

adult

breeding
adult

imm.

HAMERKOP

55

IBISES, SPOONBILLS Threskiornithidae

A family of relatively large wading waterbirds that takes its name from the genus of the African Sacred Ibis (*Threskiornis* refers to a religiously significant bird). All fly with necks and legs extended. Ibises have long, decurved bills, while spoonbills have distinctively flattened bills with a spatulate tip. Bills are adapted to capture particular vertebrate and invertebrate prey. These birds are often gregarious, and most nest colonially. They are monogamous, and both sexes undertake incubation and other parental duties. Botswana is home to three ibises belonging to separate genera and one spoonbill.

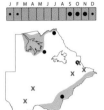

HADADA IBIS *Bostrychia hagedash*

Setswana: tshababarwa

76 cm (30 in). **Identification:** Waterbird with typical decurved ibis bill. Appears dull brown overall but has iridescent bronze mantle and green sheen on wings. In flight, legs do not protrude beyond tail, as they do in Glossy Ibis. Two allopatric subspecies are found in Botswana: *B. h. hagedash* has a dark eye, pale crescent on cheek, and bronze wing coverts; *B. h. brevirostris* has a pale eye, noticeable white crescent on cheek, and iridescent green wing coverts. **Call:** Loud *ha ha hadeda*. Common name is onomatopoeic. **Status:** Resident, breeding. **Abundance:** Uncommon in the Okavango Delta, Linyanti Swamps, and along the Chobe River, as well as in eastern Botswana along the Limpopo River and its tributaries, the Marico and Notwane Rivers. The range has expanded in southeast Botswana since the 1970s. *B. h. hagedash* occurs in eastern and southern Botswana; *B. h. brevirostris* occurs around the Okavango Delta, Linyanti Swamps, and Chobe River. **Habitat:** Freshwater wetlands: prefers rivers and channels with well-wooded margins. **Habits:** Pairs forage together, probing with bill in damp ground. Occurs in small noisy flocks when flying to communal roosts. **Conservation:** Least Concern.

GLOSSY IBIS *Plegadis falcinellus*

58 cm (22 ¾ in). **Identification:** Waterbird with typical decurved ibis bill. Appears black from a distance, but is dark chestnut overall, with iridescent green and purple on wings. When breeding, lores turn blue with a narrow white border. Immature is dark ashy brown with white speckling on throat. In flight, legs protrude well beyond tail, in contrast to Hadada Ibis. **Call:** Mostly silent. Occasional harsh squawk. **Status:** Resident, breeding. Breeds opportunistically during almost any month (e.g., when Lake Ngami is filling); however, main egg-laying months are September and October. **Abundance:** Uncommon to common in the northern wetland systems of the Okavango Delta, Linyanti Swamps, and Chobe River as well as in the Makgadikgadi Pans where it breeds in some years at Nata Delta. Scarcer in the southeast. **Habitat:** Frequents a variety of freshwater wetlands, both perennial and ephemeral, including man-made dams. **Habits:** Gregarious; feeds in shallow water. Roosts and breeds colonially in acacias, Water Figs (*Ficus verruculosa*), and *Cyperus* reedbeds. Often seen flying in large V formations. **Conservation:** Least Concern.

AFRICAN SACRED IBIS *Threskiornis aethiopicus*

Setswana: kôkôlôhutwê

M: 85 cm (33 ½ in), F: 70 cm (27 ½ in). **Identification:** Sexes are similar in plumage, but male is larger and has a longer bill than female. The head and neck are bare of feathers, revealing black skin. During breeding season, bare skin under the wings and on the sides of the breast turns bright red; ornamental blue-black plumes (secondaries) intensify in color; and legs turn copper colored. Juvenile has a mixture of black, gray, and white feathers on head and neck. In immature birds, iris and bare skin around the eyes are gray-brown; in adult, iris is brown, eye-ring is red. **Call:** Generally silent. **Status:** Resident, breeding. **Abundance:** Abundant in the Okavango Delta. Common elsewhere in the north, as well as in the east and southeast. **Habitat:** Occurs in muddy fringes of freshwater wetlands, including man-made impoundments. **Habits:** Probes with decurved bill in mud for aquatic invertebrates; also feeds on fish and frogs. Roosts and breeds colonially in reeds and acacias. **Conservation:** Least Concern. **General:** The ancient Egyptians regarded this ibis as sacred, believing it to be the incarnation of Thoth, their god of wisdom and learning.

HADADA IBIS

B. h. hagedash

B. h. brevirostris

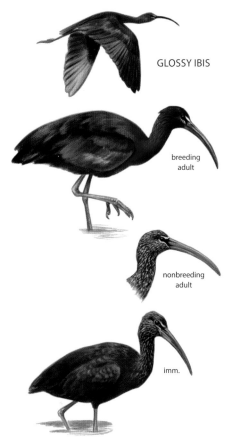

GLOSSY IBIS

breeding
adult

nonbreeding
adult

imm.

breeding
adult

juv.

imm.

adult

AFRICAN
SACRED IBIS

AFRICAN SPOONBILL *Platalea alba*

Setswana: mmaleswana

83 cm (32 ¾ in). **Identification:** Long-legged, white wading waterbird. Distinctive spoon-shaped bill is pinkish red with blue vermiculations. Juvenile has black legs (adult has red legs) and a gray bill without the "spoon," but this develops by the time they fledge. Flies with neck outstretched (not retracted, as in white egrets, p. 66). **Call:** Not very vocal; cawing *kraaak* at breeding colony. **Status:** Resident, breeding. Egg-laying can take place in virtually any month but peaks between September and November in the Okavango Delta, and between February and April elsewhere in the country. **Abundance:** Abundant in the Makgadikgadi Pans, Okavango Delta (including Lake Ngami), and Chobe River. Common in eastern and southeastern Botswana, including along the Limpopo River. **Habitat:** Found in shallows of perennial and ephemeral bodies of water, both fresh (Okavango, Chobe, Lake Ngami) and saline (Makgadikgadi). **Habits:** Solitary; feeds by sweeping bill from side to side in shallows until it contacts prey item such as fish, frogs, or aquatic invertebrates. Breeds colonially with cormorants, darters, ibises, egrets, and herons. **Conservation:** Least Concern.

HERONS, BITTERNS, EGRETS Ardeidae

A family of (mainly) waterbirds, all of which have sharp, pointed bills and long legs and necks, and fly with neck retracted. There is no clear morphological distinction between herons, bitterns, and egrets, although members of the genus *Ardea* are mostly called herons, while most egrets belong to the genus *Egretta*. The herons tend to be large and variable in coloration (but usually not white), while egrets are usually white and have long, filamentous plumes (aigrettes) in the breeding season. Bitterns are cryptically colored and exhibit "sky-pointing" behavior when disturbed. In most ardeids, the legs and bare facial skin change color during breeding. Most species make harsh croaking or deep booming calls. All 18 southern African members of this family are found in Botswana, and many have their regional strongholds in the Okavango Delta. The majority are breeding residents and nest colonially. One species, Slaty Egret, is listed as globally Vulnerable and is near endemic to the Okavango Delta; the remainder are widespread (some are cosmopolitan) and of little conservation concern.

BLACK-HEADED HERON *Ardea melanocephala*

Setswana: kôkôlôfutê, mo.gôlôri

92 cm (36 ¼ in). **Identification:** Tall, long-legged, long-necked heron. It has a black head and hind neck and a dark bill. In flight, its underwing is black and white (compare Grey Heron). **Call:** Mostly silent; loud *kraak*. **Status:** Resident, breeding. **Abundance:** Common in southeastern Botswana, particularly in the eastern hardveld; uncommon around the Makgadikgadi Pans, Okavango Delta, Linyanti Swamps, and Chobe River. **Habitat:** A terrestrial bird, it favors short grasslands; less reliant on wetlands for feeding but may nest often with Grey Herons in trees or reeds at dams, pans, and sewage ponds. **Habits:** A stand-and-wait hunter of invertebrates, small mammals, birds, and reptiles. **Conservation:** Least Concern.

GREY HERON *Ardea cinerea*

Setswana: se.ngwêpê, kôkôlêhutô

94 cm (37 in). **Identification:** Long-legged, long-necked waterbird. It is predominantly gray, but has a white head and hind neck, which distinguish it from Black-headed Heron, as does the uniformly gray underwing, visible when the bird is in flight. Bill and legs become orange-red at start of breeding. **Call:** Mostly silent; loud *kraak* in flight. **Status:** Resident, breeding. Numerous breeding sites have been recorded in Botswana, in trees or reeds (*Phragmites* and *Typha*). **Abundance:** Common throughout the Okavango wetland system (including Lake Ngami), Linyanti Swamps, and along the Chobe River; also Makgadikgadi Pans and along the Limpopo River and many wetlands in the southeast. **Habitat:** An aquatic species, it is associated with a variety of shallow, open bodies of water; compare more terrestrial habitats of Black-headed Heron. **Habits:** Solitary, stand-and-wait fisher, it also eats frogs, rodents, and occasionally birds, such as moorhen chicks. **Conservation:** Least Concern.

58

adult

imm.

AFRICAN SPOONBILL

BLACK-HEADED HERON

adult

breeding adult

imm.

juv.

adult

imm.

GREY HERON

breeding adult

adult

59

GOLIATH HERON *Ardea goliath*

143 cm (56 ¼ in). **Identification:** The largest heron in the world. Despite size, sometimes mistaken for the much smaller, slender Purple Heron, but distinguished from that species by rufous crown and black bill and legs. Slow ponderous flight. Immature, paler than adult, has heavily speckled throat and buffy upperwing coverts. **Call:** Loud, guttural barking *yak-yak-yak-yak*, repeated seven or eight times. **Status:** Resident, breeding. Lake Ngami is an important breeding area; it also breeds in the Nata River delta and the Okavango Delta. **Abundance:** Uncommon in the Okavango Delta (even though this is its stronghold in southern Africa) and at Lake Ngami; absent from the Nata River delta when the area is dry. Scarce in other areas; appears in southeastern Botswana as a rare visitor from elsewhere in southern Africa. **Habitat:** Favors shallow margins of large, permanent bodies of water. **Habits:** Solitary or in pairs. A stand-and-wait fisher, it primarily targets large fish. **Conservation:** Least Concern.

PURPLE HERON *Ardea purpurea*

85 cm (33 ½ in). **Identification:** Very slender heron with a black crown and striped face and neck. Legs are yellow with black on front of tarsus and feet, and the bill has a black upper mandible and yellow lower mandible. Slightly greater than half the size of Goliath Heron. Immature tawny brown; like adult, has bicolor bill. **Call:** Mostly silent; harsh, grating *kraaaak*, repeated. **Status:** Resident, breeding. **Abundance:** Common in the Okavango Delta, which is its stronghold in southern Africa; uncommon to rare elsewhere but regular at Phakalane Sewage Lagoons and Broadhurst sewage ponds near Gaborone. **Habitat:** A reed-bed dweller, found in wetlands with dense emergent vegetation. **Habits:** It is a skulking stand-and-wait fisher in reeds (*Phragmites*) and bulrushes (*Typha*). Roosts communally with other herons and egrets in reedbeds. **Conservation:** Least Concern.

adult

adult

juv.

GOLIATH
HERON

adult

adult

juv.

PURPLE
HERON

61

EURASIAN BITTERN *Botaurus stellaris*

Setswana: kgapu

64 cm (25 ¼ in). **Identification:** Large, compact, stocky, thick-necked heron. Overall rufous brown, with black streaking that differentiates it from immature Black-crowned Night Heron, which has prominent white spots on upperparts. **Call:** Deep, far-carrying, booming *whump, whump, whump*. The bird is more likely to be heard than seen. **Status:** Uncertain. No breeding records from Botswana. No accepted records in Botswana since 1991. **Abundance:** Rare. **Habitat:** Found in dense *Phragmites* reedbeds. **Habits:** Skulking, creeps through reeds; rarely seen on ground. Adopts typical bittern "sky-pointing" posture when disturbed. **Conservation:** Least Concern.

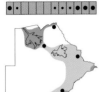

BLACK-CROWNED NIGHT HERON *Nycticorax nycticorax*

56 cm (22 in). **Identification:** Medium-size night heron. Black crown and mantle contrast with gray wings and white underparts and throat. Two or three stiff white head plumes. Immature is dark brown with white spotting, sometimes mistaken for Eurasian Bittern. **Call:** Single or repeated, loud *wak*. **Status:** Resident, breeding. **Abundance:** Abundant at Lake Ngami; locally abundant in the Okavango Delta. Both areas are strongholds for this species in southern Africa. Also common at Nata Delta and frequent at many wetlands in the east and southeast. It is nomadic in response to rain. **Habitat:** Uses dense vegetation fringing lakes, rivers, and other wetlands for roosting during the day; forages in open shallows at water edges. **Habits:** Nocturnal. Gregarious when roosting during day; forages solitarily. **Conservation:** Least Concern.

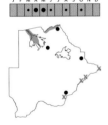

WHITE-BACKED NIGHT HERON *Gorsachius leuconotus*

53 cm (20 ¾ in). **Identification:** Medium-size night heron. It has a rufous neck, dark mantle and back, and large eye with white eye-ring. The white triangle of feathers on the back that gives it its name is difficult to see and thus not a useful identification feature. Immature has streaked breast and white spots on upperwing coverts. **Call:** Mostly silent. Harsh *kraak-kraak-kraak*. **Status:** Resident, breeding. Egg-laying peaks during April and May in the Okavango River; March, June, August, and October each has a single breeding record. **Abundance:** Uncommon, along the Okavango, Kwando, Linyanti, and Chobe Rivers, and rare on the Limpopo and Notwane Rivers. The Okavango Panhandle is the best place in southern Africa to see this species. **Habitat:** Prefers quiet backwaters of heavily wooded, slow-flowing perennial rivers. **Habits:** Shy, solitary, retiring species, made more difficult to see by its crepuscular habits. During the day, it roosts solitarily in Bicoloured Karee (*Searsia quartiniana*) and other riverside trees along the Okavango River or in Pale-bark Waterberry (*Syzygium guineense*) trees lining the Chobe River. **Conservation:** Least Concern.

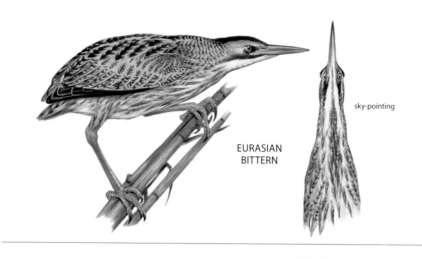

EURASIAN
BITTERN

sky-pointing

adult

imm.

juv.

BLACK-CROWNED
NIGHT HERON

WHITE-BACKED
NIGHT HERON

adult

imm.

juv.

63

LITTLE BITTERN *Ixobrychus minutus*

Setswana: kgapu

36 cm (14 ¼ in). **Identification:** Small heron. Pale rufous face, neck, and underparts contrast with dark head, mantle, and back. Pale upperwing coverts (almost white in male) contrast with dark flight feathers. Male has black crown and upperparts; in female these are brown streaked with black. Juvenile has brown-streaked neck, upperparts, and wing coverts. Two subspecies occur in Botswana: *I. m. payesii* has rufous neck and cheeks, while in *I. m. minutus* these areas are gray. **Call:** Mainly silent, but breeding birds have growling *woa* call, repeated frequently. **Status:** Two populations: *I. m. payesii*, resident, breeding (breeding bar based on data from the southern African region). *I. m. minutus*, Palearctic migrant, nonbreeding; supplements resident populations, its numbers peaking in December. **Abundance:** Common in the Okavango Delta, which supports globally important numbers and is the best place in southern Africa to see this species. Uncommon elsewhere. **Habitat:** Found in reed beds (mainly *Phragmites* and *Typha*, but also Papyrus, *Cyperus papyrus*) in standing water. **Habits:** Solitary, stand-and-wait fisher in dense vegetation (recorded bait-fishing elsewhere). **Conservation:** Least Concern.

DWARF BITTERN *Ixobrychus sturmii*

Setswana: kgapu

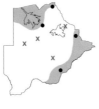

30 cm (11 ¾ in). **Identification:** Small heron (Africa's smallest). Uniformly slate-gray upperparts and wings; buffy underparts with heavy dark streaks. **Call:** Rapid, growling *roa, roa, roa* when nesting. **Status:** Intra-African migrant, breeding. Breeds prolifically after rains, and egg-laying commences as early as November if rains are early. **Abundance:** Uncommon, but more common during years of above-average rain. **Habitat:** Occurs in ephemeral pans or floodplains with inundated trees (especially acacias). **Habits:** This is a "rains migrant"— its numbers, arrival, and time of breeding vary according to rainfall. When alarmed, it may adopt the typical bittern posture with bill pointing skyward; the bold longitudinal dark brown or black streaks on its throat and breast disrupt its shape and make it difficult to see. Uses ephemeral pans for feeding and breeding. **Conservation:** Least Concern.

STRIATED HERON *Butorides striata*

41 cm (16 ¼ in). **Identification:** Small heron. Dark green crown, back, and wings. Upperwing coverts have white edges that create a scalloped appearance. Breeding birds briefly have red lores and red legs. Immature is heavily streaked below and has white spots on wings. **Call:** Invariably utters loud *chow* when flushed, sometimes repeating it a few times. **Status:** Resident, breeding. **Abundance:** Common in the Okavango, Linyanti, and Chobe wetland systems of northern Botswana, and the Limpopo, Marico, and Notwane river systems of eastern Botswana. The Okavango Delta is its stronghold in southern Africa. **Habitat:** Found along densely vegetated rivers and channels. Prefers acacias and other trees along waterways for nesting. **Habits:** Usually solitary. Lurks at water's edge in hunched position with body horizontal and legs bent. It is a stand-and-wait fisher but in the Okavango has been recorded bait-fishing by placing insects carefully on water surface to attract fish to within striking range. **Conservation:** Least Concern.

nonbreeding
adult male

adult
male

adult
female

adult
female

breeding
adult male

LITTLE BITTERN
l. m. payesii

juv.

**DWARF
BITTERN**

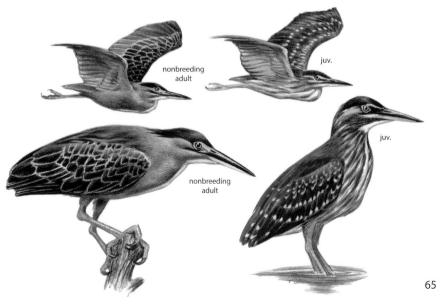

nonbreeding
adult

juv.

nonbreeding
adult

juv.

65

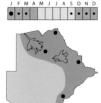

WESTERN CATTLE EGRET *Bubulcus ibis*

Setswana: mo.leane, mmamoleane, nônyane yapula, modisakgômo, le.disakgômo, nalanghê, nalanghwê wadikgômo

54 cm (21 ¼ in). **Identification:** Smallest white egret. Nonbreeding bird has yellow bill and legs. Breeding bird develops orange-buff plumes on head, breast, and back; bill and legs turn pinkish orange; and for a short while the eye is red and lores are pink. Immature has blackish legs and bill. **Call:** Mostly silent; raucous, repeated *kork* at breeding colonies. **Status:** Breeding resident; nomadic. **Abundance:** Abundant in the Okavango Delta; common elsewhere in the north and in eastern parts of the country. **Habitat:** Often associated with wetlands but forages in grasslands and woodlands. **Habits:** Flocks fly in V formation to regularly used roosts in evening. Roosts and breeds colonially in *Phragmites* reedbeds and acacias. Follows grazing herbivores, including cattle and African Buffalo, to catch flushed insects. Often congregates to forage at garbage dumps. Setswana name *modisakgômo* refers to the bird's commensal association with cattle. **Conservation:** Least Concern.

GREAT EGRET *Ardea alba*

Setswana: mo.gôlôri

95 cm (37 ½ in). **Identification:** The largest white heron; same size as Grey Heron (p. 58). Gape extends well behind eye, and legs and feet are black; these features distinguish it from Intermediate Egret. Bill is yellow in nonbreeding birds, black when breeding. At onset of breeding, base of bill and facial skin are luminous green, and the eye is orange for a short period. **Call:** Mostly silent; harsh, repeated, grating *kraaaak*, usually in flight. **Status:** Resident, breeding. **Abundance:** Widespread at wetlands throughout the country. Common at Lake Ngami, the Okavango Delta, Linyanti Swamps, and along the Chobe River. The Okavango is its stronghold in southern Africa and supports regionally, and at times globally, important numbers. The species has expanded its range in recent decades. **Habitat:** Found in shallow open water of lakes, lagoons, channels, and floodplains; also man-made impoundments. **Habits:** A stand-and-wait fisher, it feeds alone or in small groups. Large congregations can be seen along the Okavango Panhandle during the barbel (catfish) run. **Conservation:** Least Concern.

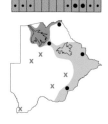

INTERMEDIATE EGRET *Egretta intermedia*

Setswana: mo.leane, mmamoleane

69 cm (27 ¼ in). **Identification:** Medium-size white egret, intermediate in size between Great and Little Egrets. Bill yellow year-round, except at onset of breeding season. Gape extends only to front of eye. Legs black, but thighs yellow; however thigh color is not a useful field feature as it is not always visible. **Call:** Mostly silent; hoarse squawk. **Status:** Resident, breeding. Breeds in northern wetlands. **Abundance:** Common in the Okavango Delta, which is its stronghold in southern Africa; common along the Chobe River at times. Uncommon elsewhere. The species is nomadic and occurs in eastern and southeastern Botswana mainly during summer. **Habitat:** Prefers shallow open water of lakes, lagoons, channels, and floodplains. **Habits:** A stand-and-wait fisher, it feeds alone. **Conservation:** Least Concern.

LITTLE EGRET *Egretta garzetta*

Setswana: mmamoleane

64 cm (25 ¼ in). **Identification:** Medium-size, slender white egret. It has a sharp bill that is black all year, and black legs with rich yellow feet. In flight, appears very long-legged, as the wings are well forward and the legs project beyond the tail. Breeding birds have a few long, ornamental head plumes and at the onset of breeding acquire violet lores and a dark orange eye (the iris is pale at other times). Juvenile has pale olive-green legs, including feet, and a gray rather than black bill; it has a pale eye. **Call:** Mostly silent; harsh, grating *kraa*. **Status:** Resident, breeding. Egg-laying starts earlier than elsewhere in the region, timed with seasonal winter flooding of the Okavango Delta. **Abundance:** Common at Lake Ngami and in the Okavango Delta, which are strongholds for the species in southern Africa and support regionally important numbers. Uncommon elsewhere. **Habitat:** Found in shallow water in a variety of wetlands. **Habits:** An active feeder, runs after small fish with wings open, stabbing into water; frequently stirs feet under water to disturb aquatic prey. May follow pelicans or Marabou Storks to catch small fish they flush. **Conservation:** Least Concern.

breeding
adult

breeding
adult

nonbreeding
adult

juv.

WESTERN
CATTLE EGRET

breeding

nonbreeding

GREAT
EGRET

breeding

nonbreeding

INTERMEDIATE
EGRET

LITTLE
EGRET

nonbreeding

breeding

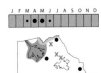

SLATY EGRET *Egretta vinaceigula*

53 cm (20 ¾ in). **Identification:** Small egret. Slate-gray plumage interrupted by wine-colored patch on throat (which extends down to belly in immature); however, this patch is not a useful field characteristic as it is not always clearly visible. Legs and feet are yellow (note, however, that they can turn grayish green with dark yellow "knees" at certain times), and at all times distinguish the species from similar Black Heron, which always has black legs and yellow feet. Plumage becomes darker when breeding, and eye also turns dark at this time. **Call:** Mostly silent; squawks during aggressive encounters with conspecifics. **Status:** Resident, breeding. **Abundance:** Common throughout the Okavango Delta, Linyanti Swamps, and along the Chobe River with very occasional records in the Makgadikgadi Pans and wetlands in the southeast. It is a range-restricted species near endemic to Botswana; the bulk of the world population (estimated at 4,000 individuals) is confined to its Okavango stronghold. **Habitat:** Found in freshwater wetlands; shallow floodplains with short emergent vegetation. **Habits:** Feeds actively and solitarily, though occasionally in larger aggregations. Never mantles wings into umbrella formation, in contrast to Black Heron. Breeds colonially in *Phragmites* reedbeds and Wild Date Palm (*Phoenix reclinata*) islands and roosts colonially. **Conservation:** Vulnerable.

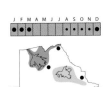

BLACK HERON *Egretta ardesiaca*

Setswana: se.khuko

55 cm (21 ¾ in). **Identification:** Small egret. Sooty-black plumage, several head plumes, and black legs with rich yellow feet distinguish it from Slaty Egret. **Call:** Mostly silent; occasional squawk. **Status:** Resident, breeding. Breeds in northern wetlands, but there are very few recorded breeding sites and only limited data on dates. Peak egg-laying occurs December to March, but the species may breed opportunistically with other herons and egrets in other months. **Abundance:** Common in the Okavango Delta, which is its southern African stronghold; uncommon elsewhere. Numbers are low in the Okavango during the dry season. Disperses to the rest of country during summer months. **Habitat:** Occurs in shallow, freshwater wetlands, drying floodplains, man-made impoundments. **Habits:** Has striking behavior of mantling wings over head, creating a canopy, when fishing, something never done by Slaty Egret. Black Herons can be gregarious at drying floodplains where fish are trapped; foraging birds leapfrog to the front of a feeding party and quickly mantle the wings and attempt to catch fish disturbed by the procession. Roosts colonially. **Conservation:** Least Concern.

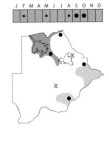

SQUACCO HERON *Ardeola ralloides*

43 cm (17 in). **Identification:** Small heron. Head and neck buffy with dark streaks. Overall buffy appearance when foraging; white wings conspicuous in flight. When breeding, has blue lores and base of bill, orange-red legs, and long head plumes. Immature lacks head plumes, and its head and sides of neck are streaked with buffy brown. **Call:** Mostly silent; low, staccato *kok*. **Status:** Resident, breeding. It breeds in the Okavango Delta in large numbers; egg-laying occurs mainly in September and October, but there are isolated records from other months. **Abundance:** Abundant in the Okavango Delta, which is its stronghold in southern Africa and is of regional if not global importance for the species; common in Linyanti Swamps and along the Chobe River. **Habitat:** Found in freshwater wetlands along water's edge, often in hippo grass (*Vossia*) or other vegetation fringing channels. **Habits:** Forages solitarily; it is a stand-and-wait fisher, camouflaged by its cryptic coloration. It has been recorded using insect bait, placed carefully on water surface, to lure fish within striking range. Roosts and breeds colonially in *Phragmites* reedbeds and acacias. **Conservation:** Least Concern.

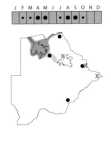

RUFOUS-BELLIED HERON *Ardeola rufiventris*

39 cm (15 ¼ in). **Identification:** Small heron. It has a slate-gray head, breast, and back; rufous wings and underparts; and rich yellow legs. Breeding birds have red lores and legs. Immature has brownish-gray upperparts and a pale buffy line down dark brown throat onto breast. **Call:** Mostly silent. Breeding bird makes growling *woa* call, repeating it frequently. **Status:** Resident, breeding. In the Okavango Delta, it breeds during April and May in response to new incoming floodwaters, and again in August and September, in synchrony with other herons and egrets at traditional heronries. **Abundance:** Common in the Okavango Delta, Linyanti Swamps, and Chobe River. In southern Africa, the bulk of the population occurs in the Okavango Delta. **Habitat:** Favors large rivers, channels, and floodplains of freshwater wetlands with tall emergent vegetation. **Habits:** Secretive, solitary when foraging. Roosts and breeds colonially with other waterbirds. **Conservation:** Least Concern.

nonbreeding
adult

SLATY
EGRET

breeding
adult

nonbreeding
adult

imm.

BLACK
HERON

umbrella
stance

breeding
adult

adult

nonbreeding
adult

SQUACCO
HERON

imm.

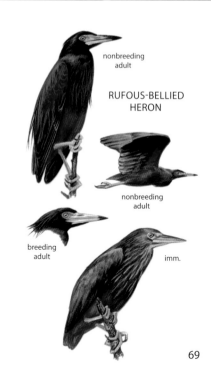

nonbreeding
adult

RUFOUS-BELLIED
HERON

nonbreeding
adult

breeding
adult

imm.

69

PELICANS Pelecanidae

Large aquatic birds that have dumpy bodies, long straight wings, short legs terminating in webbed feet, and long bills with a suspended throat pouch for catching fish. Accomplished soarers, the birds ride thermal air currents in synchronized flocks. They are gregarious while fishing and nesting. Pelicans exhibit "Cainism"—the first-hatched juvenile kills its sibling. Sexes similar, but male is significantly larger than female and has noticeably longer bill; they also differ slightly in breeding plumage. Two sedentary, resident species of the same genus occur in Botswana; pelicans have relatively few nesting sites in southern Africa.

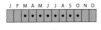

GREAT WHITE PELICAN *Pelecanus onocrotalus*

Setswana: le.ya

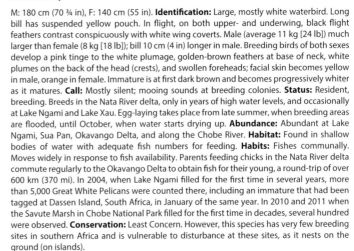

M: 180 cm (70 ¾ in), F: 140 cm (55 in). **Identification:** Large, mostly white waterbird. Long bill has suspended yellow pouch. In flight, on both upper- and underwing, black flight feathers contrast conspicuously with white wing coverts. Male (average 11 kg [24 lb]) much larger than female (8 kg [18 lb]); bill 10 cm (4 in) longer in male. Breeding birds of both sexes develop a pink tinge to the white plumage, golden-brown feathers at base of neck, white plumes on the back of the head (crests), and swollen foreheads; facial skin becomes yellow in male, orange in female. Immature is at first dark brown and becomes progressively whiter as it matures. **Call:** Mostly silent; mooing sounds at breeding colonies. **Status:** Resident, breeding. Breeds in the Nata River delta, only in years of high water levels, and occasionally at Lake Ngami and Lake Xau. Egg-laying takes place from late summer, when breeding areas are flooded, until October, when water starts drying up. **Abundance:** Abundant at Lake Ngami, Sua Pan, Okavango Delta, and along the Chobe River. **Habitat:** Found in shallow bodies of water with adequate fish numbers for feeding. **Habits:** Fishes communally. Moves widely in response to fish availability. Parents feeding chicks in the Nata River delta commute regularly to the Okavango Delta to obtain fish for their young, a round-trip of over 600 km (370 mi). In 2004, when Lake Ngami filled for the first time in several years, more than 5,000 Great White Pelicans were counted there, including an immature that had been tagged at Dassen Island, South Africa, in January of the same year. In 2010 and 2011 when the Savute Marsh in Chobe National Park filled for the first time in decades, several hundred were observed. **Conservation:** Least Concern. However, this species has very few breeding sites in southern Africa and is vulnerable to disturbance at these sites, as it nests on the ground (on islands).

PINK-BACKED PELICAN *Pelecanus rufescens*

Setswana: le.ya

128 cm (50 ½ in). **Identification:** Large, mostly gray waterbird. Long bill has pale yellow pouch and hooked orange tip. The brownish-pink back and flanks are covered by the folded wings and not a useful field characteristic. In flight, underwing, which has gray or brown coverts and dark gray primaries, appears more uniformly gray, in contrast to Great White Pelican. Breeding birds have dark gray, tufted crest, orange (male) or yellow (female) eye-ring, black smudge in front of eye, rich yellow throat pouch, and brick-red feet. **Call:** Mostly silent. **Status:** Resident, breeding. **Abundance:** Uncommon generally, but only an occasional visitor to wetlands in the southeast. Numbers breeding in the Okavango Delta at Gadikwe Lagoon and Xhamu Lediba have dwindled, while there has been a corresponding increase at nearby Lediba la Dinonyane, which now has about 50 breeding pairs. There is also a new site at Letsibogo Dam in eastern Botswana (six nests in 2005). The species has also bred in Nata River delta and on the Chobe River in the past. **Habitat:** Found in permanent wetlands; prefers large freshwater lakes and lagoons. **Habits:** Highly mobile; congregates where fish are accessible at drying pools and lagoons and often feeds alongside Great White Pelicans. Nests colonially in trees. **Conservation:** Least Concern.

GREAT WHITE
PELICAN

adult

imm.

adult

breeding
adult female

juv.

nonbreeding
adult

breeding
adult male

PINK-BACKED
PELICAN

adult

adult

breeding
adult

nonbreeding
adult

juv.

imm.

71

CORMORANTS Phalacrocoracidae

Piscivorous waterbirds that capture prey by underwater pursuit, using their webbed feet for propulsion and the hook-tipped bill to grasp (rather than spear) prey. Cormorants have partially wettable (nonwaterproof) plumage, which helps them attain negative buoyancy to save energy underwater (although reducing insulation). They are frequently seen perched with wings spread, passively warming up and drying out after diving. Strong fliers, they flap almost continuously in flight. They nest colonially, and both sexes share nest duties. Incubation commences once the first egg is laid, so hatching of chicks is staggered. Two species in two genera are found in Botswana.

REED CORMORANT *Microcarbo africanus*

Setswana: timêlêtsane, ntôdi

55 cm (21 ¾ in). **Identification:** Small, dark-plumaged piscivore with long tail. Immature has pale underparts, and is sometimes mistaken for White-breasted Cormorant, which has pure white breast and is significantly larger. **Call:** Mostly silent. **Status:** Resident, breeding Breeds communally at numerous sites in the Okavango Delta, Linyanti Swamps, and Chobe River wetland systems, as well as at Lake Ngami and man-made dams in eastern and southern Botswana. Egg-laying peaks between December and March in the south, and occurs from May to November (peaking in July and August) in the Okavango. **Abundance:** Abundant at Lake Ngami and common throughout the Okavango Delta, which is its stronghold in southern Africa. Also common in Linyanti Swamps and along the Chobe River. Also common and frequent in the east and southeast. **Habitat:** Found in freshwater wetlands, including lakes, lagoons, rivers, and channels; also frequents man-made impoundments. **Habits:** Solitary or gregarious; fishes in open water by diving. Frequently seen with wings spread, passively warming up and drying after diving. Roosts communally. **Conservation:** Least Concern.

WHITE-BREASTED CORMORANT *Phalacrocorax lucidus*

Setswana: timêlêtsane, ntôdi

90 cm (35 ½ in). **Identification:** The larger of Botswana's two cormorant species. Dark plumage, with contrasting pale underparts at all stages. It has relatively short tail and neck, angular head with turquoise eye, and yellow skin at base of hook-tipped bill. Some breeding birds have white feather patches on upper thigh and a buffy wash to throat and neck. At onset of breeding, bare facial skin briefly turns orange-red. Immature has breast mottled brownish black to varying degree but white belly. Flies with neck outstretched and head and tail slightly raised. **Call:** Mostly silent. **Status:** Resident, breeding. **Abundance:** Common in the southeast; uncommon elsewhere, and notably scarce throughout the Okavango Delta. Internationally important numbers breed at Gaborone and Letsibogo Dams and at times, Nata River delta and Bokaa Dam. **Habitat:** Found in dams and impoundments, large lakes. **Habits:** Occurs in small flocks; fishes in open water by diving and pursuing fish underwater. Often seen with wings spread, passively warming up and drying after diving. Flocks fly in V formation. Breeds in colonies (usually small, but occasionally with more than 100 nests) in trees in standing water, sometimes with African Darters and Reed Cormorants. **Conservation:** Least Concern.

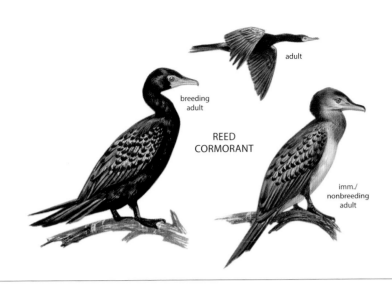

adult

breeding
adult

REED
CORMORANT

imm./
nonbreeding
adult

nuptial colors,
head detail

nonbreeding
adult

breeding
adult

imm.

WHITE-BREASTED
CORMORANT

DARTERS Anhingidae

A family of relatively large, piscivorous waterbirds, with only one African species. The long neck is kinked (due to a special hinge between the eighth and ninth vertebrae), which enables the bird to dart its head and sharp (unhooked) bill forward to spear prey. Wettable plumage results in neutral buoyancy, which facilitates the bird's underwater ambush and pursuit of fish, as do its webbed feet, used for propulsion. Molts all flight feathers simultaneously (unlike cormorants) and remains flightless for several weeks after breeding. One species occurs in Botswana.

AFRICAN DARTER *Anhinga rufa*

Setswana: timêlêtsane, ntôdi

90 cm (35 ½ in). **Identification:** Waterbird that appears black overall. It has a long, pointed bill, heron-like neck, short legs with webbed feet, and a long tail. Breeding male has a rufous neck with a white longitudinal stripe along each side. Female has browner neck. In both sexes, long white scapular feathers become more prominent during breeding. Immature has pale brown underparts, and brown wings mottled with black. Juvenile is covered in thick, buffy down. **Call:** Mostly silent; drawn-out duck-like *quaaack*, repeated. **Status:** Resident, breeding. Breeds actively thoughout the year. Egg-laying occurs in the south from November to May; in the east and northeast from January to July; in the Okavango from July to September; and at Lake Ngami throughout the year. **Abundance:** Abundant at the Okavango Delta, Linyanti Swamps, and Lake Ngami; common along the Chobe, Shashe, and Limpopo Rivers (and their tributaries) as well as at man-made dams and lakes in eastern and southeastern Botswana. The Okavango and Lake Ngami are the species's strongholds in southern Africa; the latter is a major breeding and molting area. **Habitat:** Found in freshwater wetlands, especially lakes, lagoons, and broad, slow-flowing rivers; also frequents man-made impoundments. **Habits:** Swims with body submerged and snake-like neck above water; hence colloquial name "snake-bird." Catches fish by underwater pursuit, stabbing them with dagger-like bill. Often seen with wings spread, passively warming up and drying. **Conservation:** Least Concern.

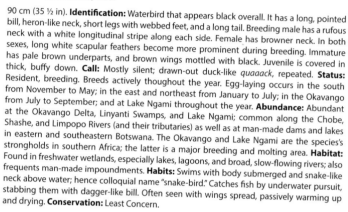

FINFOOTS Heliornithidae

A family of aquatic, freshwater birds that superficially resemble darters or grebes (p. 46). They have dagger-like bills, similar to those of darters, but lobed rather than webbed toes. Species are sexually dimorphic in plumage, and the male is larger than the female. One species is found in Botswana. It has a carpal spur on the wing.

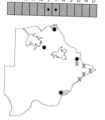

AFRICAN FINFOOT *Podica senegalensis*

M: 65 cm (25 ½ in), F: 52 cm (20 ½ in). **Identification:** Waterbird. Male has black crown and hind neck, and gray face and foreneck, separated by narrow white line. Female has a patterned brown-and-white face and neck. In both sexes, white stripe down side of neck, red bill and feet, and stiff, fan-shaped tail, which lies flat on the water surface, are reliable field characteristics. **Call:** Mostly silent. **Status:** Resident, breeding. Botswana breeding records are from the Kasane Rapids; egg-laying has been recorded there only in June and July, but the breeding season is likely to be much longer than this. **Abundance:** Regulary seen on the Chobe and Marico Rivers, scarce along the Limpopo River. **Habitat:** Favors rivers with well-wooded, overgrown banks. **Habits:** Solitary or in pairs; shy and secretive. Nods head back and forward as it swims. It feeds on small aquatic vertebrates and invertebrates it catches while swimming and diving. **Conservation:** Least Concern.

adult

drying

"snake-bird"

adult

adult

imm.

AFRICAN
DARTER

adult
male

juv.

adult
female

AFRICAN
FINFOOT

SECRETARYBIRD Sagittariidae

A monotypic African family comprising a long-legged terrestrial raptor. It hunts small vertebrates by striding through its grassland and savanna habitat and subduing prey with blows from the feet rather than the hooked bill. Although a ground dweller, it makes a platform nest on canopy of low trees; regularly raises two chicks (exhibits no Cainism, as in some other raptors). The species is listed as globally Vulnerable.

SECRETARYBIRD *Sagittarius serpentarius*

Setswana: ramolôngwana, mmamolangwane, ramolangwana, tlhamê, tlhangwe, tlhangwê, tlhêngwê

138 cm (54 ¼ in). **Identification:** Terrestrial raptor that has long legs, gray and black plumage and head plumes. In flight, long central tail feathers protrude beyond legs; extended neck is much shorter than necks of storks or cranes. Adult has dark brown iris and orange facial skin. Immature has pale eye and yellow facial skin. **Call:** Usually silent, but sometimes emits a loud, harsh, growling *eerrrr, eerrrr, eerrrr*. **Status:** Resident, breeding. **Abundance:** Locally common in Deception and Nossob Valleys (congregations of up to 50 can occasionally be seen at water holes there). Uncommon elsewhere, except in the eastern part of the country where it is scarce. **Habitat:** Occurs in open Kalahari tree and bush savannas and grasslands. **Habits:** May be solitary or in pairs. A terrestrial predator of rodents, snakes, lizards, and grasshoppers, it catches prey while striding through its preferred open grassland habitat, killing it with severe blows from the feet. **Conservation:** Vulnerable.

OSPREYS Pandionidae

A monogeneric and worldwide family of piscivorous raptors, associated in Botswana with large rivers and lakes. Ospreys hunt by plunge diving, feet first, into water. They carry fish in their talons oriented with head forward. Birds are solitary. There are three subspecies; the one that occurs in Botswana is the nominate race, a Palearctic migrant present mainly during the austral summer.

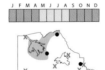

WESTERN OSPREY *Pandion haliaetus*

59 cm (23 ¼ in). **Identification:** Large fish-eating raptor with a distinctive facial mask. It has unfeathered tarsi, and has bright yellow eyes at all ages. Female has heavy streaking that forms a distinct breast band. This species is frequently confused with immature African Fish Eagle (p. 86), which may have broad, dark eye stripe similar to mask of osprey; however, osprey is more slender, has white thighs (not brown), and in flight shows a dark carpal (wrist) patch on underside of wing. Also differs from African Fish Eagle by having long and narrow wings, with only four "fingers" (primaries) at the tips, and when gliding, the carpal joints are held forward, giving the wings an angular appearance. **Call:** Usually silent in Botswana. **Status:** Palearctic migrant, nonbreeding. Birds occasionally overwinter. **Abundance:** Scarce. **Habitat:** Occurs in freshwater wetlands, including lakes and large rivers. **Habits:** Solitary. Catches fish by plunge diving, unlike African Fish Eagle. Carries fish lengthwise, with head facing forward. **Conservation:** Least Concern.

SECRETARYBIRD

adult

adult

imm.

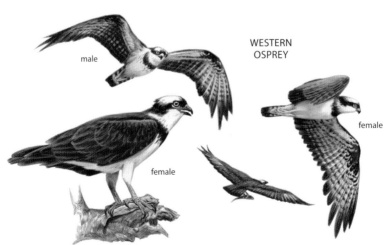

WESTERN
OSPREY

male

female

female

77

VULTURES, KITES, HAWKS, HARRIERS, BUZZARDS, EAGLES Accipitridae

Large, diverse family of diurnal raptors, including kites, vultures, buzzards, eagles, hawks, and harriers; 27 genera and 48 species are found in Botswana. All have hooked bills for tearing flesh, and most have strong talons for killing prey. There is substantial size and plumage variation within species. Taxonomic subdivisions within the family do not always aid in identification; therefore, the diurnal raptors are grouped by similarities in behavior, size and appearance in the species accounts that follow.

Vultures: Five resident species, two vagrants, all but one listed as Threatened globally. They eat carrion and are aeri scavengers that have large wings adapted for soaring in thermal air currents. They have excellent eyesight, sparsel feathered heads and long necks, powerful bills, and large, distensible crops. The two *Gyps* species are social and bree colonially (however where White-backed Vultures are scarce, they may breed solitarily); the other species occur i pairs and breed in isolation. Sexes are alike, except in White-headed Vulture. Most species lay one egg and raise single chick annually. The Setswana *le.nong* is the generic term for vulture.

PALM-NUT VULTURE *Gypohierax angolensis*

60 cm (23 ½ in). **Identification:** Smallest vulture in Botswana. Adult has pied plumage, an its red facial skin is diagnostic among vultures. However, sightings in Botswana are likel to be of immature birds, which are brown and have a yellow cere; the yellow facial skin c juvenile changes through shades of orange in the immature to red in the adult. **Call:** Most silent. **Status:** Vagrant, from south-central Africa; nonbreeding. **Abundance:** Rare. **Habitat** Preferred habitat has Kosi Palms (*Raphia australis*), which are not found in Botswana, bu vagrants can be found in any habitat type. **Habits:** Solitary. An unusual vulture in that feeds on vegetable matter (*Raphia* fruits). Scavenges on carrion and small prey items awa from preferred habitat. **Conservation:** Least Concern.

EGYPTIAN VULTURE *Neophron percnopterus*

Setswana: tlakatshôane

68 cm (26 ¾ in). **Identification:** Slender-billed vulture with a bare face and long, wedge shaped tail. Adult has yellow face, long feathers on hind crown, and mostly white plumage but black flight feathers. Juvenile is dark brown, but immature is mixture of pale and dar browns as it molts; it initially has a gray face (which becomes yellow in the second year long hind-crown feathers, and a wedge-shaped tail. Immature could be confused wit Hooded Vulture, but the long, wedge-shaped tail is very prominent. **Call:** Mostly silen **Status:** Vagrant, from elsewhere in southern Africa (probably from Angola or Namibia nonbreeding. **Abundance:** Rare. **Habitat:** Prefers open, arid areas, but as a vagrant may b seen in any habitat. **Habits:** Solitary, usually immature birds are seen, but a few sighting have been of two birds. **Conservation:** Endangered.

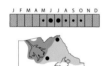

HOODED VULTURE *Necrosyrtes monachus*

Setswana: motlhanka-wamanông

70 cm (24 ½ in). **Identification:** Small, dark brown vulture. It has a slender bill, gray dow on head and neck, and bare skin on face that flushes red when the bird is excited. Adu has bluish legs and feet. Immature has heavily whiskered black face. In flight, rounde tail distinguishes it from immature Egyptian Vulture. **Call:** Mostly silent. **Status:** Residen breeding. **Abundance:** Common in the woodlands of the Okavango Delta (a majo stronghold for the species), Linyanti Swamps, and along the Chobe River. **Habitat:** Foun in mature, tall riparian woodlands; its breeding range coincides with that of its preferre nesting tree, Jackal-berry (*Diospyros mespiliformis*). **Habits:** This species is at the bottom of the dominance hierarchy when scavenging at carcasses. Its Setswana name, whic translates as "servant of the vultures," refers to its subservient nature at feeding sites. It has commensal relationship with African Wild Dogs at their dens, and follows them while the are hunting. It also consorts with Lions and eats their feces. **Conservation:** Endangered.

adult

PALM-NUT
VULTURE

imm.

adult

imm.

adult

EGYPTIAN
VULTURE

juv.

adult

juv.

adult
flushing

HOODED
VULTURE

imm.

adult

adult

imm.

79

CAPE VULTURE *Gyps coprotheres*

Setswana: le.nông lêlefatshwa

101 cm (39 ¾ in). **Identification:** The heaviest of our African vultures; much bigger than White-backed Vulture. Adult has pale eye, blue neck, a "powder-puff" ruff at base of neck, and cream-colored plumage. Male has flatter, broader head than female, which has a domed head. In flight, the secondaries appear silvery gray, rather than black like the primaries, and this is a useful way to distinguish this species from White-backed Vulture. Juvenile and immature have dark iris, pink neck, and long, lanceolate, streaked feathers forming a ruff at base of neck. In flight, buffy underwing coverts distinguish immature from adult and from White-backed Vulture; secondaries are dark gray. **Call:** Mostly silent; harsh hissing and squealing at carcass. **Status:** Resident, breeding. **Abundance:** Abundant where it breeds at Mannyelanong Hill (South-East District) and in the Tswapong Hills (Central District), and numbers there have remained stable since the 1980s. Uncommon away from breeding sites; nonbreeding adults wander widely. It is one of three raptor species endemic to southern Africa. **Habitat:** Forages over open woodlands where carcass visibility is good; avoids areas where bushes encroach. Relies on cliffs for breeding, and prefers them for roosting too. **Habits:** Birds ride thermals within sight of one another, forming a vast network, and scan the ground for carcasses; as soon as one spots carrion and descends, it triggers a chain reaction among adjacent vultures. **Conservation:** Vulnerable.

WHITE-BACKED VULTURE *Gyps africanus*

Setswana: le.nông lêletuba

95 cm (37 ½ in). **Identification:** Medium-size brown vulture. Adult has dark eyes and neck, pale buff breast, and white back, usually visible in flight. Black primaries and secondaries contrast strongly with whitish underwing coverts in flight. Juvenile (first year) has dark eyes, yellowish skin on neck covered with pale gray down, a ruff of lanceolate feathers at base of neck, and a heavily streaked, dark breast. Juvenile in flight shows conspicuous white thighs, and its dark, streaked underwing coverts and flight feathers are uniform in color; however, there is a thin white line along front edge of wing. Immature (after first year) has dark eye, slate neck skin covered with pale gray down, and paler breast. With age, underwing coverts become whitish until they contrast strongly with flight feathers. White back evident by three years of age. **Call:** Mostly silent; harsh screech at carcass. **Status:** Resident, breeding. Significant breeding populations recorded at Lesoma, Linyanti Swamps, Makgadikgadi Pans, and in trees along the Limpopo River. Egg-laying records from outside of the May–June peak period may be replacement clutches. **Abundance:** Abundant in the woodlands of the Okavango Delta, the Linyanti and Chobe Rivers, and Makgadikgadi Pans, as well as along the Limpopo River and in the Ghanzi and Kgalagadi Districts. Less common elsewhere. Currently the most numerous vulture in Botswana. **Habitat:** Found in open Kalahari tree and bush savanna and grasslands; avoids dense woodlands, which are unsuitable for foraging. **Habits:** Gregarious. Rises on thermals about two hours after sunrise; by late morning has usually fed and congregates at water holes, bathing and loafing for remainder of day. It is not uncommon to see up to 150 White-backed Vultures congregated at a carcass or water hole. **Conservation:** Endangered. Poisoning is a major threat to the survival of this species.

adult

adult

imm.

imm.

CAPE
VULTURE

adult

adult

juv.

adult

WHITE-BACKED
VULTURE

juv.

81

WHITE-HEADED VULTURE *Trigonoceps occipitalis*

Setswana: motlhanka-wamanông

85 cm (33 ½ in). **Identification:** Adult has predominantly black plumage, but has white belly, white head, and red bill with pale blue cere. Plumage pattern distinctive in flight: white belly and thighs, together with white line along trailing edge of underwing coverts, contrast with black forewing and flight feathers. Male has dark inner secondaries, while female has white inner secondaries; in both sexes these are clearly visible in flight but also in perched birds. (The species is unusual among our vultures in being sexually dimorphic.) Juvenile has black down on crown and dark brown underparts. **Call:** Mostly silent. **Status:** Resident, breeding. Generations of White-headed Vultures have nested on "Vulture Baobab" near Mombo on Chief's Island in the Okavango Delta at least since Ken Newman first documented the nest in 1991. **Abundance:** Uncommon. This species is more numerous in large protected areas (Central Kalahari Game Reserve, Kgalagadi Transfrontier Park, Chobe National Park) and the Okavango Delta and Linyanti River region than outside these areas, where numbers are low. **Habitat:** Occurs in dry woodlands and savannas but is not found in true desert. Its range coincides roughly with that of the Baobab (*Adansonia digitata*). **Habits:** Usually solitary or in pairs; sometimes up to five are seen at water holes. Often first at a carcass; although it is smaller it will dominate individual White-backed Vultures. However, multiple White-backed Vultures will displace it from a carcass, and birds waiting on the fringe may then appear to be "waiting" on the feeding birds, hence its Setswana name (shared with Hooded Vulture), *motlhanka-wamanông*, which means "servant of the vultures." Supplements scavenging diet with predation on small animals. **Conservation:** Vulnerable.

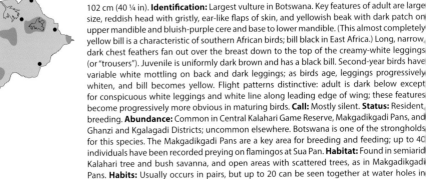

LAPPET-FACED VULTURE *Torgos tracheliotos*

Setswana: bibing, kgôsi yamanông

102 cm (40 ¼ in). **Identification:** Largest vulture in Botswana. Key features of adult are large size, reddish head with gristly, ear-like flaps of skin, and yellowish beak with dark patch on upper mandible and bluish-purple cere and base to lower mandible. (This almost completely yellow bill is a characteristic of southern African birds; bill black in East Africa.) Long, narrow, dark chest feathers fan out over the breast down to the top of the creamy-white leggings (or "trousers"). Juvenile is uniformly dark brown and has a black bill. Second-year birds have variable white mottling on back and dark leggings; as birds age, leggings progressively whiten, and bill becomes yellow. Flight patterns distinctive: adult is dark below except for conspicuous white leggings and white line along leading edge of wing; these features become progressively more obvious in maturing birds. **Call:** Mostly silent. **Status:** Resident, breeding. **Abundance:** Common in Central Kalahari Game Reserve, Makgadikgadi Pans, and Ghanzi and Kgalagadi Districts; uncommon elsewhere. Botswana is one of the strongholds for this species. The Makgadikgadi Pans are a key area for breeding and feeding; up to 40 individuals have been recorded preying on flamingos at Sua Pan. **Habitat:** Found in semiarid Kalahari tree and bush savanna, and open areas with scattered trees, as in Makgadikgadi Pans. **Habits:** Usually occurs in pairs, but up to 20 can be seen together at water holes in the Kalahari during the dry season. The species's Setswana name *kgôsi yamanông* means "chief of the vultures," and although it is dominant over other Botswana vultures, it tends to remain on the fringes at carcasses until frenzy of White-backed Vultures subsides; then the dominant bird(s) takes over. **Conservation:** Vulnerable.

adult
female

WHITE-HEADED
VULTURE

adult
male

imm.

adult
female

imm.

juv.

adult

LAPPET-FACED
VULTURE

adult

imm.

Large eagles: Four species, unified by their size alone (but see also brown eagles, p. 88). Coloration is variable; immature birds take up to seven years to attain adult plumage. These eagles have powerful talons, fully feathered legs, and broad wings. They are specialized predators of large prey in different habitats. The Setswana *ntsu* (and minor variations thereof) is a generic name for these eagles; some have their own specific names.

CROWNED EAGLE   *Stephanoaetus coronatus*

Setswana: ntsu, ntshu, ntswi

85 cm (33 ½ in). **Identification:** One of the largest eagles in Botswana, similar in size to Verreaux's and Martial Eagles; wingspan up to 1.8 m (5.9 ft). It has relatively short, broad wings with a variable number of black bars on the underside (two in adult female, three in adult male; three in juvenile female, four in juvenile male). It also has a long tail, visible in flight; and powerful legs and talons. Young birds are predominantly white, like immature Martial Eagle, but the two species occupy different habitats. **Call:** Musical chanting, rising and falling in cadence, during aerial display. **Status:** Visitor; no breeding records from Botswana. **Abundance:** Rare. Occurs in Botswana only at the western edge of its range in southern Africa. **Habitat:** A forest species, it finds limited suitable habitat in Botswana; apparently occupies Zambezi Teak (*Baikiaea plurijuga*) woodlands. **Habits:** Preys on monkeys and other similar-size mammals. Hunts within forest canopy from perch among foliage, but often takes prey on the ground. Territorial. Pairs ascend and swoop high above the forest in conspicuous nuptial displays accompanied by calling. Raises one chick; if two eggs are laid, the first-hatched chick kills its sibling (Cainism). **Conservation:** Near Threatened.

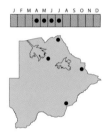

MARTIAL EAGLE   *Polemaetus bellicosus*

Setswana: ntsu, ntshu, ntswi

M: 78 cm (30 ¾ in), F: 83 cm (32 ¾ in). **Identification:** One of the largest eagles in Botswana (along with Verreaux's and Crowned Eagles); wingspan up to 2.4 m (7.9 ft). Dark head, back, and upper- and underwings contrast with white, sparsely spotted breast. Female is noticeably larger than male and has a more heavily spotted breast. The large size, spotted breast, and dark brown underwings (visible in flight) distinguish it from Black-chested Snake Eagle (p. 94). Immature is whitish and has a cowl of head feathers; it is similar to immature Crowned Eagle, but that species is a rare forest bird in Botswana. **Call:** Loud, piercing *kloo-eee, kloo-eee*. **Status:** Resident, breeding. **Abundance:** Uncommon. **Habitat:** Favors open woodlands (broad-leaved and acacia) and grasslands. **Habits:** Solitary or in pairs. Soars at great heights when hunting. A diurnal equivalent of Verreaux's Eagle-Owl (*Bubo lacteus*, p. 194), it takes prey weighing up to 8 kg, including mongooses, Suricates, jackals, hares, and monitor lizards. Frequently kills Kori Bustards. **Conservation:** Vulnerable.

adult male

juv. female

crest raised

adult

juv.

CROWNED EAGLE

adult

adult

adult

MARTIAL EAGLE

juv.

juv.

juv.

85

VERREAUX'S EAGLE *Aquila verreauxii*

Setswana: ntsu, ntshu, ntswi

M: 80 cm (31 ½ in), F: 96 cm (37 ¾ in). **Identification:** Large, jet-black eagle with white V on mantle extending back to join broad white rump; one of the largest eagles in Botswana; wingspan up to 2 m (6.6 ft). Female is significantly larger than male and has a larger white rump patch. Immature is variously mottled brown and black but always has tawny crown and nape. In flight, the large whitish "windows" on the primaries are visible from above and below, and the bulging trailing edge of the secondaries is a key feature. **Call:** Melodious, carrying *weee-yup*, mainly when breeding. **Status:** Resident, breeding. Usually lays two eggs, but raises only one chick, as the first-hatched invariably kills its younger sibling (Cainism). **Abundance:** Uncommon in the hilly areas of the eastern hardveld. **Habitat:** Occurs in rocky hills, preferring those with its favored prey, Rock Hyrax. **Habits:** Pairs hunt together, perching on rocky outcrops or soaring on updrafts. They fly fast along cliffs and surprise prey. **Conservation:** Least Concern.

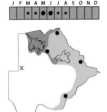

AFRICAN FISH EAGLE *Haliaeetus vocifer*

Setswana: kgoadira, kgwaadira, audi

M: 63 cm (24 ¾ in), F: 75 cm (29 ½ in). **Identification:** Adult, an African wetland icon, is unmistakable. Female is noticeably larger than male and has a broader white breast. White head and tail easily visible in flying birds of both sexes. Immature plumage is variable, changing over four or five years: it is mottled brown in first year; breast and belly become white streaked with black in second year; the dark belly, and the contrasting white breast develop at the subadult stage. General features of immature are robust appearance, unfeathered lower legs, rounded-edged white tail with dark terminal band, and white "windows" in wings. When subadult attains white head with dark band through eye, it can be mistaken for Western Osprey (p. 76); however robust body, more rounded head shape and dark eye distinguish it from that species. **Call:** Loud ringing call with head thrown back, even when soaring. Male call higher-pitched than female. **Status:** Resident, breeding. It is a winter breeder. **Abundance:** Abundant in the Okavango Delta (which is its stronghold in southern Africa), Linyanti Swamps, along the Chobe River, and along some stretches of the Limpopo River. Lake Ngami is a juvenile dispersal area, where relatively large numbers of juvenile and immature birds may be seen. **Habitat:** Prefers permanent large freshwater wetlands, such as rivers, lagoons, and floodplains. **Habits:** Solitary or in pairs, occasionally in congregations at drying pools on floodplains where fish are trapped. Hunts from high perch overlooking open water; makes sweeping dive and at last second throws feet forward to grasp fish swimming just below the surface. Immature scavenges and catches birds such as doves in addition to fishing. **Conservation:** Least Concern.

adult

adult

imm.

adult

VERREAUX'S
EAGLE

imm.

adult
mantle detail

adult

adult
female

imm.

adult

AFRICAN FISH
EAGLE

subadult

imm.

adult

87

Brown eagles: Four eagles with predominantly brown plumage, though some exhibit continuous polymorphism, while others have variable age-related plumages. All have feathered tarsi; one has tight "stovepipe" leggings. Note that Brown Snake Eagle and immature Bateleur (see snake eagles, p. 94) are also brown and could possibly be confused with species in this group, but both have unfeathered legs and a cowl of feathers that makes their head appear relatively large and rounded. The Setswana *ntsu* (and minor variations thereof) is a generic name for these eagles; some have their own specific names.

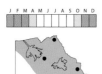

LESSER SPOTTED EAGLE   *Clanga pomarina*

Setswana: ntsu, ntshu, ntswi

62 cm (24 ½ in). **Identification:** Medium-size, migratory brown eagle. Several features distinguish it from the other brown eagles, Steppe (p. 90), Tawny (p. 90), and Wahlberg's: The gape extends below the amber eye; the tarsi are tightly feathered ("stovepipe" leggings); and in flight, the adult shows a small but distinct white primary patch above but does not have pale "windows" in the wings when seen from below. Immature has a darker amber eye, a more extensive white primary patch, and pale spots on the wing. **Call:** Mostly silent. **Status:** Palearctic migrant, nonbreeding. **Abundance:** Uncommon, although large numbers may be seen locally. Its range in Botswana, in the northern and eastern part of the country, is near the southwestern limit of its migration. **Habitat:** Ranges over a variety of woodland types. **Habits:** Solitary or in small flocks; congregates at termite alate emergences. **Conservation:** Least Concern.

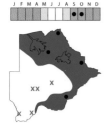

WAHLBERG'S EAGLE   *Hieraaetus wahlbergi*

Setswana: ntsu, ntshu, ntswi

58 cm (22 ¾ in). **Identification:** Medium-size migratory brown eagle that occurs in pale, brown, and dark brown morphs. Feathered tarsi. The slight crest on the head is diagnostic, as is the combination of very straight tail and long, plank-like wings in flight. **Call:** Noisy in spring after arrival, at start of nesting; a repeated *kyip-kyip-kyip*. **Status:** Intra-African migrant, breeding. It breeds during spring, laying eggs soon after its late August arrival, departing by May. (Tawny Eagle, p. 90, is mainly a winter breeder). **Abundance:** Common. **Habitat:** Found in a variety of broad-leaved and acacia woodlands; favors riparian habitats. **Habits:** Solitary or in pairs. Prone to high soaring, catches prey in aerial pursuit (birds) or on the ground (small mammals). Often perches in prominent dead trees (but does not use electric power lines, as do buzzards, pp. 96-98). **Conservation:** Least Concern.

LESSER SPOTTED
EAGLE

adult

adult

imm.

imm.

adult

imm.

imm.

adult
dark brown
morph

adult dark
brown
morph

adult pale
morph

imm.
pale
morph

imm.
dark brown
morph

adult
pale morph

imm.
pale
morph

WAHLBERG'S
EAGLE

89

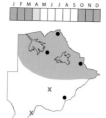

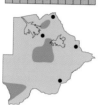

STEPPE EAGLE *Aquila nipalensis*

Setswana: ntsu, ntshu, ntswi

77 cm (30 ¼ in). **Identification:** Large, uniformly brown migratory eagle. It has a dark eye and yellow cere, and gape extends to be in line with back of eye. Tarsi are feathered and are wider than "stovepipe" leggings of Lesser Spotted Eagle (p. 88). Adult is generally darker brown than dark brown morph of Tawny Eagle (p. 90). In flight, adult has coarsely barred flight and tail feathers (when seen from below). Young birds in flight show small, light "windows" in the wings (white inner primaries), a broad white line along the wing coverts (visible from above and below), and a white rump. They also have narrow white trailing edge to wings and tail. **Call:** Mostly silent. **Status:** Palearctic migrant, nonbreeding. **Abundance:** Uncommon, although large numbers may be seen locally, especially at termite alate emergences. **Habitat:** Occurs in a variety of woodland types, as it traverses varied habitats while migrating. **Habits:** Gregarious; follows rain fronts in search of emerging termite alates. **Conservation:** Least Concern. **General:** Closely related to Tawny Eagle and regarded by some as conspecific.

TAWNY EAGLE *Aquila rapax*

Setswana: ntsu, ntshu, ntswi

71 cm (28 in). **Identification:** Very variable large brown eagle, ranging from dark rufous through tawny to pale buff. Individuals are not uniformly colored and may have shades of brown and dark streaks in the plumage. Tarsi are always well feathered. Gape extends to below center of eye. In flight, when viewed head-on, the bird has a very flat, horizontal silhouette. Almost invariably, rump and uppertail coverts are very pale. The tail is rounded. Juvenile is uniformly pale rufous brown. This species is usually paler and more rufous-toned than closely related Steppe Eagle, and the feathered tarsi have an untidy appearance when compared to those of Lesser Spotted Eagle (p. 88). **Call:** Mostly silent. **Status:** Resident, breeding. **Abundance:** Common in Savute area of Chobe National Park, eastern Moremi Game Reserve, western Makgadikgadi Pans, Central Kalahari Game Reserve, Tuli Block, and Nossob Valley; uncommon elsewhere. It is the most frequently seen of the brown eagles. **Habitat:** Found in both broad-leaved and acacia woodlands. **Habits:** Usually solitary. An efficient hunter, it preys mainly on birds, but also scavenges (and therefore is susceptible to poisoning) and pirates food from other species such as Bateleur. **Conservation:** Least Concern, but may decline as have the vultures, due to poisoning.

adult

adult

imm.

adult

imm.

adult

imm.

STEPPE
EAGLE

gape detail

gape detail

TAWNY
EAGLE

adult
rufous morph

adult
rufous morph

streaky
adult

subadult
pale morph

adult
pale morph

subadult
pale morph

imm.

imm.

adult
pale morph

91

Smaller eagles: Four small to medium-size eagles with feathered tarsi. Long-crested Eagle is distinctive in form, behavior, and habitat. Hawk-eagles and Booted Eagle are closely related and similar (as is Wahlberg's Eagle, p. 88), which however is better placed with the brown eagles for comparative identification purposes). Sexes are similar, though female is larger than male and, in some species, more boldly marked. The Setswana *ntsu* (and minor variations thereof) is a generic name for these eagles; some have their own specific names.

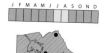

BOOTED EAGLE *Hieraaetus pennatus*

Setswana: ntsu, ntshu, ntswi

M: 48 cm (19 in), F: 50 cm (19 ¾ in). **Identification:** Compact, small eagle that occurs in brown and pale morphs; 80% of southern African birds (including those of Botswana) are pale. Key identification features are dark rufous cheeks that give face a dark appearance, light panels in the wingtips (comprising about four secondary feathers), and "landing lights": a white patch on leading edge of each wing where it meets the body, visible when bird is seen from front in flight. **Call:** Vocal when breeding; makes shrill call. **Status:** Intra-African and Palearctic migrants, nonbreeding. Three populations occur in southern Africa. One breeds in Cape Province in South Africa, laying eggs during September, and moves northward into Botswana after breeding. A second, small population breeds in Namibia in June and July, and may also disperse to Botswana. The third group is composed of Palearctic migrants, which arrive in November and depart in March. Birds are thus present in Botswana throughout the year; their numbers peak during summer. **Abundance:** Scarce. **Habitat:** Prefers a variety of woodland types; suitable nesting habitat in ravines and gorges in mountainous areas is limited in Botswana. **Habits:** Hunts on the wing for birds, small mammals, and lizards. **Conservation:** Least Concern.

AYRES'S HAWK-EAGLE *Hieraaetus ayresii*

Setswana: ntsu, ntshu, ntswi

M: 46 cm (18 in), F: 55 cm (21 ¾ in). **Identification:** Much smaller than African Hawk-Eagle, from which it differs in the following features: It has a slight crest on the head; is more heavily streaked below (streaking always extends onto thighs); and, visible in flight, it has heavily barred inner primaries (with no pale panel). It is closely related to Wahlberg's Eagle (p. 88) and Booted Eagle. Has white "landing lights," similar to Booted Eagle. Coloration of underparts varies considerably from very heavily dark blotched to very pale (intermediate is most usual). Female is usually more boldly marked than male. **Call:** Mostly silent. **Status:** Uncertain; intra-African summer migrant, but some birds are present in northern Botswana during the winter breeding season. No breeding records from Botswana, but some individuals probably do breed in Botswana. **Abundance:** Scarce. **Habitat:** Prefers moist woodlands, including riparian. **Habits:** Pairs for life. Spends long periods perched inconspicuously. Preys on small to medium-size birds (it specializes in doves and pigeons), by stooping from a height and catching them in aerial pursuit. **Conservation:** Least Concern.

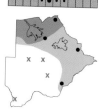

AFRICAN HAWK-EAGLE *Aquila spilogaster*

Setswana: ntsu, ntshu, ntswi

M: 60 cm (23 ½ in), F: 65 cm (25 ½ in). **Identification:** Larger than Ayres's Hawk-Eagle, it has rounder and broader wings, with pale "windows" at base of primaries, and a long tail, which has a broad, dark terminal band. Female is more heavily streaked below than male. Immature is rufous; its feathered legs and relatively small head distinguish it from immature Black-chested Snake Eagle (p. 94). **Call:** Rapid *kley, kley, kley, kley-kley*. **Status:** Resident, breeding. **Abundance:** Common. **Habitat:** Found in tall, mature woodlands; favors Mopane (*Colophospermum mopane*) woodlands. **Habits:** Occurs in pairs and pairs for life. A formidable predator of game birds (guineafowl, francolin, spurfowl) but also small mammals (Scrub Hare, mongoose), it employs a variety of hunting methods: it may be seen perched in cover (from which it makes a quick dash), quartering low over the ground, or soaring (stoops on birds in flight). **Conservation:** Least Concern.

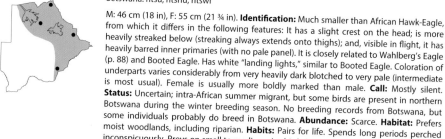
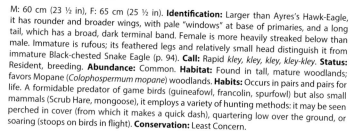

adult
pale morph

adult
pale morph

adult
dark morph

BOOTED EAGLE

adult
dark morph

dark
adult

adult

imm.

imm.

AYRES'S HAWK-EAGLE

adult

adult

imm.

imm.

AFRICAN HAWK-EAGLE

93

LONG-CRESTED EAGLE *Lophaetus occipitalis*

Setswana: mokui

M: 53 cm (20 ¾ in), F: 58 cm (22 ¾ in). **Identification:** Small, dark brown eagle with long, floppy crest. Adult male has pure white leggings, while female has brown or dirty-white leggings. In flight, distinctive wing pattern of white panels at base of primaries is conspicuous from above and below. **Call:** Piercing, long, drawn-out whistle, *weeeerr*. **Status:** Resident; no breeding records from Botswana. **Abundance:** Uncommon; notably so even in the Okavango Delta, where apparently suitable habitat exists. **Habitat:** An ecotone species, it occurs in forest-grassland mosaic and woodland patches with large trees adjacent to open wetlands. **Habits:** A perch hunter of rodents, especially vlei rats (*Otomys*). **Conservation:** Least Concern.

Snake eagles: Three species, plus Bateleur, although it is not a true snake eagle. Snake eagles are recognized by an upright posture when perched, large head (due to cowl of feathers), yellow eyes, and unfeathered tarsi. Bateleur shares these features except eye color; it has dark eyes. These species employ different hunting strategies for mainly reptile prey: two are perch hunters, one hunts from perches and by soaring, and Bateleur is a low-level glider. The Setswana *se.godi* and *se.gwedi* are generic names for the snake eagles.

BLACK-CHESTED SNAKE EAGLE *Circaetus pectoralis*

Setswana: se.gôdi, se.gwêdi

66 cm (26 in). **Identification:** Large snake eagle. Adult has dark brown plumage extending from head to chest and over the back and upperwings; its underparts are pure white without spotting (distinguishing it from larger Martial Eagle, p. 84). In flight, white underwing with brown stripes on flight feathers differentiates it from Martial Eagle. Juvenile is rufous; its unfeathered legs and relatively large head with yellow eyes distinguish it from juvenile African Hawk-Eagle (p. 92). Immature has barring on flanks and chest that is diagnostic; by maturity bars on flanks have disappeared and those on breast form black chest of adult. **Call:** Mostly silent. **Status:** Resident, breeding. **Abundance:** Common. **Habitat:** Prefers open woodlands with short grass. **Habits:** Solitary. Perch hunts and hunts by soaring, frequently hanging motionless in light breeze without flapping wings, appearing to hover. Swallows snakes whole; regurgitates them intact for nestling. **Conservation:** Least Concern

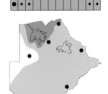

BROWN SNAKE EAGLE *Circaetus cinereus*

Setswana: se.gôdi, se.gwêdi

74 cm (29 ¼ in). **Identification:** Large, uniformly brown snake eagle. In flight, light, silvery-white underwing (without barring) is diagnostic and differentiates it from Black-chested Snake Eagle. Juvenile is brown, very similar to juvenile Black-chested. **Call:** Mostly silent. **Status:** Resident, breeding. **Abundance:** Common. By far the most commonly seen snake eagle. **Habitat:** Found in broad-leaved and acacia woodlands; prefers more wooded habitats than Black-chested Snake Eagle. **Habits:** Solitary; hunts snakes from prominent tree perch. **Conservation:** Least Concern.

WESTERN BANDED SNAKE EAGLE *Circaetus cinerascens*

Setswana: se.gôdi, se.gwêdi

58 cm (22 ¾ in). **Identification:** Medium-size snake eagle, stocky, large head, unfeathered legs. Adult is grayish brown, with faint barring on belly. A broad white band across dark tail creates single dark subterminal band that is diagnostic; bands are visible on upperside and underside. **Call:** Staccato, repeated *kok kok-kaauw*. **Status:** Resident, breeding. Little is known of its breeding habits. **Abundance:** Uncommon. The Okavango Delta, at the southern limit of the species's range, is the best place in southern Africa to see this eagle. **Habitat:** Found in riparian woodlands. **Habits:** Solitary or in pairs. Hunts from perch on lower branches of well-foliaged tree. **Conservation:** Least Concern.

LONG-CRESTED
EAGLE

adult
male

adult
male

adult

BLACK-CHESTED
SNAKE EAGLE

adult

adult
hovering

adult
soaring

imm.

imm.

juv.

BROWN SNAKE
EAGLE

adult

adult

adult

juv.

WESTERN BANDED
SNAKE EAGLE

adult

imm.

adult

95

BATELEUR *Terathopius ecaudatus*

Setswana: pêtlêkê, pêtêkê

63 cm (24 ¾ in). **Identification:** Colorful, unmistakable eagle. It has brown eyes, bare re⋯ facial skin, and unfeathered red legs; a cowl of long feathers gives the head a large, rounde⋯ appearance. The very short tail is diagnostic, whether the bird is perched or in flight. Ha⋯ "rocking" flight (reminiscent of a balancing tightrope walker). Juvenile is uniformly brown⋯ often mistaken for other large brown eagles; however, combination of bare greenish-blu⋯ facial skin and cere, dark eyes, short tail, and unfeathered tarsi revealing gray legs and fee⋯ is diagnostic. In flight, tail of juvenile projects well beyond feet. Immature is also brown⋯ overall, becoming progressively more mottled with black as it ages. By two years of age⋯ the feet reach the end of the tail when in flight, and thereafter extend beyond the tail tip⋯ The face and feet are red in the subadult stage, at about five to six years of age. **Call:** Lou⋯ bark—*kaauuw*—in flight. **Status:** Resident, breeding. **Abundance:** Common in Okavang⋯ Delta (especially at Khwai), Chobe National Park and Linyanti area (where congregations c⋯ up to 50 may be seen), Central Kalahari Game Reserve, and Kgalagadi District. Numbers hav⋯ been declining noticeably since 1990. **Habitat:** Occurs in a wide variety of broad-leaved an⋯ acacia woodlands and scrub. **Habits:** Cruises low at speed continually throughout the da⋯ in search of food. Adult preys mainly on game birds and small mammals, less frequentl⋯ on reptiles, despite similarity to snake eagles. Immature frequently scavenges at carcasses⋯ **Conservation:** Near Threatened.

Buzzards: Five *Buteo* species. They are mostly brown and resemble small eagles but have short, unfeathered tars⋯ Two sedentary species (one of which is endemic to southern Africa), one Palearctic migrant, and one rare vagrant ar⋯ illustrated here. The Red-necked Buzzard was recorded for the first time in Botswana when this book was in productio⋯ (see p. 384). The Setswana *mmankgôdi* and *mmankgwêdi* are generic names for buzzards.

LONG-LEGGED BUZZARD *Buteo rufinus*

Setswana: mmankgôdi, mmankgwêdi

59 cm (23 ¼ in). **Identification:** Variable brown buzzard (exhibits continuous polymorphism⋯ with bare yellow legs; adult has plain (unbarred), pale rufous tail. It is similar to Commo⋯ Buzzard but larger and has slightly longer legs. In flight, when seen from below, dark carpa⋯ patches are visible (but not conspicuous in dark morph), wings have dark trailing edges, an⋯ the bases of the primaries are white. **Call:** Silent in Botswana. **Status:** Vagrant, nonbreeding⋯ The species is a Palearctic migrant, but Botswana is far south of its usual range. **Abundance⋯** Rare. **Habitat:** As a vagrant, it can be found in a variety of habitats in Botswana. **Habits:** It is ⋯ perch hunter of reptiles and small mammals. Sightings should be substantiated with repor⋯ and/or photographs. **Conservation:** Least Concern.

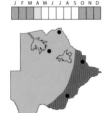

COMMON BUZZARD *Buteo buteo*

Setswana: mmankgôdi, mmankgwêdi

48 cm (19 in). **Identification:** Small raptor. Exhibits continuous polymorphism, and plumag⋯ can be pale, gray-brown, rufous, brown, or dark brown; most adults have a pale band o⋯ the lower breast. Legs are relatively short compared to those of Long-legged Buzzard⋯ **Call:** Silent in Botswana. **Status:** Palearctic migrant, nonbreeding. **Abundance:** Commo⋯ **Habitat:** Occurs in a wide range of open woodlands and shrublands. **Habits:** Gregariou⋯ during migration or at food sources; otherwise solitary. A perch hunter, it is seen on dea⋯ trees and electricity poles. **Conservation:** Least Concern.

adult male

adult male

adult female

adult female

BATELEUR

cream-backed form

subadult

juv.

juv.

adult

adult

adult

juv.

LONG-LEGGED
BUZZARD

adult
dark morph

adult
rufous morph

adult
pale morph

imm.

adult
dark morph

adult
rufous morph

imm.

COMMON
BUZZARD

AUGUR BUZZARD *Buteo augur*

58 cm (22 ¾ in). **Identification:** Large black-and-white buzzard with rufous to chestnu tail. In flight, underwing shows pure white coverts; distinct, comma-shaped carpal patch and black trailing edges to wings. Throat white in male; black in female. Immatures seen i Botswana are browner than adults and have variable dark blotching on breast and flanks pale underwing coverts; and barred secondaries. Jackal Buzzard can be distinguished from all plumages by its dark underwing coverts. **Call:** Mostly silent in Botswana. **Status:** Vagrant from mountainous areas in Namibia and Zimbabwe; nonbreeding. **Abundance:** Rare **Habitat:** Prefers hilly areas in wooded savannas and semiarid scrub; little suitable habita in Botswana. **Habits:** Solitary birds are seen in Botswana, usually perch hunting for reptiles birds, and small mammals from high vantage points. **Conservation:** Least Concern.

JACKAL BUZZARD *Buteo rufofuscus*

50 cm (19 ¾ in). **Identification:** Large buzzard with three morphs; the commonest ha black upperparts, rufous breast and tail, mottled charcoal-and-white belly, and dar throat. There are also white-breasted and very dark-breasted morphs. The white-breaste differs from Augur Buzzard in having black (not white) underwing coverts, visible in fligh Immature of all morphs may be mistaken for Common Buzzard (p. 96) but has pale hea and lacks pale breast patch seen in most Common Buzzards. **Call:** Unmusical *kweeu-kweeu* vaguely reminiscent of a jackal's call. **Status:** Visitor; no breeding records from Botswana **Abundance:** Rare but regular in Kgalagadi Transfrontier Park (where the white-breaste morph was recorded in 2011). The species's southern African range just crosses into southern and eastern Botswana. It is one of three raptor species endemic to southern Africa. **Habitat** Mainly prefers mountainous and hilly areas with scrub; in Botswana occasionally seen alone fossil riverbeds. **Habits:** Solitary perch hunter; also rides on updrafts when foraging. Adult and immatures wander widely. **Conservation:** Least Concern

***Milvus* kites:** Two sibling species of medium-size, brown scavenging hawks with deeply forked tails. One is a breeding intra-African migrant and the other a nonbreeding Palearctic migrant. Though they are sometimes lumped as one DNA analysis has shown that Black Kite and Yellow-billed Kite are separate species.

BLACK KITE *Milvus migrans*

Setswana: mmankgôdi, mmankgwêdi, malala-kokwane

55 cm (21 ¾ in). **Identification:** Brown migratory hawk. Adult has pale gray head, black bi (but yellow cere), and pale yellow eyes. In common with Yellow-billed Kite, it has long, forke tail and unfeathered slender yellow legs. Juvenile has darker brown head than adult an has brownish eyes; difficult to distinguish from juvenile Yellow-billed in the field since bot have black bills. The subspecies *M. m. migrans* has reddish-brown undertail coverts, visible i flight, while *M. m. lineatus* has pale belly and undertail coverts. **Call:** Silent, occasionally make tremulous *kleeuu-err*. **Status:** Palearctic migrant, nonbreeding. Birds start arriving in Octobe reaching their highest numbers during January and February. **Abundance:** Uncommon; muc less abundant than Yellow-billed Kite. Mainly a passage migrant through Botswana. The tw subspecies occur together throughout the country. **Habitat:** Ranges over a variety of ope woodlands when migrating. **Habits:** Occurs in large flocks, particularly during October an November; these break up as birds follow rains in search of food. **Conservation:** Least Concer

YELLOW-BILLED KITE *Milvus aegyptius*

Setswana: mmankgôdi, mmankgwêdi

55 cm (21 ¾ in). **Identification:** Brown migratory hawk. Adult has yellow bill and cere, dar red eye, and brown head. Juvenile has black bill, dark area behind eye, and more mottle appearance than adult and also than juvenile Black Kite. Flies with wings noticeably ben at the "wrist", actively twisting the wedge-shaped tail to steer. The subspecies that occur in Botswana is *M. a. parasitus*. **Call:** Tremulous *kleeu-err, ki-ki-ki*. **Status:** Intra-Africa migrant, breeding. Synchronized arrivals begin in early August and peak from September t December; departure is gradual (nonsynchronized), and numbers dwindle in March–Apr until there are none. **Abundance:** Common to abundant. **Habitat:** Not habitat specific, the species ranges over a variety of woodlands on migration. It breeds in riparian woodland **Habits:** An adaptable species, this kite has been recorded catching fish in the manner of fish eagle and engaging in kleptoparasitism. It is usually but not always seen in pairs or small numbers. However, 18,000 individuals were seen over the Boteti River in 1995, 80 were seen in Nossob Camp in Kgalagadi Transfrontier Park in 2009, and 5,000 were see over Shakawe in 2014. **Conservation:** Least Concern.

AUGUR BUZZARD

adult

adult male

imm.

juv.

adult female

imm.

adult male

JACKAL BUZZARD

adult

adult rufous-breasted morph

adult white-breasted morph

imm.

adult white-breasted morph

adult rufous-breasted morph

imm.

adult

BLACK KITE
M. m. migrans

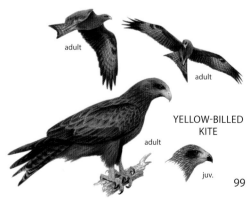

adult

adult

adult

YELLOW-BILLED KITE

adult

juv.

99

Harriers: Five species, all of which have long wings and quarter the ground in search of prey in buoyant, flapping flight. Harriers have owl-like facial disks. Botswana has one breeding resident and one vagrant Palearctic migrant associated with wetlands; and two Palearctic-breeding migrants (one of which is listed as Near Threatened globally) that favor arid open plains. The female and immature of these latter two are similar and referred to as "ringtails" for the appearance of their white rumps at the base of the dark tail. The fifth species, endemic to southern Africa, is a visitor in Botswana.

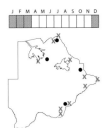

WESTERN MARSH HARRIER *Circus aeruginosus*

Setswana: se.gôdi, se.gwêdi

47 cm (18 ½ in). **Identification:** Slender, long-winged, long-tailed raptor. Most birds seen in Botswana are females and immatures. They are similar to immature African Marsh Harrier but are darker and have a well-defined, cream-colored patch on the head and throat; they lack any barring in tail or flight feathers. Male is brown, with pale head, gray flight feathers (visible along wing margin in perched bird), and black wingtips. **Call:** Silent in Botswana. **Status:** Vagrant, nonbreeding. Palearctic migrant to Africa, only occasionally recorded in Botswana. **Abundance:** Scarce, but this species may be on the increase in Botswana as there have been more sightings in recent years. **Habitat:** Found in freshwater wetlands, including lakes, large rivers, dams, and sewage ponds. **Habits:** Flight is buoyant, as the bird alternates flapping and gliding while it quarters over wetlands. **Conservation:** Least Concern.

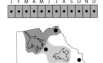

AFRICAN MARSH HARRIER *Circus ranivorus*

Setswana: se.gôdi, se.gwêdi

47 cm (18 ½ in). **Identification:** Slender, long-winged, long-tailed raptor with owl-like facial disk. Bold barring on flight feathers and banding on uppertail distinguish it from other harriers. Juvenile has pale chest band, as well as barring on flight feathers and tail. This harrier never has a white rump, as seen in female and juvenile Montagu's (p. 102) and Pallid (p. 102) Harriers **Call:** Mostly silent. **Status:** Resident, breeding. The limited data available indicate that egg-laying takes place year-round with no discernible peak. **Abundance:** Common in the Okavango wetland system, Linyanti Swamps, Makgadikgadi Pans, and along the Chobe River; scarce outside this area. The Okavango Delta is prime nesting and foraging habitat for this species; this area is its stronghold in southern Africa and is almost certainly its major global stronghold, although there are no accurate or reliable population estimates. **Habitat:** Favors permanent freshwater wetlands. **Habits:** Quarters over marshes and reed beds in buoyant flight, searching mainly for rodents. **Conservation:** Least Concern.

BLACK HARRIER *Circus maurus*

Setswana: se.gôdi, se.gwêdi

47 cm (18 ½ in). **Identification:** Slender, long-winged, long-tailed raptor. Bold black-and-white plumage, including white rump and barred tail. Juvenile also has white rump and is difficult to distinguish from female and juvenile Montagu's (p. 102) and Pallid (p. 102) Harriers. **Call:** Mostly silent. **Status:** Visitor, nonbreeding. Most sightings are during May. **Abundance:** Rare. Individuals move widely about the region and are occasionally seen in southwestern Botswana. It is one of three raptor species endemic to southern Africa. **Habitat:** Occurs in both dry and damp grasslands and scrublands. **Habits:** Hunts rodents and also small birds by quartering low over scrublands. **Conservation:** Vulnerable.

adult
male

juv.

adult
male

adult
male

adult
male

WESTERN MARSH
HARRIER

adult
female

adult
female

adult

adult

juv.

adult

juv.

AFRICAN MARSH
HARRIER

BLACK
HARRIER

adult

juv.

adult

adult

juv.

101

PALLID HARRIER *Circus macrourus*

Setswana: se.gôôtsane, se.gwêêtsane

M: 40 cm (15 ¾ in), F: 48 cm (19 in). **Identification:** Slender, long-winged, long-tailed raptor. Markedly sexually dimorphic. Adult male is pale gray with black wedges in wingtips; it lacks chestnut streaks on belly and black line along upperwing coverts shown by male Montagu's Harrier. Female and juvenile, known as "ringtails," are brown with white rump. Ringtails also typically have two or three dark bars across the underside of the secondaries (but no dark bar on the upperside). It is not possible to differentiate Pallid Harrier ringtails from Montagu's Harrier ringtails in the field. Adult male could be mistaken for Black-winged Kite (p. 110) but is more slender and longer winged and has different foraging habits. **Call:** Silent in Botswana. **Status:** Palearctic migrant, nonbreeding. **Abundance:** Uncommon in Central Kalahari Game Reserve and Makgadikgadi Pans; scarce elsewhere. Only occurs on passage in eastern and southeastern Botswana. **Habitat:** Found in grasslands and other open areas (pans, fossil riverbeds). **Habits:** Solitary, flies low over the ground, quartering to and fro in search of large insects, lizards, and rodents. Roosts on the ground at night. **Conservation:** Near Threatened.

MONTAGU'S HARRIER *Circus pygargus*

Setswana: se.gôôtsane, se.gwêêtsane

M: 40 cm (15 ¾ in), F: 47 cm (18 ½ in). **Identification:** Slender, long-winged, long-tailed raptor. Male is predominantly gray (including breast), but has pale belly streaked with chestnut. In flight, it has more extensive area of black on wingtips than male Pallid Harrier and has a distinct black line along the upperwing. Female and juvenile, known as "ringtails," are brown with white rump. It is not possible to differentiate Montagu's Harrier ringtails from Pallid Harrier ringtails in the field. **Call:** Silent. **Status:** Palearctic migrant, nonbreeding. **Abundance:** Common in the Central Kalahari Game Reserve and Makgadikgadi Pans and in southeastern Botswana; scarce elsewhere. **Habitat:** Occurs in grasslands and open savannas. **Habits:** Solitary birds are seen quartering slowly over grasslands, dropping onto prey on the ground. Roosts on the ground at night. **Conservation:** Least Concern.

PALLID HARRIER

adult male

adult male

adult female

juv.

adult male

adult female

juv.

adult male

adult female

juv.

MONTAGU'S HARRIER

adult female

adult male

adult female

adult male

juv.

juv.

adult female

adult male

adult female

juv.

Accipiters and similar hawks: Eight species of short-winged hawks, many belonging to the genus *Accipiter*. These small to medium-size raptors are pursuit hunters that depend on rapid acceleration to capture avian prey in flight, or perch hunters that take prey on the ground, using their talons. Sexes are similar, but some species show extreme size dimorphism, with female larger.

DARK CHANTING GOSHAWK *Melierax metabates*

Setswana: se.gôôtsane, se.gwêêtsane

45 cm (17 ¾ in). **Identification:** Medium-size, gray, short-winged hawk. Head and breast plain gray, belly barred, cere and legs orange-red. Barred rump and undertail coverts differentiate it from Pale Chanting and Gabar (p. 106) Goshawks, which it superficially resembles; it is much larger and longer-legged than Gabar, and its gray secondaries (visible in flight) distinguish it from Pale Chanting (see also Habitat). Immature bird has a pale eye and rufous-brown plumage; its breast is streaked and belly coarsely barred. Immatures go through scruffy transitional plumage before attaining adult coloration. **Call:** Whistling *wheee-o, wheee-o, wheee-o*. **Status:** Resident; no breeding records from Botswana. **Abundance:** Common in northern and eastern Botswana. **Habitat:** Prefers broad-leaved woodlands with tall mature trees; compare scrubbier, acacia-dominated habitat of Pale Chanting Goshawk. **Habits:** Tends to perch within tree canopy, and therefore is less conspicuous than Pale Chanting Goshawk. **Conservation:** Least Concern.

PALE CHANTING GOSHAWK *Melierax canorus*

Setswana: se.gôôtsane, se.gwêêtsane, mmankokonono

55 cm (21 ¾ in). **Identification:** Medium-size, gray, short-winged hawk. Head and breast plain gray, belly barred, cere and legs orange-red. Its white secondaries and white rump differentiate it from similar Dark Chanting Goshawk; see also Habitat. It is larger than Gabar Goshawk (p. 106) and has noticeably longer legs. The subspecies found throughout Botswana, *M. c. argentior*, is slightly paler than the nominate subspecies found in South Africa. Young bird resembles adult but is rufous brown, not gray; its rump is white. **Call:** Musical chanting, *kleeu, kleeu, klu-klu-klu-klu*. It is one of the characteristic sounds of the Kalahari dawn. **Status:** Resident, breeding. **Abundance:** Abundant throughout the country, except in the east and southeast where it is uncommon, and in Chobe District where it is scarce; it is absent from the Okavango Delta. **Habitat:** Prefers acacia woodlands and scrub, in contrast to habitat preference of allopatric Dark Chanting Goshawk. **Habits:** Solitary or in pairs. Static hunter from exposed perches. Characteristic flight path when it moves from one perch to another is a dive down to gain momentum, followed by a low, direct flight, terminating in a swoop upward to new perch. This species also has a regular foraging association with Honey Badger, Slender Mongoose, Black-backed Jackal, and snakes such as the Cape Cobra; it follows these animals in order to catch any prey items they flush. Young bird forages by walking on the ground, like a small Secretarybird. Exhibits cooperative polyandry when breeding. **Conservation:** Least Concern.

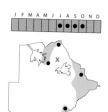

BLACK SPARROWHAWK *Accipiter melanoleucus*

M: 45 cm (17 ¾ in), F: 60 cm (23 ½ in). **Identification:** Largest accipiter in Botswana, where pale and rarer dark morphs occur. Upperparts are black in both morphs; breast and belly are white in pale morph but variable in dark morph, which may be almost completely black below except for white throat. Sexes show extreme size dimorphism; female is twice as heavy as male. Juvenile occurs in two color morphs (which do not correspond to the adult morphs), with underparts either rufous (more common) or white, both with dark streaking. Unfeathered tarsi prevent confusion between immature rufous morph and immature African Hawk Eagle (p. 92). **Call:** Male makes plaintive *kee-yoo* call; female a harsh *kek-kek-kek*. **Status:** Resident, breeding. **Abundance:** Scarce, but overlooked. Its presence in Botswana is near the western edge of its southern African range. **Habitat:** A forest species with limited prime habitat in Botswana; occurs in dense riparian woodlands, may roost or nest in exotic plantation trees, especially *Eucalyptus*. **Habits:** A persistent and tenacious pursuit predator, it specializes in large doves and game birds up to the size of Helmeted Guineafowl (p. 28). **Conservation:** Least Concern.

adult

juv.

adult

adult

juv.

DARK CHANTING GOSHAWK

juv.

adult

adult

adult

juv.

PALE CHANTING GOSHAWK
M. c. argentior

melanistic adult

adult

juv.

juv. rufous morph

adult dark morph

adult pale morph

BLACK SPARROWHAWK

adult

105

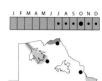

AFRICAN GOSHAWK *Accipiter tachiro*

M: 38 cm (15 in), F: 45 cm (17 ¾ in). **Identification:** Medium-size, short-winged hawk that shows marked sexual dimorphism. Male is much smaller than female and has slate-gray upperparts and white underparts barred with rufous brown. Female has brown upperparts and white underparts barred in brown. Both sexes have yellow legs and gray cere. Little Sparrowhawk (p. 108) is similar but has white rump. Immature is brown above and has brown tear-shaped spots on white breast. The subspecies *A. t. tachiro* has a distinct brown wash to underparts; *A. t. sparsimfasciatus* has fine gray barring with little brown on underparts. **Call:** Repetitive *chik … chik … chik*, during display flight. **Status:** Resident; no breeding records from Botswana. **Abundance:** Rare, except in Kasane and Maun areas, where it is more common. The species occurs in Botswana near the southern and western limits of its range. The nominate subspecies is present in the northern part of the country; *A. t. sparsimfasciatus* is restricted to the Tuli Block in the far east. **Habitat:** A forest species, found in dense riparian areas. **Habits:** Preys on birds, catching them in aerial pursuit. It has a prolonged and conspicuous circling display flight during which it calls frequently. **Conservation:** Least Concern.

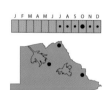

GABAR GOSHAWK *Micronisus gabar*

Setswana: segôôtsane

M: 28 cm (11 in), F: 36 cm (14 ¼ in). **Identification:** Small, short-winged hawk with gray head and chest, lightly barred belly, pale bars on tail, and orange cere and legs. White rump, visible in flight, is a key field feature; Shikra and Ovambo Sparrowhawk (p. 108) lack white rumps. Up to 25% of the species's population in all forms may be melanistic (all-black) morph, which lacks white rump; it has red cere and red legs that are black in front, which separate it from melanistic Ovambo Sparrowhawk. Juvenile is rufous, with brown streaking on breast and barring on belly, and is the only juvenile accipiter to have a white rump; its pale yellow eyes gradually turn red with age. Melanistic juvenile has black plumage and pale orange eye, cere, and legs. **Call:** Piping *tuii-tuii-tuii-tuii* (often mimicked by Fork-tailed Drongo). **Status:** Resident, breeding. **Abundance:** Common. **Habitat:** Favors open woodlands, especially acacia, including acacia-dominated riparian communities. **Habits:** Virtually every small water hole in Kalahari tree and bush savanna and arid scrub savanna has a resident bird, hunting doves and small seedeaters from the cover of surrounding shady trees, its flight direct and fast. Often seen tearing open weaver nests to get chicks. Nests in association with social spiders (*Stegodyphus* spp.), which cover the base of the nest with their webs, making it difficult to detect from below. **Conservation:** Least Concern.

SHIKRA *Accipiter badius*

M: 27 cm (10 ¾ in), F: 30 cm (11 ¾ in). **Identification:** Small short-winged hawk. Upperparts are slate gray, underparts are white with pale rufous (not gray) barring (superficially similar to much larger African Goshawk). Female has slightly browner upperparts than male. Yellow cere and red (male) or orange-red (female) eye are key features, and plain gray back and tail, without white rump or tail spots, is a useful field characteristic for separating it from the other small, short-winged hawks. Juvenile is brown above and has white underparts that are heavily blotched with brown on the breast, and barred with brown on the belly. It has a yellow eye that becomes darker with age. Legs and cere yellow. **Call:** High-pitched *tsieu, tsieu, tsieu*. **Status:** Resident, breeding. The few Botswana breeding records indicate that egg-laying peaks in October. **Abundance:** Common. Botswana is toward the southern limit of the species's range. **Habitat:** Occurs in a variety of woodlands and moist savannas, including Kalahari tree and bush savanna. **Habits:** Unique among small accipiters in preying largely on reptiles, which it hunts from exposed perches. **Conservation:** Least Concern.

adult
male

adult
female

juv.
female

adult
male

adult
male

adult
female

imm.
male

juv.
male

AFRICAN
GOSHAWK

GABAR
GOSHAWK

adult

melanistic
adult

juv.

adult

melanistic
adult

adult

adult

juv.

adult

SHIKRA

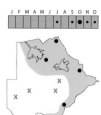

LITTLE SPARROWHAWK *Accipiter minnulus*

M: 23 cm (9 in), F: 27 cm (10 ¾ in). **Identification:** Very small short-winged hawk; smallest accipiter in Botswana. Adult male has gray upperparts, female has slightly browner; both sexes have white underparts barred with gray, and rufous-tinged flanks. When bird is seen close-up, yellow eye, eye-ring, cere, and legs are diagnostic. White rump and two white tail spots are visible when bird is perched or in flight. Much smaller than African Goshawk (p. 106), which has gray cere and lacks white rump and tail spots. Also smaller than Shikra (p. 106), which has red eye and lacks white rump and tail spots. Juvenile is brown above and has white underparts heavily marked with brown tear-shaped spots. The subspecies *A. m. tropicalis* has finer barring on the breast and paler flanks than *A. m. minullus*. **Call:** Rapid high-pitched *kew-kew-kew-kew*. **Status:** Resident, breeding. Although egg-laying usually takes place in spring, there is one July record. **Abundance:** Uncommon. Botswana is near the southern and western extent of the species's range. Both southern African subspecies are found here: *A. m. tropicalis* is restricted to the extreme north of the country, while *A. m. minullus* is more widespread. **Habitat:** Prefers forests and moist woodlands with tall trees, such as riparian and Zambezi Teak (*Baikiaea plurijuga*) woodlands. **Habits:** This hawk is a specialized hunter that preys almost entirely on small birds. **Conservation:** Least Concern.

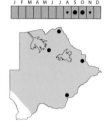

OVAMBO SPARROWHAWK *Accipiter ovampensis*

M: 31 cm (12 ¼ in), F: 40 cm (15 ¾ in). **Identification:** Falcon-like accipiter with relatively long wings and short tail. Female is one-third larger than male. Adult normally gray, but occasionally melanistic (only 1-2% of the population). Upperparts plain gray (no white rump); underparts are completely barred in dark gray from base of bill down. Head appears small, with large bill; cere is yellow-orange or red; eye is dark red-brown. Legs are usually orange but may be yellow-orange or red. The dark tail, which has three paler bars with a central line created by the white feather shafts (most visible on the upperside), is diagnostic in all forms. Tail pattern and yellow-orange legs and cere differentiate melanistic morph from melanistic Gabar Goshawk (p. 106). Juveniles occur in one of two forms—rufous, with rufous underparts, or pale, with white underparts. Young birds also have a distinctive dark patch behind eye and a white eyebrow. **Call:** Rapid, whistled *keep-keep-keep-keeep* ascending in tone. **Status:** Resident, breeding. **Abundance:** Uncommon. Botswana is at the southern limit of the species's range. **Habitat:** Found in acacia and mixed woodlands. Favors a mosaic of tall woodlands and open areas. **Habits:** Specialized bird hunter, it perches high up in edges of tall woodlands and pursues small birds in open areas; female takes dove-size birds, male targets smaller birds. **Conservation:** Least Concern.

LITTLE
SPARROWHAWK

adult

adult

adult

juv.

adult

juv.

OVAMBO
SPARROWHAWK

adult

juv.
rufous form

juv.
pale form

melanistic
adult

juv.
rufous form

adult

109

Miscellaneous kites and hawks: This is an arbitrary grouping of six distinctive, unrelated raptors.

BLACK-WINGED KITE *Elanus caeruleus*

Setswana: phakalane

30 cm (11 ¾ in). **Identification:** Small raptor. Predominantly gray and white, it has a black shoulder patch that is diagnostic. Ruby-red eye is visible at close quarters. Immature is brownish above, with a scalloped appearance on wings and mantle due to buff edges to feathers; it has a pale brown eye, which changes through orange to red. **Call:** Mostly silent. **Status:** Resident, breeding. **Abundance:** Uncommon throughout the country except in years of high rodent numbers, when it is locally common. **Habitat:** Found in grasslands and open Kalahari tree and bush savanna. **Habits:** A static perch hunter, usually solitary, it specializes in diurnal rodents. Regularly hunts by hovering, one of the largest birds to do so. When excited, pumps tail up and down. **Conservation:** Least Concern. **General:** The Setswana name *phakalane* is also used loosely for a variety of kestrels and small gray falcons.

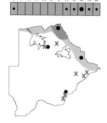

LIZARD BUZZARD *Kaupifalco monogrammicus*

36 cm (14 ¼ in). **Identification:** Small gray hawk that superficially resembles Gabar Goshawk (p. 106). White throat with black line down the center is diagnostic. In flight, shows white rump and white bar (occasionally two) across tail; the latter is a useful feature to separate it from goshawks and sparrowhawks (pp. 104-108). **Call:** Long, drawn-out melodious whistle followed by a series of shorter notes: *wheeo, we-we-we-we-we*. **Status:** Resident, breeding. **Abundance:** Scarce, except in the vicinity of Kasane town (between Pandamatenga and Kasane), where it is uncommon. Botswana is at the southern limit of the species's range. **Habitat:** Prefers moist, tall, mature woodlands, such as Zambezi Teak (*Baikiaea plurijuga*) and broad-leaved woodlands. **Habits:** Solitary perch hunter, it perches in the open, as it is primarily an insect-eater and for this reason is not usually mobbed by small birds. When moving from one perch to another, its characteristic flight path is a dive down to gain momentum, followed by a low, uniform flight, terminating in an upward swoop to new perch. **Conservation:** Least Concern. **General:** The specific name *monogrammicus* means "with a single mark" and refers to the line down the throat.

AFRICAN CUCKOO-HAWK *Aviceda cuculoides*

40 cm (15 ¾ in). **Identification:** Small raptor. Mostly gray, with bold brown barring on belly. Small crest and short legs are noticeable field features. In flight, rufous barring on underwing coverts is distinctive. Male has red eye; female has yellow eye. Immature has same general size and shape as adult but is brown above and white with bold brown spots below. **Call:** Whistled *teee-oooo* in flight. **Status:** Resident; no breeding records from Botswana. **Abundance:** Rare. Its range reaches into Botswana at its southwestern limits. **Habitat:** Prefers moist woodlands, especially riparian woodlands in the Okavango Delta; also found in Zambezi Teak (*Baikiaea plurijuga*) woodlands in Chobe District. **Habits:** Secretive and easily overlooked, it perches in the canopy of a tree and makes short flights to the ground to capture insects or small reptiles., It may be seen soaring over its territory. **Conservation:** Least Concern.

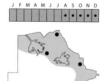

AFRICAN HARRIER-HAWK *Polyboroides typus*

Setswana: se.gôôtsane, se.gwêêtsane

63 cm (24 ¾ in). **Identification:** Large, gray hawk that looks floppy in flight. The unfeathered face with bare yellow cheeks (which flush red when the bird is excited) is unique among hawks. It has a small head, and long, slender, yellow "double-jointed" legs (see Habits). In flight, it shows broad wings and a conspicuous white bar in tail. Juvenile is dark chocolate brown and has a cowl of large, soft feathers on the head that can form a broad crest. Immature has blotched and mottled appearance as it changes irregularly before attaining gray adult plumage. **Call:** Mostly silent. A tremulous *suuu-eee-ooo* in flight. **Status:** Resident, breeding. **Abundance:** Common in well-wooded areas in the north and east of the country, particularly around the Okavango Delta and the Tuli Block. **Habitat:** Prefers dense woodlands and riparian vegetation; often associated with densely wooded ravines and cliffs, especially in eastern Botswana. **Habits:** Solitary or in pairs. Probes cracks and crevices with its long, dexterous legs and feet in search of lizards, nesting birds, and small mammals. The leg's tibio-tarsal joint can bend backward and forward. **Conservation:** Least Concern.

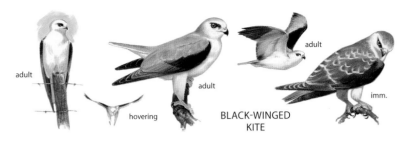

adult

hovering

adult

adult

imm.

**BLACK-WINGED
KITE**

**LIZARD
BUZZARD**

adult

adult

adult

imm.

adult

imm.

adult
female

adult
female

imm.

adult
male

adult
male

adult
male

**AFRICAN
CUCKOO-HAWK**

hunting
posture

flushing
adult

adult

juv.

adult

juv.

**AFRICAN
HARRIER-HAWK**

111

BAT HAWK *Macheiramphus alcinus*

45 cm (17 ¾ in). **Identification:** Dark brown raptor. In flight, it has a falcon-like shape, with broad-based, angular, pointed wings. It has a large head with a distinctive crest; large, yellow owl-like eyes; and a slight beak with an enormous gape. White eyelids and white streaks on the nape that form false eyes are diagnostic. Juvenile and immature have variable amounts of white on underparts. This species can be confused with African (p. 116) and Eurasian (p. 116) Hobbies, which are also crepuscular and forage over rivers; when silhouetted these birds are difficult to separate. Eurasian Hobby is paler below (although heavily streaked) and African Hobby is rufous below; both are smaller than Bat Hawk and are slender and fast flying. **Call:** Mostly silent; plaintive whistling, not unlike that of Water Thick-knee. **Status:** Resident, breeding. Breeds in the Okavango Delta; a single-egg clutch is the norm. **Abundance:** Scarce. **Habitat:** Found in riparian woodlands. **Habits:** A highly specialized, crepuscular and nocturnal predator of a narrow spectrum of prey species (mainly bats), it hunts over rivers. It has a large gape and swallows the bat whole, on the wing. It also hunts Red-billed Queleas and other small birds. Roosts during the day among tree foliage. **Conservation:** Least Concern.

EUROPEAN HONEY BUZZARD *Pernis apivorus*

55 cm (21 ¾ in). **Identification:** Small-headed, long-tailed raptor related to kites. It exhibits continuous polymorphism, and plumage is variable. Pale and intermediate birds recorded in Botswana. In flight, undertail has distinctive dark subterminal band and less conspicuous double band at the tail's base. **Call:** Silent in Botswana. **Status:** Palearctic migrant, nonbreeding. **Abundance:** Scarce. Seen more widely and frequently during recent years, mainly in northern Botswana. **Habitat:** Favors mature, tall woodlands. **Habits:** Solitary. It has a specialized diet and hunts in trees and on the ground for its main food, the larvae of ground-dwelling wasps. (In spite of its name, it does not eat honey.) **Conservation:** Least Concern.

FALCONS Falconidae

Long-winged, diurnal raptors with notched, hooked bills. Thirteen species occur in Botswana. In a group of its own (genus *Polihierax*), the specialized Pygmy Falcon is an African falconet, a diminutive shrike-like species that roosts and breeds in association with the Sociable Weaver. The remaining 12 species belong to the genus *Falco*. These are grouped, somewhat arbitrarily, into kestrels (six species) and true falcons (six species). The kestrels are shorter-winged and perch hunt or hover before diving onto their prey (mostly invertebrates) on the ground; this group includes the Amur and Red-footed Falcons, which are essentially kestrels. The true falcons, which include the hobbies, are aerial hunters and stoop to catch their prey (mainly birds); they are all solitary or occur in pairs. The migratory species of *Falco* are highly gregarious. All species of the genus *Falco* are sexually dimorphic in size (female larger) and/or plumage. *Phakalane* is a generic Setswana name for falcons and kestrels, although it is also applied specifically to the Black-winged Kite (p. 110).

PYGMY FALCON *Polihierax semitorquatus*

20 cm (7 ¾ in). **Identification:** Smallest diurnal raptor in Botswana (it weighs a mere 60 g [2 oz]). Adult has white underparts and red eye-ring, cere, and legs. Male has all-gray upperparts; female has gray upperparts except chestnut back. The species cannot be confused with any other raptor in Botswana. **Call:** Squeaky *twee TWIK, twee-twee TWIK*. **Status:** Resident, breeding. **Abundance:** Common; found in the extreme southwest. **Habitat:** Favors arid scrub savannas with scattered large trees, especially Camel Thorns (*Acacia erioloba*), growing in open grassy areas. **Habits:** This falconet is a specialized lizard predator; the bulk of its diet comprises sand lizards, agamas, and skinks, but it also takes other reptiles, small birds, and invertebrates. It perch hunts in shrike-like fashion, pouncing on prey on the ground. It sometimes bobs head and wags tail up and down; it has undulating flight. Closely associated with Sociable Weaver, it is an obligate user of the weaver's nest chambers for breeding and roosting. Those in use by the falcon have distinctive white-rimmed entrances from accumulation of the birds' droppings. **Conservation:** Least Concern.

112

adult

BAT HAWK

imm.

juv.

adult

juv.

EUROPEAN HONEY BUZZARD

adult pale morph

adult pale morph

adult pale morph

imm. pale morph

adult pale morph

adult intermediate morph

adult dark morph

imm. intermediate morph

male

male

female

female

PYGMY FALCON

113

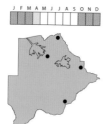

LESSER KESTREL *Falco naumanni*

Setswana: phakalane

M: 26 cm (10 ¼ in), F: 32 cm (12 ½ in). **Identification:** Slender, long-winged, long-tailed kestrel. Male easily recognizable by plain gray head, plain chestnut back and upperwing coverts, gray greater coverts, and black primaries and secondaries. Female is tawny rufous above with black barring on wings, and buffy below with dark streaks. Immature resembles female. Rock Kestrel of both sexes can be differentiated from Lesser male by its gray-streaked head, black spots on wings, lack of gray wing bar, and chestnut secondaries (when seen from above). The two females are very similar, but female Rock Kestrel has gray-streaked head and is rich chestnut above and below, with dark spotting on underparts. Immature Lesser's rufous tail with black bars (viewed from above) differentiates it from Rock Kestrel, which has a gray tail barred with black. **Call:** High-pitched *chi, chi, chi* at roosts. **Status:** Palearctic migrant, nonbreeding. It is a passage migrant, seen traveling southward in late October with the onset of rainstorms and returning northward during March and April. **Abundance:** Uncommon. This species passes through Botswana in small and medium-size flocks on its way to and from South Africa; no communal roosts are known in Botswana. **Habitat:** Found in semiarid grasslands. **Habits:** Highly gregarious; solitary birds unlikely to be seen. This kestrel hunts insects from exposed perches or by hovering. Individual birds with satellite transmitters have been recorded foraging around their roosting sites for a day or two (or three) before moving to new area. **Conservation:** Vulnerable.

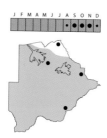

ROCK KESTREL *Falco rupicolus*

Setswana: phakalane

M: 30 cm (11 ¾ in); F: 33 cm (13 in). **Identification:** Small, rufous kestrel. Adult of both sexes has gray-streaked head and rufous back spotted with black. Immature has brownish head and gray tail with black bars (viewed from above). **Call:** High-pitched *kee-kee-kee-kee*. **Status:** Resident, breeding. **Abundance:** Uncommon, but more frequent in eastern hardveld. **Habitat:** Occurs in a wide range of habitats, from grasslands to semiarid scrub; prefers habitat near rocky areas, where it nests. **Habits:** Solitary or in pairs. A conspicuous perch hunter, it also hovers. It preys on small mammals, birds, reptiles, and insects. **Conservation:** Least Concern.

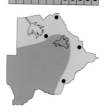

GREATER KESTREL *Falco rupicoloides*

Setswana: phakalane

M: 33 cm (13 in); F: 36 cm (14 ¼ in). **Identification:** Medium-size buffy kestrel, heavily barred with black. Adult of both sexes has pale eye; although not easy to see in the field, it is unique to this kestrel. Immature has dark eye. **Call:** Mostly silent; shrill *keer-kik-kik*. **Status:** Resident, breeding. **Abundance:** Common in the Kalahari in central, western, and southern Botswana; uncommon in eastern and northern Botswana. The Kalahari is the center of its abundance in southern Africa. **Habitat:** Found in grasslands and open Kalahari tree and bush savanna. **Habits:** It is a conspicuous, solitary perch hunter. **Conservation:** Least Concern.

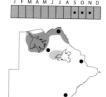

DICKINSON'S KESTREL *Falco dickinsoni*

Setswana: phakalane

M: 26 cm (10 ¼ in), F: 30 cm (11 ¾ in). **Identification:** Small kestrel. Adult of both sexes has pale gray head that contrasts with dark gray back and upperwing coverts. Pale rump and barred tail are diagnostic and separate it from Sooty Falcon (p. 118). (Rump and tail also distinguish it from Grey Kestrel, which has not been recorded in Botswana.) **Call:** Mostly silent; tremulous *keee-keee-keee*. **Status:** Resident, breeding. There are limited data on egg-laying, which occurs in spring. **Abundance:** Common north of 20° S (the latitude of the Nata-Maun-Sehithwa road); it occurs in Chobe National Park, the Linyanti area, Okavango Delta, and Makgadikgadi Pans. The Okavango Delta is its stronghold in southern Africa. **Habitat:** Prefers open savannas with *Hyphaene* palms and Baobab (*Adansonia digitata*) trees. The species is endemic to the Zambezian region. **Habits:** This kestrel perch hunts from tops of dead trees, scanning for insects and lizards. It is subject to irruptive movements. **Conservation:** Least Concern.

male

male

female

female

LESSER
KESTREL

male

male

ROCK
KESTREL

female

adult

GREATER
KESTREL

adult

juv.

adult

adult

DICKINSON'S
KESTREL

115

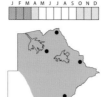

AMUR FALCON *Falco amurensis*

Setswana: phakalane

M: 28 cm (11 in), F: 30 cm (11 ¾ in). **Identification:** Small kestrel; wings shorter than those c true falcons. Male is dark gray, with rufous lower belly and vent; in flight, white underwin coverts differentiate it from male Red-footed Falcon. Female is slate gray above and ha white underparts with barring and blotching, and whitish underwing coverts with som black markings; the white underparts and underwing coverts distinguish it from female Red footed Falcon. **Call:** Mostly silent. **Status:** Palearctic migrant; nonbreeding. **Abundance** Uncommon; outnumbered by Red-footed Falcon. It is seen on migration passage throug Botswana. Only one temporary communal roost recorded, in Palapye, Central District in 2007. **Habitat:** Found in open grasslands and also clearings in woodlands. **Habits** Gregarious, often in large flocks. Perch hunts and hover hunts for arthropods such a grasshoppers and termite alates. This bird covers 22,000 km (13,700 mi) annually during it migration, much of it over the sea; from its breeding grounds in northeastern Asia it trave via India and across the Indian Ocean to southern Africa. **Conservation:** Least Concern.

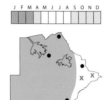

RED-FOOTED FALCON *Falco vespertinus*

Setswana: phakalane

M: 28 cm (11 in), F: 31 cm (12 ¼ in). **Identification:** Small kestrel; wings shorter than those c true falcons. Male is dark blue-gray, with dull red tarsi and rufous lower belly and undertai in flight, dark underwing coverts distinguish it from male Amur Falcon. Female has slate gray back with dark barring; unstreaked rufous-buff underparts, extending from side of hea down to belly; and buffy underwing coverts. Orange-red cere and legs (not useful field mark except to avoid confusion with juvenile Eurasian Hobby, which has yellow cere and legs Immature is similar to female but has gray streaking on underparts and buffy edges to da gray back feathers. **Call:** Mostly silent. **Status:** Palearctic migrant, nonbreeding. **Abundance** Uncommon but outnumbers Amur Falcon. Migrating birds mainly pass through Botswan Only one temporary communal roost recorded, in Palapye, Central District, in 2007. **Habitat** Favors open grassy clearings in woodlands and arid savannas. **Habits:** Gregarious, in flocks c 10 to 50 birds. Diurnal aerial predator of insects, sometimes hovers while searching. Follow rain fronts in search of termite alates and other insects. Roosts communally in tall eucalypt **Conservation:** Near Threatened.

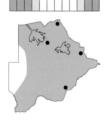

EURASIAN HOBBY *Falco subbuteo*

M: 28 cm (11 in), F: 36 cm (14 ¼ in). **Identification:** Small, long-winged falcon. Adult of bot sexes has black hood and moustachial stripe, dark slate back and wings, and white underpart heavily streaked and blotched, except belly and leggings, which are rich chestnut. Immatur has similar pattern but is browner and lacks chestnut on belly and thighs. Due to habit c catching bats at dusk, sometimes mistaken for Bat Hawk (p. 112), which is larger and ha very dark underparts and underwing. Immature more likely to be confused with femal Amur Falcon, but hobby is larger, longer-winged, and more heavily marked on underpart **Call:** Mostly silent. **Status:** Palearctic migrant, nonbreeding. **Abundance:** Scarce. **Habitat** Found in broad-leaved and acacia woodlands; also riparian woodlands. **Habits:** Crepuscula solitary hunter of small birds, insects (especially dragonflies), and bats on the wing, ofte along rivers. It is a high-speed, maneuverable flier. Its movements are linked to rainfall, an it is most likely to be seen during late afternoons in summer following rain. Termite alate are a favored food item, and flocks of several dozen hobbies may congregate at termit emergences. **Conservation:** Least Concern.

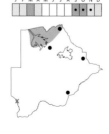

AFRICAN HOBBY *Falco cuvierii*

M: 27 cm (10 ¾ in), F: 32 cm (12 ½ in). **Identification:** Inconspicuous, small, long-winge falcon. Adult of both sexes has dark slate upperparts, cap, and prominent moustachial strip and plain rufous underparts. Immature has dark streaking on rufous underparts. Sometime mistaken for Bat Hawk (p. 112), due to habit of catching bats at dusk, but Bat Hawk larger and has very dark underparts and underwing. Immature superficially resemble female Red-footed Falcon, due to rufous underparts, but Red-footed Falcon lacks da cap and mustache. **Call:** Mostly silent. **Status:** Intra-African migrant; no breeding record from Botswana. **Abundance:** Scarce. The species's range just reaches northern Botswan **Habitat:** Found in broad-leaved woodlands with open clearings; often associated wit *Hyphaene* palms. **Habits:** Solitary. Crepuscular; hunts bats, insects, and birds at dusk, ofte along rivers. Joins other raptors at termite alate emergences. **Conservation:** Least Concer

AMUR
FALCON

adult
female

adult
male

adult
male

juv.

adult
female

RED-FOOTED
FALCON

adult
male

adult
male

juv.

adult
male

adult
female

adult
female

adult
female

EURASIAN
HOBBY

juv.

adult

adult

adult

juv.

adult

adult

adult

AFRICAN
HOBBY

SOOTY FALCON *Falco concolor*

M: 32 cm (12 ½ in), F: 36 cm (14 ¼ in). **Identification:** Small, long-winged falcon. Adult of both sexes has uniformly bluish-gray plumage. It occurs in pale gray and dark gray morphs; the pale morph has been observed in Makgadikgadi Pans. The eye-ring, cere, and legs are yellow. Wingtips protrude beyond tail when bird is at rest; this differentiates it from the gray-plumaged kestrels. **Call:** Mostly silent. **Status:** Vagrant from northeastern Africa, nonbreeding. It is a possible summer visitor during its migration passage. **Abundance:** Rare. This species has not been reliably reported in Botswana since 1988. **Habitat:** Traverses a variety of habitats but forages in open woodlands and grasslands. **Habits:** Crepuscular, spends most of day roosting in well-foliaged trees. Hunts insects, bats, and small birds in flight. Travels solitarily or in pairs when migrating. **Conservation:** Near Threatened.

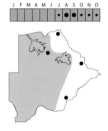

RED-NECKED FALCON *Falco chicquera*

M: 30 cm (11 ¾ in), F: 36 cm (14 ¼ in). **Identification:** Small, dashing, long-winged falcon. Adult of both sexes has rufous nape and crown, and its back and underparts are finely barred in black. In flight, when seen from below, it shows clean, fine barring on body and wings, a white throat separated from barred breast by rufous band, a dark subterminal tail band, and dark wingtips. Juvenile has darker brown head and rufous (but still finely barred) underparts. **Call:** Mostly silent; strident trilling. Recently fledged juveniles have noisy twittering, begging call. **Status:** Resident, breeding. Late instances of egg-laying (during November and December) are usually replacement clutches after early failure. **Abundance:** Locally common in the Okavango Delta, Makgadikgadi Pans, Ghanzi farms, and Nossob Valley; uncommon elsewhere. **Habitat:** Found in *Hyphaene* palm savannas and margins of floodplains; also in acacia savannas, where it is associated with water holes. **Habits:** Crepuscular. Catches small birds on the wing after rapid aerial pursuit. Often hunts in association with Gabar Goshawks at water holes in the Kalahari. Nests in *Hyphaene* palms in the northern part of its range, but uses Cape Crow nests in Camel Thorns (*Acacia erioloba*) in Kgalagadi District. **Conservation:** Least Concern.

LANNER FALCON *Falco biarmicus*

Setswana: phakwe

M: 36 cm (14 ¼ in), F: 48 cm (19 in). **Identification:** Large, long-winged falcon. Adult (of both sexes) is easily distinguished from Peregrine Falcon by rufous crown and pinkish-buffy underparts. Immature has creamy-brown crown and dark streaking on underparts (compare immature Peregrine, which has dark cap and more finely streaked breast and belly). **Call:** Harsh *kek-kek-kek*. **Status:** Resident, breeding. The population is supplemented by intra-African migrants. Migrating birds pass through Central Kalahari Game Reserve in substantial numbers during summer, and the species is five times more abundant in summer than winter, peaking in January. **Abundance:** Locally abundant in Central Kalahari Game Reserve and Kgalagadi Transfrontier Park; common throughout remainder of range. The summer influx of birds is from south-central Africa, rather than from South Africa. **Habitat:** Found in open habitats such as fossil riverbeds and pans in Kalahari tree and bush savanna. **Habits:** This is the common large falcon of the country. Pairs are resident around Kalahari water holes. The species soars more than Peregrine Falcon but frequently catches birds in fast, low-level flight. Hunts Red-billed Queleas at their roosts and breeding sites. **Conservation:** Least Concern.

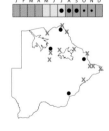

PEREGRINE FALCON *Falco peregrinus*

F. p. minor: M: 34 cm (13 ½ in), F: 43 cm (17 in). *F. p. calidus*: M: 42 cm (16 ½ in), F: 54 cm (21 ¼ in). **Identification:** Large, long-winged falcon. Adult of both sexes has all-black head, and white, barred underparts; these features differentiate it from Lanner Falcon. Two subspecies occur in Botswana. *F. p. calidus* is larger, paler, and its underparts are barred from the throat downward. The smaller *F. p. minor* has a white chest and barred belly; immature of *F. p. minor* is browner and prominently streaked below. **Call:** Harsh *kek-kek-kek*. **Status:** *F. p. minor*: resident; no breeding records from Botswana, but suspected to nest in Lepokole Hills, in Tswapong Hills, and near Selebi-Phikwe, all in Central District. *F. p. calidus*: Palearctic migrant, nonbreeding. **Abundance:** *F. p. minor* is scarce; *F. p. calidus* is rare. The two subspecies occur throughout the country. **Habitat:** Resident birds usually occur in closed woodlands near cliffs (used for roosting, breeding, and as hunting perches); migrants range over a variety of habitats. **Habits:** Flight direct; the species is specialized for high-speed pursuit and capture of aerial prey. Red-billed Queleas are an important component of the diet. The species soars less often than Lanner Falcon. *F. p. minor* is essentially a cliff nester but will nest in trees. **Conservation:** Least Concern. No trade in this species is permitted due to CITES listing.

SOOTY FALCON

adult
pale gray
morph

juv.

juv.

RED-NECKED FALCON

adult

adult

adult

juv.

adult

adult

adult

juv.

LANNER FALCON

juv.

adult
F. p. calidus

adult
F. p. calidus

juv.

adult
F. p. minor

adult
F. p. minor

PEREGRINE FALCON

119

BUSTARDS   Otididae

Birds of this family are cryptically colored ground dwellers that lack a hind toe and never perch. They are omnivorous. Species are sexually dimorphic; most are polygynous and have traditional breeding arenas (leks) where mating takes place. No pair bonds are formed between the sexes. The large species inflate throat pouches in terrestrial courtship displays; smaller species have spectacular, noisy aerial displays. The seven species found in Botswana are divided on the basis of size into large or medium-size bustards (five species) and smaller korhaans (two species). Most are sedentary, and one is endemic to southern Africa.

LUDWIG'S BUSTARD   *Neotis ludwigii*

M: 88 cm (34 ¾ in), F: 81 cm (32 in). **Identification:** Large cursorial bird. Combination of gray-brown throat and foreneck, rufous-brown hind neck, and small black-and-white wing panel is diagnostic among bustards. **Call:** Male has loud booming call during breeding season. **Status:** Resident; no breeding records from Botswana. It breeds following rains. **Abundance:** Rare. Its range just reaches southwestern Botswana, but it is a regular visitor to the Nossob Valley in the Kgalagadi Transfrontier Park. **Habitat:** Found in arid scrub savannas with open plains and fossil riverbeds. **Habits:** Solitary or in small groups. Male has spectacular, conspicuous display during breeding, inflating gray throat pouch into large balloon. **Conservation:** Endangered. Collision with power lines is a major threat to this species.

DENHAM'S BUSTARD   *Neotis denhami*

Setswana: kgorithamaga

M: 110 cm (43 ¼ in), F: 85 cm (33 ½ in). **Identification:** Large cursorial bird. Combination of gray throat, rufous-brown hind neck, and large black-and-white wing panel is diagnostic among bustards. The subspecies found in Botswana, *N. d. jacksoni*, has a paler hind neck and darker back than *N. d. stanleyi*, which is found in South Africa. **Call:** Mostly silent. **Status:** Intra-African migrant; breeding status uncertain. Botswana birds, which are found in the north of the country in summer, are mostly intra-African migrants of the subspecies *N. d. jacksoni* at the southern limit of their range. However, occasional birds are seen during winter, and there is one (March 2014) record of a small chick, indicating that the species may occasionally be a breeding visitor. **Abundance:** Scarce. Reliable places to see this species in northern Botswana are Nxai Pan, Savute Marsh, Selinda, Pandamatenga, and Moremi Game Reserve. **Habitat:** Occurs in open grasslands and clearings in Kalahari tree and bush savanna. **Habits:** Usually solitary, but small groups, with a maximum of five individuals, have been seen occasionally. Male has spectacular display during breeding season, inflating throat into conspicuous white balloon. This bustard undertakes local movements. **Conservation:** Near Threatened.

KORI BUSTARD   *Ardeotis kori*

Setswana: kgôri, kgwêri

M: 135 cm (53 ¼ in), F: 112 cm (44 in). **Identification:** Large cursorial bird. Combination of gray neck, black collar, and small black-and-white wing panel is diagnostic among bustards. Sexes alike, but male much larger and heavier than female. **Call:** Low-frequency, booming *duf, duf, duf-duf* sound; can be heard over significant distance early on still mornings during breeding season (summer). **Status:** Resident, breeding. **Abundance:** Common at Savute Marsh, Nxai Pan, Central Kalahari Game Reserve, Khutse Game Reserve, Tuli Block, and Kgalagadi Transfrontier Park. Uncommon elsewhere. Botswana is the stronghold for the southern African subspecies, *A. k. kori*. **Habitat:** Occurs in Kalahari tree and bush savannas with open short-grass areas adjacent to shrublands with longer grass. **Habits:** Solitary, no lasting pair bond. Female and offspring form small, temporary group. Males display on expanded leks by inflating throat, drooping the wings, cocking the short tail, and strutting about. This is the world's heaviest flying bird (heaviest on record was a male of 22 kg [49 lb]). Flight is ponderous, especially that of male, which is reluctant to get airborne. **Conservation:** Near Threatened. **General:** This is one of only a few birds whose English name is taken directly from the Setswana. Traditionally, the Kori Bustard had been regarded as a royal bird in Botswana, and its meat was strictly reserved for chiefs; today it is the official national bird. It is the subject of the proverb *Kgori e bona mae, lerapo ga ele bone*: "The Kori sees the eggs but does not see the trap!"

120

male

female

adult

LUDWIG'S
BUSTARD

male
display

adult

female

male

DENHAM'S
BUSTARD
N. d. jacksoni

adult

adult

male
display

KORI
BUSTARD
A. k. kori

121

WHITE-BELLIED BUSTARD *Eupodotis senegalensis*

Setswana: mo.kagatwê, kegamakalo

50 cm (19 ¾ in). **Identification:** Small bustard with white belly (in both sexes). Male slightly larger than female. The subspecies found in Botswana, *E. s. barrowii*, is distinguished from the other four found elsewhere in Africa by the following features: Male crown is black in front and blue-gray at the rear; the white face has indistinct malar stripe; the throat is black, the foreneck blue-gray, the hind neck rufous. Female has tawny face and neck, white throat. **Call:** Garrulous *tuk-warra*, repeated. **Status:** Uncertain; no breeding records from Botswana. **Abundance:** Rare in Pitsane grasslands in the extreme southeast. Botswana is near the northern limit of the species's range. There have been no sightings of this species in the country since the early 1990s. **Habitat:** Prefers open, tall grasslands. **Habits:** A sedentary bustard, lives in small family groups. Forages in early morning and late afternoon for plant material and invertebrates. **Conservation:** Least Concern.

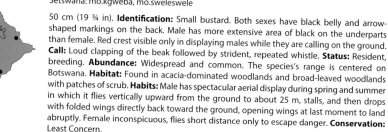

RED-CRESTED KORHAAN *Lophotis ruficrista*

Setswana: mo.kgwêba, mo.sweleswele

50 cm (19 ¾ in). **Identification:** Small bustard. Both sexes have black belly and arrow-shaped markings on the back. Male has more extensive area of black on the underparts than female. Red crest visible only in displaying males while they are calling on the ground. **Call:** Loud clapping of the beak followed by strident, repeated whistle. **Status:** Resident, breeding. **Abundance:** Widespread and common. The species's range is centered on Botswana. **Habitat:** Found in acacia-dominated woodlands and broad-leaved woodlands with patches of scrub. **Habits:** Male has spectacular aerial display during spring and summer in which it flies vertically upward from the ground to about 25 m, stalls, and then drops with folded wings directly back toward the ground, opening wings at last moment to land abruptly. Female inconspicuous, flies short distance only to escape danger. **Conservation:** Least Concern.

NORTHERN BLACK KORHAAN *Afrotis afraoides*

Setswana: tlatlawê, mo.tlatlagwê, tlatlagwê, mo.tlatlawe, mo.tlatlawa, mo.tlatlawê

50 cm (19 ¾ in). **Identification:** Small bustard. Male slightly larger than female. Male has black head, neck, and underparts, and brown-barred back and wings. Female has black on belly, and brown barring on wings and extending onto neck. Both sexes have yellow legs and red base to bill. In flight, white primaries are conspicuous (hence alternative name White-quilled Korhaan). The two subspecies found in Botswana differ subtly in the barring on the back. **Call:** Noisy *tlatlawe*. The Setswana names are onomatopoeic, taken from the call. **Status:** Resident, breeding. Egg-laying is governed by rain; occurrences recorded during winter would have followed substantial late rains. **Abundance:** Abundant in the central and western parts of Botswana; common to uncommon elsewhere in its range. *A. a. damarensis* is widespread across the southern two-thirds of the country; *A. a. etoschae* is found from Makgadikgadi Pans northward. The species is endemic to southern Africa. **Habitat:** Found in open grasslands. **Habits:** Solitary. During summer, males can be seen on breeding arenas (leks) following solitary females and vying for the opportunity to mate. Male conspicuous during display flight, making loud, clattering calls and gliding down with legs dangling and wings whirling; patrols display arena with feathers on crown and throat puffed up, which gives head a square appearance. Dull red base to bill flushes bright scarlet during these displays. Female more sedentary and cryptic in plumage and behavior. **Conservation:** Least Concern.

BLACK-BELLIED BUSTARD *Lissotis melanogaster*

Setswana: mo.kgwêba

M: 65 cm (25 ½ in), F: 58 cm (22 ¾ in). **Identification:** Medium-size bustard with long legs and neck. Both sexes have spotted back. Male has black line down throat and neck terminating at black belly. Female is browner and has buffy throat and white belly; long slender neck distinguishes it from White-bellied and other bustards. **Call:** Explosive *woop*, given by displaying male as it progressively extends its neck and head skyward, followed by a *wick* as the head is quickly retracted. **Status:** Resident; no breeding records from Botswana. **Abundance:** Uncommon in Gumare (on the western edge of the Okavango Delta), Savute Marsh when dry, and the Linyanti area; scarce elsewhere in the north. **Habitat:** Found in dense tall grasslands and open woodlands with long grass. Attracted to edges of wetlands. **Habits:** Solitary. **Conservation:** Least Concern.

WHITE-BELLIED BUSTARD
E. s. barrowii

male

male

female

male crest display

male

male

RED-CRESTED KORHAAN

female

male

male

NORTHERN BLACK KORHAAN
A. a. damarensis

female

male

male

BLACK-BELLIED BUSTARD

male

male calling

female

123

CRANES Gruidae

Tall, elegant grassland and wetland birds that have long tertial wing feathers that project over the tail. Cranes feed and nest on the ground, and when they fly, they do so with their long necks extended (compare Ardeidae, p. 58, and Ciconiidae, p. 50). They are monogamous and pair for life and have dancing courtship displays and bugling unison calls. Three species occur in Botswana: the closely related Blue and Wattled Cranes, both listed as globally Vulnerable, and the Grey Crowned Crane, which is Endangered. Blue and Wattled Cranes have the same Setswana name, *mo.gôlôri (mo.gôlôdi)*.

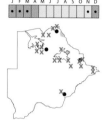

GREY CROWNED CRANE *Balearica regulorum*

Setswana: le.owang

105 cm (41 ¾ in). **Identification:** Unmistakable tall waterbird with "decorative" gold crest (crown) and red throat wattle. Pale gray body and neck contrast with the darker back. Adult has a bare white cheek patch; this is covered with creamy feathers in immature, which has a shorter crown. In flight, white upper and underwing coverts contrast with dark flight feathers. **Call:** Bisyllabic trumpet: *may hem, may hem.* **Status:** Resident, breeding. **Abundance:** Scarce. Most sightings, including chicks, are from Nata Sanctuary; irregular sightings from the Okavango Delta, Makgadikgadi Pans, Chobe River, and bodies of water in Tuli Block. **Habitat:** Occurs in freshwater wetlands and associated grasslands. **Habits:** Seen in pairs and small flocks of up to 17 birds. Roosts in wetlands. Occasionally occurs with Wattled Crane. **Conservation:** Endangered.

BLUE CRANE *Grus paradisea*

Setswana: mo.gôlôri, mo.gôlôdi

110 cm (43 ¼ in). **Identification:** Tall, stately, blue-gray bird with large, bulbous head. Long black tertial feathers project over tail. **Call:** Harsh but musical trumpeting. **Status:** Visitor; may be locally extinct as a breeding bird (although breeding recorded as recently as 2000). **Abundance:** Rare. This species, a southern African endemic, is now a visitor in Botswana. Up until 1997, it was recorded in the southeastern corner of the country at Kgoro Pan and Good Hope (one record near Lobatse in 2003), and in Makgadikgadi Pans, where it bred until about 2000. These birds are no longer seen, and it is presumed that they were relict pairs that have now died or moved elsewhere. The most recent sightings were in 2004, at Phokoje Pan in the Central Kalahari Game Reserve. **Habitat** Found in open grasslands. **Habits:** Occurs in pairs. Ground dwelling, it forages in grasslands with short, sparse growth. **Conservation:** Vulnerable.

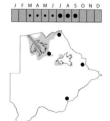

WATTLED CRANE *Grus carunculata*

Setswana: mo.gôlôdi, mo.gôlôri

150 cm (59 in). **Identification:** Tall, stately waterbird. Adult has gray cap, red facial skin, white neck, and pair of white, pendulous wattles at base of bill. Wings are slate gray with long black tertial feathers that project over the tail. First-year immature has white head (no gray cap) and smaller wattles. Sexes can be determined only when pair is calling in unison: at end of call, male briefly raises both wings above his back. **Call:** Guttural, drawn-out trumpeting. **Status:** Resident, breeding. Main egg-laying period (July to September) follows floods in the Okavango Delta. **Abundance:** Common in Jao-Boro river system in the Okavango Delta throughout the year and in localized areas in Makgadikgadi Pans during summer. The Okavango Delta currently supports the largest single population of this species in the world, numbering approximately 1,300 individuals. Scarce in Linyanti Swamps and at Lake Ngami. **Habitat** A floodplain specialist, it is found on seasonally inundated, large-scale, low-lying floodplains. **Habits:** Monogamous, pairs for life; seen in trios, which are adults with single offspring. Large flocks of several hundred form at front of annual Okavango floodwaters; however, the spectacular flocks of 800 to 1,000 birds documented in the late 1990s are no longer seen. Small flocks (4 to 20 birds) move to grassy outlying pans away from the Okavango during summer. **Conservation:** Vulnerable.

adult

GREY CROWNED
CRANE

adult

imm.

adult

BLUE
CRANE

adult

juv.

WATTLED
CRANE

adult

juv.

adult

adult head
detail

FLUFFTAILS Sarothruridae

A family of secretive, diminutive ground dwellers containing a single genus, *Sarothrura* (which means "broom tail" or "brush-shaped tail"). Although fluffy, the tail is not a useful field characteristic for identifying the genus or species. Flufftails are related to the rallids, and occupy similar rank habitat, but differ in being sexually dimorphic. The birds make hooting, ventriloquial calls. Two species occur in Botswana.

BUFF-SPOTTED FLUFFTAIL *Sarothrura elegans*

16 cm (6 ¼ in). **Identification:** Tiny, secretive, rail-like bird. Male has orange-brown head and upper chest, buff-spotted back, white spots on belly, and a barred rufous tail. Female is buff-spotted above, and has black and brown barring below and a barred buffy tail (and lacks rufous head and breast of male). **Call:** Haunting, ventriloquial *wooooooo-eeeeeeeee*. **Status:** Vagrant, nonbreeding. **Abundance:** Rare. This is an intra-African migrant that may occur in Botswana during its passage. Only two records: one from Maun in December 1991 and the most recent—a specimen from Sunday Pan in Central Kalahari Game Reserve— is from April 1995. **Habitat:** Prefers dense moist vegetation in or near woodlands. **Habits:** Presence usually indicated by call, which, however, may be confused with that of Common Buttonquail. **Conservation:** Least Concern.

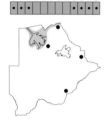

RED-CHESTED FLUFFTAIL *Sarothrura rufa*

16 cm (6 ¼ in). **Identification:** Tiny, secretive, rail-like bird. Male has black plumage with short white streaks, a white-spotted black tail, and a chestnut-red head, the color of which extends to lower breast, distinguishing it from Buff-spotted Flufftail. Female is brown overall, much darker than female Buff-spotted, and has a white-spotted black tail. **Call:** Low *woop* given together with rapid *gu-duk, gu-duk, gu-duk*; also strident *tuwi-tuwi-tuwi*, repeated several times. **Status:** Resident; no breeding records from Botswana. **Abundance:** Scarce. Although information on this species is limited, the Okavango is certainly a stronghold. It can be locally common in preferred habitat, for example at Xakanaxa in Moremi Game Reserve **Habitat:** Found in a variety of wetlands with exposed mud and areas of flooded *Miscanthus* grass. **Habits:** Sits very tight and does not flush easily; consequently seldom seen. **Conservation:** Least Concern.

RAILS, CRAKES, COOTS Rallidae

A diverse group of skulking waterbirds, including rails, crakes, swamphens, gallinules, moorhens, and coots. Twelve species occur in Botswana, including residents (some of which are nomadic) and Palearctic and intra-African migrants. Those that breed in Botswana nest over or near water and construct their nests from aquatic weeds. All are monogamous except the Striped Crake, which is polyandrous.

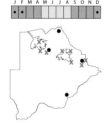

BAILLON'S CRAKE *Porzana pusilla*

17 cm (6 ¾ in). **Identification:** Tiny, secretive rallid. Plumage pattern similar to that of African Crake (p. 130), but Baillon's is much smaller and has limited barring on underbelly. **Call:** Harsh, repeated rattle. **Status:** Resident and possibly Palearctic migrant; no breeding records from Botswana. Timing of breeding probably conforms with that of populations in the rest of the region. **Abundance:** Scarce. Fewer than 20 records, from the Okavango Delta, Lake Ngami, Nata River delta, Nthane, Gweta, Francistown, and Shashe Dam. But undoubtedly underrecorded. **Habitat:** Found in dense vegetation of marshes, ephemeral pans, flooded grasslands, and edges of open water. **Habits:** Seen at widely scattered localities. It undertakes local movements driven by changes in habitat. **Conservation:** Least Concern.

**BUFF-SPOTTED
FLUFFTAIL**

male

female

**RED-CHESTED
FLUFFTAIL**

male

female

**BAILLON'S
CRAKE**

adult

juv.

BLACK CRAKE *Amaurornis flavirostra*

Setswana: kokwana yanoka

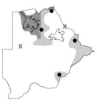

21 cm (8 ¼ in). **Identification:** Skulking rallid, more easily seen than other crakes. Adult has all-black plumage, a dark red iris, red eye-ring, and greenish-yellow bill. Legs and feet are bright red during breeding season, dull red in nonbreeding birds. Juvenile has brown iris and pink bill with a black bar; by immature stage the bill changes to dark green and the iris and skin around eye become red. Immature has dull brownish-black body plumage and brown wings. **Call:** Harsh, grating duet; often the first indication of its presence in its dense habitat. **Status:** Resident, breeding. Egg-laying may take place during any month **Abundance:** Abundant in the Okavango Delta; common elsewhere. The Okavango has the highest reporting rates for this species in southern Africa. **Habitat:** Found in dense, permanent, emergent aquatic vegetation, especially *Miscanthus* grasses. **Habits:** Occurs in pairs and small family parties (it is a cooperative breeder). Molts all its flight feathers simultaneously, and is flightless for up to three weeks during this time, which occurs over the breeding season when the birds are incubating. **Conservation:** Least Concern. **General:** The Setswana name means "little river chicken."

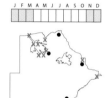

CORN CRAKE *Crex crex*

28 cm (11 in). **Identification:** Secretive rallid. Tawny overall but has distinctive chestnut upper and underwing coverts, visible when bird is perched and in flight. Male has blue-gray stripe over eye, and this color extends to sides of breast; less obvious on female. Immature light brown overall, similar to adult female. **Call:** Silent. **Status:** Palearctic migrant, nonbreeding. **Abundance:** Scarce; most records from Okavango Delta but also near Gaborone. **Habitat:** Prefers moist, rank grasslands, sometimes adjacent to water. **Habits:** When flushed, takes off with fast wingbeats, legs dangling. **Conservation:** Least Concern. Recently removed from the IUCN's Red List, where it had been classified as Vulnerable, because monitoring of populations in Russia showed that predicted declines had not taken place, and the species is stable.

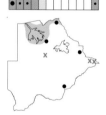

STRIPED CRAKE *Aenigmatolimnas marginalis*

20 cm (7 ¾ in). **Identification:** Secretive rallid. Male tawny overall. Female has blue-gray head and neck, the color extending to the belly. Both have white streaks on back and wings. When bird takes off it shows striking contrast between gray, striped plumage and the reddish (almost orange-red) undertail. Nonbreeding birds have pale green or yellow-orange eye-ring; this turns bright orange in breeding. Immature is brown above, without streaking, head and neck are rufous. Juvenile is covered in black down. **Call:** Female has loud ticking call, given at night. **Status:** Intra-African migrant, breeding. Present during late summer; breeding follows rains. **Abundance:** Generally scarce, but the occurrence of this species is influenced by the level of local rainfall, and the birds are more abundant during wetter years, sometimes present in relatively large numbers in the Okavango Delta, Chobe River floodplains and large pans on the Zimbabwe border; occasionally at pans in eastern Botswana. Breeding records are from near Maun (Ngamiland District) and near Kasane (Chobe District). **Habitat:** Prefers shallow, temporarily flooded pans in grasslands. **Habits:** Submerges underwater at approach of danger; flushes only when surprised at close quarters. The polyandrous female issues its call at night to attract males. **Conservation:** Least Concern.

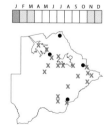

SPOTTED CRAKE *Porzana porzana*

23 cm (9 in). **Identification:** Secretive rallid. Adults are tawny overall; male is grayer, while female is browner and has a white throat. Both sexes have spotted neck, breast, and underparts (diagnostic among the crakes), a short, yellow bill with orange-red base, and buff undertail coverts. **Call:** Mostly silent. **Status:** Palearctic migrant, nonbreeding. **Abundance:** Scarce. The Okavango Delta and Central District are the main areas of the species's occurrence in southern Africa, although even there it is infrequently recorded. The most recent accepted records are from January 2003, at both the Boteti River near Maun and a pan near South Gate, Moremi Game Reserve, and from 1997, at the Shashe Dam. **Habitat:** Found in dense, flooded grasses and sedges at ephemeral wetlands and by rivers. **Habits:** Wanders widely in search of suitable habitat, the location of which varies according to rainfall. **Conservation:** Least Concern.

breeding
adult

BLACK
CRAKE

imm.

juv.

CORN
CRAKE

STRIPED
CRAKE

adult
male

adult
female

imm.

male

SPOTTED
CRAKE

female

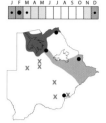

AFRICAN CRAKE *Crex egregia*

22 cm (8 ¾ in). **Identification:** Secretive rallid. Has streaked brown back, white throat, gray breast and barred black-and-white belly. Smaller and shorter-billed than African Rail, which occupies different habitats. Juvenile brown, duller than adult. **Call:** Series of *kruck kruck-kruck* notes. **Status:** Intra-African migrant, breeding. Egg-laying takes place following adequate summer rains. Occasional winter records. **Abundance:** Scarce to locally common in some years. The moist grasslands of the Okavango Delta and Lake Ngami are strongholds for this species in southern Africa; also common at times along edge of Boteti River as far south as Makgadikgadi Pans. **Habitat:** Found in moist or inundated grasslands adjacent to wetlands, or dry grasslands in open woodlands. **Habits:** The species is irruptive in response to rains. Flies with legs dangling when flushed. **Conservation:** Least Concern.

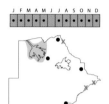

AFRICAN RAIL *Rallus caerulescens*

28 cm (11 in). **Identification:** Secretive rallid. Adult has plain brown upperparts, gray breast and barred black-and-white belly and flanks. The long red bill and red legs are diagnostic among rails. Juvenile is sooty overall but has a white throat and center of breast. **Call:** Descending trill, *creee, ke-ke-ke-ke-kee*. **Status:** Resident, breeding. The few breeding records available fall within the pattern for the rest of the region (July to May). **Abundance:** Scarce but probably overlooked; heard regularly and seen occasionally in wetlands in Gaborone Game Reserve adjacent to Broadhurst sewage ponds. **Habitat:** Prefers reedbeds and dense rank growth in freshwater wetlands. **Habits:** Frequently forages on mud, in shallow water and on floating vegetation. **Conservation:** Least Concern.

COMMON MOORHEN *Gallinula chloropus*

Setswana: kgokgonoka, mmamathêbê

34 cm (13 ½ in). **Identification:** Sooty-black rallid. Adult has red frontal shield, yellow-tipped red bill, and greenish-yellow legs with bright red thighs. Raises tail when walking, revealing white underside with black central stripe. Immature has dark gray body plumage, brown wings, and brown bill; its undertail coverts are white and it has white flank stripes. Lesser Moorhen is smaller and grayer, has a mostly yellow bill, and occupies different habitat. **Call:** Staccato *kerrruk* and variety of clucking notes. **Status:** Resident, breeding. The species is an opportunistic breeder; the late winter–spring peak in egg-laying is among birds nesting at Lake Ngami when the annual floodwaters arrive. In other areas, egg-laying peaks during February with the rains. **Abundance:** Common. **Habitat:** Frequents wide range of permanent natural and artificial wetlands with fringing vegetation. **Habits:** A successful, widespread species, it exploits even small permanent water holes in the Central Kalahari Game Reserve and the Ghanzi District. It was one of the first species to colonize Lake Ngami when it filled in 2004 after being dry for decades. **Conservation:** Least Concern. **General:** The Setswana name *kgokgonoka* means "river chicken."

LESSER MOORHEN *Gallinula angulata*

Setswana: kgokgonoka, mmamathêbê

23 cm (9 in). **Identification:** Small rallid. Adults have slate-gray body plumage, dark brown back and wings; male is darker than female and has brighter yellow-and-red bill. Juvenile has buffy body plumage, olive-brown back and wings, and a yellow bill with blackish ridge along upper mandible; immature becomes progressively grayer as it ages, until it differs from adult female only in this blackish ridge on yellow bill. **Call:** Clucking notes, repeated *duk, duk, duk*. **Status:** Intra-African migrant, breeding. A "rains migrant," it breeds prolifically in northern Botswana following substantial rains. Occasionally overwintering birds are seen, but there is no evidence for a regular overwintering population. **Abundance:** Uncommon; ranges from common in years of above-average rainfall to almost absent in other years. It may be locally abundant, as in pans in Chobe National Park in early 2000. Occurs in Botswana at the southwestern limit of its continental range. Northern Botswana is its main area of occurrence in southern Africa. **Habitat:** Found in ephemeral wetlands with ample cover provided by emergent vegetation. **Habits:** May be seen trampling down emergent grass stems to feed on the seed heads. **Conservation:** Least Concern.

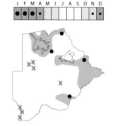

AFRICAN
CRAKE

AFRICAN
RAIL

imm.

adult

adult

COMMON
MOORHEN

imm.

adult
male

LESSER
MOORHEN

adult
female

juv.

ALLEN'S GALLINULE *Porphyrio alleni*

Setswana: mmamathêbê

26 cm (10 ¼ in). **Identification:** Small rallid. Adult has rich purple-blue body plumage, red bill, and long red legs. The frontal shield is powder blue in breeding male, lime green in breeding female, brownish in nonbreeding birds. Juvenile is black with pale pink spot at base of black bill; plumage becomes buffy and by immature stage it is brownish overall. **Call:** Repeated, clucking *duk, duk, duk*. **Status:** Intra-African migrant, breeding. Present mainly during summer; a few birds overwinter in permanent wetlands such as the Okavango Delta. **Abundance:** Uncommon although in some years can be locally common, as on the Boteti River in 2000. The Okavango Delta is the bird's stronghold in southern Africa. Rare in eastern and southeast Botswana. Its range in Botswana is at the southwestern limit of its continental range. **Habitat:** Found in wetlands with floating-leaved plants, including ephemeral pans and floodplains; prefers shorter and more grass-dominated vegetation than African Swamphen. **Habits:** Clambers about in reeds and tangled waterside vegetation searching for food, frequently flicking tail. Solitary or in small groups. **Conservation:** Least Concern.

AFRICAN SWAMPHEN *Porphyrio madagascariensis*

Setswana: mmamathêbê

43 cm (17 in). **Identification:** Large, secretive rallid. Adult has rich purple-blue plumage (*porphyrio* means purple) and a red frontal shield and bill. White "powder-puff" undertail coverts are revealed when tail is cocked. Immature is grayish-brown overall. **Call:** Loud, nasal cackles and shrieks. **Status:** Resident, breeding. **Abundance:** Uncommon. The species rapidly colonized Lake Ngami when *Typha* reedbeds became established; also recorded at Savute Marsh soon after flooding. Frequents sewage ponds in southeastern Botswana, notably Phakalane and Broadhurst. **Habitat:** Found in reedbeds and other dense aquatic vegetation fringing still or slow-flowing waters. **Habits:** Omnivorous; plant material forms major component of diet. Uses feeding platforms comprised of short lengths of sedge stems; it holds plant stems with its long, dexterous toes before cutting them with massive bill to extract the soft stem pulp. Disperses at night, when subject to predation by Verreaux's Eagle-Owl. **Conservation:** Least Concern.

RED-KNOBBED COOT *Fulica cristata*

Setswana: kgokgonoka, mmamathêbê

39 cm (15 ¼ in). **Identification:** Plump rallid. Adult has all-black plumage and a white frontal shield and bill. When breeding, two fleshy red knobs atop frontal shield become swollen. Immature is brown-gray, lacks red knobs. **Call:** *Cronk*, uttered several times in succession. **Status:** Resident, breeding. Egg-laying peaks from July to October at Lake Ngami but in March and April in the rest of the country (the first coinciding with flooding, the other with rains). **Abundance:** Abundant in the southeast; common elsewhere. Strangely, it is virtually absent from the Chobe system and the Okavango Delta, although common at the fringes of the delta at Lake Ngami and along the Thamalakane and Boteti Rivers. **Habitat:** Prefers open freshwater lakes, slow-flowing rivers, dams, and sewage ponds. **Habits:** Gregarious during nonbreeding season. Nomadic and opportunistic, as evidenced by its colonization of Lake Ngami since it flooded in 2004. **Conservation:** Least Concern.

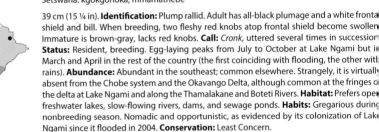

breeding
adult female

imm.

breeding
adult male

**ALLEN'S
GALLINULE**

adult

imm.

subadult

**AFRICAN
SWAMPHEN**

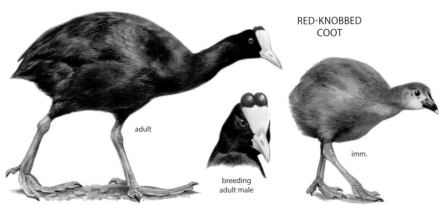

**RED-KNOBBED
COOT**

adult

breeding
adult male

imm.

THICK-KNEES Burhinidae

A family of cryptically colored waders that have long legs with thickened tibiotarsal joints (hence "thick-knee," although technically the tibiotarsal joint is the ankle) and no hind toe. The eyes are noticeably large, in line with the birds' nocturnal habits, and the bill is short and stout. The generic name *Burhinus* means large or great nose, referring to the bill, but this is not a striking feature of the two Botswana species.

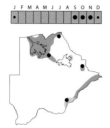

WATER THICK-KNEE *Burhinus vermiculatus*

Setswana: mo.ngwangwa wamolapô

40 cm (15 ¾ in). **Identification:** Large, plover-like wader. Back and wings are buffy with brown streaks and vermiculations. The dark gray panel above white bar on the wing is diagnostic, separating it from its congener. In flight, large white patches are conspicuous on black outer wings. **Call:** Loud, plaintive, piping *ti-ti-ti-ti-ti*, rising in tone and then falling, *tee … tee … tee … teee … teee*. **Status:** Resident, breeding. Egg-laying takes place over early summer. **Abundance:** Common in the Okavango Delta, Linyanti Swamps, and along the Chobe River; uncommon elsewhere. The Okavango Delta is its stronghold in southern Africa. **Habitat:** Favors sandbanks and shorelines of perennial rivers and lakes; may also be found on concrete bunds at sewage ponds. **Habits:** Gregarious; birds are crepuscular and nocturnal. **Conservation:** Least Concern.

SPOTTED THICK-KNEE *Burhinus capensis*

Setswana: mo.ngwangwa, mo.ngwangwa wamotlhaba, tswangtswang, kgoadira, kgwaadira

43 cm (17 in). **Identification:** Large, plover-like terrestrial wader found in dryland habitats. The plumage pattern of brownish-black, buff, and white spots marking upperparts and wings is diagnostic and separates it from the Water Thick-knee. It also lacks wing bar seen in its congener. In flight, small white patches are conspicuous on black outer wings. Juvenile has luminous green eye. Two subspecies occur in Botswana: *B. c. damarensis* is paler and grayer than the nominate. **Call:** Loud, yelping *whe-whe-whe-whe*. **Status:** Resident, breeding. **Abundance:** Common throughout its range. *B. c. damarensis* is found in southwestern Botswana, while *B. c. capensis* occurs throughout the remainder of the country. **Habitat:** Occurs in wide range of arid and semiarid habitats from grasslands to stony open savannas. **Habits:** Gregarious during nonbreeding season. Mainly nocturnal. When disturbed on roads at night, takes off vertically. During the day rests in shade under bushes. **Conservation:** Least Concern.

STILTS, AVOCETS Recurvirostridae

Large, slender, black-and-white waders with extremely long legs and slender bills. The bill is either straight and long-pointed (stilts) or uniquely upcurved (avocets). These birds wade in relatively deep water to feed on aquatic invertebrates visible on the surface; they may also do this while swimming, since they have partially webbed toes. They also feed tactilely by probing in sediments underwater. Lacking a hind toe, stilts and avocets never perch. They are monogamous ground nesters that produce precocial young. One stilt and one avocet occur in Botswana.

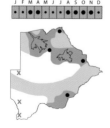

BLACK-WINGED STILT *Himantopus himantopus*

38 cm (15 in). **Identification:** White waterbird with black wings, exceptionally long, red legs, and a sharp-pointed black bill. Immature has soft gray head and hind neck, dark gray-brown back and wings, pale orange legs, and orange base to lower mandible. **Call:** Noisy *kik, kik, kik* or a single *kijk*. **Status:** Resident, breeding. Breeds throughout the year, with a peak in egg-laying between August and November at Lake Ngami, and between December and April in the rest of the country. **Abundance:** Abundant at Lake Ngami, Makgadikgadi Pans, and the Chobe River, which at times support globally significant numbers; common elsewhere. **Habitat:** Prefers open shallow waters of lakes, dams, rivers, sewage ponds and pans. **Habits:** Feeds in shallow water by picking invertebrates off the water surface. **Conservation:** Least Concern. **General:** Relative to body size, this species has the longest legs of any bird.

WATER
THICK-KNEE

SPOTTED
THICK-KNEE
B. c. capensis

adult

imm.

adult

BLACK-WINGED
STILT

PIED AVOCET *Recurvirostra avosetta*

44 cm (17 ¼ in). **Identification:** Long-legged, black-and-white wader with sharp, upturned bill. Immature is dark brown where adult is black. **Call:** Clear musical *kluit* is given by flock members in unison. **Status:** Resident, breeding. The few Botswana breeding records conform with the pattern in the remainder of the region. **Abundance:** Common to locally abundant in the Makgadikgadi Pans, which can hold globally significant numbers of nonbreeding birds, and uncommon in the southeast, mainly at sewage ponds and seasonal pans. Scarce in the Okavango Delta. **Habitat:** Prefers saline bodies of water. **Habits:** Scythe water surface with unique bill to catch invertebrates. **Conservation:** Least Concern.

LAPWINGS, PLOVERS Charadriidae

Large family that has fourteen representatives in Botswana: six large lapwings (genus *Vanellus*), seven small plovers (*Charadrius*), and a single plover of the genus *Pluvialis*, which is intermediate between lapwings and plovers. All have relatively short bills (shorter than head length) and necks, and relatively long legs; their feet generally lacking a hind toe (therefore they do not perch). Most forage visually, using run-stop-search behavior, and thus have relatively large eyes. The lapwings are sedentary wading waterbirds, except the Crowned, which is terrestrial. Sexes are alike, and all species have bony growths at the carpal joint, developed into prominent spurs in some species. The plovers are all aquatic waders with little or no sexual dimorphism; most are residents, but a few are Palearctic migrants.

LONG-TOED LAPWING *Vanellus crassirostris*

Setswana: thatswane wadikubu, thatswana yadikubu

31 cm (12 ¼ in). **Identification:** Large boldly marked lapwing with white crown, face, and throat contrasting with black nape and breast. In flight, the pure white wings (except for a few black outer primaries) are an obvious feature and give rise to alternative name White-winged Plover. Immature has blackish crown and black feathers with buffy margins on hind neck and breast. **Call:** High-pitched chittering, *kik-k-k-k-k*. **Status:** Resident, breeding. **Abundance:** Abundant in the Okavango Delta, where it occurs in globally important numbers. The delta is its stronghold in southern Africa. Rare away from the northern wetlands, but some records in the Makgadikgadi Pans. **Habitat:** Favors floating vegetation of freshwater wetlands such as swamps, lakes, and rivers. **Habits:** Territorial; mostly found in pairs along edge of water or on floating vegetation. **Conservation:** Least Concern. **General:** In Setswana the bird is known as "plover of the hippos."

SPUR-WINGED LAPWING *Vanellus spinosus*

26 cm (10 ¼ in). **Identification:** Large, boldly marked, black, brown, and white lapwing. Adult has black crown, white cheeks and sides of neck, and prominent carpal spurs (in both sexes). **Call:** Metallic *tik, tik, tik*, similar to call of Blacksmith Lapwing. **Status:** Vagrant, nonbreeding. **Abundance:** Rare. This species was first recorded in Botswana in 1989 on the Chobe River floodplain; this is in line with its gradual expansion southward through central African countries, but no confirmed record since 1989. **Habitat:** Prefers bare, open ground, usually near water. As a vagrant, it can be expected at any body of water. **Habits:** Solitary. **Conservation:** Least Concern.

BLACKSMITH LAPWING *Vanellus armatus*

Setswana: le.thulatshipi, le.itaatshipi, thatswane êphatshwa, thatswane yanoka, le.thatswana, mmalapaneng

30 cm (11 ¾ in). **Identification:** Large, boldly marked, black, gray, and white lapwing. Immature has gray wings mottled with brown and black and may be mistaken for Spur-winged Lapwing. **Call:** Metallic *klink* call. **Status:** Resident, breeding. Breeds throughout the year; egg-laying peaks from July to September in the northern wetlands (following flooding), and during March in the rest of the country (following rains). **Abundance:** Abundant in the Okavango wetland system, Linyanti Swamps, and along the Chobe, Boteti, Nata, and Limpopo Rivers, as well as at Lake Ngami and Lake Xau. **Habitat:** Prefers moist short grasslands and mudflats adjacent to lakes, dams, rivers, lagoons, and channels. **Habits:** Seen in pairs when breeding, in flocks thereafter. Noisy and aggressive, dive-bomb intruders, with its carpal spurs visible, when it is breeding. **Conservation:** Least Concern. **General:** English and Setswana names allude to the call's metallic quality.

adult

adult

imm.

PIED
AVOCET

LONG-TOED
LAPWING

SPUR-WINGED
LAPWING

adult

imm.

adult

BLACKSMITH
LAPWING

WHITE-CROWNED LAPWING *Vanellus albiceps*

30 cm (11 ¾ in). **Identification:** Large, boldly marked lapwing. Adult has white breast and black-and-white panel on wing, visible in standing bird. Top of head is white; the face is adorned with prominent yellow wattles. Spurs at the wing's carpal joint are often visible. **Call:** Strident *peep-peep-peep*. **Status:** Resident, breeding. **Abundance:** Scarce. The Chobe River has emerged as the species's stronghold in Botswana; uncommon along the Limpopo River. Absent from the Okavango Delta (not seen there since 2000). **Habitat:** Favors sandbanks along large tropical rivers. **Habits:** Pairs are territorial; nonbreeders form small flocks. A habitat specialist, it is found only where there are exposed sandbars along large rivers. It nests on these sandbanks. **Conservation:** Least Concern.

CROWNED LAPWING *Vanellus coronatus*

Setswana: le.rweerwee, le.rrane, le.erane, le.thêêtsana, le.thêêtswane, le.thatswane, thatswane yalebala

31 cm (12 ¼ in). **Identification:** Large terrestrial lapwing. Adult has brown upperparts and breast, white belly, and black-and-white crown ringing the head. Two subspecies occur in Botswana: *V. c. xerophilus* has a broad white crown ring; *V. c. coronatus* has more black in center of crown. Immature of both subspecies similar to adult, but colors duller, including red on bill and legs, and brown feathers on back and mantle have buffy margins, creating scalloped appearance. **Call:** Strident *weerwe*, repeated. **Status:** Resident, breeding. **Abundance:** Abundant. *V. c. xerophilus* is widespread throughout most of Botswana; *V. c. coronatus* is restricted to the Tuli Block, in the extreme east of the country. **Habitat:** Prefers dry, short, overgrazed grasslands, even alongside roads. Usually found away from water. **Habits:** Occurs in pairs or small groups. Forages on ground by making short runs, pausing, and pecking at insects and other invertebrates with tail raised. Light buoyant flight; flies in loose flocks, calling noisily. Chases small and large raptors vigorously and vociferously. **Conservation:** Least Concern. **General:** The commonly used Setswana name *le.rweerwee* is onomatopoeic and derived from the bird's alarm call. The alternative name *thatswane yalebala* means "plover of the open space (or clearing)."

AFRICAN WATTLED LAPWING *Vanellus senegallus*

35 cm (13 ¾ in). **Identification:** Largest African lapwing. Plumage is brown above (wings plain brown at rest); below it has streaked neck, brown breast, and blackish belly bar. Legs are yellow. Face has yellow wattle with red flange above on either side of black-tipped yellow bill; yellow eye-ring; prominent white forehead. Immature similar to adult but has heavily streaked brown head, including forehead, and shorter wattles. **Call:** Strident *kek-kek-kek-kek* alarm call. **Status:** Resident, breeding. The few Botswana breeding records conform with those from the remainder of the region. **Abundance:** Common in the Okavango wetland system, Linyanti Swamps, and along the Chobe River; scarce on the Limpopo River and in the southeast. **Habitat:** Favors wet, short grasslands adjacent to wetlands. **Habits:** Occurs in pairs along water's edge. It is territorial when breeding. **Conservation:** Least Concern.

GREY PLOVER *Pluvialis squatarola*

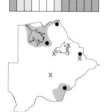

29 cm (11 ½ in). **Identification:** Large gray plover, with speckled gray-and-black wings and back. In flight, it is identifiable by its white rump, bold white wing bar, and black axillaries—commonly referred to as its "dirty armpits." **Call:** Plaintive *plur-plu-weee*. **Status:** Vagrant, nonbreeding. It is a Palearctic migrant that only passes through Botswana. **Abundance:** Scarce. **Habitat:** Primarily a coastal species, seen at bodies of water with open, exposed mud in Botswana while on its migration passage. **Habits:** A visual feeder, it stands and watches for prey on mud surface. **Conservation:** Least Concern.

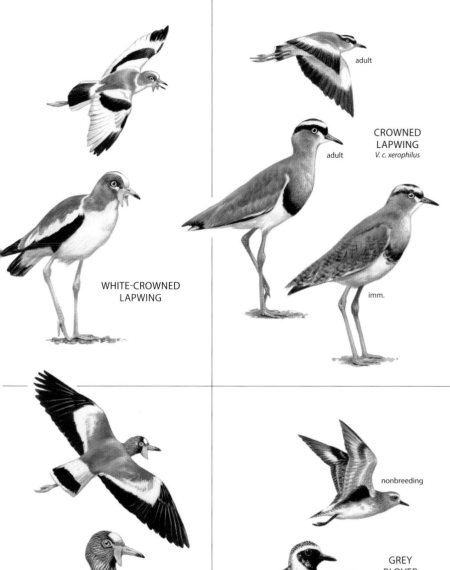

adult

CROWNED
LAPWING
V. c. xerophilus

adult

imm.

WHITE-CROWNED
LAPWING

nonbreeding

breeding

GREY
PLOVER

nonbreeding

AFRICAN WATTLED
LAPWING

139

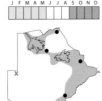

COMMON RINGED PLOVER *Charadrius hiaticula*

19 cm (7 ½ in). **Identification:** Small wader. Its complete white collar above broad blac breast band is diagnostic, even when breast band is incomplete in birds in nonbreedir plumage. **Call:** Whistling *too-lee, too-lee, too-lee*. **Status:** Palearctic migrant, nonbreedin **Abundance:** Uncommon. **Habitat:** Found on shores and mudflats adjacent to lakes ar dams. **Habits:** Usually solitary, but occasionally in small flocks of 20 or more. Displays ru stop-search foraging behavior. **Conservation:** Least Concern. **General:** The first Botswar record of the species was from the Peterhouse expedition in 1966, during which th scientific society from Zimbabwe's Peterhouse School collected bird specimens around th Makgadikgadi Pans.

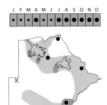

KITTLITZ'S PLOVER *Charadrius pecuarius*

Setswana: thatswane

13 cm (5 in). **Identification:** Small wader with black facial markings. Combination of whi neck collar and buffy breast, extending to belly, is diagnostic among small plovers. Can b confused with inland subspecies of White-fronted Plover (p. 142). Immature also has buf breast, although it is paler and less extensive; its head markings are less bold than those adult. **Call:** Trilling *terit, tritritritrit*. **Status:** Resident, breeding. Part of the population consis of intra-African migrants that migrate regularly within Africa. Some individuals also mak irregular nomadic movements in response to availability of bodies of water. **Abundanc** Abundant at Lake Ngami (where numbers exceed 0.5% of the regional population), Lak Xau, and Mopipi Dam. Common elsewhere. **Habitat:** Found in short grass and dry mudfla near water; also at sewage ponds. **Habits:** Often seen in small groups. Covers eggs in ne scrape when leaving nest (especially when danger threatens) by kicking small pebbles ov them. This makes the nest very difficult to find. **Conservation:** Least Concern.

THREE-BANDED PLOVER *Charadrius tricollaris*

Setswana: thatswane

18 cm (7 in). **Identification:** Small wader with distinctive breast pattern of two black ban separated by a white one. Has red eye-ring and red bill tipped with black. **Call:** Rattlir *wick, wick, wick, wick, wickwickwickwick*. **Status:** Resident, breeding. **Abundance:** Commc throughout its range in Botswana. **Habitat:** Found in shallows and on mudflats adjacent any body of freshwater with an open shoreline; often on concrete bunds at sewage pond **Habits:** Forages visually, picking invertebrates from mud surface with its short bill. Vibrate foot in shallow water to disturb prey. **Conservation:** Least Concern.

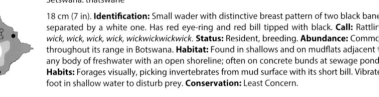

GREATER SAND PLOVER *Charadrius leschenaultii*

24 cm (9 ½ in). **Identification:** Medium-size wader. Appears in rather nondescri nonbreeding plumage when in southern Africa. Note large bill and gray-brown patch on sides of breast; these do not join to form a breast band (compare Caspian Plover). Als distinguished from Caspian Plover by broad, dark eye patch. **Call:** Soft ringing *tree-ree-re* **Status:** Vagrant, nonbreeding. It is a Palearctic migrant to coastal areas, seldom four inland. **Abundance:** Rare; one record from Nata Delta in August 2005. **Habitat:** As a vagrar it can be expected at any body of water. **Habits:** Solitary; feeds on mudflats. **Conservatio** Least Concern.

CASPIAN PLOVER *Charadrius asiaticus*

19 cm (7 ½ in). **Identification:** Medium-size dryland wader. It has a faint, gray-brow undivided breast band when in Botswana (in nonbreeding plumage), at which time th sexes are indistinguishable. Bold, pale supercilium to rear of eye and longer legs differentia it from Greater Sand Plover. Males may be seen in partial or full breeding plumage aft molting in summer before they migrate northward. **Call:** Sharp *tyup*. **Status:** Palearct migrant, nonbreeding. **Abundance:** Common in northern Central Kalahari Game Reserv Nxai Pan National Park, Makgadikgadi Pans, and Mopipi Dam. Short grasslands adjace to Lake Ngami also support significant numbers. **Habitat:** Found in short grasslands c fossil riverbeds and pans. **Habits:** Gregarious; flocks of more than 1,000 individuals hav been recorded at Mopipi Dam and Lake Ngami. Forages with typical plover run-stop-searc technique. **Conservation:** Least Concern.

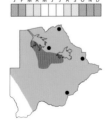

breeding
adult

nonbreeding
adult

imm.

adult

COMMON RINGED
PLOVER

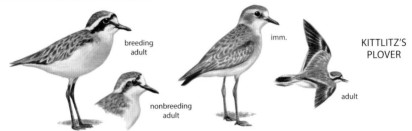

breeding
adult

nonbreeding
adult

imm.

adult

KITTLITZ'S
PLOVER

adult

imm.

adult

THREE-BANDED
PLOVER

nonbreeding

breeding

nonbreeding

GREATER SAND
PLOVER

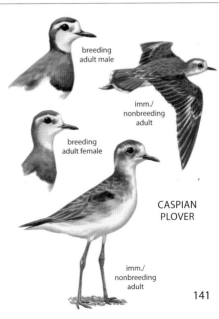

breeding
adult male

imm./
nonbreeding
adult

breeding
adult female

CASPIAN
PLOVER

imm./
nonbreeding
adult

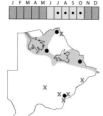

WHITE-FRONTED PLOVER *Charadrius marginatus*

18 cm (7 in). **Identification:** Small wader. Botswana hosts the inland subspecies C. *m mechowi*, described here; it is much buffer below than the coastal subspecies C. *m marginatus*, which is occasionally recorded. Adult has white lores, broad black forehea and thin black eye stripe. White collar on hind neck, but this is not always clearly visibl Wings do not project beyond tail in standing bird. The dorsal color is much paler than th of all stages of Kittlitz's Plover (p. 140), which has bolder facial markings and a broad blac eye stripe. Can be confused with immature and nonbreeding Chestnut-banded Plove which has pale chestnut collar on hind neck and wings that project beyond short tail. **Cal** Soft *chirit*. **Status:** Resident, breeding. The few Botswana egg-laying records conform wit those from other inland waters. **Abundance:** Scarce. The best place to see this species i Botswana is along the lower Shashe River and at Shashe Dam. **Habitat:** Found in large rive with sandbanks; also seen in salt pans and dams. **Habits:** Partially covers eggs with san when disturbed at nest. **Conservation:** Least Concern.

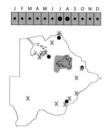

CHESTNUT-BANDED PLOVER *Charadrius pallidus*

15 cm (6 in). **Identification:** Small wader. Easy to identify when in breeding plumag by conspicuous chestnut breast band. Crown, hind neck, and mantle gray-brown all plumages. Nonbreeding and immature have a faint chestnut breast band and lac a pale collar on hind neck, which distinguishes them from White-fronted Plover. **Cal** High-pitched, squeaky *chee-reeoo, chee-reeoo*. **Status:** Resident, breeding. **Abundanc** Common in the Makgadikgadi Pans, especially Sua and Rysana Pans, which suppo globally important numbers, exceeding 1% of the world population of 18,000 birds. Scarc elsewhere. Botswana is home to the nominate subspecies, *C. p. pallidus*, which is endem to southern Africa. **Habitat:** Found in saline pans and alkaline lakes. **Habits:** Widely space individuals forage along saline mudflats, using run-stop-search technique. **Conservatio** Near Threatened.

PAINTED SNIPES Rostratulidae

A distinctive family related to jacanas (p. 144) but only distantly to true snipes (p. 146). Mating is polyandrous, and species exhibit reverse sexual dimorphism in plumage pattern and size. One species, of genus *Rostratula*, occurs in Botswana. The generic name means "having a small bill," but this is relative to the true snipes. Nevertheless, the bill is a key feature; it has a slightly down-turned bulbous tip and, unlike that of true snipes, is not pitted.

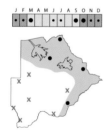

GREATER PAINTED-SNIPE *Rostratula benghalensis*

M: 23 cm (9 in) , F: 26 cm (10 ¼ in). **Identification:** Cryptically marked wader. Female, mor brightly colored than male, has dark chestnut neck and breast and reddish-brown bill. Female wing coverts are dull metallic green with fine black lines; male's are buffy with regular golde blotches. Both sexes have relatively short (compared to true snipes) down-turned bill wit bulbous tip. Immature resembles male. In flight, legs trail well beyond tail, and lateral whit rump patches are visible from below. **Call:** Female more vocal, calling *wukoo-ooo, wukoo ooo, bow, bow, bow* to attract males, mostly at night. **Status:** Resident, breeding. Egg-layin peaks in March for those birds using ephemeral pans; the September–October peak is from birds breeding opportunistically at Lake Ngami. The species is highly nomadic; part of th population may be intra-African migrants. **Abundance:** Common during summer but ofte overlooked in winter unless flushed. The Okavango Delta may support regionally importan numbers of this species. **Habitat:** Found in wetlands (especially well-vegetated rivers an streams, and ephemeral pans) with exposed mud adjacent to cover. **Habits:** Solitary or i small, loose flocks. Moves widely following rains to locate suitable habitat. Walks with bobbin hindquarters. Probes for aquatic invertebrates in shallow water, sometimes submerging hea as it does so. This is a polyandrous species—the female has more than one mate, and males ar responsible for incubation and raising the chicks. **Conservation:** Least Concern.

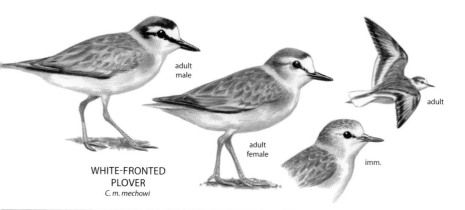

adult
male

adult
female

adult

imm.

**WHITE-FRONTED
PLOVER**
C. m. mechowi

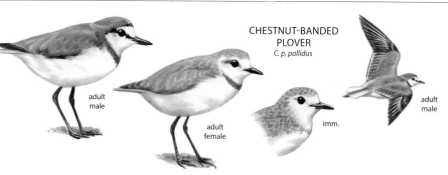

**CHESTNUT-BANDED
PLOVER**
C. p. pallidus

adult
male

adult
female

imm.

adult
male

male

male

female

female

**GREATER
PAINTED-SNIPE**

JACANAS Jacanidae

A family of waterbirds with long toes for walking on floating vegetation. The two species that occur in Botswana display contrasting mating systems. The Lesser Jacana is monogamous, and the sexes are similar. The African Jacana is polyandrous and exhibits reverse sexual dimorphism. Both species build floating nests of waterweed (*Ceratophyllum* and *Lagarosiphon* spp.) and lay highly glossed and patterned eggs that are narrowly pointed at one end and nearly flat at the other. Young are precocial; adult carries chicks under wing when danger threatens.

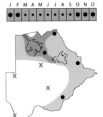

AFRICAN JACANA *Actophilornis africanus*

Setswana: mo.gatsa-kwêna, mo.gatsê-kwêna, kgaitsadia-kwêna, kgaitsadiê-kwêna

M: 23 cm (9 in), F: 32 cm (12 ½ in). **Identification:** Waterbird with long legs and toes. Adult of both sexes has chestnut body plumage, golden upper breast, white neck, and pale blue frontal shield (absent in juvenile). **Call:** Noisy, ringing *yowk, yowk, yowk*, as well as various quieter *krrrrk* calls. **Status:** Resident, breeding. **Abundance:** Abundant in the Okavango wetland system, Linyanti Swamps, along the Chobe River, and at Lake Ngami. The Okavango Delta supports the species's largest population concentration in southern Africa. **Habitat:** Prefers still or slow-flowing water with floating vegetation, especially Blue Water Lily (*Nymphaea nouchali*). **Habits:** This is a polyandrous species and displays reverse sexual dimorphism (the female is noticeably larger than the male). Each female has several mates in succession, which undertake all incubation and chick-raising duties. In response to danger, chicks dive underwater or are carried away under the male's wing (see illustration). This species molts all primaries simultaneously and is temporarily flightless. **Conservation:** Least Concern. **General:** The species names in Setswana mean, variably, "spouse of the crocodile" or "in-law of the crocodile."

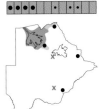

LESSER JACANA *Microparra capensis*

M: 15 cm (6 in), F: 16 cm (6 ¼ in). **Identification:** Small waterbird with long legs and toes. Adult is half the size of adult African Jacana, but resembles chick of that species. However, adult Lesser Jacana has chestnut crown and eye stripe, and can be distinguished by wing pattern in flight: it has pale upperwing coverts, black flight feathers with white trailing edges, and an otherwise black underwing. **Call:** Soft, hooting *poop, poop, poop, poop.* **Status:** Resident, breeding. Egg-laying takes place mainly during summer, but birds also lay opportunistically in other months when suitable conditions prevail in the Okavango Delta. **Abundance:** Abundant in the Okavango Delta, which supports globally important numbers of the species and is its southern African stronghold; scarce on the Chobe River. **Habitat:** Favors still or slow-flowing water of lagoons, floodplains, and ephemeral pans with floating vegetation such as Broad-leaved Pondweed (*Potamogeton thunbergii*). **Habits:** May be solitary or in pairs, occasionally in loose aggregations (279 counted on three small, drying lagoons in the Okavango in January 2003). Usually raises wings vertically on alighting, showing black undersides. Monogamous, and both sexes share incubation and chick raising. In response to danger, chicks dive underwater or are carried away under the parent's wing. Has unusual molt pattern, replacing flight feathers sequentially, starting with the outermost primary. **Conservation:** Least Concern.

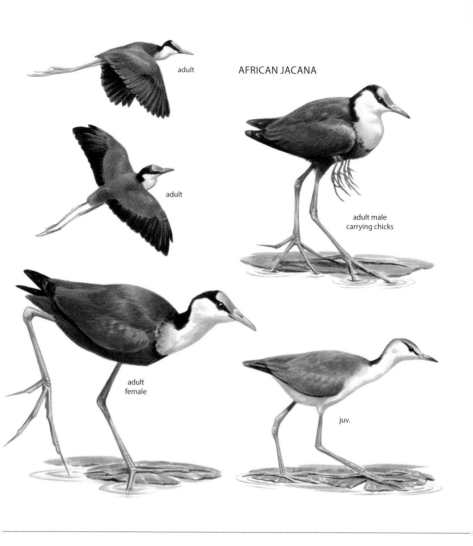

adult

AFRICAN JACANA

adult

adult male
carrying chicks

adult
female

juv.

LESSER JACANA

adult

juv.

adult

SANDPIPERS, SNIPES, PHALAROPES Scolopacidae

Large family of wading birds in which the bill is equal to or longer than head length. All members of the family share a foraging strategy: They probe in mud and detect prey by touch and they are continually moving when feeding. Scolopacids have smaller eyes than lapwings and plovers (p. 136), since they are not visual feeders. The family is represented by 26 species in Botswana. Most are migrants and occur in drab nonbreeding plumage, and resident species are also generally grayish brown. The two snipes (this page) are cryptically colored waders with exceptionally long bills. The two phalaropes (this page) are small polyandrous waders that have lobed toes for swimming. Page 148 shows four large, long-billed species. The eight *Tringa* species (pp. 150-152) are medium-size waders with long, almost straight bills. Page 154 features four unrelated, distinctive waders; all are easily identifiable by beaks, silhouettes, and behavior. The six gray *Calidris* waterbirds (pp. 156-158) are small to medium-size waders with slightly decurved bills.

GREAT SNIPE *Gallinago media*

28 cm (11 in). **Identification:** Long-billed wader. Cryptic coloration includes bold blac chevrons on breast, flanks, and vent. Underwings relatively dark in flight. Bill slightly shorte than that of African Snipe. **Call:** Mostly silent. **Status:** Vagrant, nonbreeding. This snipe a Palearctic migrant, occasionally seen during winter months. **Abundance:** Rare. **Habitat** Occurs in a variety of wetlands. **Habits:** Birds take off in straight flight when flushed, unlik African Snipe. **Conservation:** Near Threatened.

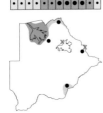

AFRICAN SNIPE *Gallinago nigripennis*

28 cm (11 in). **Identification:** Long-billed wader. Wings cryptically marked with dark brow and black; belly mainly white. Two subspecies are found in Botswana: *G. n. angolensis* ha a longer bill than *G. n. nigripennis*. **Call:** Babbler-like *chur, chur, chur*, reputedly made b female. Male produces whirring, drumming sound during aerial display, more frequentl heard during winter months. **Status:** Resident, breeding. May breed during any mont when conditions are favorable, but main egg-laying peak is during late winter. **Abundanc** Common during winter months in the Okavango Delta and Linyanti Swamps, less s along the Chobe River. The Okavango is the bird's stronghold in southern Africa. The tw subspecies are allopatric: *G. n. angolensis* occurs in the north; *G. n. nigripennis* occurs in th south and east. **Habitat:** Found in temporary and permanent bodies of water with sho emergent vegetation and exposed mud. **Habits:** Has zigzagging takeoff flight, whic distinguishes it from the rare Great Snipe. Male has a spectacular breeding display durin which it makes aerial dives and produces a drumming sound, made as air is forced throug the stiff, fanned tail feathers. **Conservation:** Least Concern.

RED PHALAROPE *Phalaropus fulicarius*

M: 20 cm (7 ¾ in), F: 22 cm (8 ¾ in). **Identification:** Small to medium-size wader, slightly large than Red-necked Phalarope. Has short, thick bill, dark gray eye patch, and plain gray bac differing in all these respects from Red-necked. Occurs in Botswana in gray nonbreedin plumage; it only fits its name in its reddish breeding plumage (see illustration, but note th plumage has molted by the time the birds arrive here). **Call:** Mostly silent. **Status:** Vagran nonbreeding. A visitor from the Palearctic, normally a coastal species, rarely seen inlan **Abundance:** Rare; only four records to date. **Habitat:** As a vagrant, it could occur at an body of water. **Habits:** Solitary birds seen, sometimes swimming in deeper water than Rec necked. Phalaropes are polyandrous, and females are larger and more colorful (in breedin plumage) than males. **Conservation:** Least Concern.

RED-NECKED PHALAROPE *Phalaropus lobatus*

M: 17 cm (6 ¾ in), F: 19 cm (7 ½ in). **Identification:** Small to medium-size wader. Has fin needle-like black bill, black eye patch, and scallop-edged gray feathers on back, whic separate it from Red Phalarope. The red neck it is named for (see illustration of adults i breeding plumage) is conspicuous by its absence in the nonbreeding bird that visi Botswana. **Call:** Mostly silent. **Status:** Vagrant, nonbreeding. A Palearctic breeder, it migrate to coastal areas and is seldom seen inland. **Abundance:** Rare. **Habitat:** As a vagrant, it coul occur at any body of water. **Habits:** Has unique habit of spinning in tight circles in wate when feeding. Phalaropes are polyandrous; hence females are larger and more brightl colored in breeding plumage. **Conservation:** Least Concern.

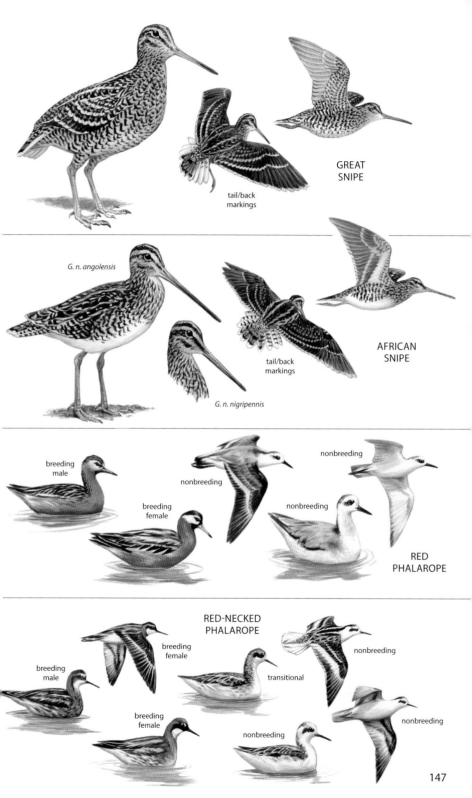

GREAT
SNIPE

tail/back
markings

G. n. angolensis

AFRICAN
SNIPE

tail/back
markings

G. n. nigripennis

breeding
male

nonbreeding

nonbreeding

breeding
female

nonbreeding

RED
PHALAROPE

RED-NECKED
PHALAROPE

breeding
female

nonbreeding

transitional

breeding
male

breeding
female

nonbreeding

nonbreeding

147

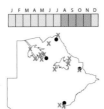

EURASIAN CURLEW *Numenius arquata*

55 cm (21 ¾ in). **Identification:** Largest scolopacid in the world. Very long decurved bill three times the length of its head, longer than that of Whimbrel, which is twice head length. Head marked with faint streaking. White, wedge-shaped rump visible in flight. **Call:** Repetitive *cur-loo, cur-loo*. **Status:** Vagrant, nonbreeding. A Palearctic migrant to southern Africa, it is a vagrant inland, present during summer months. A few birds overwinter at bodies of water such as Lake Xau. **Abundance:** Scarce. **Habitat:** Found in mudflats along edge of lakes and salt pans; occasionally seen at ephemeral pans. **Habits:** Solitary. Feeds by probing deeply in mud. **Conservation:** Near Threatened.

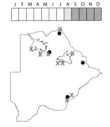

WHIMBREL *Numenius phaeopus*

43 cm (17 in). **Identification:** Very large wader with long, decurved bill twice the length of its head. Head marked with buffy supercilium and dark crown with pale central stripe. White rump and back visible in flight. **Call:** Trilling *tuituituitui*. **Status:** Vagrant, nonbreeding. A Palearctic migrant to the region, sighted during summer months. **Abundance:** Scarce. **Habitat:** Primarily a coastal species in southern Africa; uses lakes, dams, and salt pans when on migration passage in spring. **Habits:** Solitary. Feeds by probing in mud. **Conservation:** Least Concern.

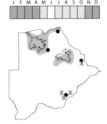

BLACK-TAILED GODWIT *Limosa limosa*

42 cm (16 ½ in). **Identification:** Large wader with long, straight bill, basal half of which is pink. Upperparts relatively plain gray in nonbreeding plumage. In flight, black tail, square white rump, and prominent white bar across upperwing distinguish it from Bar-tailed Godwit. **Call:** Mostly silent. **Status:** Vagrant, nonbreeding. It is a Palearctic migrant, occurring mainly during summer months. **Abundance:** Scarce (but recorded more regularly in recent years; more common than Bar-tailed Godwit). **Habitat:** Found in shallow lakes, dams, rivers, and channels with muddy substrate. **Habits:** Solitary or in small groups. Probes deeply on mudflats for aquatic invertebrates. **Conservation:** Near Threatened.

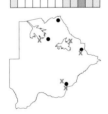

BAR-TAILED GODWIT *Limosa lapponica*

39 cm (15 ¼ in). **Identification:** Wader with long, slightly upcurved bill, basal half of which is pink. Smaller and shorter-legged than Black-tailed Godwit. Upperparts brown-gray and more mottled than Black-tailed in nonbreeding plumage. In flight, white tail with black bars further distinguishes it from Black-tailed Godwit, as do wedge-shaped white rump, which extends up the back, and lack of white wing bar. **Call:** Mostly silent. Bisyllabic *wick-wick* in flight. **Status:** Vagrant, nonbreeding. A Palearctic migrant to coastal areas of southern Africa, but a vagrant inland; occurs during summer months. **Abundance:** Rare. **Habitat:** Birds on migration passage use any large bodies of water. **Habits:** Solitary or in small flocks. Probes mud with long bill. **Conservation:** Least Concern.

EURASIAN CURLEW

WHIMBREL

BLACK-TAILED GODWIT

breeding adult

nonbreeding adult

imm.

breeding adult

nonbreeding adult

BAR-TAILED GODWIT

breeding adult

nonbreeding adult

imm.

nonbreeding adult

breeding adult

149

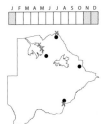

SPOTTED REDSHANK *Tringa erythropus*

30 cm (11 ¾ in). **Identification:** Large wader with long bill (one and a half times head length) with red base to lower mandible, and long red legs. In flight, white of rump extends as a thin line up the back. **Call:** Sharp *p-wee*, repeated. **Status:** Vagrant, nonbreeding. A Palearctic migrant, present during summer months. **Abundance:** Rare. **Habitat:** As a vagrant, it can turn up at any body of water. **Habits:** Feeds on mudflats, and wades and swims in relatively deep water, occasionally upending. **Conservation:** Least Concern.

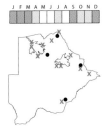

COMMON REDSHANK *Tringa totanus*

28 cm (11 in). **Identification:** Large wader with shorter bill than Spotted Redshank and red base to upper and lower mandible. Bright orange-red legs (compare Ruff, p. 154, which has dull orange legs). In flight, differs from Spotted Redshank by showing white trailing edge to wing and pointed, wedge-shaped white rump. **Call:** Mostly silent; *tee-wi-wi* in flight. **Status:** Vagrant, nonbreeding. A Palearctic migrant, present during summer months. **Abundance:** Scarce. **Habitat:** As a vagrant, can turn up at any large body of water, such as Lake Ngami or Lake Xau. **Habits:** Runs rapidly on mudflats when foraging for aquatic invertebrates.

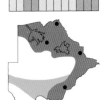

COMMON GREENSHANK *Tringa nebularia*

32 cm (12 ½ in). **Identification:** Large, robust wader with slightly upturned bill that is much longer than head. Legs and base of bill gray-green. Shows broad white V on back as it flies away. **Call:** Trisyllabic *tjuu-tjuu-tjuu*, invariably given as the bird flies off. **Status:** Palearctic migrant, nonbreeding. Birds are present mainly during summer, but many individuals overwinter at bodies of water such as Lake Xau. **Abundance:** Common. The Okavango Delta and Makgadikgadi Pans are the bird's strongholds in southern Africa. **Habitat:** Favors shallow water of ephemeral and perennial bodies of water. **Habits:** Solitary or in small flocks; occasionally large aggregations such as 350 at Nata Delta and 868 at Rysana Pan. Forages in shallow water. **Conservation:** Least Concern.

MARSH SANDPIPER *Tringa stagnatilis*

Setswana: mo.salakatane, mo.sêlêkatane

24 cm (9 ½ in). **Identification:** Large, slender wader with long, straight, needle-like bill and long, dull yellow legs. Paler and slimmer than Common Greenshank. In flight, the long legs extend well beyond tail. **Call:** Piping *tew-tew-tew*. **Status:** Palearctic migrant, nonbreeding. It is present mainly from late August to April; sightings peak between October and December. A few birds overwinter at bodies of water such as Lake Xau. **Abundance:** Common. **Habitat:** Found in shallow water of ephemeral and perennial bodies of water. **Habits:** Feeds in shallow water over mud; solitary or in loose flocks of up to 200 birds. **Conservation:** Least Concern.

SPOTTED
REDSHANK

nonbreeding

nonbreeding

COMMON
REDSHANK

nonbreeding

breeding

COMMON
GREENSHANK

nonbreeding

nonbreeding

nonbreeding

breeding

nonbreeding

MARSH
SANDPIPER

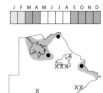

GREEN SANDPIPER *Tringa ochropus*

23 cm (9 in). **Identification:** Medium-size wader. Similar to Wood Sandpiper in size and appearance, but white supercilium indistinct behind the eye (which has prominent white eye-ring). Dark brown streaking on breast ends abruptly where it meets the white underparts, while in Wood Sandpiper the streaking fades into the white belly. Also, back darker and less spotted than that of Wood Sandpiper. In flight, shows blackish underwing and white rump. Longer-legged than Common Sandpiper (p. 154), which shows dark rump in flight. **Call:** Whistled *twee-twee-twee*. **Status:** Palearctic migrant, nonbreeding. **Abundance:** Scarce. **Habitat:** Found at edges of large rivers, lakes, sewage ponds, dams, and streams. **Habits:** Solitary. Does not bob hindquarters like Common Sandpiper. **Conservation:** Least Concern. **General:** In Europe, this bird nests in trees, in old nests of thrushes and other birds, which is unusual for a sandpiper, since most nest on the ground.

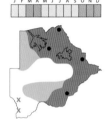

WOOD SANDPIPER *Tringa glareola*

Setswana: mo.salakatane, mo.sêlêkatane

20 cm (7 ¾ in). **Identification:** Medium-size wader with straight bill same length as head. Bill black with olive base; white supercilium prominent behind eye; upperparts dark with white spots; legs yellowish. Similar to Green Sandpiper, which is darker above with fewer white markings and has greener legs and a heavily streaked breast that ends abruptly at white belly, forming a clear breast band. Both species show white rump in flight, but underwing of Wood Sandpiper is pale gray. Longer-legged than Common Sandpiper (p. 154), which has white shoulder patch and lacks white rump in flight. **Call:** High-pitched *tee-tee-tee-tee* when flushed. **Status:** Palearctic migrant, nonbreeding. Present from August to April, it is seen in higher numbers during southward migration from October to December and again during northward passage in March and April. Some birds overwinter. **Abundance:** Abundant throughout its range in the north, east, and southeast; absent from the drier parts of the country. Lake Ngami (when mud is exposed) and the Makgadikgadi Pans are two of the southern African strongholds for this species. It is the most commonly seen sandpiper in Botswana. **Habitat:** Found at edges of ephemeral and perennial bodies of water, plentiful at sewage ponds; catholic in its habitat preferences. **Habits:** Solitary birds or small flocks forage in shallow water. Bobs hindquarters when agitated. **Conservation:** Least Concern.

GREATER YELLOWLEGS *Tringa melanoleuca*

31 cm (12 ¼ in). **Identification:** Large wader. Slightly smaller than the similar Common Greenshank (p. 150), but bill (which is much longer than head) may be straight or slightly upturned, legs are yellow, and bird in flight shows square white rump and gray-brown back. **Call:** Similar to that of Common Greenshank but softer. **Status:** Vagrant, nonbreeding. This species is a Nearctic migrant. **Abundance:** Rare. First and only accepted record is from the Majale River, Mashatu Game Reserve (2000). **Habitat:** As a vagrant, can turn up at any body of water. **Habits:** Solitary. Feeds in water. **Conservation:** Least Concern.

LESSER YELLOWLEGS *Tringa flavipes*

24 cm (9 ½ in). **Identification:** Medium-size wader with long yellow legs. Smaller than Greater Yellowlegs, it has noticeably shorter (only slightly longer than head) and straighter bill than that species. In flight, shows square white rump patch. More robust than Marsh Sandpiper (p. 150). Similar to Common Redshank (p. 150) and Wood Sandpiper (p. 152); differs from former mainly in leg color, and from latter by absence of white supercilium. **Call:** Mostly silent. **Status:** Vagrant, nonbreeding. This species is a migrant from the Nearctic. **Abundance:** Rare. Only one confirmed sighting to date, from Dead Tree Island, Moremi Game Reserve (2009). **Habitat:** As a vagrant, can turn up at any body of water. **Habits:** Solitary. Probes in shallow water when feeding. **Conservation:** Least Concern.

GREEN
SANDPIPER

adult

worn
plumage

adult

WOOD
SANDPIPER

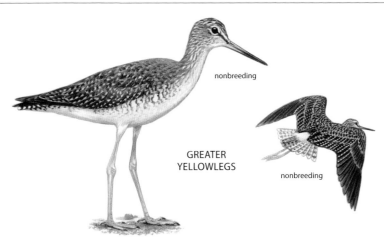

nonbreeding

GREATER
YELLOWLEGS

nonbreeding

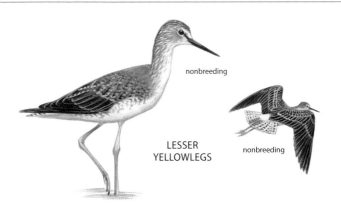

nonbreeding

LESSER
YELLOWLEGS

nonbreeding

153

COMMON SANDPIPER *Actitis hypoleucos*

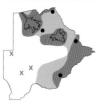

Setswana: mo.salakatane, mo.sêlêkatane

20 cm (7 ¾ in). **Identification:** Medium-size, short-legged wader with horizontal, crouched posture and relatively long tail. It has dark upperparts with a distinct white crescent in front of shoulder, formed by body feathers. In flight, shows dark rump. Straight bill equals head length. **Call:** High-pitched *seep-seep-seep*, usually on takeoff. **Status:** Palearctic migrant, nonbreeding. Present from August to April, its numbers peak during October when it is on southward passage, and again in March and April, during northward passage. Some birds overwinter. **Abundance:** Common throughout its range in the north, east, and southeast; absent from the drier parts of the country. **Habitat:** Found on sandbanks and mudflats along edges of lakes, rivers, dams, and sewage ponds. **Habits:** Forages along edge of water. Bobs hindquarters frequently and in exaggerated manner, especially after landing and after every short movement. It flies low over water, making a few flickering wingbeats and then gliding a short distance. **Conservation:** Least Concern.

TEREK SANDPIPER *Xenus cinereus*

23 cm (9 in). **Identification:** Medium-size wader with long (one and a half times head length), slightly upturned black bill with orange base, and short orange-yellow legs. **Call:** Mostly silent. **Status:** Vagrant, nonbreeding. A Palearctic migrant to coastal areas, it is a vagrant inland. **Abundance:** Rare. **Habitat:** Primarily a coastal species, in Botswana it is found on mudflats adjacent to lakes, dams, and large rivers. **Habits:** Active feeder; runs around with head and long bill well forward, chasing invertebrates, changing direction abruptly. Probes in mud with long bill. Occasionally bobs hindquarters. **Conservation:** Least Concern.

RUDDY TURNSTONE *Arenaria interpres*

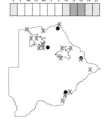

23 cm (9 in). **Identification:** Medium-size wader with distinctive overall shape due to short legs, dumpy body, and small head with short, thick, pointed bill. Dark chest band contrasts with white lower breast and belly. Often appears in Botswana in transitional plumage, showing variable amounts of rich chestnut. Legs orange. **Call:** Rapid *trik-trik-trik*. Also rattling *wickwickwickwick* call similar to that of Three-banded Plover (p. 160). **Status:** Palearctic migrant, nonbreeding. Passes through Botswana mainly during September and early October. **Abundance:** Scarce. **Habitat:** Primarily a coastal species, in Botswana it uses sandbanks on rivers, salt pans, lakes, and dams as stopovers. **Habits:** Solitary. Uses wedge-shaped bill to turn debris to reveal food items. Feeds frenetically prior to departure, and increases mass (with stored fat) by 50%. **Conservation:** Least Concern.

RUFF *Philomachus pugnax*

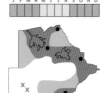

M: 28 cm (11 in), F: 22 cm (8 ¾ in). **Identification:** Medium-size wader with black, slightly decurved bill equal in length to head. It has pale scalloped edges to feathers on back and wings and orange-yellow legs. (Legs may be reddish, in which case may be mistaken for Common Redshank, p. 150, which, however, does not have scallop-edged feathers). It is usually predominantly buffy-brown, but there is an uncommon white morph (male), which has orange legs and an orange base to the bill. It also often has pale feathers surrounding base of bill. Sexes similar in nonbreeding plumage, but male (120–200 g) is significantly larger than female (80–140 g). Most of the birds seen in Botswana are females (known as reeves). **Call:** Mostly silent. **Status:** Palearctic migrant, nonbreeding. Present in summer; a few birds overwinter at bodies of water such as Lake Xau and Lake Ngami. **Abundance:** Abundant. **Habitat:** Frequents shallow water and mudflats along freshwater bodies; also short grasslands adjacent to water. **Habits:** Gregarious; flocks of 2,000 to over 5,000 occasionally seen in the Makgadikgadi Pans. Frequently raises mantle feathers when feeding. It is the longest-distance terrestrial migrant; it flies 16,000 km (one way) in little over a week. **Conservation:** Least Concern.

COMMON
SANDPIPER

TEREK
SANDPIPER

breeding

nonbreeding

transitional

RUDDY
TURNSTONE

nonbreeding

nonbreeding

nonbreeding

RUFF

male
transitional

nonbreeding
male

nonbreeding
female

155

RED KNOT *Calidris canutus*

24 cm (9 ½ in). **Identification:** Stocky, medium-size wader with short (equal to head length) straight bill. Usually nondescript in Botswana, where it occurs in nonbreeding plumage, though may show chestnut wash to underparts when in transitional plumage prior to departure in autumn. **Call:** Mostly silent; apparently has abrupt *knut* call, from which name is derived. **Status:** Vagrant, nonbreeding. A Palearctic migrant to coastal shorelines, very rare vagrant inland. **Abundance:** Rare. There have been no sightings since 1978. **Habitat:** Vagrants in Botswana are seen at large bodies of water such as lakes and dams. **Habits:** Solitary. **Conservation:** Least Concern.

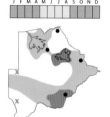

CURLEW SANDPIPER *Calidris ferruginea*

19 cm (7 ½ in). **Identification:** Small to medium-size wader with medium-length (slightly longer than head), decurved bill. Has prominent pale eye stripe. In flight, shows white rump. Birds seen in March–April may be in varying degrees of transitional plumage; some may have a ruddy coloration and be close to full breeding plumage. **Call:** High-pitched trilling. **Status:** Palearctic migrant, nonbreeding. Present from September to April, but highest numbers are seen in October and again April, corresponding with southward and northward movements. A few birds overwinter at bodies of water such as Lake Xau and Lake Ngami. **Abundance:** Common. **Habitat:** Found on mudflats along edges of lakes, dams and sewage ponds. **Habits:** Occurs in flocks, which are sometimes large; 750 seen at Bokaa Dam in October 2009. Actively moves across mud, continually probing for invertebrates as it walks. **Conservation:** Least Concern.

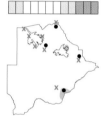

SANDERLING *Calidris alba*

21 cm (8 ¼ in). **Identification:** Palest sandpiper in Botswana, it has light gray upperparts and white underparts. In contrast to other scolopacids, its stout, pointed bill is slightly shorter than head length. Conspicuous black "shoulder" patch (on wing) visible in standing bird. **Call:** Mostly silent. **Status:** Palearctic migrant, nonbreeding. Essentially a coastal bird in southern Africa, recorded inland mainly when on southward passage, from October to early December. **Abundance:** Scarce. **Habitat:** Seen on sandbanks along large rivers and edges of lakes and dams in Botswana. **Habits:** Solitary or in small flocks. Runs along mudflats when foraging. **Conservation:** Least Concern.

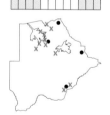

PECTORAL SANDPIPER *Calidris melanotos*

21 cm (8 ¼ in). **Identification:** Medium-size, brownish-gray sandpiper with slightly decurved black bill with orange base. The heavily streaked breast band, contrasting with white belly, dark brown back and wings (lacking wing bar shown by several other small scolopacids), and yellowish legs aid in identification. **Call:** Mostly silent; *kriek-kriek* when flushed. **Status:** Vagrant, nonbreeding. Palearctic migrant, present from October to April. **Abundance:** Rare. **Habitat:** As a vagrant, can turn up at any body of water. **Habits:** Usually solitary, but up to five have been seen together; mixes with other small waders. **Conservation:** Least Concern.

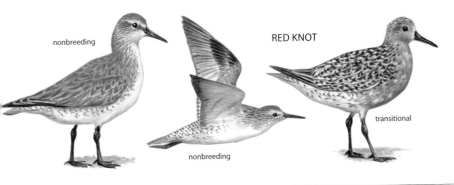

nonbreeding

RED KNOT

nonbreeding

transitional

nonbreeding

nonbreeding

transitional

CURLEW
SANDPIPER

transitional

nonbreeding

SANDERLING

nonbreeding

transitional

PECTORAL
SANDPIPER

nonbreeding

nonbreeding

TEMMINCK'S STINT *Calidris temminckii*

14 cm (5 ½ in). **Identification:** Very small wader with slightly decurved, shortish, blac bill. Plain grayish-brown back, breast, and head. Very similar to Little Stint, but has shorte yellow or grayish-green legs, and tail projects slightly beyond wingtips in standing bird. Ha darker breast than Little Stint; also has all-white outer tail feathers (visible as bird flies of in contrast to Little Stint's gray outer tail feathers. **Call:** A loud trill, very different from the of Little Stint. **Status:** Vagrant, nonbreeding. Palearctic species. **Abundance:** Rare. Only on Botswana record, from Savute Marsh (1986). **Habitat:** As a vagrant, it can turn up at a varie of wetlands. **Habits:** Forages along partly vegetated, muddy water's edge, with distinctiv creeping action. **Conservation:** Least Concern.

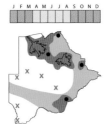

J F M A M J J A S O N D

LITTLE STINT *Calidris minuta*

13 cm (5 in). **Identification:** Very small, squat wader with short, straight, black bill. Legs ar usually black (occasionally greenish yellow) and wings project beyond tail in standing bir Also has whiter breast than Temminck's Stint. In flight, shows white wing bar and white side to rump; outer tail feathers gray, not white (compare Temminck's Stint). Plumage variable on arrival in Botswana and just before departure, some individuals may have rufous was to face, upperparts, and sides of breast. **Call:** Indistinct chittering, very different to call o Temminck's Stint. **Status:** Palearctic migrant, nonbreeding. Present in summer; a few bird overwinter at bodies of water such as Lake Xau. **Abundance:** Common to locally abundan **Habitat:** Found at muddy edges of lakes, dams, and lagoons. **Habits:** Forages in flock sometimes large flocks of up to 2,000, rapidly probing mud while walking. **Conservatio** Least Concern.

COURSERS, PRATINCOLES Glareolidae

A family of ground-dwelling birds divided into two distinct subfamilies, pratincoles and coursers. The pratincoles have long wings, short legs, and a hind toe; the coursers have shorter wings, long legs, and lack a hind toe (and therefore never perch). Eight species occur in Botswana; all nest on the ground and have precocial young (including the Palearctic-breeding Black-winged Pratincole). The three pratincoles are aerial insectivores, while the five coursers are terrestrial insectivores.

BURCHELL'S COURSER *Cursorius rufus*

Setswana: se.golagola

21 cm (8 ¼ in). **Identification:** Small terrestrial wader with rufous plumage. The combinatio of blue-gray hind crown and narrow horizontal band across upper belly is diagnostic. I flight, shows white trailing edge to secondaries. **Call:** Mostly silent. **Status:** Uncertair no breeding records from Botswana. **Abundance:** Rare. Endemic to southern Afric the species is nomadic, and Botswana is at the northern and eastern limit of its main Namibian and South African range. Easily overlooked, but has undoubtedly declined sinc 1964, when Smithers regarded c widespread. **Habitat:** Found in open, overgrazed c burned grasslands and bare salt pans. **Habits:** Diurnal; occurs in small flocks. Runs quickl, stops, and bobs its head and hindquarters; may move backward or sway from side to sid **Conservation:** Least Concern.

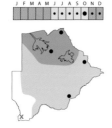

J F M A M J J A S O N D

TEMMINCK'S COURSER *Cursorius temminckii*

Setswana: se.golagola

20 cm (7 ¾ in). **Identification:** Small, rufous terrestrial wader. Combination of rufous hin crown and black belly is diagnostic. In flight, shows no white trailing edge to secondarie (compare Burchell's Courser). **Call:** High-pitched *keerr, keerr, keerr-keerr*. **Status:** Resider breeding. The species is nomadic, and the population also includes intra-African migrant Egg-laying takes place between June and December, which indicates that it is mainl the resident birds breeding, as the main influx of migrants is between January and Apr **Abundance:** Common. **Habitat:** Occurs in arable fields; open, sparsely vegetated pans; an bare clearings in open woodlands. Has a preference for burned areas, and occupies ther quickly. **Habits:** Solitary or in pairs or small groups. Diurnal. **Conservation:** Least Concern.

TEMMINCK'S STINT

nonbreeding

nonbreeding

LITTLE STINT

nonbreeding

nonbreeding

transitional

transitional

BURCHELL'S COURSER

TEMMINCK'S COURSER

159

BRONZE-WINGED COURSER *Rhinoptilus chalcopterus*

27 cm (10 ¾ in). **Identification:** Terrestrial wader with dark brown back and wings, and pale underparts with single dark breast band. It has a large, dark eye, accentuated by a red eye-ring, and a dark brown cheek patch. Legs are purplish red (compare Three-banded Courser). Unfortunately, the bird's most outstanding features—iridescent bronze and green markings on the flight feathers, for which it is named, and violet tips to the primaries—are not visible in the field. **Call:** Occasionally, at night, gives peculiar, somewhat yodeling call. **Status:** Resident (summer visitor only in some areas); no breeding records from Botswana. It probably breeds during the dry season as it does elsewhere in southern Africa. Population is supplemented by influx of migrants, mainly immature birds dispersing from breeding grounds, from November to April. **Abundance:** Scarce to Common **Habitat:** Favors open woodlands, such as those of Mopane (*Colophospermum mopane*) and other broad-leaved species, and Kalahari tree and bush savanna. **Habits:** Solitary or in pairs. Crepuscular; rests in shade during the day, feeds in open areas (including roads) at twilight. Often overlooked due to its crepuscular habits. **Conservation:** Least Concern **General:** The metallic-looking primary feather tips fluoresce strongly under ultraviolet light, which has led some to hypothesize that they may be visible at night and perhaps help migrating birds stay together.

DOUBLE-BANDED COURSER *Rhinoptilus africanus*

Setswana: se.golagola, se.golagolane, se.gôlagôla

24 cm (9 ½ in). **Identification:** Terrestrial wader, distinguished by two black breast bands separated by buffy area. The subspecies that occur in Botswana (*R. a. africanus* and *R. a. traylori*) look very similar to one another but are darker then *R. a. sharpei*, found in Namibia and paler than *R. a. granti*, found in South Africa. **Call:** High-pitched trilling rendered as *chikee-chikee-chikee-kee-kee-kee*. Also a thin, plaintive *pee-wee* in flight. **Status:** Resident breeding. Breeds opportunistically throughout the year (there is however a slight increase between August and March). **Abundance:** Common. *R. a. africanus*, is widespread throughout most of Botswana, except in the northeast, where it is replaced by *R. a. traylori* in most of Ngamiland District, in Chobe District, and the northern part of Central District **Habitat:** Found in dry pans, open short-grass plains, and calcareous areas. **Habits:** Solitary or in pairs, sometimes in small groups of up to four. Crepuscular. This species has evolved a unique and successful breeding strategy suited to its arid environment. It invariably lays a single, relatively large egg but has multiple broods. Each chick is raised individually to fledging before the next clutch (of one egg) is laid. It invests the minimum amount of effort per breeding attempt in case suitable conditions do not prevail for long. As would be expected, egg-laying can take place during any month when suitable conditions prevail **Conservation:** Least Concern.

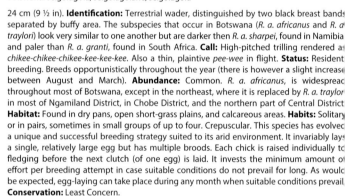

THREE-BANDED COURSER *Rhinoptilus cinctus*

26 cm (10 ¼ in). **Identification:** Terrestrial wader with three distinct bands on neck and chest. It is larger than Double-banded Courser and has separate black and rufous breast bands as well as a rufous-and-black neck band. Broad supercilium, rufous cheeks, and narrow moustachial stripe form a distinctive head pattern. Legs are yellow or pale gray **Call:** Strident, squeaky whistle. **Status:** Resident, breeding. The limited number of Botswana breeding records conforms with the egg-laying peak seen elsewhere in southern Africa **Abundance:** Scarce. Botswana is near the southern limit of the species's range. The old Hunters' Road in the eastern part of the country and Kasane are probably the best places to see this species in Botswana. **Habitat:** Found in woodlands with open areas of short grass, particularly stands of Mopane (*Colophospermum mopane*) and of acacia growing on alluvial soil adjacent to watercourses. **Habits:** Solitary or in pairs. Nocturnal, rests in shade during the day. Remains motionless when detected, relying on its camouflaging plumage Eggs become embedded in the soil during incubation and cannot be turned; chicks hatch through the upper exposed part of the egg. **Conservation:** Least Concern.

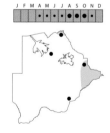

BRONZE-WINGED
COURSER

DOUBLE-BANDED
COURSER

THREE-BANDED
COURSER

161

COLLARED PRATINCOLE *Glareola pratincola*

Setswana: le.tlhapêlapula

25 cm (9 ¾ in). **Identification:** Short-legged, long-winged waterbird. It has dark brown crown, back, and wings, with pale brown extending onto breast; the belly is white. Breeding bird has buffy-yellow throat fringed with black and a red gape extending to base of bill. In flight ocher-red underwings and white trailing edge to wings (due to white-tipped secondaries) distinguish it from Black-winged Pratincole. Juvenile has brown, mottled throat and breast and scaly pattern to upperparts. **Call:** Melodious *kik-kik, kik-kik*, interspersed with occasional *cheeuu*. Similar to call of Black-winged Pratincole. **Status:** Resident, breeding. Population supplemented in summer by influx of intra-African migrants. **Abundance:** Abundant in the Okavango Delta, Lake Ngami, Linyanti Swamps, and Chobe River floodplains. The Okavango Delta, Lake Ngami, and the Chobe River floodplains are its strongholds in southern Africa. At Lake Ngami, where over 10,000 individuals have been recorded, it occurs in globally important numbers. **Habitat:** Found in freshwater wetlands in areas of moist, short grass. **Habits:** Large flocks hawk insects in the air. **Conservation:** Least Concern.

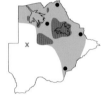

BLACK-WINGED PRATINCOLE *Glareola nordmanni*

Setswana: le.tlhapêlapula

25 cm (9 ¾ in). **Identification:** Short-legged, long-winged waterbird. Occurs in nonbreeding plumage in Botswana, in which dark upperparts and breast contrast with white belly. (It does not attain breeding bird's buffy-yellow throat narrowly edged with black while here.) In flight shows black underwings; lacks white trailing edge to wings shown by Collared Pratincole. Its tail is forked but shorter than that of Collared. **Call:** Melodious *kik-kik, kik-kik*, interspersed with occasional *cheeuu*. Similar to call of Collared Pratincole. **Status:** Palearctic migrant, nonbreeding. Most birds are seen between November and March; their numbers peak in January. Botswana is an important nonbreeding area for this species. **Abundance:** Abundant at Lake Ngami, where more than 10,000 individuals have been recorded, and at Lake Xau, where 17,700 were recently seen (2014). Common in Makgadikgadi Pans and Nxai Pan, and between Deception Valley and Orapa, including Mopipi Dam. Uncommon at Bokaa Dam (although regularly seen there) and at Kgoro Pan. Numbers appear to be declining. **Habitat:** Found in grasslands, fallow fields, sometimes near water. Prefers drier habitats than Collared Pratincole. **Habits:** Gregarious; hawks insects in the air and on the ground. Responds to abundance of insects after storms. **Conservation:** Near Threatened.

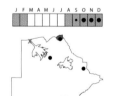

ROCK PRATINCOLE *Glareola nuchalis*

Setswana: le.tlhapêlapula

18 cm (7 in). **Identification:** Short-legged, long-winged waterbird. Plumage is gray-brown, except for white collar on hind neck. It has short red legs and red bill with black tip. These features, its smaller size, and its habitat preferences differentiate it from the other pratincoles. **Call:** Squeaky, high-pitched *keek-keek-keek*. **Status:** Intra-African migrant, breeding. The birds arrive along the Chobe River floodplains in August and wait for water levels at the Kasane Rapids to subside and expose the rocks on which they breed; egg laying peaks when water levels are lowest. **Abundance:** Rare, but locally common around the Kasane area (small numbers breed at the Kasane Rapids). Sometimes overshoots on migration; hence, there is a record from Jwaneng in Southern District. **Habitat:** Found along large tropical rivers, it has specific habitat requirements for breeding: exposed rocks (for nesting) in fast-flowing water. **Habits:** Aerial insectivore found in pairs or small groups. However, post-breeding flocks of up to 200 individuals may be seen along the Chobe River. **Conservation:** Least Concern.

breeding

nonbreeding

breeding

**COLLARED
PRATINCOLE**

nonbreeding

nonbreeding

breeding

**BLACK-WINGED
PRATINCOLE**

**ROCK
PRATINCOLE**

adult

adult

imm.

SKUAS, JAEGERS Stercorariidae

A family of gull-like marine birds. They are mainly brown and have a stout bill hooked at the tip, sharp, curved claws, and long middle tail feathers. They are piratical, chasing other seabirds and stealing the food that they disgorge. Only one vagrant has been recorded in Botswana.

LONG-TAILED JAEGER *Stercorarius longicaudus*

38 cm (15 in). **Identification:** Long-winged, gull-like seabird. Unmistakable, due to its dark, tern-like wings and hooked bill. The long, central tail streamers are reduced or missing during the nonbreeding season, when the bird is present in southern Africa. **Call:** Silent. **Status**: Vagrant, nonbreeding. A Holarctic breeder, it migrates to coastal areas of southern Africa during summer. **Abundance:** Rare. Recorded only once, along the Chobe River 3 km (2 mi) west of Kasane. **Conservation:** Least Concern.

GULLS, TERNS, SKIMMERS Laridae

Large family of predominantly marine species, but some species occur inland. Eight larids occur in Botswana: three gulls, four terns, and a skimmer. Two of the gulls are vagrants from the Palearctic, the third is a breeding resident. They have white, gray, and black plumage, webbed feet, and general-purpose bills. Terns have long, slender wings and webbed toes; they feed on aquatic animals by plunge diving or surface dipping. Of the terns, one is a vagrant from the Palearctic, one is a Palearctic migrant, and the other two are breeding residents. In Botswana, they all prefer large bodies of water such as lakes. The skimmer, a breeding resident, is tern-like in appearance, with its exceptionally long narrow wings, but has a unique bill with an elongated lower mandible.

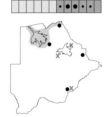

AFRICAN SKIMMER *Rynchops flavirostris*

39 cm (15 ¼ in). **Identification:** Large, black-and-white tern-like bird. Unique red bill has elongated lower mandible. Juvenile has brown upperparts, with black showing through as it matures; bill also changes to red, starting from base, as lower mandible becomes progressively longer. **Call:** Ringing, yelping *keek, keek, keek.* **Status:** Resident, breeding. During spring and summer, numbers are supplemented by an influx of intra-African migrants, which come to Botswana to breed. **Abundance:** Common between July and December, when breeding and tending to chicks; uncommon during rest of year. The Okavango Delta is the bird's stronghold in southern Africa; its main breeding sites are along the Okavango Panhandle (subject to disturbance by fishermen). It also breeds at Xigera Lagoon in Moremi Game Reserve, at sites on the Boro River (also in Moremi), and along the Chobe River. It apparently bred at Mopipi Dam and Lake Ngami in the past. During summer post-breeding, birds disperse throughout the Okavango Delta to Lake Ngami and the Botet River. Rare in southern Botswana. **Habitat:** Prefers open water of lakes, lagoons, and large slow-flowing rivers. Nests on exposed sandbanks when water levels are low. **Habits:** Flies above water, skimming the surface with the lower mandible to detect and capture small fish by touch. **Conservation:** Near Threatened.

imm.

LONG-TAILED
JAEGER

breeding
adult

nonbreeding
adult

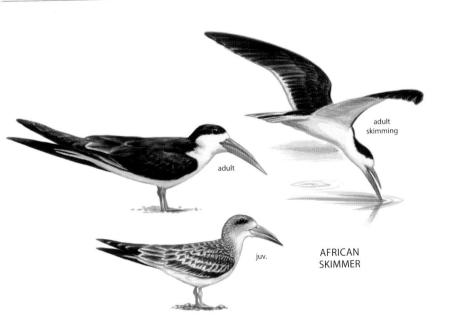

adult skimming

adult

juv.

AFRICAN
SKIMMER

BLACK-HEADED GULL   *Chroicocephalus ridibundus*

37 cm (14 ½ in). **Identification:** Medium-size gull. It has brown hood (when in breeding plumage), indistinct white eye-ring, and red bill tipped with black. In nonbreeding plumage it has dark smudge on ear coverts. Dark hood often not prominent in birds seen in Botswana, can be only slightly darker than gray hood of Grey-headed Gull In flight, generally paler in appearance than Grey-headed: Black-headed upperwing shows much more white or leading edge, with black confined to tips of primaries. **Call:** Mostly silent. **Status:** Vagrant (from the Palearctic), nonbreeding. **Abundance:** Rare. Most sightings are from Lake Ngami one is from the Chobe River. **Habitat:** Seen at large bodies of water, especially lakes. **Habits:** Usually seen with Grey-headed Gulls. **Conservation:** Least Concern.

J	F	M	A	M	J	J	A	S	O	N	D
•	•	•	•	•	•	•	•	•	•	•	•

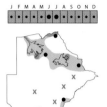

GREY-HEADED GULL   *Chroicocephalus cirrocephalus*

42 cm (16 ½ in). **Identification:** Medium-size gull. It has pale gray hood (when breeding), red bill and legs, and pale eye. In flight, upperwing shows broad area of black at tip and relatively small white panel at base of primaries; compare Black-headed Gull. Immature has white head with gray smudge over ear coverts. **Call:** Noisy, ringing *kraah*. **Status:** Resident breeding. At Lake Ngami, egg-laying peaks in midwinter. **Abundance:** Uncommon. Can be locally common at Lake Ngami, the Nata Delta and along the Chobe River. **Habitat:** An inland gull, it favors shallow open bodies of water. **Habits:** Gregarious and noisy. Circles and dive-bombs humans in vicinity of nests. Nests in small colonies on short, emergent vegetation in open water (such as Lake Ngami). **Conservation:** Least Concern.

LESSER BLACK-BACKED GULL   *Larus fuscus*

58 cm (22 ¾ in). **Identification:** Large gull. It has slate-black wings, yellow legs, relatively slender yellow bill, and pale eye. Only the nominate subspecies (*L. f. fuscus*) is found in Botswana; it has a blackish mantle. **Call:** Mostly silent; yelping, repeated *kow*. **Status:** Vagrant (from the Palearctic), nonbreeding. **Abundance:** Rare. **Habitat:** Seen at large rivers and lakes, salt pans. **Habits:** Solitary (in Botswana but not elsewhere). Forages in open water and scavenges along shores. **Conservation:** Least Concern.

166

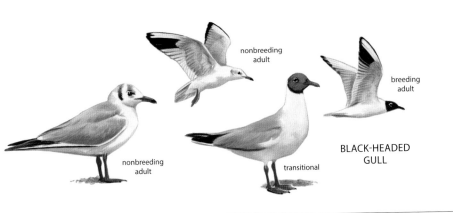

nonbreeding
adult

breeding
adult

nonbreeding
adult

transitional

**BLACK-HEADED
GULL**

breeding
adult

nonbreeding
adult

breeding
adult

**GREY-HEADED
GULL**

imm.

imm.

**LESSER
BLACK-BACKED GULL**
L. f. fuscus

nonbreeding
adult

nonbreeding
adult

imm.

167

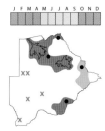

WHITE-WINGED TERN *Chlidonias leucopterus*

21 cm (8 ¼ in). **Identification:** Long-winged, gray lake tern. Smaller than Whiskered Tern. Appears in Botswana in nonbreeding plumage. In flight, white rump (at all ages) is diagnostic among Botswana's terns (it is shared only by Gull-billed Tern, a rare vagrant that is much paler). Dark patch behind each eye, giving appearance of "headphones." Before birds depart in autumn, some show traces of black breeding plumage, which can be quite extensive on head, body, and underwing coverts. **Call:** High-pitched, repeated *queek*. **Status:** Palearctic migrant, nonbreeding. Most sightings are in summer, but some birds overwinter. **Abundance:** Common. The Okavango Delta, Lake Ngami, Makgadikgadi Pans, and sewage ponds and dams in southeastern Botswana are important areas for this species when it is in southern Africa. **Habitat:** A lake tern, it is found in open still water with floating surface vegetation. **Habits:** Takes aquatic invertebrates by dipping into the water surface; also takes insects in aerial pursuit. **Conservation:** Least Concern.

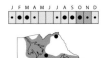

WHISKERED TERN *Chlidonias hybrida*

24 cm (9 ½ in). **Identification:** Larger of the two lake terns found in Botswana. It has black cap and dark gray underparts when breeding. Nonbreeding bird is similar to White-winged Tern (the other lake tern) but does not have black patch behind eye. Male has longer bill than female. Juvenile is distinguished from nonbreeding adult by mottled brown back. **Call:** Harsh, unmusical *kreek*. **Status:** Resident, breeding. Population is supplemented by local migratory population during summer months. Birds breed opportunistically at Lake Ngami when it floods (sometimes before they are in full breeding plumage); hence, breeding peaks from August to October. Elsewhere in the country, egg-laying peaks in summer (October –March). Nests are made on floating vegetation. **Abundance:** Abundant at Lake Ngami, where the species breeds prolifically and numbers reach globally important levels. Common in the Okavango Delta and Makgadikgadi Pans, which are also strongholds for the species in southern Africa. **Habitat:** Favors open water of lakes, lagoons, and slow-flowing rivers that have surface vegetation. **Habits:** Forages in loose groups over water, employing light, dipping flight to pick aquatic invertebrates off the water surface; also makes shallow plunges to catch small fish. Flocks rest on emergent aquatic vegetation when not feeding. **Conservation:** Least Concern.

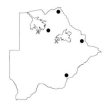

GULL-BILLED TERN *Gelochelidon nilotica*

37 cm (14 ½ in). **Identification:** Medium-size, pale tern. It can occur in breeding plumage in Botswana, at which time it has a black crown and relatively thick black bill. Nonbreeding bird has virtually white crown, but black through eye and thick black bill. White rump at all stages. When perched, it has upright posture and appears taller than Whiskered or White-winged Terns. **Call:** Mostly silent. **Status:** Vagrant (from the Palearctic), nonbreeding. **Abundance:** Rare. Recorded at Lake Ngami and Lake Xau. **Habitat:** Found at large inland lakes. **Habits:** Solitary. Doesn't normally plunge dive, but will pick insects off the water surface. **Conservation:** Least Concern.

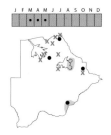

CASPIAN TERN *Hydroprogne caspia*

51 cm (20 in). **Identification:** Largest tern in Botswana. It has black crown and nape and large red bill. In flight, black wingtips are clearly visible at all ages. Juvenile similar to adult with dark cap, but has brown edges to wing coverts. **Call:** Harsh *kraaa*. **Status:** Resident breeding. **Abundance:** Scarce. There are fewer than 10 breeding sites in southern Africa; in Botswana it breeds at Lake Xau and Nata River delta. It is also seen at Lake Ngami and occasionally on the Chobe River and at dams in eastern and southeastern Botswana. **Habitat:** Found at saline and freshwater lakes and pans. **Habits:** Hovers before plunge diving into water, beak first, to catch small fish. Nests on the ground on small islands. **Conservation:** Least Concern.

breeding
adult

nonbreeding
adult

nonbreeding
adult

transitional

**WHITE-WINGED
TERN**

transitional

breeding
adult

nonbreeding
adult

breeding
adult

**WHISKERED
TERN**

juv.

nonbreeding
adult

nonbreeding
adult

nonbreeding
adult

nonbreeding
adult

**GULL-BILLED
TERN**

breeding
adult

nonbreeding
adult

breeding
adult

breeding
adult

breeding
adult

juv.

**CASPIAN
TERN**

SANDGROUSE Pteroclidae

Cryptically colored, dove-like ground dwellers that favor arid areas. This is one of only two families worldwide in which the diet is exclusively seeds from the time of the birds' hatching. Birds forage in pairs on the ground; they also nest on the ground. Fast, strong fliers with long, pointed wings, they flock to water at specific times daily. Males have specially adapted belly feathers that can soak up water to be carried to the chicks; during breeding season, males can be seen "belly wetting." Four species are found in Botswana, one of which is a biome-restricted species confined to the Kalahari-Highveld. The Setswana *le.gwaragwara* is a generic name for sandgrouse and is derived from the noise the birds make when they take off.

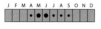

BURCHELL'S SANDGROUSE *Pterocles burchelli*

Setswana: le.gwaragwara

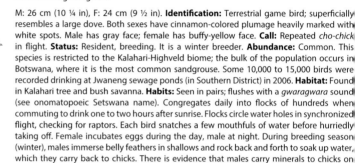

M: 26 cm (10 ¼ in), F: 24 cm (9 ½ in). **Identification:** Terrestrial game bird; superficially resembles a large dove. Both sexes have cinnamon-colored plumage heavily marked with white spots. Male has gray face; female has buffy-yellow face. **Call:** Repeated *cho-chick* in flight. **Status:** Resident, breeding. It is a winter breeder. **Abundance:** Common. This species is restricted to the Kalahari-Highveld biome; the bulk of the population occurs in Botswana, where it is the most common sandgrouse. Some 10,000 to 15,000 birds were recorded drinking at Jwaneng sewage ponds (in Southern District) in 2006. **Habitat:** Found in Kalahari tree and bush savanna. **Habits:** Seen in pairs; flushes with a *gwaragwara* sound (see onomatopoeic Setswana name). Congregates daily into flocks of hundreds when commuting to drink one to two hours after sunrise. Flocks circle water holes in synchronized flight, checking for raptors. Each bird snatches a few mouthfuls of water before hurriedly taking off. Female incubates eggs during the day, male at night. During breeding season (winter), males immerse belly feathers in shallows and rock back and forth to soak up water, which they carry back to chicks. There is evidence that males carry minerals to chicks on muddied breast feathers. **Conservation:** Least Concern. Classified as a game bird; may be hunted from October to March inclusive.

NAMAQUA SANDGROUSE *Pterocles namaqua*

Setswana: le.gwaragwara, le.gorwagorwana, le.gorogorwane

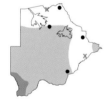

M: 28 cm (11 in), F: 24 cm (9 ½ in). **Identification:** Terrestrial game bird; superficially resembles a large dove. Male has plain head and breast, with a white-and-brown band at the breast's lower border. Female has streaking on breast and barring below it. Both sexes have long, pointed tail. **Call:** Musical, repeated *kelkiewyn*—also rendered as *look at YOU*—given mainly in flight. **Status:** Resident, breeding. Breeds year-round but mainly during winter. **Abundance:** Abundant in Kgalagadi Transfrontier Park; common elsewhere in its range. Breeds as far north as Tale Pan in Ngamiland. **Habitat:** Found on calcareous gravel plains with scattered low shrubs or grass tufts in arid scrub savannas. **Habits:** Congregates into large flocks to drink at water holes at or just after sunrise. Female incubates eggs during day, male at night. **Conservation:** Least Concern. Classified as a game bird; may be hunted from October to March inclusive.

YELLOW-THROATED SANDGROUSE *Pterocles gutturalis*

Setswana: le.gwaragwara, photi-mpha-bogôgô

30 cm (11 ¾ in). **Identification:** Large terrestrial game bird that superficially resembles a large dove. Both sexes have yellow throat, but male's is bordered below by black. **Call:** Harsh, creaking *kaw-kaw* in flight. **Status:** Resident, breeding. Part of the population comprises intra-African migrants, which move northward during winter to breed and depart during summer. **Abundance:** Scarce; occurs mainly in the northern part of the country, but recorded as far south as Ramotswa near Gaborone. Chobe District and Makgadikgadi Pans are its strongholds in Botswana and southern Africa. This species has declined over the last few decades and is not frequently seen. **Habitat:** Prefers short, open grasslands growing on black clay soils, usually near water. **Habits:** Usually seen in small groups, but when fresh water is available in the Makgadikgadi Pans during summer, there is an influx of migrants, and larger groups may be seen. It comes to drink between two and four hours after sunrise daily, but occasionally in late afternoon. **Conservation:** Least Concern. Classified as a game bird; may be hunted from October to March inclusive. The status of this species is seriously in need of review throughout southern Africa.

BURCHELL'S SANDGROUSE

male

female

male

female

male
belly-soaking

NAMAQUA SANDGROUSE

male

female

male

female

YELLOW-THROATED SANDGROUSE

male

female

male

female

DOUBLE-BANDED SANDGROUSE *Pterocles bicinctus*

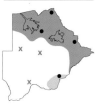

Setswana: le.gwaragwara

25 cm (9 ¾ in). **Identification:** Terrestrial game bird; superficially resembles a large dove. Male has bold black-and-white face pattern and buffy-yellow breast with white and black bands at lower border (compare male Namaqua Sandgrouse, p. 170). Female has black-and-brown barring on breast and belly. Two subspecies occur in Botswana: in *P. b. bicinctus* male has broad breast bands and fine barring on the belly, and female is relatively pale; *P. b. multicolor* is more richly colored (both sexes). **Call:** Musical whistle, rendered as *wee-chee choo-chip-will.* **Status:** Resident, breeding. There are egg-laying records from most months of the year, but the species is mainly a winter breeder. **Abundance:** Common. *P. b. bicinctus* occurs in the north of the country; *P. b. multicolor* is found in eastern and southern Botswana. **Habitat:** Found in open clearings in woodlands, especially Mopane (*Colophospermum mopane*). **Habits:** Seen in pairs or small family parties, except when congregating to drink. Arrives at water to drink about 20 minutes after sunset daily. Female incubates eggs during the day, male at night. **Conservation:** Least Concern. Classified as a game bird; may be hunted from October to March inclusive.

PIGEONS, DOVES Columbidae

This family takes its name from the genus *Columba*, which means pigeon, although most members are called doves (technically there is no difference between pigeon and dove although larger species are generally called pigeons). All are plump birds with small heads, short legs, and distinctive bills. In their crops they produce a secretion called "pigeon's milk," which is fed to the young. The chicks feed by inserting their bills into the parent's mouth. All members of this family drink water regularly by sucking it up (rather than scooping a beakful and raising the head to swallow it). Ten species occur in Botswana: seven indigenous members and two alien species of the subfamily Columbinae and one member of the subfamily Treroninae. Columbinae species are generally gray or brown seedeaters, while the *Treron* pigeon is a brightly colored arboreal frugivore. The Setswana *le.eba* is a generic name for doves.

ROCK DOVE *Columba livia*

Setswana: le.eba

33 cm (13 in). **Identification:** Large, familiar urban pigeon. Unmistakable, though plumage colors vary. **Call:** Soft hooting and cooing. **Status:** Resident, breeding. **Abundance:** Common; it has increased in numbers and range with the expansion of high-rise buildings in Botswana, which it uses as breeding sites. **Habitat:** Prevalent in urban environments and industrial areas. **Habits:** Gregarious; feeds on the ground in urban areas. Flocks take off with loud clattering of wings. **Conservation:** Least Concern. **General:** This is an alien, human-commensal species; descended from the wild Rock Dove of North Africa and Europe.

AFRICAN GREEN PIGEON *Treron calvus*

Setswana: le.eba lamotšhaba, le.ebarope

29 cm (11 ½ in). **Identification:** Colorful, parrot-like frugivore in a pigeon's body. Two subspecies occur in Botswana: *T. c. damarensis*, which has the yellowest plumage among the subspecies of the region, has distinctively green-yellow head, breast, and belly; by contrast *T. c. glaucus* has the most greenish-gray toned plumage and a pale, not blue, eye. **Call:** Very unpigeon-like: high-pitched, fluting whistles, followed by several harsh croaks, and ending with quiet clicking notes. **Status:** Resident, breeding. **Abundance:** Abundant in the Okavango wetland system, Linyanti Swamps, and along the Chobe River, as well as in the Tuli Block. The Okavango is a stronghold for this species in southern Africa. *T. c. damarensis* is found around the Okavango Delta and the Chobe River; *T. c. glaucus* occurs in the extreme east of the country, and is also found in South-East District but is uncommon there. **Habitat:** Found in riparian woodlands, preferring those with wild figs (*Ficus* spp.). **Habits:** Found in flocks in tree canopy feeding on fruits. When disturbed, remains motionless and is difficult to see; explodes from cover with clattering of wings. **Conservation:** Least Concern. Classified as a game bird; may be hunted throughout the year.

DOUBLE-BANDED
SANDGROUSE
P. b. bicinctus

male

female

male

female

ROCK DOVE

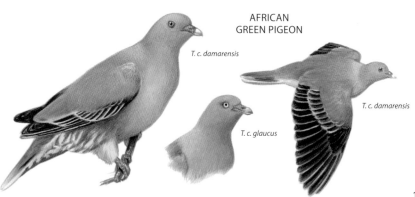

AFRICAN
GREEN PIGEON

T. c. damarensis

T. c. glaucus

T. c. damarensis

173

RED-EYED DOVE *Streptopelia semitorquata*

Setswana: le.eba, le.tseba

35 cm (13 ¾ in). **Identification:** Largest of the collared doves in Botswana. The specific name *semitorquata* refers to the half-collar on the hind neck. It has a red or orange eye with a dull red eye-ring. Outer tail feathers have gray tips, visible in flight. **Call:** Cooing, six-note phrase *co-coo coo-coo-coo-coo*, repeated. It is also rendered as *I-am, a-red-eyed-dove*. **Status:** Resident, breeding. **Abundance:** Abundant in the Okavango wetland system, Linyanti Swamps, and along the Chobe, Boteti, and Limpopo Rivers. **Habitat:** Occurs in riparian vegetation. **Habits:** Solitary birds or large flocks are seen feeding on the ground. Frequently nests over water in swamp vegetation such as *Phragmites* reeds. Male has conspicuous display known as "towering" in which it flies up steeply above tree canopy, clapping wings and then descends in a gliding flight with wings and tail splayed out rigidly. Male also performs bowing display with neck inflated during courtship. **Conservation:** Least Concern. Classified as a game bird; may be hunted throughout the year.

MOURNING COLLARED DOVE *Streptopelia decipiens*

Setswana: le.eba lamotsebe

30 cm (11 ¾ in). **Identification:** Collared dove; smaller and more slender than Red-eyed Dove. It has a yellow eye with a red eye-ring. Outer tail feathers have white tips, visible in flight. **Call:** Mournful descending *ko-krroooo*, followed by cooing notes. **Status:** Resident, breeding. **Abundance:** Abundant in the Okavango wetland system, Linyanti Swamps, and along the Chobe River; common along the Boteti and Limpopo Rivers. The Okavango Delta is its southern African stronghold. **Habitat:** Found in riparian woodlands and other woodland types not far from water. **Habits:** Feeds on the ground, where it pecks open large fruits of the Fever-berry (*Croton megalobotrys*) and ingests the seeds. This bird's range in Botswana mirrors that of the Fever-berry (*mo.tsebe*), and in Setswana it is called "dove of the Crotons." Courting male performs bowing display to female. **Conservation:** Least Concern. Classified as a game bird; may be hunted throughout the year.

RING-NECKED DOVE *Streptopelia capicola*

Setswana: le.phôi, mo.hiri, mo.kuru

27 cm (10 ¾ in). **Identification:** Small, pale gray dove with black ring on hind neck. In flight it shows white outer tail feathers, a key feature. A thin black line extending from base of bill to eye, visible only close-up, is diagnostic. Two subspecies occur in Botswana: *S. c. onguati* is very pale; *S. c. tropica* is slightly darker. **Call:** Cooing, rendered as *Work har-der, work har-der* or *How's faa-ther, how's faa-ther*. It is one of the most characteristic background sounds throughout Botswana. **Status:** Resident, breeding. **Abundance:** Abundant. One of Botswana's most abundant and widespread species. *S. c. onguati* is widespread throughout the country; *S. c. tropica* occurs in the extreme north of Chobe District and along the Limpopo River. **Habitat:** Catholic in choice of habitat, it is present in all vegetation types throughout the country. **Habits:** Solitary or in pairs, but large numbers congregate at Kalahari water holes to drink one or two hours after sunrise. Feeds on seeds on the ground. Male has conspicuous display known as "towering" in which it flies up steeply above tree canopy, clapping wings, and then descends in a gliding flight with wings and tail rigidly outspread. Male also performs bowing display with neck inflated during courtship. Monogamous birds pair for life. **Conservation:** Least Concern. Classified as a game bird; may be hunted throughout the year.

LAUGHING DOVE *Spilopelia senegalensis*

Setswana: tsôkwane, tsôdutsôkwane, tsôditsôkwane

25 cm (9 ¾ in). **Identification:** Relatively small, pinkish-gray dove without collar. Black spotting on rufous breast is a key identification feature. White tips to outer tail feathers are visible when bird takes off. **Call:** Chuckling coos from which the name Laughing Dove is derived. **Status:** Resident, breeding. **Abundance:** Abundant. One of Botswana's most abundant and widespread species. **Habitat:** Catholic in its choice of habitat, found in various open savannas; uses drier habitats than the collared doves. **Habits:** Solitary, except at Kalahari water holes where it congregates to drink in the early morning. Feeds primarily on seeds on the ground. Male has conspicuous display known as "towering" in which it flies up steeply above tree canopy, clapping wings, and then descends in a gliding flight with wings and tail splayed out rigidly. Male also performs bowing display to female with neck inflated. **Conservation:** Least Concern. Classified as a game bird; may be hunted throughout the year.

RED-EYED
DOVE

MOURNING
COLLARED DOVE

RINGED-NECKED
DOVE
S. c. onguati

LAUGHING
DOVE

175

EUROPEAN TURTLE DOVE *Streptopelia turtur*

Setswana: le.eba

27 cm (10 ¾ in). **Identification:** Larger than Laughing Dove (p. 174). It has brown, scaled appearance to wings and a black-striped neck patch that is diagnostic. Lacks black collar on hind neck (compare collared doves, p. 174). **Call:** Purring *kurrr, kurrr*, repeated. **Status:** Vagrant (from the Palearctic), nonbreeding. **Abundance:** Rare. **Habitat:** As a vagrant, it can turn up in a variety of habitats, but may be found near water in arid woodlands (as was the case with the two records to date). **Habits:** Solitary; feeds on seeds on the ground. **Conservation:** Least Concern.

J F M A M J J A S O N D

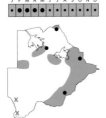

SPECKLED PIGEON *Columba guinea*

Setswana: le.ebarope, le.tsebarope, le.hukutiba

33 cm (13 in). **Identification:** Large gray pigeon. It has rufous-maroon wash over back and upperwing coverts, white spots on wing, and red skin around pale eye. **Call:** Series of coos starting softly, becoming louder and then slowing slightly toward end. **Status:** Resident, breeding. **Abundance:** Abundant in the east and southeast. The population is increasing elsewhere, and its range is expanding significantly with the development of high-rise buildings in urban centers, which the birds use as roosting and breeding sites. **Habitat:** Formerly restricted to rocky habitats in the eastern hardveld, but now more widespread and associated with towns and villages and agricultural activity. **Habits:** Flocks fly out among fields to feed on seeds on the ground. **Conservation:** Least Concern.

J F M A M J J A S O N D

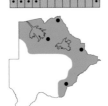

EMERALD-SPOTTED WOOD DOVE *Turtur chalcospilos*

Setswana: mo.kudunyane, mo.kudinyane, tshêbêru

20 cm (7 ¾ in). **Identification:** Small, pinkish-brown dove. It has several iridescent green wing spots, a dark bill, and chestnut primaries, which are conspicuous in flight. The subspecies found in Botswana, *T. c. volkmanni*, is the palest in the region and has a whitish belly. **Call:** Mournful cooing, from which is derived an African saying, translated as: "My mother is dead, my father is dead, all my relatives are dead, and my heart goes *du du du-du du-du du-du du-du-du-du-du*." **Status:** Resident, breeding. **Abundance:** Abundant throughout its range in northern and eastern Botswana. **Habitat:** Found in tall, deciduous woodlands with understory of scrub and thickets. **Habits:** Solitary; forages on the ground. Rises steeply when flushed, showing chestnut in wings. **Conservation:** Least Concern.

J F M A M J J A S O N D

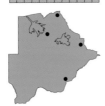

NAMAQUA DOVE *Oena capensis*

Setswana: rankudinyane, rankurunyane, ramokudinyane, ramokuditshêphê, rankudunyane

26 cm (10 ¼ in). **Identification:** Small dove. Its long, slender black tail is diagnostic among doves. Male is pale gray with a black face and throat and has a bicolor bill with a red base and yellow tip. Dark wing spots are iridescent purple in the right light. Female is pale brown and has a black bill. Both sexes show cinnamon coloring in wings when in flight. Juvenile has dark mottling on upperwing coverts and shoulder. **Call:** Soft, hooting *kuh-whoo*, repeated. **Status:** Resident, breeding. **Abundance:** Abundant. One of Botswana's most abundant and widespread species. **Habitat:** Catholic in its choice of habitat, occurs in a variety of semiarid woodlands. **Habits:** Usually solitary or in pairs. Feeds on seeds on bare ground. It is nomadic in response to rainfall and seed availability. **Conservation:** Least Concern. **General:** This is the smallest dove in Africa (excluding its long tail) and is the only sexually dimorphic dove in Botswana.

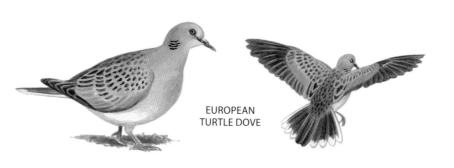

EUROPEAN
TURTLE DOVE

SPECKLED
PIGEON

EMERALD-SPOTTED
WOOD DOVE
T. c. volkmanni

NAMAQUA
DOVE

adult
male

adult
female

imm.

TURACOS Musophagidae

An endemic African family of large, arboreal, plant-eating birds. All are poor fliers, but the birds bound nimbly along branches on semi-zygodactyl feet (position of outer toe varies). They are long-tailed, with short, rounded wings, and most have erectile crests. Their plumage colors come from unique pigments: turacoverdin (green) and turacin (red). The chicks are semi-precocial and covered in thick down when they hatch; they have a carpal claw that enables them to clamber about in the vicinity of the nest. Four species occur in Botswana: The three forest species are mainly green or blue and have bright crimson flight feathers; the single savanna species is gray.

ROSS'S TURACO *Musophaga rossae*

51 cm (20 in). **Identification:** Large indigo-blue turaco. It has a yellow frontal shield, a crimson crest, and bright red flight feathers. **Call:** Guttural *kok-kok-kokokok-kok*. **Status** Vagrant; no breeding records from Botswana. **Abundance:** Rare. This species was first recorded in Botswana by Tim Liversedge, who collected a specimen at Ikoga on the Okavango River in October 1974. The second substantiated sighting was along the Linyanti River in August 2011. This species may be seen more frequently during decades when the Zambezi, Okavango, and Linyanti Rivers have above-average water levels, as at these times the riparian forest forms a well-developed corridor from Zambia into Botswana, along which the species can move. **Habitat:** Occurs in dense riparian forests. **Habits:** Solitary in Botswana, frugivorous. **Conservation:** Least Concern. **General:** The specimen collected by Liversedge is currently housed in the National Museum of Zimbabwe in Bulawayo.

PURPLE-CRESTED TURACO *Tauraco porphyreolophus*

42 cm (16 ½ in). **Identification:** Large, predominantly green turaco. It has a rounded, violet-mauve crest and bright red flight feathers. The nominate subspecies occurs in Botswana **Call:** Raucous *kok-kok-kok-kok*, rising in pitch and ending in drawn-out *kook-kook-kook* **Status:** Visitor; no breeding records from Botswana. **Abundance:** Rare. Near its western limit, the range of *T. p. porphyreolophus* extends westward along the Zambezi Valley into Botswana—when conditions are favorable. However, there have been no records of it since 1999. **Habitat:** Occurs in riparian forests with dense thickets; also in Zambezi Teak (*Baikiaea plurijuga*) woodlands. **Habits:** Frugivorous canopy dweller; bounds along branches **Conservation:** Least Concern.

GREY GO-AWAY-BIRD *Corythaixoides concolor*

Setswana: mo.koe, mo.koê, mo.kue, mo.kuê

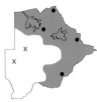

49 cm (19 ¼ in). **Identification:** All-gray turaco, with erectile crest and long tail. **Call** *Mo-ko-weee* or *go-waaaay*. Setswana name is onomatopoeic and derived from the call **Status:** Resident, breeding. **Abundance:** Abundant. One of Botswana's most abundant and widespread species. **Habitat:** Occurs in a variety of woodland types, including both dry acacia-dominated and broad-leaved woodlands. **Habits:** Solitary or in small groups forms larger groups in dry season (e.g., 40-50 by Notwane River on fruiting trees of the alien *Melia azedarach*); seen foraging within tree canopy or perched on top giving alarm on spotting danger (usually large raptor). Its flight is cumbersome and floppy. It feeds on tender shoots, flowers, and fruit, and is frequently seen eating clay along the Okavango River and elsewhere to supplement vegetarian diet. It is a cooperative breeder; three or more helpers feed the chicks. **Conservation:** Least Concern. **General:** There is a Setswana belief that if a child imitates the call of the Grey Go-away-bird, his or her mouth will crack.

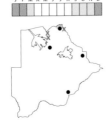

SCHALOW'S TURACO *Tauraco schalowi*

45 cm (17 ¾ in). **Identification:** Large, predominantly green turaco. It has a long, pointed white-tipped green crest and bright red flight feathers. **Call:** Harsh, growling *korr, korr* repeated. **Status:** Resident; no breeding records from Botswana. **Abundance:** This species extends only marginally into northern Botswana, where it is scarce in the area between Kasane and Kazungula towns. The species's range extends only marginally into northern Botswana. Four specimens collected at the Kasane Rapids by Austin Roberts in 1930 were the first Botswana records. It was seen recently (2014) near Khwai River, north of Moremi Game Reserve. It has not been seen in the Linyanti Swamps area since 1988. **Habitat:** Occurs in dense riparian woodlands. **Habits:** A forest-canopy frugivore, it bounds along branches and makes short flights to adjacent trees, during which its crimson underwing is visible **Conservation:** Least Concern.

ROSS'S TURACO

PURPLE-CRESTED
TURACO

GREY
GO-AWAY-BIRD

SCHALOW'S
TURACO

COUCALS, CUCKOOS Cuculidae

Members of this family have zygodactyl feet (with the first and fourth toes directed backward) and fairly strong, arched bills. They also all have 10 primary feathers and 10 tail feathers, but beyond this there are few visible unifying features. The Botswana representatives are divided into two distinct subfamilies: the Cuculinae, which includes 11 cuckoos belonging to four genera, all brood parasites; and the Centropodinae, five species of coucals belonging to one genus, all of which are nonparasitic. The species in each subfamily have various features in common, but also have major anatomical differences, which makes these groupings complex.

Cuckoos: Short-legged birds that have slender bodies and long wings and tails. They are arboreal and specialize in feeding on caterpillars. Most are migratory. The subfamily's representatives in Botswana are three *Clamator* cuckoos black or gray and white, all crested; three glossy *Chrysococcyx* cuckoos, which have iridescent green plumage and are sexually dimorphic; four *Cuculus* cuckoos, lacking crests and hawk-like in appearance; and one *Pachycoccyx* cuckoo which appears to have some affinities with *Clamator*.

LEVAILLANT'S CUCKOO *Clamator levaillantii*

Setswana: mo.rôkapula, phêtlhamedupe

39 cm (15 ¼ in). **Identification:** Large, black-and-white cuckoo, with black streaking on throat and breast. Two color morphs exist, one with a white breast and the other with black Black-breasted morph has not been recorded in Botswana; it is either rare here or does not occur at all. Juvenile is dark brown but has characteristic striping on throat, and a black bill that differentiates it from juvenile Jacobin Cuckoo, which has a yellow bill; it is usually seen in the company of its foster parents (babblers). **Call:** Clamorous *kleeuw, kleeuw*, followed by trilling *chirirrrriri*. Similar to call of Jacobin Cuckoo. **Status:** Intra-African migrant, breeding There may be an irruption of nonbreeding visitors if conditions are suitable—for example an outbreak of armyworms (*Spodoptera*). **Abundance:** Common. **Habitat:** Occurs in tall mature woodlands, both broad-leaved and acacia. **Habits:** Solitary or in pairs. Forages in upper canopy of woodlands; it is particularly active and noisy immediately after rain. The species is a brood parasite; hosts are mainly babblers (Arrow-marked Babbler is recorded in Botswana), rarely Kurrichane Thrush. It sometimes lays two eggs in the host's nest, and the young cuckoo does not evict other eggs or chicks, so babbler flocks can be seen with two cuckoo chicks in tow. This species exhibits pre-incubation development of the egg—that is the embryo is already developing in the egg when it is laid. **Conservation:** Least Concern.

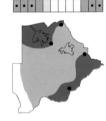

JACOBIN CUCKOO *Clamator jacobinus*

Setswana: nônyane yapula, tlhôtlhamedupe, tlhatlhamedupe

34 cm (13 ½ in). **Identification:** Similar to Levaillant's Cuckoo but much smaller. Three subspecies, virtually indistinguishable in the field, occur. *C. j. jacobinus* and *C. j. pica* have pure white, unstreaked throat and breast. *C. j. serratus* has two color morphs: a pied morph that has fine black streaking on white throat and breast and an entirely black morph (both sexes occur in both morphs). Juvenile of both morphs has a yellow bill and dark yellow eye-ring (which differentiates it from juvenile Levaillant's Cuckoo); dark morph juvenile can be distinguished from adult Black Cuckoo (p. 186) by white patch in the wing. **Call:** Loud clamorous, discordant whistles, especially after rain. A commonly repeated call is *Peeuw, peeuw, peeuw-peeuw, peeuw*. **Status:** *C. j. serratus*: common intra-African migrant, breeding *C. j. pica*: uncommon migrant from northern India and tropical Africa; no breeding records but may breed in Botswana. *C. j. jacobinus*: rare migrant from southern India and Sri Lanka nonbreeding. Note that *C. j. serratus* lays a white egg; *C. j. jacobinus* and *C. j. pica* lay blue green eggs; hence it is clear that all Botswana breeding records to date are from *C. j. serratus* alone. **Abundance:** *C. j. serratus*, which occurs over much of Botswana, is common (both morphs); *C. j. pica*, found in Ngamiland and Chobe Districts, is uncommon; *C. j. jacobinus* restricted to northeastern Botswana along the border with Zimbabwe, is rare. **Habitat** Found in a variety of woodland types, particularly acacia woodlands. **Habits:** Usually in pairs but loose associations of several individuals may be seen in the upper stratum of woodlands where the birds feed primarily on caterpillars and call noisily. The species is a brood parasite African Red-eyed and Dark-capped Bulbuls are its main hosts in Botswana, and Chestnut vented Warbler is also a recorded host in Botswana. Host eggs and chicks not evicted by adult or juvenile cuckoo, but mixed broods are rarely raised to fledging. **Conservation:** Least Concern. **General:** The Setswana name *nônyane yapula* means "rainbird."

adult
white-breasted
morph

LEVAILLANT'S
CUCKOO

JACOBIN CUCKOO
C. j. serratus

adult
black morph

adult
pied morph

juv.

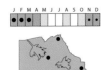

GREAT SPOTTED CUCKOO *Clamator glandarius*

39 cm (15 ¼ in). **Identification:** Adult has white-spotted upperparts, a gray crest, and white underparts. Immature is darker and has a black cap and rich chestnut primaries, visible in perched and flying bird. In flight, with its long wings, the bird looks like a small raptor. The two subspecies present in Botswana are indistinguishable in the field. **Call:** Chattering descending *chow-chow-chow, chow-chow*. **Status:** Two populations: *C. g. choragium*, intra-African migrant, breeding; and *C. g. glandarius*, intra-African migrant, nonbreeding. The latter is possibly dominant in Botswana. One winter record in August. **Abundance:** Uncommon. **Habitat:** Occurs in broad-leaved and acacia woodlands. **Habits:** Forages within tree canopy for caterpillars, but may call from conspicuous perch. The species is a brood parasite; hosts include Burchell's, Cape, Red-winged, and Meves's Starlings, and Cape Crow. There are no Botswana records of Pied Crow, which is the main host elsewhere in Africa, or of Common Myna as hosts. **Conservation:** Least Concern.

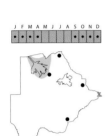

THICK-BILLED CUCKOO *Pachycoccyx audeberti*

36 cm (14 ¼ in). **Identification:** Adult has plain, gray to blackish upperparts, white underparts, and long, indistinctly barred tail. No crest. The heavy bill is usually dark above and yellow below. Yellow eyelids are conspicuous when the bird is seen close-up (all stages). Juvenile is pale gray above, with white spots on wings; resembles adult Great Spotted Cuckoo more than adult Thick-billed. **Call:** Persistent, repeated, whistled *weee-eeep, weee-eeep*. **Status:** Uncertain; possible resident (there are some winter records); no breeding records from Botswana. **Abundance:** Uncommon to rare. This African species may be expanding its range in Botswana, as there are now more sightings in the Okavango Delta. **Habitat:** Occurs in riparian woodlands and Mopane (*Colophospermum mopane*) woodlands. **Habits:** Elusive, but performs display of haphazard flight in tree canopy, accompanied by calling. Occasionally several adults display together. It is a brood parasite whose only host is Retz's Helmetshrike; ranges of the two species overlap, but there are no breeding records from Botswana. **Conservation:** Least Concern.

adult

adult

subadult

imm.

GREAT SPOTTED
CUCKOO

imm.

adult

imm.

adult

THICK-BILLED
CUCKOO

DIEDERIK CUCKOO *Chrysococcyx caprius*

19 cm (7 ½ in). **Identification:** Small cuckoo with metallic-green and white plumage and white spotting in wings. Both sexes have strong eye stripe extending in front of and behind the eye, white in male, buffy in female. Male has red iris and eye-ring. Immature has the white wing spots, and a distinctive orange-red bill; underparts are white with streaks on throat and spots on breast and belly (rather than horizontally barred, as sometimes pictured). **Call:** The *dee-dee-dee-deederik* call, from which the English name is derived, is apparently made by male; female issues a plaintive *deea, deea, deea*. **Status:** Intra-African migrant, breeding. **Abundance:** Common. **Habitat:** Occurs in a variety of woodland habitats but not usually found in Mopane (*Colophospermum mopane*) woodlands. **Habits:** Solitary. A leaf-gleaning bird, it specializes in feeding on caterpillars within the canopy foliage. Males use regular calling posts. The species is secretive and more frequently heard than seen, except in the vicinity of weaver colonies, where the birds are actively pursued by weavers trying to prevent them from parasitizing their nests. Recorded hosts for this brood parasite in Botswana are Cape Sparrow, Southern Masked Weaver, African Paradise Flycatcher, Lesser Masked Weaver, Red-headed Weaver, Southern Red Bishop, and Brown-crowned Tchagra. **Conservation:** Least Concern.

KLAAS'S CUCKOO *Chrysococcyx klaas*

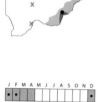

18 cm (7 in). **Identification:** Small, metallic-green and white cuckoo. Lacks white wing bar shown by Diederik Cuckoo. Male distinguished from male Diederik by green half-collar extending onto sides of breast. Both sexes have a narrow blue-green eye-ring, and a small white or buffy patch behind and above eye that is diagnostic. Lack of white in front of eye separates the species from Diederik Cuckoo. Female and immature have brownish head and face. **Call:** Bisyllabic whistle, rendered as *may-kie*, repeated several times; given by male only, when perched. **Status:** Intra-African migrant, breeding. **Abundance:** Uncommon. **Habitat:** Occurs in a variety of woodland types. **Habits:** Solitary. A leaf-gleaner, it specializes in feeding on caterpillars within the canopy foliage. Secretive, more frequently heard than seen. Males use fixed calling posts. The species is a brood parasite; known hosts in Botswana include Long-billed Crombec, Marico and Copper Sunbirds, Pririt Batis, and White-browed Scrub-Robin. **Conservation:** Least Concern.

AFRICAN EMERALD CUCKOO *Chrysococcyx cupreus*

20 cm (7 ¾ in). **Identification:** Male is striking: uniformly iridescent green upperparts and upper breast, bright yellow lower breast and belly. Close-up view reveals vivid blue-green eye-ring and slate-blue feet. Female and juvenile are bronzy above and heavily barred on underside; both lack white patch behind eye (compare female Klaas's Cuckoo). Birds at all stages have white on outer tail feathers. **Call:** Loud whistle, rendered as *pretty-Geor-gie*. **Status:** Intra-African migrant; no breeding records from Botswana. **Abundance:** Rare, except in Kasane, Kazungula, and Lesoma in northern Chobe District, where it is uncommon. **Habitat:** Found in riparian forests. **Habits:** Solitary. It is a leaf-gleaner, confined to the upper canopy of forest trees, more frequently heard than seen. Males use fixed calling posts. The species is a brood parasite; hosts include Grey-backed Camaroptera. **Conservation:** Least Concern.

DIEDERIK CUCKOO

adult male

adult male

adult female

imm.

juv.

KLAAS'S CUCKOO

adult male

adult male

adult female

imm.

AFRICAN EMERALD CUCKOO

male

female

185

BLACK CUCKOO *Cuculus clamosus*

Setswana: makokwe

30 cm (11 ¾ in). **Identification:** All-black cuckoo without a crest. Could be confused with juvenile black-morph Jacobin Cuckoo (p. 180), which also lacks crest, but Jacobin has white wing patches. Female Black Cuckoo has indistinct pale barring on belly. **Call:** Monotonous, mournful dirge, rendered as *I'm-so-saaad*, repeated endlessly (even during night). Also has a whirling call, *yow-yow-yow-yow*, rising to a crescendo and then fading. **Status:** Intra-African migrant, breeding. **Abundance:** Common. **Habitat:** Found in broad-leaved and acacia woodlands. **Habits:** More frequently heard than seen, it gleans foliage for caterpillars in the tree canopy. Males use fixed calling posts. The species is a brood parasite; known hosts in Botswana include Crimson-breasted Shrike and Swamp Boubou. **Conservation:** Least Concern.

RED-CHESTED CUCKOO *Cuculus solitarius*

29 cm (11 ½ in). **Identification:** Fast-flying, long-tailed, accipiter-like gray cuckoo with black upper mandible and yellow base to lower mandible. Its chestnut upper breast is diagnostic among cuckoos in Botswana. Juvenile is black above with faint buffy feather edges, barred black and white below, with black throat and black bill. Resembles a small sparrowhawk in flight. **Call:** Repetitive trisyllabic whistle, rendered *Piet-may-frou* or *quid pro quo*. Calls incessantly, day and night, during summer. **Status:** Intra-African migrant; no breeding records from Botswana (surprisingly, given the bird's abundance). **Abundance:** Common in east and southeast; scarce in Ngamiland District. Transits through the north when migrating to and from its destination in southern Botswana and South Africa. **Habitat:** Favors tall, mature, wooded habitats, including evergreen riparian woodlands and woodlands on rocky hills. **Habits:** Solitary, true to its specific name *solitarius*, and covert in its habits. Feeds on caterpillars. More frequently heard than seen. Males use fixed calling posts. The species is a brood parasite, but there are no Botswana breeding records, despite the presence of many of its documented hosts. **Conservation:** Least Concern.

AFRICAN CUCKOO *Cuculus gularis*

32 cm (12 ½ in). **Identification:** Fast-flying, long-tailed, accipiter-like gray cuckoo. Lacks rufous breast shown by Red-chested Cuckoo; has more yellow at base of bill than Common Cuckoo. Undertail pattern useful in differentiating this species and Common Cuckoo: African has barred undertail coverts and undertail. **Call:** Bisyllabic *hoo-hoo* or *hoop-hoop* is diagnostic. Very similar to call of African Hoopoe, but accent is on slightly higher-pitched second syllable. Note that Common Cuckoo does not call when in Botswana. **Status:** Intra-African migrant, breeding. **Abundance:** Scarce to common. **Habitat:** Found in a variety of woodlands, both broad-leaved and acacia, but prefers the latter. **Habits:** Feeds on caterpillars within tree foliage. More frequently heard than seen. Males use fixed calling posts. The species is a brood parasite; the only known host in Botswana is Fork-tailed Drongo. **Conservation:** Least Concern.

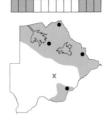

COMMON CUCKOO *Cuculus canorus*

33 cm (13 in). **Identification:** Fast-flying, long-tailed, accipiter-like gray cuckoo. Lacks rufous breast shown by Red-chested Cuckoo; bill has yellow only at base of lower mandible (compare African Cuckoo). Undertail pattern is useful in differentiating this species and African Cuckoo: Common has finer barred undertail coverts and a blackish undertail. Female polymorphic; rufous (hepatic) morph has been recorded in Chobe and Ngamiland Districts. Two subspecies occur in Botswana, the dark *C. c. canorus* and the paler *C. c. subtelephorus*. **Call:** Silent when in Botswana. **Status:** Palearctic migrant, nonbreeding. **Abundance:** Uncommon in most of its range (not as plentiful as African Cuckoo); scarce in South-East District. *C. c. canorus* occurs throughout most of Botswana; *C. c. subtelephorus* is a vagrant to the northeastern part of the country. **Habitat:** Catholic in habitat choice; occurs in variety of woodland types. **Habits:** As it is nonbreeding in Botswana, it makes no territorial advertisement and is unobtrusive. **Conservation:** Least Concern.

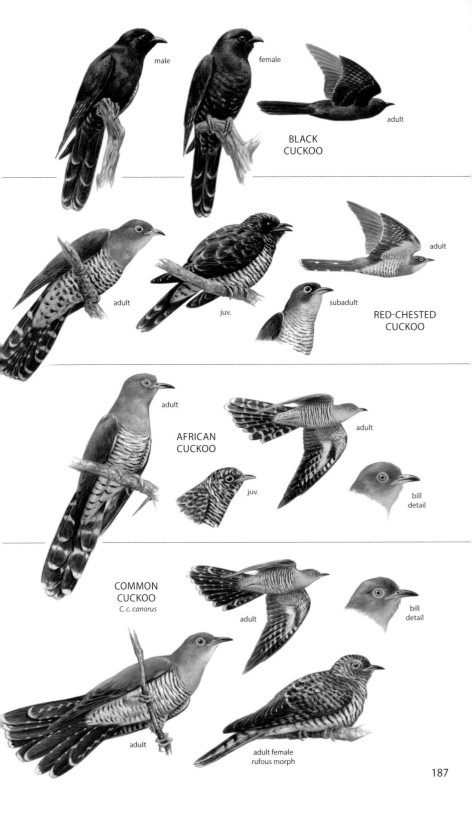

male

female

adult

BLACK CUCKOO

adult

adult

juv.

subadult

RED-CHESTED CUCKOO

adult

AFRICAN CUCKOO

adult

juv.

bill detail

COMMON CUCKOO
C. c. canorus

adult

bill detail

adult

adult

adult female
rufous morph

Coucals: Are all in the genus *Centropus*, the name of which is derived from the long claw that all species have on the hind toe (or hallux). They have similar plumage colors and bubbling calls and are terrestrial and sedentary (the Black Coucal is an exception in some respects). Coucal chicks void a foul-smelling fluid thought to deter predators. The Setswana name *le.fututu* is onomatopoeic, derived from the bubbling call, and used generically for all coucals.

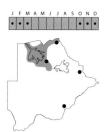

COPPERY-TAILED COUCAL *Centropus cupreicaudus*

Setswana: le.fututu, tuutuu, tlhômêlêdi

47 cm (18 ½ in). **Identification:** Largest coucal in Botswana. It has dark head and mantle, russet wings, creamy white underparts, and long dark tail. Rump and uppertail coverts are blackish and distinctly darker than the otherwise russet upperparts; in flight, this blackish back color separates the russet-brown wings (compare Senegal Coucal). This species has a noticeably larger bill than the other coucals. **Call:** Bubbling call, similar to the sound of outpouring water. Also frequently gives a harsh alarm call, *tchak-tchak-tchak*. **Status:** Resident, breeding. **Abundance:** Abundant. The Okavango is its stronghold in southern Africa. It is a Zambezian endemic. **Habitat:** Restricted to swamps and marshes with rank vegetation, including Papyrus (*Cyperus papyrus*) and *Phragmites* reedbeds, in contrast to the other coucals. Also floodplain margins. **Habits:** Solitary or in pairs. Skulks in rank vegetation searching for prey. Has clumsy flapping flight but is nimble on the ground. **Conservation:** Least Concern.

SENEGAL COUCAL *Centropus senegalensis*

Setswana: le.fututu, tuutuu, tlhômêlêdi

39 cm (15 ¼ in). **Identification:** Medium-size coucal with dark head and mantle, russet wings, creamy white underparts, and long dark tail. Back and upperwings uniformly orange-brown. This uniform rufous coloration along the bird's upperside is a key feature in flying bird (compare Coppery-tailed Coucal). This species lacks barring on rump and uppertail coverts (compare White-browed Coucal). Rare rufous morph with russet breast recorded in Okavango Delta in 2002 could be mistaken for Black Coucal (p. 190). **Call:** Bubbling call, similar to sound of outpouring water. **Status:** Resident, breeding. **Abundance:** Abundant in northern wetlands. Scarce along the Limpopo River. The Okavango is one of its strongholds in southern Africa. **Habitat:** Favors rank grass and thickets in savannas and dense riparian woodlands. Can occur in relatively dry habitats away from water. **Habits:** Solitary or in pairs, seen in lower stratum of habitat; often forages by walking on ground, searching for invertebrates. Has clumsy flapping flight. **Conservation:** Least Concern.

BURCHELL'S COUCAL *Centropus burchellii*

Setswana: le.futut, tuutuu, tlhômêlêdi, mo.gofa

41 cm (16 ¼ in). **Identification:** Medium-size coucal with dark head and mantle, russet wings, buffy underparts, and long dark tail. Rump and uppertail coverts are barred. The subspecies that occurs in Botswana, *C. b. burchellii*, has prominent streaking on sides of neck and flanks; this streaking is most consistent in immature birds. Immature has pale supercilium; residual juvenile barring on mantle and wings differentiate it from White-browed Coucal, which occupies an allopatric range. **Call:** Bubbling call, similar to the sound of outpouring water. **Status:** Resident; no breeding records from Botswana. Probably breeds during summer months, as it does elsewhere in southern Africa. **Abundance:** Uncommon to common throughout its range in eastern Botswana, especially along the Limpopo River drainage. The species is endemic to southern Africa. **Habitat:** Favors rank growth and thickets in woodlands along drainage lines, often but not invariably near water; also occurs in emergent vegetation around sewage ponds and other wetlands. **Habits:** Solitary or in pairs. Skulks close to the ground, searching actively for invertebrates and small vertebrates. Has clumsy flapping flight. **Conservation:** Least Concern.

WHITE-BROWED COUCAL *Centropus superciliosus*

Setswana: le.fututu, tuutuu, tlhômêlêdi

41 cm (16 ¼ in). **Identification:** Medium-size coucal, with dark head and mantle, russet wings, brownish-gray underparts, and long dark tail. In combination, white supercilium and heavily streaked throat are diagnostic among Botswana's coucals. Underparts finely barred and streaked. Adult similar to immature Burchell's Coucal, which has a pale supercilium, but the two species' ranges are mutually exclusive. **Call:** Bubbling call, similar to the sound of outpouring water. **Status:** Resident, breeding. **Abundance:** Common in the Okavango wetland system, Linyanti Swamps, and along the Chobe River. **Habitat:** Found in thickets and tangled undergrowth near water. **Habits:** Solitary or in pairs. It is a skulking ground forager and has a clumsy flapping flight. **Conservation:** Least Concern.

COPPERY-TAILED COUCAL

SENEGAL COUCAL

adult

juv.

adult

BURCHELL'S COUCAL
C. b. burchellii

adult

imm.

juv.

WHITE-BROWED COUCAL

adult

imm.

189

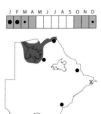

BLACK COUCAL *Centropus grillii*

M: 33 cm (13 in), F: 37 cm (14 ½ in). **Identification:** Small coucal. During breeding season, both sexes are easily recognized by all-black body and head, and rich rufous wings. Nonbreeding birds have dark brown upperparts, crown and mantle streaked with buff, and buffy underparts. Immature is buffy overall, heavily barred and streaked, with dark brown tail. **Call:** Female gives bisyllabic, popping call, *pop-pop, pop-pop*, repeated at intervals. **Status:** Intra-African migrant, breeding. Limited Botswana breeding records conform with data from the rest of southern Africa. **Abundance:** Uncommon. The Okavango Delta is one of the species's strongholds in southern Africa. **Habitat:** Prefers rank, moist grasslands particularly of *Imperata* grasses. **Habits:** Solitary or in pairs. Flushes reluctantly and flies short distance before flopping back into grass. Female conspicuous when calling from prominent bush, in hunched posture. This is a polyandrous species; the female is dominant over the male and more vocal and conspicuous, and the male undertakes all incubation and chick rearing. **Conservation:** Least Concern.

OWLS Strigidae

Large family of nocturnal, predatory birds that are cryptically colored and have downward-pointing bills (but kill prey with their talons). Most have yellow eyes, which are often surrounded by a round facial disk, and give a hooting call. Many species have ear tufts (not connected to the ears), which are absent from the Tytonidae owl family (p. 196). Botswana has seven genera and nine species, ranging from diminutive owlets to the giant Verreaux's Eagle-Owl. They feed on prey ranging from insects to large birds, monkeys, and small antelopes. Monogamous, they nest in holes or natural cavities in trees, among rocks, or in other birds' nests. Most occur solitarily or in pairs; some of the larger species that duet are commonly found in pairs (e.g., Spotted Eagle-Owl, Pel's Fishing Owl, African Wood Owl). The Setswana *mo.rubise* is the generic name for owls.

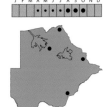

SOUTHERN WHITE-FACED OWL *Ptilopsis granti*

Setswana: kukuruma, mo.rubise

27 cm (10 ¾ in). **Identification:** Medium-size owl with blackish ear tufts and a white face bracketed with black. Adult has orange-red eyes. Male is paler than female and has a central white streak running down its breast and belly (absent in the female). During the day, adult avoids detection by drawing itself into tall, thin posture with ear tufts raised and eyes closed to slits. Immature has pale orange to orange-yellow eyes and less obvious ear tufts. **Call:** Bubbling *hoot, who-ho-ho-ho ho-oooo*. The Setswana name *kukuruma* is onomatopoeic, derived from the call. **Status:** Resident, breeding. **Abundance:** Scarce to common. **Habitat:** Found in dry acacia woodlands and Kalahari tree and bush savanna. **Habits:** Nocturnal, usually solitary; rodent specialist. **Conservation:** Least Concern.

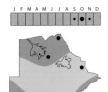

AFRICAN SCOPS OWL *Otus senegalensis*

Setswana: se.kopamarumo

16 cm (6 ¼ in). **Identification:** Diminutive; smallest owl in Botswana. Gray plumage resembles tree bark. Two color morphs: gray (common) and rufous brown (present in small numbers throughout the population). **Call:** Staccato *purrup*, repeated at intervals. **Status:** Resident, breeding. **Abundance:** Common. The Okavango Delta and southern Kalahari, including Kgalagadi District, are strongholds for this species in southern Africa. It is also common throughout Ngamiland, Chobe, and North-East Districts but less common elsewhere. **Habitat:** Found in tall woodlands; prefers Mopane (*Colophospermum mopane*) woodlands and Kalahari (acacia) tree and bush savanna. **Habits:** Nocturnal, usually solitary; feeds mainly on insects but also small birds and rodents. During the day, it perches motionless on a small branch near the trunk, thus obscuring its outline. **Conservation:** Least Concern. **General:** At 65 g (2.3 oz), this is the smallest southern African owl; it is only 3% of the weight of Verreaux's Eagle-Owl.

breeding
adult

breeding
adult

BLACK
COUCAL

sub-adult

juv.

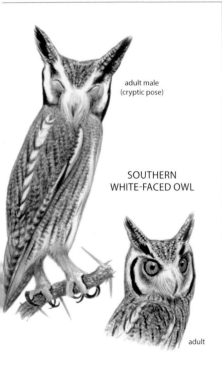

adult male
(cryptic pose)

SOUTHERN
WHITE-FACED OWL

adult

adult
gray morph

AFRICAN
SCOPS OWL

adult
rufous-brown
morph

191

AFRICAN WOOD OWL *Strix woodfordii*

Setswana: mo.rubise

33 cm (13 in). **Identification:** Medium-size owl. It has round head, without ear tufts, and yellow beak and feet. There is some variation in plumage coloration: most individuals are dark brown, but a few have rufous head and underparts. **Call:** Hooting duet: the male call *hoo-hoo, hu-hu-hu, hoo-hoo*, and the female repeats that at a slightly higher pitch. **Status:** Resident, breeding. **Abundance:** Uncommon. Regularly seen only in Shakawe village and south along the Okavango Panhandle; also occurs at Linyanti Swamps. **Habitat:** A forest species, found in thickly wooded riparian habitats. **Habits:** Nocturnal; roosts in trees with thick foliage during the day. Solitary or in pairs. **Conservation:** Least Concern.

AFRICAN BARRED OWLET *Glaucidium capense*

Setswana: mo.rubisana

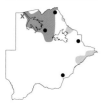

21 cm (8 ¼ in). **Identification:** Diminutive owlet. Barred wings, back, and tail (and lack of false eyes on back of head) distinguish this species from Pearl-spotted Owlet. Bold white spots along wings and small triangular brown blotches on the breast are key field characteristics. Its feet are relatively small, suited to small invertebrate prey. Only the subspecies *G. c. ngamiense*, originally described from a specimen collected in Maun (Ngamiland District), is found in Botswana. **Call:** Series of purring calls, starting softly and increasing in volume, *croo-croo-croo-CROO*. **Status:** Resident, breeding. **Abundance:** Common. The Okavango Delta is its stronghold in southern Africa. **Habitat:** Found in tall, mature woodlands, especially riparian and Mopane (*Colophospermum mopane*) woodlands. **Habits:** Solitary. Nocturnal, but partially diurnal in areas where undisturbed. A perch hunter, it is a nocturnal equivalent of shrikes; its diet mainly invertebrates. It nests in natural cavities in trees but is too large to use woodpecker holes. **Conservation:** Least Concern.

PEARL-SPOTTED OWLET *Glaucidium perlatum*

Setswana: mmankgôtlhwê, ma.kgôtlhwê, pelekekae

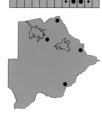

19 cm (7 ½ in). **Identification:** Diminutive owlet. Wings, back, and tail are spotted (not barred), and it has a streaky (not blotched) breast; these features distinguish it from African Barred Owlet. Black markings create a false face on the back of the head. It has relatively thick legs and large feet, specialized for taking large prey. **Call:** Series of piercing whistles: ascending *tu, tu, tu, tu*, then descending *tia, tia, tia, tia*. It is frequently and ably imitated by Fork-tailed Drongo. **Status:** Resident, breeding **Abundance:** Common. **Habitat:** Occurs in arid acacia-dominated savannas, such as Kalahari tree and bush savanna, and mature, open deciduous woodlands. **Habits:** Solitary. Nocturnal equivalent of small sparrowhawks and goshawks; regularly active during the day. Although it weighs just 75 g (2.6 oz) (slightly more than African Scops Owl, p. 190), it has been recorded taking prey as large as a Laughing Dove; the largest prey item on record is a Ring-necked Dove (double its weight). **Conservation:** Least Concern.

AFRICAN
WOOD OWL

no false
eyes

AFRICAN BARRED
OWLET
G. c. ngamiense

false
eyes

PEARL-SPOTTED
OWLET

VERREAUX'S EAGLE-OWL *Bubo lacteus*

Setswana: mmankgôtlhô

62 cm (24 ½ in). **Identification:** Africa's largest and heaviest owl. It has uniformly gray-brown plumage, dark eyes, and conspicuous pink eyelids. **Call:** Jumbled, irregular series of deep hoots and grunts. Immature has loud, often-heard, whistled begging call. **Status:** Resident, breeding. **Abundance:** Common in Linyanti area, Savute, Okavango Delta, and Tuli Block; uncommon to scarce elsewhere. **Habitat:** Favors mature woodlands, from riparian woodlands to Kalahari tree and bush savanna with mature Camel Thorns (*Acacia erioloba*). **Habits:** Nocturnal, solitary or in pairs. Feeds on a variety of prey from insects to game birds to small and medium-size mammals. An extremely powerful, rapacious owl, has been recorded killing a Pel's Fishing Owl (Okavango Delta, 2008) and killing and eating an African Fish Eagle (Okavango Delta, 2011). It takes over nests of vultures (Lappet-faced Vulture documented) and eagles (African Fish Eagle, Bateleur) for breeding, and also nests on tops of Red-billed Buffalo Weaver and Hamerkop nests. **Conservation:** Least Concern.

SPOTTED EAGLE-OWL *Bubo africanus*

Setswana: mmankgôtlhô, mo.rubise

45 cm (17 ¾ in). **Identification:** Large owl with ear tufts. Underparts are lightly blotched over fine gray barring. Two color morphs occur: gray morph, which has yellow eyes, is more common; less frequently seen rufous morph has yellow-orange eyes. Cape Eagle-Owl (*Bubo capensis*), which doesn't currently occur in Botswana but comes very close in Zimbabwe, can be differentiated by its bold chest and belly markings. **Call:** Two-note hoot, *hu whooo* by male, often followed by higher pitched *huu ho huuu* of female. **Status:** Resident, breeding. **Abundance:** Common throughout the southern half of the country; scarce in the north (Ngamiland and Chobe Districts). **Habitat:** Catholic in its choice of habitats; found throughout Kalahari tree and bush savanna and also in eastern hardveld where suitable breeding sites among rocks are to be found. **Habits:** Nocturnal equivalent of eagles and buzzards; perch hunts, taking wide variety of prey. Occurs in pairs, pairs for life. **Conservation:** Least Concern.

PEL'S FISHING OWL *Scotopelia peli*

Setswana: nqumu, mo.ng-amolapô, nônyane yaditlhapi

63 cm (24 ¾ in). **Identification:** Unmistakable large, ginger-colored owl, almost the size of Verreaux's Eagle-Owl. It has dark eyes and unfeathered legs, and lacks ear tufts. Immature is paler than adult. **Call:** Booming, two-note duet between birds of a pair, *hoom … hoom*. Chick makes a loud, eerie call to solicit food. **Status:** Resident, breeding. **Abundance:** Common in the Okavango Panhandle and Delta. Uncommon along the Chobe River and the Limpopo River; however, it has been recorded breeding in both places. The Okavango is its stronghold in southern Africa; it is apparently absent from Linyanti Swamps. **Habitat:** Found in riparian woodlands; a key component is large trees with suitable hunting perches overhanging permanent slow-flowing water. Its favored nesting tree is Jackal-berry (*Diospyros mespiliformis*). **Habits:** Nocturnal counterpart of African Fish Eagle. Solitary or in pairs. It perch hunts over still backwaters in complete darkness, plunging feet-first to catch fish near the water surface. The Setswana name *nônyane yaditlhapi* means "bird of the fishes." **Conservation:** Least Concern.

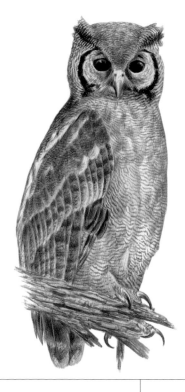

VERREAUX'S
EAGLE-OWL

SPOTTED
EAGLE-OWL

PEL'S
FISHING OWL

195

MARSH OWL *Asio capensis*

Setswana: mo.rubise

37 cm (14 ½ in). **Identification:** Medium-size owl. It has dark eyes and a buffy-gray (neve white) facial disk. Because of its habitat preference, it is frequently misidentified as Africa Grass Owl, which has a white facial disk. Also, in flight, feet do not protrude beyond ta as they do in the grass owl. **Call:** Croaking, frog-like *qurark*. **Status:** Resident, breeding Peak egg-laying months are March to May, but it occasionally breeds in other months **Abundance:** Locally common. The species is nomadic; it moves seasonally into suitabl habitat, such as moist grasslands around Lake Ngami. It is regularly recorded in foss riverbeds in the Central Kalahari Game Reserve and in Makgadikgadi Pans, also aroun wetlands in and near Gaborone. **Habitat:** Found in marshes, swamps, and rank grasse along drainage lines or near pans; frequently seen in dry grasslands and shrub savannas **Habits:** Gregarious, especially just after breeding season. Nocturnal and crepuscular; ofte seen during early mornings and late afternoons, particularly when breeding and more foo is needed for chicks. It preys on rodents in manner of a harrier, and occupies similar habitats Roosts communally in thick grass on the ground; may be found in loose aggregations of u to 35 birds when roosting. **Conservation:** Least Concern.

BARN OWLS Tytonidae

Nocturnal raptors that have dark, forward-facing eyes set in a prominent, heart-shaped facial disk. The disk focuses sound and enables these owls to hunt by auditory clues from rodent prey. Specially adapted flight feathers allow them to fly silently. They kill with their sharp talons, not the downward-pointing bill. Botswana has two species of the genus *Tyto*, both of which give harsh screeching calls. The heart-shaped facial disk and downward-pointing bill differentiate them from the typical owls in the family Strigidae (p. 190). The Setswana *mo.rubise* is the generic name for owls.

WESTERN BARN OWL *Tyto alba*

Setswana: se.kea, mo.rubise

32 cm (12 ½ in). **Identification:** Medium-size, pale owl: Has facial disk, off-white underparts and golden-buff upperparts flecked with white. *T. a. affinis* is the subspecies found throughout Botswana. **Call:** Eerie, purring screech. **Status:** Resident, breeding. Egg-layin occurs throughout year, but the peak during late summer and into winter correlates with rodent abundance. **Abundance:** Common. Populations fluctuate in accordance with it prey numbers. **Habitat:** Found in a wide variety of woodland types and more open habitats often occurs in association with human habitation. **Habits:** Nocturnal and crepuscula equivalent of a harrier, it perch hunts and quarters over open areas with light buoyant fligh It is a very efficient predator of rats and mice, as indicated by records of a nest (containing six eggs) stockpiled with 80 mice, and another nest holding four young owls and 73 mice Nests in tree holes, rock crevices, roofs of buildings, Hamerkop nests, wells and other sites **Conservation:** Least Concern.

AFRICAN GRASS OWL *Tyto capensis*

Setswana: le.kutikurru, mo.rubise

36 cm (14 ¼ in). **Identification:** Medium-size owl with dark brown back and wings, and rich buff underparts. Coloration and habitat differentiate this species from Western Barr Owl. In flight, its feet project beyond the short tail, differentiating it from Marsh Owl, which occupies similar habitat. **Call:** Soft, cricket-like clicking. **Status:** Uncertain; no recent records and no breeding records from Botswana. **Abundance:** Rare. This species may be extirpated in Botswana. It has declined in neighboring South Africa since 1970 due to degradation of it grassland habitat. There is a specimen in the Botswana National Museum of a bird shot in the Notwane grasslands (now Broadhurst sewage ponds and Gaborone Game Reserve), and Penr (1994) reported a few sight records, but there have been no recent, substantiated sightings other than one of two birds in July 1998 by Gaborone Dam and another in the same area in February 1999; also one unconfirmed report near Francistown. **Habitat:** Prefers permanently moist, but not inundated, tall, rank grasses. **Habits:** Strictly nocturnal, terrestrial species. Preys on rodents. **Conservation:** Least Concern.

MARSH OWL

WESTERN
BARN OWL
T. a. affinis

AFRICAN
GRASS OWL

197

NIGHTJARS Caprimulgidae

Family of nocturnal insectivores. Nightjars have small beaks but large gapes that are adorned with rictal bristles, which facilitate the catching of insects in the air. Botswana's seven species have cryptic plumage for camouflage during the day, when they roost (usually) on the ground among leaf litter. They are difficult to differentiate from one another. They vary in the presence of white or buff spots on the wing and the extent of white or buff on the tail feathers; the combination of the two is diagnostic for each species. For birds in the hand, the position, size and color of the spots on the ninth primary (the second to front wing feather which has a distinct emargination on its leading edge) and on the two outer tail feathers are useful identification features. Calls are particularly useful. Most species either whistle or churr; those with whistled calls are generally found in woodlands, while those with churring calls occur in open habitats. Wing-clapping performed by males in display flight. One species trills like an insect. Nightjars are the nighttime equivalent of swifts and swallows, and because they are dependent on insects, which flourish and dwindle in response to seasonal fluctuations in precipitation, many are migratory to a greater or lesser extent. The Setswana *mmamphuphame* is the generic name for nightjars.

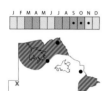

FIERY-NECKED NIGHTJAR   *Caprimulgus pectoralis*

Setswana: mmamphuphama

24 cm (9 ½ in). **Identification:** Has "fiery" collar—rufous with bright buff streaks—that extends around hind neck, and rufous cheeks. Male has white spots on four main wing feathers and very large white tips to two outer tail feathers. Female has white or buffy wing spots and small white tail tips. A rufous morph occurs in Botswana (photographed at Pandamatenga in Chobe District), Two subspecies occur in Botswana: *C. p. shelleyi* has a very broad and rufous collar as compared to *C. p. fervidus*. **Call:** This nightjar is a whistler. Tremulous whistling, rendered as *Good lord, deliver-us*. **Status:** Resident, breeding. Numbers are supplemented by breeding intra-African migrants, especially between July and October; there is also a peak in numbers in March and April as birds return northward. **Abundance:** Common in Ngamiland and Chobe Districts; uncommon elsewhere. *C. p. fervidus* covers most of the species's range in Botswana; *C. p. shelleyi* may occur in the extreme north. **Habitat:** Occurs in tall, mature woodlands. **Habits:** Nocturnal aerial insectivore; most active at twilight and on moonlit nights. Roosts on the ground during the day. Monogamous; lays eggs at full moon or during the week following, so there will be a waxing moon when the eggs hatch. **Conservation:** Least Concern.

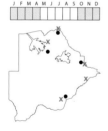

EUROPEAN NIGHTJAR   *Caprimulgus europaeus*

Setswana: mmamphophame

27 cm (10 ¾ in). **Identification:** Large nightjar with long wings (they reach distal third of tail in perched bird). Male usually has white spots on first three primaries and white tips to the outer two tail feathers. Female has no white wing or tail spots. Five of the six subspecies, all similar in appearance, may be seen in southern Africa; the most common subspecies in Botswana is *C. e. europaeus*. **Call:** Silent in Botswana. **Status:** Palearctic migrant, nonbreeding. **Abundance:** Rare. **Habitat:** Occurs in a wide range of open habitats, a reflection of its wide range in Eurasia. **Habits:** The only nightjar in Botswana to roost lengthwise along a branch (rather than on the ground) during the day. Like other nightjars, it occupies the niche of nocturnal aerial insectivore; most active at twilight and on moonlit nights. **Conservation:** Least Concern.

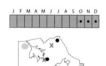

FRECKLED NIGHTJAR   *Caprimulgus tristigma*

Setswana: mmamphuphama

28 cm (11 in). **Identification:** One of the largest nightjars in Africa. It is the easiest nightjar to identify due to its vermiculated plumage pattern and specific habitat requirements. It has a noticeably large, flattened head and enormous eyes. The two subspecies found in Botswana, *C. t. lentiginosus* and *C. t. granosus*, are very similar in appearance and difficult to differentiate in the field. **Call:** This nightjar is a whistler. Bi- or trisyllabic, whistled *bow-wow* or *bow-wow-wow*. **Status:** Resident, breeding. **Abundance:** Uncommon, restricted by its habitat requirements but locally common in Gaborone area. *C. t. lentiginosus* is found at Tsodilo Hills (Ngamiland) and on the hills at Savute (Chobe National Park); *C. t. granosus* occurs in eastern Botswana. **Habitat:** Found in hilly areas, such as those in eastern hardveld, and rocky outcrops (e.g., in Tsodilo Hills). **Habits:** Nocturnal; during the day it rests on rocky substrate, where it relies on its camouflage to escape detection. Most active at twilight and on moonlit nights. Monogamous; lays eggs on bare rock. **Conservation:** Least Concern.

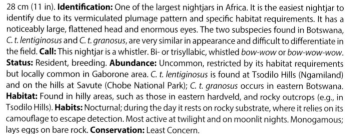

198

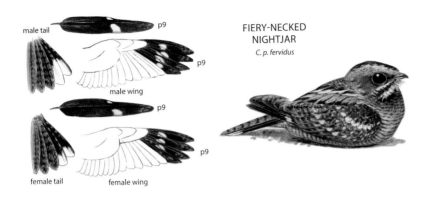

**FIERY-NECKED
NIGHTJAR**
C. p. fervidus

male tail

p9

male wing

p9

female tail

female wing

p9

p9

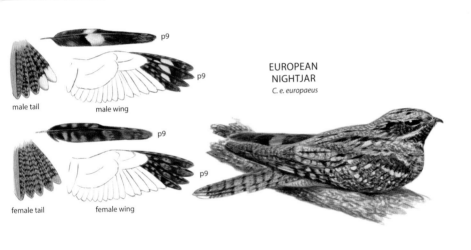

**EUROPEAN
NIGHTJAR**
C. e. europaeus

male tail

male wing

p9

p9

female tail

female wing

p9

p9

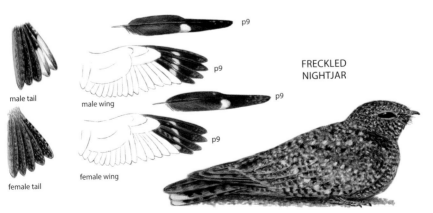

**FRECKLED
NIGHTJAR**

male tail

male wing

p9

p9

female tail

female wing

p9

p9

199

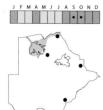

SWAMP NIGHTJAR *Caprimulgus natalensis*

Setswana: mmamphuphama

23 cm (9 in). **Identification:** Black markings on lores, ear coverts, throat, and neck are key identification features. Plumage has dark and spotted appearance overall. Male has white spots on four main wing feathers, and the outer web of the outermost tail feather and half the outer web of the adjacent feather are white. Female has buff spots on four wing feathers and is buffy on tail where male is white. The subspecies found in Botswana is *C. n. carp* **Call:** This nightjar has both churring- and whistling-type calls: rapid series of *chop* sound a tremulous *wha-hu-hu-hu-hu-hu* in flight. **Status:** Resident; no breeding records from Botswana. **Abundance:** Scarce. At the southern limit of its continental range, it occurs in the Linyanti Swamps, along the Chobe River, and in the Okavango Delta. **Habitat:** A species of freshwater wetlands, found at edges of short, moist grasslands between riparian woodland and swamps or floodplains. **Habits:** Nocturnal aerial insectivore; most active at twilight and on moonlit nights. Monogamous; lays eggs on ground. **Conservation:** Least Concern.

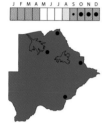

RUFOUS-CHEEKED NIGHTJAR *Caprimulgus rufigena*

Setswana: le.tsôbu, mmaubane, mmamphuphame

24 cm (9 ½ in). **Identification:** Rufous cheeks only faintly evident: It has an evenly colored silvery-gray plumage. Male has white spots on four main wing feathers and large white tips to two outer tail feathers. Female has buff spots on three main wing feathers and no white in tail. Two subspecies are found in Botswana: the nominate is slightly larger than *C. r. damarensis* which is paler and grayer. **Call:** This nightjar is a churrer. Monotonous churring continues for a protracted period; it is similar to that of Square-tailed Nightjar but unvarying in pitch or speed. **Status:** Intra-African migrant, breeding. **Abundance:** Common. Its stronghold in southern Africa is in Botswana. The subspecies found over most of the country is *C. r. damarensis*; *C. r. rufigena* occurs in eastern Botswana. **Habitat:** Found in open, arid Kalahari tree and bush savanna. This is a dry-country nightjar and is the only species to penetrate into the Kalahari. **Habits:** Nocturnal aerial insectivore; most active at twilight and on moonlit nights. It roosts among leaf litter on the ground during the day. Monogamous; lays eggs on ground. **Conservation:** Least Concern.

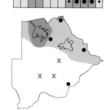

SQUARE-TAILED NIGHTJAR *Caprimulgus fossii*

Setswana: mmamphuphama

25 cm (9 ¾ in). **Identification:** Male has prominent white bars on the upperwing coverts and white tips to the secondaries. The male's wing spots are white and extend across the six main wing feathers; the outer tail feather is white for its full length. These features are buffy in female. *C. f. griseoplurus* is the prevalent subspecies in Botswana; *C. f. welwitschii* is paler **Call:** This nightjar is a churrer. Its continuous churring is similar to that of Rufous-cheeked Nightjar but varies in pitch and speed—as if "changing gear." **Status:** Resident, breeding Part of the population regularly migrates out of Botswana (northward) during the dry season **Abundance:** Common in Ngamiland around the Okavango Delta, and in northern Chobe District. Uncommon elsewhere. The species occurs in Botswana at the southern and western limit of its continental range. *C. f. griseoplurus* covers most of the species's range in Botswana *C. f. welwitschii* may occur in the north of the country. **Habitat:** Occurs in open woodlands associated with water and open, sandy pans. Its range in Botswana corresponds with range of Mopane (*Colophospermum mopane*). **Habits:** Nocturnal aerial insectivore; most active at twilight and on moonlit nights. Monogamous; lays eggs from full moon to last quarter, so the chicks hatch when the next month's moon is waxing. **Conservation:** Least Concern.

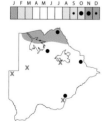

PENNANT-WINGED NIGHTJAR *Caprimulgus vexillarius*

Setswana: mmamphuphama

27 cm (10 ¾ in). **Identification:** Male has two long wing extensions ("pennants"), up to 77 cm (30 ¼ in) long. Both sexes have small head and mottled crown. In flight, female lacks any white spots in wings or tail. **Call:** Cricket-like trill, distinctive among nightjars. **Status:** Intra-African migrant; no breeding records from Botswana. Sightings of this species peak in midsummer. **Abundance:** Scarce; unpredictable in occurrence. **Habitat:** Occurs in broad-leaved woodlands, including Zambezi Teak (*Baikiaea plurijuga*) and Mopane (*Colophospermum mopane*). **Habits:** Nocturnal aerial insectivore, but may be seen during late afternoon. Most active at twilight and on moonlit nights. Roosts on the ground during the day. This species, unique among nightjars, is thought to be polygamous, the male mating with more than one female. Males arrive in Botswana before females and are most vocal and visual at this time. They have a spectacular display flight. **Conservation:** Least Concern.

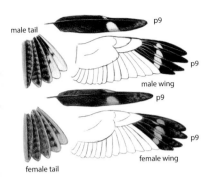

male tail

p9

p9

male wing

p9

p9

female wing

female tail

SWAMP NIGHTJAR
C. n. carpi

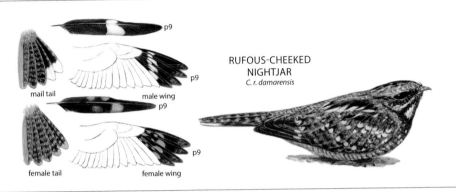

mail tail

p9

male wing

p9

p9

female tail

female wing

p9

RUFOUS-CHEEKED NIGHTJAR
C. r. damarensis

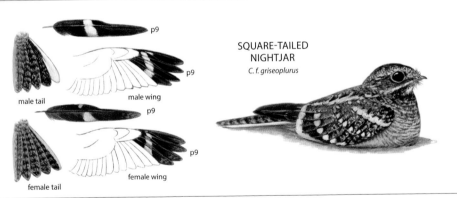

p9

male wing

p9

p9

male tail

female wing

p9

female tail

SQUARE-TAILED NIGHTJAR
C. f. griseoplurus

p9

p9

female wing

female tail

male

female

PENNANT-WINGED NIGHTJAR

201

SWIFTS Apodidae

Diurnal aerial insectivores that have large gapes adapted for catching prey on the wing. Swifts are highly streamlined, fast fliers with scythe-shaped wings. All have black (or dark gray) plumage, and many have white rumps. They have strident twittering calls and build saucer-shaped nests of feathers and other material glued together with their saliva. Nonpasserines, and hence unrelated to swallows and martins (p. 274), they cannot perch but rather cling to vertical surfaces when not flying. Extremely aerial, swifts are never seen on the ground (some species even sleep on the wing). There are nine species in four genera in Botswana; most belong to the genus *Apus*, which means footless and alludes to their highly reduced legs and feet. The Setswana *pêolane*, with minor dialectal spelling variations, is a generic name for swifts as well as for swallows.

BRADFIELD'S SWIFT *Apus bradfieldi*

Setswana: pêolane

18 cm (7 in). **Identification:** Gray-brown swift. Pale edges to breast feathers give underparts a scaled appearance. Primaries and secondaries of underwing are uniformly dark gray. **Call:** High-pitched, shrill scream. **Status:** Visitor; no breeding records from Botswana. **Abundance:** Rare. The core range of this species is in Namibia; it extends marginally into Botswana. **Habitat:** Occurs in rocky habitats in semiarid areas. **Habits:** An aerial insectivore, it forages at height over open country. **Conservation:** Least Concern.

COMMON SWIFT *Apus apus*

Setswana: pêolane

17 cm (6 ¾ in). **Identification:** Plain, nearly uniformly dark-colored swift with pale, off-white throat. May be confused with African Black Swift, but the two differ in call and range. Two sympatric subspecies may be found throughout Botswana: *A. a. apus* has darker plumage and small pale throat, while *A. a. pekinensis* (a rare visitor) is paler oveall and has a prominent white throat. **Call:** Mostly silent. **Status:** Palearctic migrant, nonbreeding. Arrival in October and November is concentrated over a short time period; departure during March and April is more leisurely. **Abundance:** Common to abundant. Large flocks of more than 10,000 individuals may be seen foraging at the approach of, or following, rainstorms, as occurred at Samedupe on the Boteti River in Ngamiland in 1995. In 1980, in South-East District, flocks of 2,000 birds were seen over Lobatse town and of several thousand over Pitsane village. **Habitat:** Occurs over any habitat. **Habits:** Completely aerial when in Botswana; feeds and sleeps in flight. These swifts spend nine months of the year in the air, often above the limits of human vision. **Conservation:** Least Concern.

AFRICAN BLACK SWIFT *Apus barbatus*

Setswana: pêolane

19 cm (7 ½ in). **Identification:** In flight, seen from below, has jet-black plumage and white throat; feathers of underparts have white fringes when fresh. From above, contrastingly paler, more gray-brown-toned inner secondaries and secondary coverts are diagnostic. May be confused with Common Swift, but compare calls and ranges. **Call:** High-pitched, shrill scream. **Status:** Intra-African migrant; no breeding records from Botswana. Sightings from the Kasane area are probably birds from the breeding colony at nearby Victoria Falls. This species is likely to breed in the Tswapong Hills (Central District); peak egg-laying months are likely to be the same as for other parts of the region. **Abundance:** Rare. **Habitat:** Found mainly near cliffs and gorges. **Habits:** An aerial insectivore, it forages at height over open country. Gregarious; occurs in large flocks when breeding, but often only seen in ones or twos in Botswana. **Conservation:** Least Concern.

BRADFIELD'S
SWIFT

COMMON
SWIFT
A. a. apus

fresh
plumage

worn plumage

AFRICAN BLACK
SWIFT

BÖHM'S SPINETAIL *Neafrapus boehmi*

9 cm (3 ½ in). **Identification:** Small swift with white underparts, white rump, and very short tail. **Call:** Mostly silent; soft twittering. **Status:** Vagrant from elsewhere in southeastern Africa; no breeding records from Botswana. **Abundance:** Rare. **Habitat:** Found in Mopane (*Colophospermum mopane*) woodlands with Baobabs (*Adansonia digitata*). **Habits:** Occurs in pairs or small parties; often seen around Baobabs, in which it nests. Flight is bat-like and erratic. **Conservation:** Least Concern.

LITTLE SWIFT *Apus affinis*

Setswana: pêolane

13 cm (5 in). **Identification:** Small swift with square tail, and broad, rectangular white rump extending onto flanks. **Call:** High-pitched, shrill twittering. **Status:** Resident, breeding. The population is supplemented by intra-African migrants, also breeding, the numbers of which peak between September and April. **Abundance:** Common in Southern and South-East Districts and in the eastern hardveld of Central District; uncommon around the Makgadikgadi Pans, Okavango Delta, and northern Chobe District. **Habitat:** Occurs over a wide range of vegetation types, excluding semiarid Kalahari tree and bush savanna. Nests colonially on buildings, on cliffs, and under bridges. **Habits:** Gregarious aerial insectivore; it occurs regularly over water and drinks frequently. **Conservation:** Least Concern.

HORUS SWIFT *Apus horus*

Setswana: pêolane

15 cm (6 in). **Identification:** Swift with a shallow forked tail and a rectangular patch of white on the rump that wraps around the flanks. **Call:** Mostly silent; shrill screams at breeding sites. **Status:** Not well known; apparently an intra-African migrant, but there may be a resident population, since a few sightings occur throughout the year. Breeding: Although there are few Botswana records, egg-laying dates appear to conform with the pattern for the rest of the region, in which egg-laying can take place during any month. **Abundance:** Rare. Its range in southern Africa extends marginally into the northern and eastern parts of Botswana. **Habitat:** Occurs over a range of vegetation types. **Habits:** It nests in abandoned tunnel nests of species such as bee-eaters. **Conservation:** Least Concern.

WHITE-RUMPED SWIFT *Apus caffer*

Setswana: pêolane

16 cm (6 ¼ in). **Identification:** Swift with a deeply forked tail and a narrow white rump. The secondaries have a pale trailing edge, and the throat is white. **Call:** High-pitched, shrill scream. **Status:** Intra-African migrant, breeding. Egg-laying generally takes place between September and April, although there is one late record from May. **Abundance:** Common in the southern part of its range; uncommon elsewhere. **Habitat:** Occurs over a wide range of vegetation types. **Habits:** Prefers to use old nests of Greater and Lesser Striped Swallows minus the entrance tunnel, which it breaks off. **Conservation:** Least Concern.

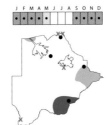

BÖHM'S
SPINETAIL

LITTLE
SWIFT

HORUS
SWIFT

WHITE-RUMPED
SWIFT

205

ALPINE SWIFT *Tachymarptis melba*

Setswana: pêolane

20 cm (7 ¾ in). **Identification:** Large, robust swift, with white throat and white bel[l] separated by gray breast band. Only the subspecies *T. m. africanus*, which has a dark breas[t] band, is found in Botswana. **Call:** High-pitched twittering. **Status:** Intra-African migran[t] breeding. Birds on migration move through Botswana mainly from August to October an[d] again in April and May. **Abundance:** Scarce. **Habitat:** Occurs over a wide range of vegetatio[n] types, excluding Kalahari tree and bush savanna. **Habits:** A powerful flier, it ranges widel[y] Often seen in company of other swifts. Pairs for life. **Conservation:** Least Concern.

AFRICAN PALM SWIFT *Cypsiurus parvus*

Setswana: pêolane

15 cm (6 in). **Identification:** Small, slender swift with long, attenuated wings and ta[il] Plumage is gray-brown. Two subspecies occur in Botswana: *C. p. hyphaenes* is much paler an[d] grayer than *C. p. myochrous*. **Call:** High-pitched, thin twittering. **Status:** Resident, breedin[g] **Abundance:** Abundant around the Okavango Delta (its stronghold in southern Africa) an[d] in Linyanti Swamps; common throughout the rest of its range in Botswana, though les[s] common in South-East District, where it has only been established since 1980. Exotic palm[s] (planted in towns) have enabled it to extend its range. *C. p. hyphaenes* occurs in the norther[n] part of the country, coinciding with the range of *Hyphaene* palms; *C. p. myochrous* is foun[d] in the eastern part. **Habitat:** Found in any habitat with palm trees, whether indigenou[s] or exotic (palm trees are crucial for breeding). **Habits:** Aerial insectivore, active main[ly] at dawn and dusk; it forages in the vicinity of palm trees. Can be seen around heronrie[s] and communal roosts of a variety of birds, collecting down feathers in flight for its nes[t] construction. Nest comprises a few feathers stuck with the bird's saliva onto palm frond[s] eggs are also "glued" to the nest with saliva. **Conservation:** Least Concern.

TROGONS Trogonidae

Colorful, medium-size birds with short, rounded wings and long tails. Their bills are short, and broad at the base. The legs are weak, the feet zygodactyl. Mainly forest dwellers, trogons glean leaves and branches for insects or fruit. One species occurs in Botswana, a beautiful but cryptic arboreal bird that is sexually dimorphic; both sexes have green backs and frequently turn them toward observers, which makes them difficult to spot.

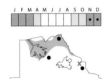

NARINA TROGON *Apaloderma narina*

32 cm (12 ½ in). **Identification:** Cryptic; bottle-green upperparts. Male has green throat and[d] uniformly crimson underparts. Female has cinnamon forehead, throat, and upper breast, grading through pink to crimson belly and undertail. The subspecies *A. n. rufiventris*, in[n] which the female has a deep red belly and undertail, is found in Botswana. **Call:** Ventriloquial hooting. This species calls frequently between September and December, and this is the[e] best way to locate it. **Status:** Intra-African migrant, breeding. The few Botswana egg-laying records indicate that November and December are the most important months. **Abundance:** Scarce. Botswana is at the western extremity of the species's range. The best place to see it is along the Okavango Panhandle downstream from Shakawe village. It is occasionally seen in Kasane Forest Reserve and as far south as Pandamatenga, where seen in 2012; it has not been seen recently in the Linyanti area. **Habitat:** Occurs in dense riparian woodlands. **Habits:** Usually solitary. Perches motionless in the canopy's middle stratum and makes short sallies after invertebrates on the tree foliage. It turns its back on an approaching observer, thereby concealing bright coloring of its underparts. **Conservation:** Least Concern.

**ALPINE
SWIFT**
T. m. africanus

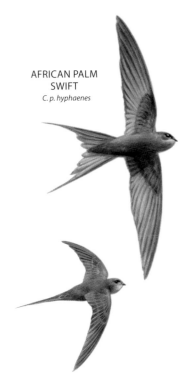

**AFRICAN PALM
SWIFT**
C. p. hyphaenes

male

female

**NARINA
TROGON**
A. n. rufiventris

MOUSEBIRDS Coliidae

An African family of six species, three of which occur in Botswana. Mousebirds superficially resemble mice, not only in coloration and in having long tails, but in the way they clamber through foliage in the manner of rodents. The body feathers are hair-like and do not grow in tracts, creating the impression of fur. Birds are often seen hanging from branches by their flexible feet (rather than perching), sunning themselves to aid digestion of their strictly vegetarian food (leaves and other plant matter). The Setswana *mo.ririmotlhobê* (*mo.ririntlhofê*) is the generic name for mousebirds.

SPECKLED MOUSEBIRD *Colius striatus*

Setswana: mo.ririmotlhobê, mo.ririntlhofê

33 cm (13 in). **Identification:** Frugivorous bird with crested head, soft plumage, and long, stiff tail. Uniformly brown above and below, but black face and bicolor beak (black upper and whitish lower mandible) are distinctive. Juvenile lacks black face and has reverse bill coloration, greenish-white above and black below. The subspecies found in Botswana is *C. s. minor*, which has a dark throat and upper breast. **Call:** Rasping *zeek, zeek*. **Status:** Resident; no breeding records from Botswana. Main egg-laying months probably conform with those of the region. **Abundance:** Uncommon. Botswana is on the western extremity of the species's range in southern Africa. **Habitat:** Found in canopy of fruiting trees in thickets adjacent to dams, wooded drainage lines, and gardens. **Habits:** Clambers about in foliage. Its flight is floppy (unlike direct flight of Red-faced Mousebird), and flock members fly individually in staggered formation. **Conservation:** Least Concern.

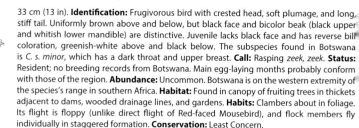

WHITE-BACKED MOUSEBIRD *Colius colius*

Setswana: mo.ririmotlhobê, mo.ririntlhofê

31 cm (12 ¼ in). **Identification:** Predominantly gray mousebird. The white bill tipped with black, and the white lower back, visible in flight, are distinctive. **Call:** Whistled *zee, we-witt*; also chattering *ki-ki-ki-ki*. **Status:** Resident, breeding. **Abundance:** Uncommon, although may be locally common as in the Gaborone area. The species is a southern African endemic. **Habitat:** Found in dry acacia woodlands, particularly along drainage lines; also in gardens. **Habits:** Gregarious. **Conservation:** Least Concern.

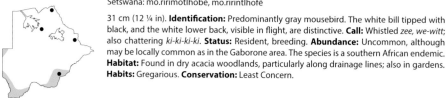

RED-FACED MOUSEBIRD *Urocolius indicus*

Setswana: le.tsiababa, mo.ririmotlhobê, mo.ririntlhofê

32 cm (12 ½ in). **Identification:** Blue-gray mousebird with distinctive red face. Juvenile lacks red face (its bare facial skin is greenish), and its bill is greenish with a dark tip. The subspecies found in Botswana is *U. i. transvaalensis*. **Call:** Whistling *tsia-ba-ba*, often given in flight. The Setswana name *le.tsiababa* is onomatopoeic. **Status:** Resident, breeding. There is one breeding record from June, outside the normal span of egg-laying months. **Abundance:** Common to abundant; this is the most numerous and widespread mousebird in Botswana. **Habitat:** Found in canopy of fruiting trees in riparian woodlands; also acacia woodlands, where it feeds on mistletoe (*Viscum* spp.). **Habits:** Gregarious; small flocks fly in tight formation in strong, direct flight. May form large flocks of 100-plus at roost or when sunning. Forages by clambering in trees. **Conservation:** Least Concern.

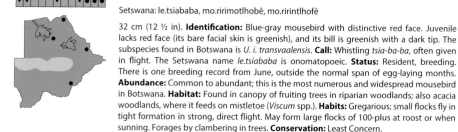

208

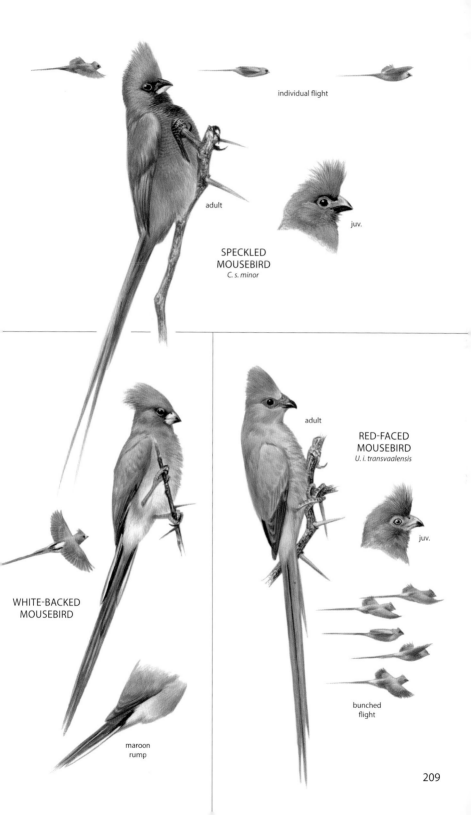

individual flight

adult

SPECKLED
MOUSEBIRD
C. s. minor

juv.

RED-FACED
MOUSEBIRD
U. i. transvaalensis

adult

juv.

WHITE-BACKED
MOUSEBIRD

maroon
rump

bunched
flight

ROLLERS Coraciidae

Members of this family are multicolored, principally in shades of blue and brown. During the breeding season, rollers become very garrulous and perform a spectacular rolling, tumbling, jinking display flight (whence the name "roller"). Five species occur in Botswana, all of which are perch hunters that take a variety of invertebrate and small vertebrate prey items. The Setswana *le.tlêrêtlêrê* and *majêkê* are generic names for rollers.

PURPLE ROLLER *Coracias naevius*

Setswana: le.tlêrêtlêrê, majêkê

33 cm (13 in). **Identification:** Heavily built, largest-bodied roller. It has olive-green upperparts and a dark mauve breast heavily streaked with white. **Call:** Not very vocal; harsh grating cawing calls during display. **Status:** Resident, breeding. **Abundance:** Uncommon to common. **Habitat:** Occurs in a variety of woodland types, including both broad-leaved and acacia woodlands. **Habits:** Solitary or in pairs. Hunts from perch, diving down to catch prey on the ground. It has a spectacular rocking display flight. **Conservation:** Least Concern

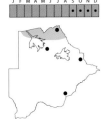

RACKET-TAILED ROLLER *Coracias spatulatus*

Setswana: le.tlêrêtlêrê, majêkê

37 cm (14½ in), incl. tail streamers. **Identification:** Slender, elongate roller. It is predominantly blue, and appears bluer overall than Lilac-breasted Roller. In adult (both sexes), long tail streamers with spatulate ends are diagnostic when present (they are molted during winter). Immature lacks tail streamers, but has deep blue primary wing coverts. **Call:** Usually silent; harsh *chow* and *cheer* calls during courtship display. **Status:** Resident, breeding. **Abundance:** Scarce. Botswana is on the southwestern edge of the species's range. The best place to see it is in the wooded swath from Kasane and Kazuma Forest Reserves across to the Chobe Forest Reserve and Goha Gate in Chobe National Park. **Habitat:** Found in mature, dense Mopane (*Colophospermum mopane*) and Zambezi Teak (*Baikiaea plurijuga*) woodlands. **Habits:** Most often seen in pairs and small family groups. It usually perches below the canopy, and is much more discreet than Lilac-breasted Roller. Flight is undulating. In breeding season it performs the characteristic zigzagging roller display, flying up and dropping with closed wings. **Conservation:** Least Concern.

LILAC-BREASTED ROLLER *Coracias caudatus*

Setswana: le.tlêrêtlêrê, majêkê

36 cm (14½ in), incl. tail streamers. **Identification:** Medium-size roller with overall pinkish appearance. It is the only roller with lilac throat and breast. Its long outer tail feathers have pointed rather than spatulate ends (compare Racket-tailed Roller). **Call:** Mostly silent; series of harsh *ghaak, ghaak* calls during display. **Status:** Resident, breeding. It can have two broods per season. **Abundance:** Abundant. One of Botswana's most abundant and widespread species. **Habitat:** Occurs in a variety of open woodlands (both broad-leaved and acacia); prefers ecotone between woodland and open grassland. **Habits:** Solitary or in pairs. It has a spectacular breeding display: calling loudly, it flies high and then dives down twisting from side to side, looping up periodically into a steep stall before diving down again. **Conservation:** Least Concern.

EUROPEAN ROLLER *Coracias garrulus*

Setswana: le.tlêrêtlêrê, majêkê

31 cm (12¼ in). **Identification:** Large, stocky roller. Appears blue overall. Combination of square tail and blue head and breast is diagnostic. Subspecies *C. g. garrulus* has "clean" blue plumage, while *C. g. semenowi* has a green or brown wash to the plumage and looks "dirty." **Call:** Mostly silent in Botswana. **Status:** Palearctic migrant, nonbreeding. **Abundance:** Scarce. *C. g. garrulus* (which breeds in Europe) is widespread throughout Botswana; *C. g. semenowi* (which breeds in the Middle East region) may be seen in the eastern half of the country. **Habitat:** Tolerates wide range of habitats; found in a variety of open woodlands. **Habits:** Migrates in large flocks; these are conspicuous just after arrival and preceding departure. Seen in small loose groups during remainder of summer. Perch hunts. It has a loose, floppy-winged flight that is diagnostic among rollers. **Conservation:** Near Threatened

PURPLE
ROLLER

RACKET-TAILED
ROLLER

LILAC-BREASTED
ROLLER

EUROPEAN ROLLER
C. g. garrulus

211

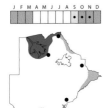

BROAD-BILLED ROLLER *Eurystomus glaucurus*

Setswana: le.tlêrêtlêrê, majêkê

29 cm (11 ½ in). **Identification:** Small, dark-plumaged roller. It is the only roller with a bright yellow bill. It has cinnamon-brown upperparts and purple underparts. Only one subspecies occurs in Botswana, *E. g. suahelicus*. **Call:** Noisy during breeding; harsh cawing call. **Status:** Intra-African migrant, breeding. **Abundance:** Uncommon to common. The Okavango Delta is its principal wintering ground in southern Africa. **Habitat:** Found in tall, mature riparian and other moist woodlands. **Habits:** Solitary or in pairs. The birds' arrival is highly synchronized over a short period in early October, and breeding commences immediately. **Conservation:** Least Concern.

KINGFISHERS Alcedinidae

Kingfishers are generally small, robust birds with disproportionally long, dagger-like bills. They mostly perch hunt for fish or insects. Nine species occur in Botswana. For identification purposes, they can be divided into two groups: four aquatic species, which are all piscivorous and nest in tunnels in the ground; and five dryland species, which are insectivorous and breed in tunnels in the ground, except Woodland and Striped Kingfishers, which utilize tree holes or cavities. The fish-eaters are all resident; the insect-eaters are a combination of resident species and intra-African migrants. The Setswana *se.inwêdi* is a generic name for kingfishers; the fish-eating species are also known as *se.tshwaraditlhapi* (which means "catcher of fishes").

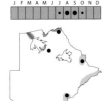

GIANT KINGFISHER *Megaceryle maxima*

Setswana: se.inwêdi, se.tshwaraditlhapi

M: 42 cm (16 ½ in), F: 46 cm (18 in). **Identification:** Largest kingfisher in Botswana; aquatic. Adult of both sexes has black upperparts heavily spotted with white. Sex can be determined by underside coloring, especially in flight: Male has chestnut breast, white belly, and white underwing coverts. Female has white throat and breast streaked with black, chestnut belly, and chestnut underwing coverts. **Call:** Loud, ringing *kahk-kahk-kahk*, mixed with rapid trilling *kakakakak*. **Status:** Resident, breeding. **Abundance:** Common along the Okavango, Linyanti, and Chobe Rivers (surprisingly scarce in the alluvial fan of the Okavango Delta). It extends its range to the lower Boro, Thamalakane, Kunyere, and N'habe Rivers during periods of high flooding. Scarce to uncommon in the east and southeast. **Habitat:** Freshwater wetlands; frequents rivers and tree-lined channels, and will visit small ponds nearby. **Habits:** Solitary or in pairs. Occasionally hovers when fishing, but prefers perch hunting. Nesting takes place along the Okavango and Chobe Rivers when the water level is low and banks are exposed. **Conservation:** Least Concern.

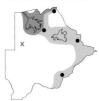

PIED KINGFISHER *Ceryle rudis*

Setswana: se.inwêdi, se.tshwaraditlhapi

25 cm (9 ¾ in). **Identification:** Second largest kingfisher in Botswana; aquatic. Both sexes have black-and-white plumage. Male has double breast band; female has only upper band. **Call:** Noisy, twittering *kwit, kwit, kwit-kwit, kwit*. **Status:** Resident, breeding. Egg-laying in the Okavango wetland system peaks in May and June, dictated by the annual floods; this is out of synchrony with that in the rest of southern Africa, where the main laying months are August to November. **Abundance:** Abundant. The Okavango wetland system is a center of abundance in southern Africa. **Habitat:** Freshwater wetlands; exploits almost any body of water with fish, even ephemeral pans. **Habits:** Occurs in pairs or small groups; may roost, and sometimes breed, gregariously. This species perch hunts but also by hovering above the water; it hover fishes more habitually than any other kingfisher. In the northern wetlands, nesting is synchronized with flooding which is unseasonal; hence the late summer to midwinter peak. May breed colonially. **Conservation:** Least Concern.

**BROAD-BILLED
ROLLER**
E. g. suahelicus

male

female

**GIANT
KINGFISHER**

male

female

hovering

**PIED
KINGFISHER**

213

MALACHITE KINGFISHER *Corythornis cristatus*

Setswana: se.inwêdi, se.tshwaraditlhapi

14 cm (5 ½ in). **Identification:** Diminutive aquatic kingfisher. Adult has barred turquoise and-black crested crown and orange cheeks, the combination of which is diagnostic. Bill red. Juvenile has black bill and feet, which change with age to red (feet first); these and the orange cheeks distinguish it from the slightly larger Half-collared Kingfisher, which has blue cheeks an red legs and feet. African Pygmy Kingfisher is distinguished by orange supercilium and viole ear coverts. Two subspecies of Malachite Kingfisher occur in Botswana: *C. c. longirostris* ha orange-buff on underparts with white on the belly extending to the chest, while *C. c. cristatus* i all orange-buff below. **Call:** Sharp *peep-peep*, given as bird flies off. **Status:** Resident, breeding **Abundance:** Common to abundant. *C. c. cristatus* is found in the eastern part of the countr along the Limpopo River, where it is scarce to common; *C. c. longirostris* is abundant in the Okavango wetland system, Linyanti Swamps, and along the Chobe River. **Habitat:** Freshwate wetlands; prefers reed-lined standing water. **Habits:** Usually solitary. Perch hunts from lov reed. Breeds when water levels in the northern wetlands are low and banks are exposed **Conservation:** Least Concern.

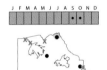

HALF-COLLARED KINGFISHER *Alcedo semitorquata*

Setswana: se.inwêdi, se.tshwaraditlhapi

18 cm (7 in). **Identification:** Small, predominantly blue aquatic kingfisher. Combination c black bill, blue cheeks, and red legs and feet is diagnostic. Female has reddish base to lowe mandible. Juvenile Malachite Kingfisher has a black bill and is sometimes mistaken for th species, but has orange cheeks and black legs and feet. **Call:** Not very vocal; soft *tseep-tseep* **Status:** Resident, breeding. **Abundance:** Rare (rarest kingfisher in Botswana), except alon the Chobe River at the Kasane Rapids, where it is uncommon but seen regularly. In recer years it has been absent from the upper and middle Limpopo River and from the Okavang Delta, where previously recorded; also absent from the southeast, where last seen in mi to late 1970s. **Habitat:** Freshwater wetlands; favors fast-flowing wooded rivers, often nea rapids. **Habits:** Solitary. Perch hunts from low spot, often from exposed roots. All breedin records to date are from the Chobe River, where egg-laying takes place when the water i low and banks are exposed. **Conservation:** Least Concern.

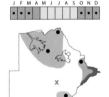

AFRICAN PYGMY KINGFISHER *Ispidina picta*

Setswana: se.inwêdi

13 cm (5 in). **Identification:** Diminutive dryland kingfisher. The combination of orang supercilium and violet ear coverts is diagnostic. It further differs from Malachite Kingfishe in lacking a crest. Juvenile has pale plumage and black bill. **Call:** High-pitched *tseep-tseep tseep*. **Status:** Intra-African migrant; no breeding records from Botswana. The specie almost certainly breeds in eastern and northeastern Botswana (Tuli Block and Francistow area) as birds have been netted with mud on their bills (from excavating nest tunnel and there are breeding records from adjacent areas of South Africa and Zimbabwe. Sma numbers are also recorded in Botswana from May to July; these may be birds at the end c the northward passage from South Africa, which commences in late February. **Abundance** Scarce. It could be recorded anywhere in the northern part of Botswana, but is unlikely t be seen here as it migrates through at night; its destination within the country is easter Botswana, where birds spend the summer. **Habitat:** Prefers woodlands. During migratio it can occur in almost any habitat (e.g., there have been sightings in Central Kalahari Gam Reserve). **Habits:** Individuals passing through northern Botswana are often recorded afte collisions with buildings in the darkness. This kingfisher nests in tunnels in riverbanks or i the sides of Aardvark burrows. **Conservation:** Least Concern.

adult

crest
raised

juv.

**MALACHITE
KINGFISHER**
C. c. longirostris

adult
male

juv.

adult
female

**HALF-COLLARED
KINGFISHER**

adult

juv.

**AFRICAN PYGMY
KINGFISHER**

STRIPED KINGFISHER *Halcyon chelicuti*

Setswana: se.inwêdi

18 cm (7 in). **Identification:** Small dryland kingfisher with red-and-black bill. Distinctive white collar encircles neck. Smaller than Brown-hooded Kingfisher. Occasional leucistic (pale-pigmented) individuals have been recorded in the Okavango Delta. **Call:** Pair calls antiphonally: *keep-kirrrr*. Territorial call is a ringing trill, similar to an old-fashioned telephone ring: *tirrrrr, deeooo-deeooo-deeooo*. **Status:** Resident, breeding. **Abundance:** Common to scarce. **Habitat:** Found in open woodlands, both broad-leaved and acacia. Favors tall, riparian trees. **Habits:** Solitary or in pairs. Insectivorous. Pairs perform wing-opening display, usually accompanied by calling. Nests in tree holes, preferring those excavated by Black-collared Barbet. **Conservation:** Least Concern.

BROWN-HOODED KINGFISHER *Halcyon albiventris*

Setswana: se.inwêdi

H. a. orientalis: 20 cm (7 ¾ in); *H. a. vociferans:* 22 cm (8 ¾ in). **Identification:** Medium-size dryland kingfisher. Adult has red bill, brown head streaked with black, and sides of breast and flanks streaked brownish. Male has black mantle and wing coverts; female and juvenile have dark brown. Two subspecies occur: *H. a. orientalis* is noticeably smaller than *H. a. vociferans.* Occasional leucistic (pale-pigmented) individuals have been recorded. **Call:** Whistle, rendered as *pity-for-you*; also a strident *chee-chee-chee-chee.* **Status:** Resident, breeding. **Abundance:** Common in the eastern hardveld; absent from areas of Kalahari tree and bush savanna. Rare in the Okavango Delta. *H. a. orientalis* is found around the Okavango Delta and in northern Chobe District; *H. a. vociferans* occurs in the eastern parts of the country from North-East District south to South-East District. **Habitat:** Found in moist woodlands, including riparian; gardens. **Habits:** Usually solitary or in pairs. Insectivorous. Although a dryland kingfisher, it nests in a tunnel excavated in earth bank, not necessarily near water. **Conservation:** Least Concern.

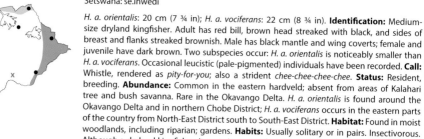

WOODLAND KINGFISHER *Halcyon senegalensis*

Setswana: se.inwêdi, nonyane yapula

23 cm (9 in). **Identification:** Medium-size, dryland kingfisher. Red-and-black bill coupled with black legs distinguishes adult from all other kingfishers. However, adults with completely red bills have been recorded repeatedly. Juvenile has predominantly black bill; upper mandible progressively turns red. **Call:** Loud *chip-chirrrrrrr*, repeated from early morning until well into the night. **Status:** Intra-African migrant, breeding. **Abundance:** Common. **Habitat:** Found primarily in riparian woodlands and Mopane (*Colophospermum mopane*) woodlands **Habits:** Perch hunts, catching insects on the ground. Performs wing-opening display, often while calling. Males call from near prospective nesting holes in trees on arrival in October. Maintains long-term pair bond, although mates overwinter in separate localities in north-central Africa. **Conservation:** Least Concern. **General:** The species's name has changed from Woodland Kingfisher to Red-and-black-billed Kingfisher to Angola Kingfisher and back to Woodland.

GREY-HEADED KINGFISHER *Halcyon leucocephala*

Setswana: se.inwêdi

21 cm (8 ¼ in). **Identification:** Relatively small dryland kingfisher with an all-red bill. Grayish head and breast and chestnut belly are distinctive. **Call:** Weak, chattering trill, *chee-che-che-che.* **Status:** The Botswana population consists of both breeding intra-African migrants and a greater number of nonbreeding intra-African migrants. Breeding takes place before the majority of nonbreeding visitors arrives. **Abundance:** Scarce. In wet years, birds occur in greater numbers and extend farther southward in Botswana. **Habitat:** Found in tall, mature woodlands, both broad-leaved and acacia. **Habits:** Solitary or in pairs. Insectivorous. Breeds in terrestrial burrow, where it sometimes serves as host to Greater Honeyguide, a brood parasite. It is a nocturnal migrant. **Conservation:** Least Concern.

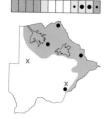

STRIPED
KINGFISHER

pair bond
display

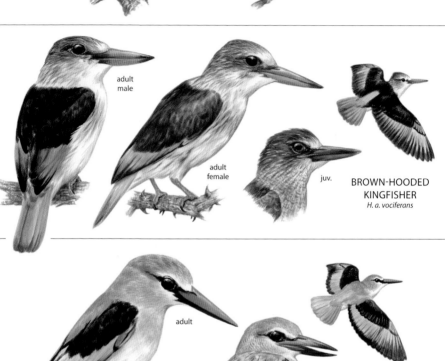

adult
male

adult
female

juv.

BROWN-HOODED
KINGFISHER
H. a. vociferans

adult

juv.

WOODLAND
KINGFISHER

GREY-HEADED
KINGFISHER

217

BEE-EATERS Meropidae

A family of slender, lively, aerial insectivores. They have brightly colored plumage; long, pointed wings; sharp, slightly decurved bills; and small, weak legs and feet. True to their name, they eat mainly species of the order Hymenoptera (wasps and bees). All nest in tunnels in the ground. Only one genus, *Merops* (which means "bee-eater") occurs in Botswana, represented by seven morphologically and ecologically similar species. However, the genus is diverse in terms of survival strategies, and Botswana hosts both resident and migrant (intra-African or Palearctic) populations, both breeding (solitary or colonial) and nonbreeding. The Setswana *se.sêlamarumô* is the generic name for bee-eaters, while *morôkapula* applies mainly to the migratory bee-eaters and recognizes them as harbingers of rain.

SOUTHERN CARMINE BEE-EATER *Merops nubicoides*

Setswana: morôkapula, se.sêlamarumô

35 cm (13 ¾ in), incl. tail streamers. **Identification:** Pink and red adult unmistakable. Pink throat becomes very pronounced in breeding bird. Juvenile has pink or pale bluish throat, brown wings, and a pinkish breast suffused with pale blue. **Call:** Melodious *turk, turk*. **Status:** Intra-African migrant, breeding. The species is present mainly from September to March, but it is nomadic following breeding, and sightings are possible in every month of the year. **Abundance:** Common to abundant throughout the Okavango wetland system, Linyanti Swamps, and Chobe River floodplains, which are the southern African strongholds for this species; it is also common in eastern Botswana. There are large and important breeding colonies in the banks of the Okavango River along the panhandle at Mohembo, Shakawe, and Red Cliffs. There are also large colonies in flat ground in the Kwando-Linyanti area; the colony in flat ground at Xakanaxa in Moremi Game Reserve is currently abandoned following high flooding. **Habitat:** Occurs in open woodlands and floodplains. **Habits:** Birds start breeding when the northern rivers are low and banks are exposed for their tunnel nests. Post-breeding, the birds disperse from the Okavango, Chobe, and Linyanti wetlands during summer and then appear in the southeast between January and March. May be seen hawking insects in flight low over open habitats. Occasionally the species is associated with mammalian herbivores, which disturb insects, and has the unique habit of using Kori Bustard as mobile perch at Savute Marsh and the Selinda Spillway. It will also follow vehicles if they flush insects. **Conservation:** Least Concern.

WHITE-FRONTED BEE-EATER *Merops bullockoides*

Setswana: se.sêlamarumô

23 cm (9 in). **Identification:** Predominantly green bee-eater. Combination of white forehead and cheek stripe and red throat is diagnostic. It lacks tail streamers and has more rounded wings in flight than the migratory bee-eaters. **Call:** Nasal *naaauuu*. **Status:** Resident, breeding. **Abundance:** Common to abundant. **Habitat:** Prefers large rivers in broad-leaved woodlands and wooded grasslands. Visitor in southeast (3-4 records) probably from Limpopo River. **Habits:** Gregarious; nests colonially in vertical, sandy riverbanks. Breeding groups form large, relatively stable clans. They commence breeding during July when riverbanks are exposed. The species is a cooperative breeder; the use of helpers increases chick survival. **Conservation:** Least Concern.

EUROPEAN BEE-EATER *Merops apiaster*

Setswana: morôkapula, se.sêlamarumô

25 cm (9 ¾ in), incl. tail streamers. **Identification:** Brown upperparts and blue underparts make this migratory bee-eater distinctive. Immature has pale plumage and could be mistaken for Blue-cheeked Bee-eater (p. 220) at a distance. **Call:** Liquid *quirk, quirk, quirrikirk*, given in flight. **Status:** Palearctic migrant; no breeding records from Botswana, although there is a breeding population in South Africa. Its arrival in Botswana in spring coincides with the coming of rain. **Abundance:** Common. **Habitat:** Found in a variety of woodlands, excluding the arid scrub savanna of Kgalagadi District. **Habits:** Aerial insectivore; forages in small, loose flocks a few hundred meters above the ground as it migrates throughout Botswana. The melodious, bell-like call is often the first indication of its presence. **Conservation:** Least Concern.

breeding
adult

juv.

**SOUTHERN
CARMINE BEE-EATER**

**WHITE-FRONTED
BEE-EATER**

nonbreeding

breeding

**EUROPEAN
BEE-EATER**

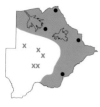

LITTLE BEE-EATER *Merops pusillus*

Setswana: se.sêlamarumô

16 cm (6 ¼ in). **Identification:** Diminutive, mainly green bee-eater. Combination of square tail and ocher underparts with black breast band is diagnostic, especially in conjunction with size and overall color. Only one subspecies is found throughout Botswana, *M. p. argutus* (originally described from a specimen collected at the Nata River). **Call:** Soft *tree-tree-tree.* **Status:** Resident, breeding. **Abundance:** Common to abundant. **Habitat:** Found in open woodlands with low bushes and shrubs; also in the Okavango and Chobe areas, in reeds and papyrus along rivers and lagoons. **Habits:** Occurs in small groups. An aerial insectivore, it hunts from a low perch, catching insects in flight after a short sally. Groups may roost shoulder to shoulder at night. **Conservation:** Least Concern.

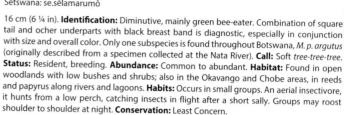

SWALLOW-TAILED BEE-EATER *Merops hirundineus*

Setswana: se.sêlamarumô

21 cm (8 ¼ in). **Identification:** Small bee-eater, predominantly green above and below. Long, metallic-blue tail with distinct fork at end is diagnostic. Only the subspecies *M. h. hirundineus* is found in Botswana. Similar Little Bee-eater has a short tail and ocher underparts. **Call:** Soft *kweep kweep.* **Status:** Resident (however, part of the population is thought to be migratory), breeding. **Abundance:** Common throughout its range in Botswana, except in the east where it is replaced by Little Bee-eater. It is a characteristic bird of the Kalahari. **Habitat:** Found in a variety of habitats including Kalahari tree and bush savanna. **Habits:** Solitary or in pairs, but may roost in groups on winter nights and huddle together on cold mornings. Hawks insects in the tree canopy, up to 20 m above the ground, and thereby avoids competing with Little Bee-eater, which forages lower. **Conservation:** Least Concern.

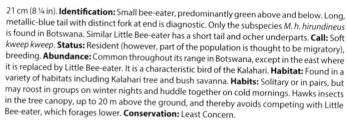

OLIVE BEE-EATER *Merops superciliosus*

Setswana: morôkapula, se.sêlamarumô

30 cm (11 ¾ in), incl. tail streamers. **Identification:** Large, predominantly green bee-eater. Adult is distinctive with its dark olive-brown cap, russet throat, and long tail streamers. Some birds show blue cheeks and a pale yellow throat and may be confused with immature Blue-cheeked Bee-eater, which has a green crown. The subspecies found in Botswana is *M. s. superciliosus.* **Call:** High-pitched, repeated *twip, twip.* **Status:** Vagrant from coastal Mozambique; no breeding records from Botswana. **Abundance:** Rare. Accepted records to date are only from Kasane. **Habitat:** Uses woodlands adjacent to large rivers. **Habits:** Gregarious. Hawks insects from a high perch, often a dead tree. **Conservation:** Least Concern.

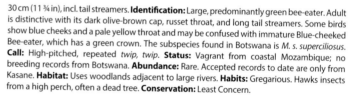
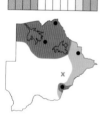

BLUE-CHEEKED BEE-EATER *Merops persicus*

Setswana: morôkapula, se.sêlamarumô

32 cm (12 ½ in), incl. tail streamers. **Identification:** Large, predominantly green bee-eater. The green crown is its only consistent identification feature but is diagnostic in conjunction with the bird's size. Facial colors become abraded and are not reliable field characteristics. Immature, which is paler than adult, may be mistaken for rare Olive Bee-eater, recorded only in the Kasane area. **Call:** Musical, repeated *prreeoo.* **Status:** Palearctic migrant, nonbreeding. The birds' influx into Botswana in spring coincides with the arrival of rain fronts. **Abundance:** Common. Its strongholds in southern Africa are the Okavango Delta and Makgadikgadi Pans. In eastern and southeastern Botswana, it may be seen from October to April. **Habitat:** Prefers woodlands near water. **Habits:** Gregarious. An aerial predator that specializes in catching dragonflies, it forages at altitude when on migration passage, and perches on low bushes to spot prey during summer. **Conservation:** Least Concern.

LITTLE BEE-EATER
M. p. argutus

adult

juv.

SWALLOW-TAILED BEE-EATER
M. h. hirundineus

adult

juv.

OLIVE BEE-EATER
M. s. superciliosus

BLUE-CHEEKED BEE-EATER

adult

imm.

HOOPOES Upupidae

Hoopoes have buff, black, and white plumage, a fan-like crest, decurved bill, and short legs. There is slight color dimorphism between the sexes. The birds have erratic, undulating, buoyant flight. They are mainly terrestrial feeders, but nest in tree holes and other cavities, which become fouled with feces, since chicks void them within the nest. In addition, nestlings and female produce a pungent-smelling secretion from the enlarged preen gland, thought to be a predator deterrent. This monogeneric family has a single species in Botswana, African Hoopoe, which was previously considered a subspecies of Eurasian Hoopoe.

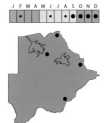

AFRICAN HOOPOE *Upupa africana*

Setswana: mmadilêpê, pupupu, pêtlô, nyônywane yamahuphu, le.rênkêtê

26 cm (10 ¼ in). **Identification:** Russet, black, and white plumage. Erectile crest is frequently and conspicuously flared. Male has more white in wings (visible at rest or in flight) and is generally more rufous-toned than female and immature. **Call:** Bi- or trisyllabic *hoop-hoop[-hoop]*. The names hoopoe, *Upupa*, and the Setswana *pupupu* are onomatopoeic. Gives noisy *cherrr* at nest when feeding mate or chicks. **Status:** Resident, breeding. An intra-African migratory population, also breeding, supplements resident numbers in summer. **Abundance:** Common. **Habitat:** Found in a variety of habitats, including Kalahari tree and bush savanna. **Habits:** Forages solitarily or in pairs on bare ground or short grass, probing with decurved beak for insects and their larvae. It may be seen in tree canopy when nesting, as it is a cavity nester. It is a host to the brood parasite Greater Honeyguide. **Conservation:** Least Concern.

WOOD HOOPOES Phoeniculidae

A family of elongate, slender birds that have iridescent dark plumage and decurved bills for probing in cracks and crevices for invertebrate food. They nest in natural tree cavities, which become foul smelling from lack of nest hygiene and smelly secretions from the preen gland. The family is endemic to Africa. Two species occur in Botswana; they have dissimilar calls and different breeding systems. (The family is sometimes split into two based on these differences.)

GREEN WOOD HOOPOE *Phoeniculus purpureus*

Setswana: le.tshêga-nôga

33 cm (13 in). **Identification:** Long, slender bird with decurved red bill. Dark plumage has iridescent green sheen. White spots in tail are conspicuous in flight. Male has longer (by a third), more curved bill than female. Immature has black bill; however, it is not as decurved as black bill of Common Scimitarbill. Only one subspecies is found in Botswana, *P. p. angolensis*. **Call:** Loud cackling, given by one or more flock members; similar to call of babblers. **Status:** Resident, breeding. **Abundance** Common in Ngamiland, Chobe, and North-East Districts, and in eastern Central District south to Kgatleng and South-East Districts. Uncommon elsewhere in its range. **Habitat:** Favors mature broad-leaved woodlands, including Mopane (*Colophospermum mopane*), but also found in acacia woodlands with large trees such as Camel Thorn (*Acacia erioloba*). **Habits:** Arboreal. Occurs in flocks, which are territorial; clashes between neighbors include bowing displays and loud group vocalizations. A cooperative breeder; only the dominant pair breeds, and the whole flock assists with feeding the female and nestlings. **Conservation:** Least Concern. **General:** The genus name *Phoeniculus* means "scarlet bill." The Setswana *le.tshêga-nôga* (literally, "laugher at snake") refers to laugh-like call.

COMMON SCIMITARBILL *Rhinopomastus cyanomelas*

Setswana: sebôdu

26 cm (10 ¼ in). **Identification:** Small, slender wood hoopoe with a strongly decurved black bill. Both sexes have small white spots in tail. Male otherwise uniformly dark blue (iridescent in certain light). Female and immature have brown face and throat (extending onto breast). Juvenile frequently has white, fleshy gape. Two subspecies occur, *R. c. cyanomelas* and *R. c. schalowi*, adults of which have differing arrangements of white spots on wings and tail. **Call:** High-pitched, whistled *sweep, sweep, sweep*. **Status:** Resident, breeding. **Abundance:** Uncommon to common. *R. c. cyanomelas* is widespread throughout Botswana; *R. c. schalowi* may occur in northern Chobe District. **Habitat:** Found in a variety of habitats, including arid Kalahari tree and bush savanna and mixed woodland and scrub. **Habits:** Solitary or in pairs. Forages in tree canopy, probing into small crevices. The species is monogamous and nests in cavities. **Conservation:** Least Concern. **General:** The Setswana name refers to the bird's unpleasant smell.

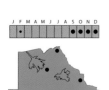

adult

male wing

female

AFRICAN HOOPOE

adult

juv.

adult

GREEN WOOD HOOPOE
P. p. angolensis

male

female

male

COMMON SCIMITARBILL
R. c. cyanomelas

223

HORNBILLS Bucerotidae

A fairly uniform group of birds that have robust, decurved bills (males often have an ornamental casque), long tails, short legs, and flap-and-glide, undulating flight. Six species are found in Botswana, all of which exhibit the family's unique breeding behavior: The female seals herself into a tree-cavity nesting hole, molts her flight feathers, incubates eggs, and broods young, while provisioned by the male. This nesting behavior is the basis for a Setswana proverb, *Kôrwê ke bapala tsetse*, "the male (hornbill) fends for the nursing mother." The *Tockus* species give either clucking calls, uttered with head down, or piping whistles issued with the head pointing upward; the *Bycanistes* hornbill has a loud braying, trumpeting call. The Setswana *kôrwê* and *kôrô* are generic names for hornbills.

SOUTHERN YELLOW-BILLED HORNBILL *Tockus leucomelas*

Setswana: kôrwê, kôrô

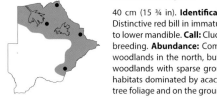

50 cm (19 ¾ in). **Identification:** Small gray hornbill with white spots on wing coverts. Large yellow beak, diagnostic in both sexes (that of male is larger) and immature. Bare pink skin around eye is also distinctive. Only one subspecies, *T. l. leucomelas*, is found in Botswana. **Call:** Clucking *kok, kok, kok*, given with head down and wings raised. **Status:** Resident breeding. **Abundance:** Common. One of Botswana's most abundant and widespread species. **Habitat:** Found in dry, open woodlands, both broad-leaved (especially Mopane, *Colophospermum mopane*) and acacia. **Habits:** Occurs in pairs or small family groups; feeds on the ground. Studies of breeding birds have shown that weak chicks may be eaten by the female or fed to siblings, before or after they die. **Conservation:** Least Concern.

SOUTHERN RED-BILLED HORNBILL *Tockus rufirostris*

Setswana: kôrwê, kôrô

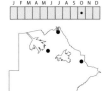

40 cm (15 ¾ in). **Identification:** Small, gray hornbill with white spots on wing coverts. Distinctive red bill in immature and adult. Male bill is slightly longer, and has blackish base to lower mandible. **Call:** Clucking *kok, kok, kok*, given with the head down. **Status:** Resident breeding. **Abundance:** Common. **Habitat:** Found in Mopane (*Colophospermum mopane*) woodlands in the north, but occurs in other broad-leaved woodlands in the east; prefers woodlands with sparse ground cover. Avoids Kalahari tree and bush savanna and other habitats dominated by acacia. **Habits:** Occurs in pairs and small family parties. Forages in tree foliage and on the ground for insects. **Conservation:** Least Concern.

CROWNED HORNBILL *Tockus alboterminatus*

Setswana: kôrwê, kôrô

52 cm (20 ½ in). **Identification:** Medium-size hornbill with dark brown upperparts and throat and white lower breast and belly. Bill red with yellow base; that of male has distinct casque, which differentiates it from closely related Bradfield's Hornbill. Plumage is overall darker than Bradfield's, and the two birds are largely allopatric. **Call:** High-pitched whistle, very similar to that of Bradfield's Hornbill, uttered with bill pointed upward. **Status:** Resident, breeding. The limited breeding information from Botswana generally concurs with the timing of egg laying elsewhere in southern Africa. **Abundance:** Rare. The species's range just extends into Botswana, in northern Chobe District, where it bred in Kazungula, near Kasane town, for several consecutive years from 2004 to 2013. **Habitat:** A forest-edge species, in Botswana found only in riparian woodlands along the Chobe River. **Habits:** Arboreal; pairs or family parties forage for fruit among foliage of riverside trees. **Conservation:** Least Concern.

BRADFIELD'S HORNBILL *Tockus bradfieldi*

Setswana: kôrwê, kôrô

54 cm (21 ¼ in). **Identification:** Medium-size hornbill with gray-brown head and brown upperparts. Bill orange; male has slightly larger casque than female (though it is smaller than that of Crowned Hornbill). **Call:** High-pitched whistle, very similar to that of Crowned Hornbill, uttered with bill pointed upward. **Status:** Resident, breeding. There are very few Botswana breeding records. Birds move locally, and there is an influx of birds during winter. **Abundance:** Locally common. This is a range-restricted species virtually confined to northern Botswana and northeastern Namibia. Savute in Chobe National Park is a good place to see it. **Habitat:** Catholic in habitat use; found in broad-leaved, acacia, and mixed woodlands. **Habits:** Occurs in pairs and small family parties. Forages in trees during summer when fruit is readily available; forages on ground during dry season for invertebrates and reptiles. **Conservation:** Least Concern.

SOUTHERN
YELLOW-BILLED
HORNBILL
T. l. leucomelas

male
display

SOUTHERN
RED-BILLED
HORNBILL

CROWNED
HORNBILL

BRADFIELD'S
HORNBILL

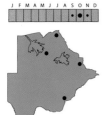

AFRICAN GREY HORNBILL *Tockus nasutus*

Setswana: kôrwê, kôrô, kôrômodimo, kôrwêmodimo, kôrwê-badimo, kôrwê-modingwar kôrômosi

46 cm (18 in). **Identification:** Small gray hornbill. Male has large black casque extending within 2 cm of bill tip; lower edge of upper mandible is yellow, creating a longitudinal stri along each side of beak. Female's upper mandible, including small casque, is ivory yello except the tip, which is red (lower mandible is also red-tipped). Immature has small casqu **Call:** Piping whistle, *peee, peeepee, peeepee*, repeated, given with bill pointed skywar wings are flicked open with each note. **Status:** Resident, breeding. Egg-laying commenc after the first rains. **Abundance:** Common. **Habitat:** Prefers tall, mature, mixed woodlan (including riparian) but during dry season may be found in less well-wooded habita **Habits:** Usually solitary or in pairs, occasionally loose flocks. Flies with exaggerated wir flaps, alternating with dipping glide, before landing clumsily. Primarily a canopy feeder, makes short sallies from perch to pursue prey of invertebrates and small vertebrates b may also forage for fallen fruit by hopping on the ground. **Conservation:** Least Concern.

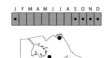

TRUMPETER HORNBILL *Bycanistes bucinator*

Setswana: kôrwê, kôrô

58 cm (22 ¾ in). **Identification:** Large, black-and-white hornbill. Male has large gr casque that extends to the end of the bill. Female's casque is half the bill length. **Ca** Loud, distinctive braying or child-like wailing, repeated several times. **Status:** Resident; breeding records from Botswana. **Abundance:** Scarce, but seen regularly throughout yea The species's presence in Botswana, around the Chobe River, is at the western extrem of its range. **Habitat:** Favors riparian woodlands. **Habits:** Pairs and small groups of up five forage in tree canopy for fruits. Up to 12 birds regularly roost in the Baobab (*Adansor digitata*) at Mowana Safari Lodge in Kasane town. **Conservation:** Least Concern.

GROUND HORNBILLS Bucorvidae

Endemic African family with one genus (*Bucorvus*, which means "huge crow") of large, black terrestrial carnivorous birds that have robust, decurved bills. The toes are joined together at the base so the bird walks on the tips only; this is one of the ways in which the family differs from the Bucerotidae (p. 224). It also differs in breeding behavior: Gregarious, occurring in small groups, these are cooperative breeders (the largest in the world), and the breeding female is not incarcerated in the nest hole and does not molt flight feathers. Ground hornbills generally lay two eggs but invariably raise only one chick (there are no genuine records of both being raised), due to passive fratricide (first-hatched chick monopolizes food). Facial skin and throat pouch color vary according to age and/or sex. One species occurs in Botswana.

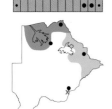

SOUTHERN GROUND HORNBILL *Bucorvus leadbeateri*

Setswana: le.hututu

110 cm (43 ¼ in). **Identification:** Turkey-size ground dweller with jet-black plumag except for white primaries, visible in flight. Facial skin and throat pouch are red; female h variable amount of dark blue on throat pouch below bill. Juvenile has dirty khaki-wh facial skin and throat pouch, which become redder over several years as it matures. **Ca** Booming *hu-tu-tu* call, usually uttered in duet at dawn. Setswana name is onomatopoe **Status:** Resident, breeding. **Abundance:** Scarce in the eastern part of its range; commc in the Okavango Delta, including Moremi Game Reserve, the Linyanti area, and Savute Chobe National Park. Its range in parts of southern Africa has contracted markedly in rece decades. **Habitat:** Prefers moist tropical woodlands, especially broad-leaved woodlan interspersed with open grassland. Preferred nesting tree in Botswana is the Apple-le (*Philenoptera violacea*). **Habits:** A terrestrial predator of mice, bird nestlings, snakes, lizarc toads, spiders, grasshoppers, and other arthropods, it hunts by scanning the ground wh walking. Occurs in small family parties. Only the alpha pair in a group forms a breeding un helpers are of both sexes. The species was recently recorded "double-brooding"—raisir two chicks in succession in a single year. **Conservation:** Vulnerable.

AFRICAN GREY
HORNBILL

female

male
display

male

TRUMPETER
HORNBILL

male

female

SOUTHERN GROUND
HORNBILL

adult
male

adult
female

juv.
(one year)

227

BARBETS Lybiidae

Members of this African family are small birds related to woodpeckers and honeyguides. They have powerful, often notched or toothed bills adapted to a frugivorous diet and also used for excavating nest holes. All are mainly arboreal and have zygodactyl feet for clinging to vertical surfaces. Four resident species occur in Botswana. All are heavy fliers with high wing loading, as their wings are small relative to their body mass.

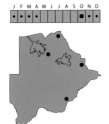

ACACIA PIED BARBET   *Tricholaema leucomelas*

Setswana: tlhôlabaêng, mmamokae, mmamongae, mo.rogolwane, mo.teenyane, mogôrôs

18 cm (7 in). **Identification:** Small barbet, recognized by red forehead, black throat, black and-white upperparts, and white underparts. Only one subspecies occurs in Botswana, *l. centralis*, which has limited black on throat, forming a "bib," and has unmarked whitish underparts. **Call:** Nasal *peh-peh*; sounds like a child's toy trumpet. Also gives a quieter *poop poop-poop* used as territorial advertisement. **Status:** Resident, breeding. **Abundance** Common. **Habitat:** A habitat generalist, especially common in dry acacia-dominate habitats such as Kalahari tree and bush savanna. **Habits:** Solitary or in pairs. Territorial. **I** is parasitized by Lesser Honeyguide, as are other barbets. **Conservation:** Least Concern.

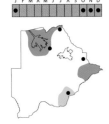

BLACK-COLLARED BARBET   *Lybius torquatus*

Setswana: kopaopê, kôpaope, kôpaôpê, kôkwapê, kwakwapê, kokomore, kôkômore

20 cm (7 ¾ in). **Identification:** Chunky bird with conspicuous red head and black colla Juvenile has black forehead and crown that extend back to join black collar, confinin red to sides of face. Two subspecies are found in Botswana: *L. t. bocagei* (illustrated) ha a vermiculated pattern on the back and a plain yellow belly; *L. t. torquatus* has a plain da back and a pale yellow belly streaked with black. Rare yellow-headed form exists (due t a pigment deficiency known as schizochroism), but there are no Botswana records. **Cal** Loud duet, repeated for 10 seconds or more, often rendered as *two-puddly, two-puddly* bu closer to *cu-kukuk, cu-kukuk, cu-kukuk*. Harsh grating *kerrr, kerrr* often precedes the due **Status:** Resident, breeding. **Abundance:** *L. t. bocagei* is common in the Okavango Delta; *L.* *torquatus* is common in South-East District and in eastern Botswana. **Habitat:** Prefers mois woodlands (including riparian). **Habits:** Occurs in small groups of up to 10 birds, found i the canopy of riparian trees, where they feed on fruits. The species excavates its own nes hole (the Setswana name *kokomore*, which literally translates as "knocker on trees," is als used for woodpeckers). It is a cooperative breeder. Group members take turns at nest t prevent incursion of Lesser Honeyguide, a brood parasite. The barbet often produces tw broods per breeding season, even though the chicks have a relatively long fledging perio **Conservation:** Least Concern.

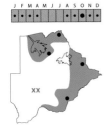

CRESTED BARBET   *Trachyphonus vaillantii*

Setswana: kôkôpa, kopaopê, kôpaope, kôpaôpê, kôkwapê, kwakwapê, mo.fadi, kokonyamere, se.kokonyane

24 cm (9 ½ in). **Identification:** Chunky, unmistakable, multicolored barbet with conspicuou crest and heavy bill. Both southern African subspecies occur in Botswana: birds of subspecie *T. v. nobilis* are paler than those of *T. v. vaillantii*. **Call:** Metronomic trilling, similar to soun of an alarm clock. **Status:** Resident, breeding. **Abundance:** Common. *T. v. nobilis* (originall described from a specimen collected at Lake Ngami) occurs in the north; *T. v. vaillantii* in th east and south. **Habitat:** Found in a variety of woodlands, particularly broad-leaved, but als the mixed woodlands of the eastern hardveld and acacia woodlands. **Habits:** Solitary or pairs. Territorial; calls from prominent position on a treetop. It excavates its own nest hol The species is a host for brood parasite Lesser Honeyguide. There is a record of honeyguide entering an occupied Crested Barbet nest, attacking the adult, and killing some of th chicks; presumably, this was done to prompt the barbets to re-lay, so the honeyguide could synchronize their brood parasitism with the hosts' breeding cycle. **Conservatio** Least Concern.

ACACIA PIED
BARBET
T. l. centralis

yellow-headed
form

BLACK-COLLARED
BARBET
L. t. bocagei

CRESTED BARBET
T. v. nobilis

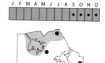

YELLOW-FRONTED TINKERBIRD *Pogoniulus chrysoconus*

Setswana: mo.thudi

12 cm (4 ¾ in). **Identification:** Diminutive barbet; Botswana's only representative of the tinkerbird genus. The yellow forehead patch is diagnostic among tinkerbirds (occasional individuals with orange foreheads are seen in South Africa but not yet recorded in Botswana). Only one subspecies occurs in Botswana, *P. c. extoni* (the type specimen for which was collected in 1871 at Kanye in Southern District). **Call:** Monotonous tink-tink-tink-tink or pop-pop-pop-pop, given by male. **Status:** Resident, breeding. There are very few Botswana breeding records, but they conform with egg-laying times for the rest of the region. **Abundance:** Uncommon. Occurs in Botswana at the western edge of its continental range at these latitudes. **Habitat:** Found in broad-leaved and mixed woodlands. **Habits:** Solitary and highly territorial. Male calls from treetops but is difficult to locate, due to small size and ventriloquial nature of call. Feeds on fruits of mistletoe (*Viscum* spp.) and helps disperse the seeds. **Conservation:** Least Concern.

HONEYGUIDES, HONEYBIRDS Indicatoridae

A family with a peculiar mix of characteristics. All species are brood parasites; their eggs are thick-shelled to minimize damage during laying (which is often hasty), and the hatchlings have hooked bills for killing young of the host. They are polygynous; males use fixed calling posts to attract females. The birds are able to digest wax, which honeyguides obtain from honeycombs and honeybirds obtain from eating scale insects. The birds have an undulating flight, during which they show white outer tail feathers. All have zygodactyl feet with two toes facing forward and two backward. Two genera occur in Botswana, each containing two species. Only one, the Greater Honeyguide, lives up to the name and reliably guides people to bee nests.

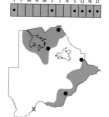

GREATER HONEYGUIDE *Indicator indicator*

Setswana: tshêtlho, tshêtlhô, tshêtlo

20 cm (7 ¾ in). **Identification:** Large brown honeyguide. Adult of both sexes has four pairs of conspicuous white outer tail feathers, pale-edged wing coverts, and an olive or yellow shoulder patch (which is often hard to see and is not a useful field feature). Male has distinctive pink bill, black throat, and pale cheek patch. Female has a dark bill and lacks black throat and pale cheek patch of male. Juvenile is distinctive: it has a yellow breast and buffy belly, and dark brown upperparts. **Call:** Territorial call is repetitive, ringing vic-terr, vic-terr, issued from calling post by male. Guiding call is an insistent chatter. **Status:** Resident, breeding. There are few Botswana egg-laying records, but one is from June (which is unusual). **Abundance:** Uncommon. **Habitat:** A woodland species, found in riparian strips and deciduous broad-leaved woodlands. **Habits:** Solitary and arboreal; it has fast, dipping flight. The species has the unique habit of guiding humans to bee nests (but has never been reliably recorded guiding Honey Badgers or any other mammal). The species is a brood parasite of a wide range of hosts that breed in tunnel nests in banks and in tree holes; in Botswana, African Hoopoe and Cape Starling have been recorded as hosts. Multiple females may lay eggs in the same host nest. It is believed this species lays eggs that match those of its hosts, not because the host discriminates but because of intraspecific competition: Other female honeyguides preferentially puncture competing honeyguides' eggs if they recognize them. **Conservation:** Least Concern.

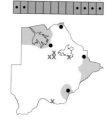

LESSER HONEYGUIDE *Indicator minor*

15 cm (6 in). **Identification:** Smaller than Greater Honeyguide. Olive-green back and mantle, and black malar stripe are key identification features. In flight, shows four pairs of white outer tail feathers (a honeyguide characteristic). Two subspecies occur in Botswana: *I. m. teitensis* is markedly paler (and has a less-distinct malar stripe) than the nominate. **Call:** Tew, blip, blip, blip, blip, given from calling post. **Status:** Resident, breeding. **Abundance:** Uncommon. *I. m. teitensis* occurs in northern and eastern Botswana, *I. m. minor* in southeastern Botswana. **Habitat:** Found in savannas, riparian woodlands, and thickets. **Habits:** Solitary or in pairs; unobtrusive. Moves around in tree canopy hawking insects or visiting bee and barbet nests. Its nostrils are raised, presumably to prevent them from getting blocked with wax and honey when the bird feeds on beeswax. It is a brood parasite of hole-nesters, with a record of Black-collared Barbet as host in Botswana; also parasitizes other barbets, and bee-eaters elsewhere in southern Africa. It has been recorded entering an occupied Crested Barbet nest, attacking the adult, and killing some of the chicks, presumably to cause the barbets to re-lay so it could synchronize its brood parasitism with the hosts' breeding cycle. **Conservation:** Least Concern.

orange
variant

**YELLOW-FRONTED
TINKERBIRD**
P. c. extoni

adult
male

imm.

adult
female

**GREATER
HONEYGUIDE**

**LESSER
HONEYGUIDE**
I. m. teitensis

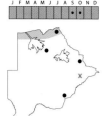

GREEN-BACKED HONEYBIRD *Prodotiscus zambesiae*

12 cm (4 ¾ in). **Identification:** Resembles a flycatcher in size, appearance, and behavior. White outer tail feathers (three pairs) are conspicuous in flight. Has olive-green back, similar to Lesser Honeyguide (p. 230), which is larger, but no malar stripe. **Call:** Chattering *chee, chee, chewit, chewit, chewit, chee, chee.* **Status:** Resident; no breeding records from Botswana. **Abundance:** Rare. This is a Zambezian species, with a range extending only marginally into extreme northern Botswana. **Habitat:** Found in Zambezi Teak (*Baikiaea plurijuga*) woodlands. **Habits:** Solitary or in pairs; often in mixed species bird parties. It has a distinctive dipping display flight, during which one bird chases another, and the white outer tail feathers are visible. Hawks insects from a perch, like a flycatcher. Also eats wax obtained from the waxy coverings of scale insects. Known to parasitize broods of African Yellow White-eye. **Conservation:** Least Concern.

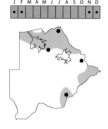

BROWN-BACKED HONEYBIRD *Prodotiscus regulus*

13 cm (5 in). **Identification:** Resembles a flycatcher in size, appearance, and behavior. White outer tail feathers (three pairs) are conspicuous in flight. Bill is slender and slightly decurved (alternative name is Sharp-billed Honeyguide). Brown back differentiates it from Green-backed Honeybird. **Call:** Insect-like *dzeeeee*, repeated at intervals. **Status:** Resident; no breeding records in Botswana. **Abundance:** Scarce. The best place to see this species is in the Zambezi Teak (*Baikiaea plurijuga*) woodlands of northern Chobe District. **Habitat:** Prefers Zambezi Teak woodlands and riparian woodlands but may be found in a variety of other mesic woodlands. **Habits:** Solitary or in pairs. It makes short aerial sallies from a perch to catch insects; it also eats wax, obtained from the waxy coverings of scale insects. It has a dipping display flight in which white outer tail feathers are visible. It is a brood parasite; host birds are camaropteras, cisticolas, and prinias. **Conservation:** Least Concern.

WOODPECKERS Picidae

Members of this family have chisel-like bills for excavating nest holes and procuring invertebrate prey (aided in this by their long sticky tongues). They have zygodactyl feet and stiffened tail feathers, which support the bird while it clings to vertical branches and trunks. All five Botswana species are sexually dimorphic. They are arboreal and have a dipping flight, and some species advertise their territories by drumming with the bill on a dead, hollow branch. They occupy similar niches and are morphologically similar. Key identification criteria are color of forehead, crown, and malar stripe, and whether the breast is streaked, spotted, or barred. Calls are also useful for identification. The Setswana name *kokomore* (literally, "knocker on trees") is commonly used for woodpeckers. Other names, such as *kôkôpa, kopaopê, kokolamere, kokonamore, kokonyamere, kwanyakwanya, mo.kônkônyana, rêmaditlhare*, and *qoqonamuti*, reflect dialectal differences and are used in some parts of Botswana.

OLIVE WOODPECKER *Dendropicos griseocephalus*

Setswana: kokomore, kôkôpa, kopaopê, kokolamere, kokonamore, kokonyamere, kwanyakwanya, mo.kônkônyana, rêmaditlhare, qoqonamuti

20 cm (7 ¾ in). **Identification:** The only unspeckled woodpecker species in Botswana. Both sexes have plain olive upperparts, a red rump, and gray head, but male has red crown. *D. g. ruwenzori,* the subspecies found in Botswana, has a bright red belly patch in both sexes. **Call:** Loud *weet* or *weter.* **Status:** Visitor; no breeding records from Botswana. **Abundance:** Rare. The range of *D. g. ruwenzori* just extends into the extreme northern part of Chobe District; there has been only one sighting, in Kasane in 2003. **Habitat:** Occurs in riparian woodland and Zambezi Teak (*Baikiaea plurijuga*) woodlands. **Habits:** Clambers along branches extracting invertebrates with chisel-like bill. **Conservation:** Least Concern.

GREEN-BACKED
HONEYBIRD

BROWN-BACKED
HONEYBIRD

male

female

OLIVE
WOODPECKER
D. g. ruwenzori

233

BENNETT'S WOODPECKER *Campethera bennettii*

Setswana: qoqonamuti

23 cm (9 in). **Identification:** Male has red forehead and crown and red malar stripe. Female has black forehead spotted with white (but note differences between subspecies), red crown, white malar stripe, and chestnut cheeks and throat. Two subspecies occur: In the nominate, both sexes have boldly spotted underparts. *C. b. capricorni* is easily recognizable by its plain breast and underparts with a yellowish wash; the female sometimes has a white forehead with black spots. **Call:** Chattering *chirrit, chirrit, chirrit,* often in duet. Often groups of three or four birds gather on a tree trunk and flap their wings and call excitedly. **Status:** Resident, breeding. **Abundance:** Common. *C. b. bennettii* is widespread throughout the country; *C. b. capricorni* occurs from Ngamiland across to northern Chobe District. **Habitat:** Found in mature woodlands dominated by broad-leaved species such as Mopane (*Colophospermum mopane*) and bushwillow (*Combretum* spp.), but also in acacia woodlands. **Habits:** Solitary or in pairs or small family groups. It forages low, frequently on the ground (a useful field feature). This species does not drum with bill. It has strong, dipping flight. **Conservation:** Least Concern.

GOLDEN-TAILED WOODPECKER *Campethera abingoni*

Setswana: kokomore, kôkôpa, kopaopê, kokolamere, kokonamore, kokonyamere, kwanyakwanya, mo.kônkônyana, rêmaditlhare, qoqonamuti

21 cm (8 ¼ in). **Identification:** This woodpecker has a streaked breast (not spotted, as in Bennett's Woodpecker). Male has red forehead and crown and red malar stripe. Female has black forehead spotted with white, red crown, and speckled malar stripe. *C. a. anderssoni* has a more heavily streaked throat and breast than the nominate, which gives it a darker appearance. **Call:** Single, nasal shriek, *weeauu.* **Status:** Resident, breeding. **Abundance:** Common. *C. a. anderssoni* occurs in southwestern Botswana; *C. a. abingoni* is found throughout the remainder of the country. **Habitat:** Found in a range of habitat types, including Kalahari tree and bush savanna; *C. a. anderssoni* occurs in arid scrub savanna. **Habits:** Arboreal. Solitary or in pairs. Seldom drums. Has fast, dipping flight. **Conservation:** Least Concern.

CARDINAL WOODPECKER *Dendropicos fuscescens*

Setswana: kokomore, kôkôpa, kopaopê, kokolamere, kokonamore, kokonyamere, kwanyakwanya, mo.kônkônyana, rêmaditlhare, qoqonamuti

15 cm (6 in). **Identification:** Botswana's smallest woodpecker. Both sexes have a streaked breast. Male has brown forehead, red crown, and black malar stripe. Female has brown forehead, black crown, and black malar stripe. *D. f. stresemanni* has lightly streaked, pale yellow underparts while *D. f. harei* has whitish underparts more heavily streaked with dark gray. **Call:** Rapid, rattling *kree-kree-kreek.* **Status:** Resident, breeding. **Abundance:** Common; it is the most commonly recorded woodpecker in Botswana. *D. f. stresemanni* occurs in Ngamiland, Chobe and North-East Districts, while *D. f. harei* is found in the southern half of the country. **Habitat:** Occupies a variety of habitat types, including Kalahari tree and bush savanna and mixed woodlands. **Habits:** Solitary or in pairs, it is seen clambering on vertical stems or hanging below horizontal branches with its zygodactyl feet. Drums with bill on hollow logs but not loudly, due to its small size. **Conservation:** Least Concern.

BEARDED WOODPECKER *Dendropicos namaquus*

Setswana: kokomore, kôkôpa, kopaopê, kokolamere, kokonamore, kokonyamere, kwanyakwanya, mo.kônkônyana, rêmaditlhare, qoqonamuti

24 cm (9 ½ in). **Identification:** Largest woodpecker in Botswana. Both sexes have gray underparts with fine white barring and bold black-and-white facial markings. Male has black forehead and red crown. Female has black forehead and crown. **Call:** Easily recognizable *wik-wik-wik.* **Status:** Resident, breeding. **Abundance:** Common. **Habitat:** Found in a variety of habitats, excluding arid scrub savanna. **Habits:** Drums loudly from calling post and can be identified by its drumming alone, which is significantly louder than that of other local woodpeckers. It has fast, dipping flight. **Conservation:** Least Concern.

male
C. b. capricorni

male
C. b. bennettii

female
C. b. bennettii

BENNETT'S
WOODPECKER

male

female

GOLDEN-TAILED
WOODPECKER
C. a. abingoni

male

female

CARDINAL
WOODPECKER
D. f. stresemanni

male

female

BEARDED
WOODPECKER

235

PARROTS Psittacidae

Arboreal frugivores. Their zygodactyl feet (with two toes facing forward and two backward) are an adaptation for clambering about among foliage, and they have stout, strongly curved bills for feeding on fruits, seeds, nuts, and grains. Parrots hold food in one dexterous foot and raise it to the beak, a feeding action shared only with owls. All three Botswana species are sedentary breeding residents that nest in holes, and their fledging period is almost double the incubation period (an unusual feature shared with only four other African families). Birds are monogamous and have long-term pair bonds. International trade in any member of this family is prohibited by the Convention on International Trade in Endangered Species of Fauna and Flora (CITES). The Setswana *papalagae* is the generic name for parrots.

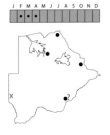

ROSY-FACED LOVEBIRD *Agapornis roseicollis*

17 cm (6 ¾ in). **Identification:** Small green parrot with pink face. The blue rump and pale bill are diagnostic; other lovebirds that could potentially occur in Botswana have green rumps and red bills. **Call:** Shrill, whistled shriek. **Status:** Resident; no breeding records from Botswana. **Abundance:** Rare. The Namibian population reaches its eastern limit in southwestern Botswana. A feral population of escapees has established itself recently in Maun, in Ngamiland District; from sightings of juveniles, breeding among them is inferred **Habitat:** Prefers arid scrub savannas along fossil riverbeds. **Habits:** Gregarious and arboreal, feeds primarily on seeds (limited fruit intake) in tree canopy. Roosts and breeds in Sociable Weaver nests. Tucks nesting material into rump feathers and flies with it to nest site. **Conservation:** Least Concern.

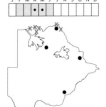

BROWN-NECKED PARROT *Poicephalus fuscicollis*

Setswana: papalagae

32 cm (12 ½ in). **Identification:** Largest parrot in Botswana. Red marking on wings and thighs is diagnostic. Female sometimes has orange forehead or, more rarely, a wholly orange crown. Juvenile of both sexes always has orange forehead. **Call:** Loud piercing shrieks, given when perched and in flight. **Status:** Visitor, breeding. Only one Botswana egg-laying record, the date of which conforms with data from the region. **Abundance:** Rare. The subspecies *P. f. suahelicus*, found in south-central Africa, reaches into Botswana's Chobe and Ngamiland Districts along the Namibian border at the southern limit of its range. **Habitat:** Favors Zambezi Teak (*Baikiaea plurijuga*) and Mopane (*Colophospermum mopane*) woodlands and well-wooded watercourses. **Habits:** Arboreal. Congregates in flocks during summer when feeding on seeds of Manketti-tree (*Schinziophyton rautanenii*), Kiaat (*Pterocarpus angolensis*), and fruits of African Mangosteen (*Garcinia livingstonei*), Jackal-berry (*Diospyros mespiliformis*), and figs (*Ficus* spp.). **Conservation:** Least Concern.

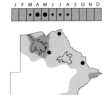

MEYER'S PARROT *Poicephalus meyeri*

Setswana: hêgha, hêka, papalagae

23 cm (9 in). **Identification:** Medium-size parrot. It has brown upperparts, turquoise-blue underparts, and yellow shoulders. Two subspecies occur in Botswana: *P. m. transvaalensis* has greener underparts, and adult usually has a yellow crown; *P. m. damarensis* adult has yellow on crown greatly reduced or absent. **Call:** High-pitched shrieks, sometimes in duet. **Status:** Resident, breeding. **Abundance:** Common. The Okavango Delta is the stronghold for this species in southern Africa. *P. m. transvaalensis* occurs in eastern Botswana from Kasane through Francistown down to the Gaborone area; *P. m. damarensis* is found in Ngamiland and Chobe Districts. **Habitat:** Prefers open woodlands with watercourses. Often associated with Sausage Tree (*Kigelia africana*). **Habits:** Occurs in pairs or small groups. Arboreal, feeds on fruits and seeds in tree canopy. Breeds in late summer–autumn to avoid competition for nest cavities with Burchell's Starling; this is also the time when arthropod larvae are available and eaten to supplement the vegetarian diet. **Conservation:** Least Concern.

ROSY-FACED
LOVEBIRD

BROWN-NECKED
PARROT
P. f. suahelicus

male

female

female

juv.

MEYER'S
PARROT

adult
P. m. damarensis

adult
P. m. damarensis

adult
P. m. transvaalensis

juv.

237

BATISES Platysteiridae

An endemic African family of small, pied flycatcher-like birds that are told apart by the variable rufous markings on the females. Batises are arboreal and hawk insects within the foliage of the tree canopy; they have rictal bristles at the base of the bill to facilitate prey capture. All construct cup-shaped nests on horizontal branches and camouflage them with lichens. The family is related to the helmetshrike (p. 240) and bushshrike (p. 242) families. Three species in genus *Batis* occur in Botswana. They all have a black facial mask and contrasting eye. The Setswana *jôkôsekêi* is the generic name for batises.

CAPE BATIS *Batis capensis*

Setswana: jôkôsekêi

13 cm (5 in). **Identification:** Small, flycatcher-like forest bird. Adult has orange-red eye and rufous flanks and wing panel. Male has black breast band and dark rufous flanks. Female has rich rufous breast band and chin. The two subspecies potentially found in Botswana differ slightly: *B. c. hollidayi* has a rufous-olive mantle (both sexes), while that of *B. c. kennedyi* is gray. **Call:** Trisyllabic whistle, *weeuu, weeuu, weeuu*. **Status:** Visitor; no breeding records from Botswana. **Abundance:** Rare. The species is a southern African endemic. *B. c. hollidayi* has been recorded in eastern Botswana, in two sightings at Sunnyside Farm on the Botswana side of the Limpopo River (Central District) in August 1988. It seems likely that this record indicates a latitudinal movement in winter from South Africa rather than a small resident population. It is possible that *B. c. kennedyi* may also extend into eastern Botswana from Zimbabwe. **Habitat:** Essentially a forest bird, in Botswana found in tangled undergrowth of riparian woodlands. **Habits:** Forages for insects within tree canopy, hopping from branch to branch or making short flights to catch prey. **Conservation:** Least Concern.

CHINSPOT BATIS *Batis molitor*

Setswana: jôkôsekêi

13 cm (5 in). **Identification:** Small, pied flycatcher-like bird. Iris pale yellow in adult, white in immature. Male lacks any russet coloration and has unmarked flanks (hence previous common name of White-flanked Flycatcher); it is similar to male Pririt Batis, which has flanks speckled with gray or black. (Chinspot and Pririt Batis are largely allopatric, with little overlap in their ranges.) Female easily identified by rich chestnut chin spot and broad breast band. Only one subspecies is found in Botswana, *B. m. palliditergum*. **Call:** Distinctive three-note call, rendered as *three-blind-mice*. **Status:** Resident, breeding. **Abundance:** Abundant. **Habitat:** Found in a variety of moist woodland types. **Habits:** Usually in pairs. Forages in tree canopy for insects, hopping from branch to branch or making short, bouncy flights. **Conservation:** Least Concern.

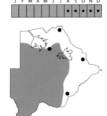

PRIRIT BATIS *Batis pririt*

Setswana: jôkôsekêi

12 cm (4 ¾ in). **Identification:** Small black, gray, and white flycatcher-like bird. Female has pale rufous throat and breast. Both sexes have gray or black speckles on flanks, which distinguish them from Chinspot Batis. (This species and Chinspot are largely allopatric, with relatively little range overlap.) **Call:** Similar to call of Chinspot Batis, but longer, not restricted to three notes, and gradually descending. **Status:** Resident, breeding. **Abundance:** Common. **Habitat:** Found in dry habitats, especially Kalahari tree and bush savanna, often along drainage lines. **Habits:** Occurs in pairs; forages within tree canopy. This species is a host for brood parasite Klaas's Cuckoo. **Conservation:** Least Concern.

CAPE BATIS
B. c. hollidayi

male

female

CHINSPOT BATIS

male

female

male

female

PRIRIT BATIS

239

HELMETSHRIKES Prionopidae

An endemic African family containing one genus, *Prionops*, the name of which refers to the serrated wattle surrounding the eye and thus highlights a key feature of the group. Taxonomically, helmetshrikes are placed between the batises (p. 238) and bushshrikes (p. 242) and have features of both: They construct cup-shaped nests on horizontal branches, and they glean insects from tree foliage or hawk them in the air or on the ground. Two species occur in Botswana, both cooperative breeders. They usually fly in a staggered sequence from tree to tree, issuing a whistled call accompanied by bill clicking.

WHITE-CRESTED HELMETSHRIKE *Prionops plumatus*

Setswana: le.ranthata, tlabore

18 cm (7 in). **Identification:** Pied bird with facial disk of stiff feathers (a helmetshrike characteristic). In adult, eye and wattle surrounding it are yellow. Immature has dark eye, lacking the wattle, and is dark gray on nape and ear coverts. **Call:** *Cherow, cherow, cherow,* given by group, often mixed with bill clicking. **Status:** Resident, breeding. **Abundance:** Common to abundant. **Habitat:** Favors deciduous broad-leaved woodlands and acacia savannas. **Habits:** Gregarious, always in small flocks, which forage low in trees and shrubs, and fly from tree to tree. Cooperative breeder; helpers assist with nest construction, incubation, and chick rearing. **Conservation:** Least Concern.

RETZ'S HELMETSHRIKE *Prionops retzii*

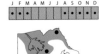

19 cm (7 ½ in). **Identification:** Black helmetshrike with white vent and tail tips, and red bill and eye wattle. Immature is gray-brown, with white vent, and lacks eye wattle. Only the nominate subspecies, *P. r. retzii*, occurs in Botswana. **Call:** Harsh group call, *chi-rew, chi-rew,* repeated with bill snapping. **Status:** Resident, breeding. There are limited egg-laying data from Botswana, but timing appears to conform with records from elsewhere in the region. **Abundance:** Uncommon to locally common, but less so than White-crested Helmetshrike. Its range in Botswana is at the southern and western edge of the species's range in Africa. The Okavango is a stronghold for this species. **Habitat:** Prefers tall, moist deciduous woodlands and riparian woodlands. **Habits:** Gregarious; small flocks forage high in canopy of tall trees, flying from tree to tree. The species is a known host for Thick-billed Cuckoo but has not been recorded being parasitized by it in Botswana. **Conservation:** Least Concern.

BROADBILLS Eurylaimidae

Small, arboreal birds, broadbills have dorsoventrally flattened bills and wide gape for catching insect prey. Monogamous, they construct purse-shaped, pendent nest of grass and other plant material. One species occurs in Botswana. It resembles a squat flycatcher with a broad bill but has a distinctive display flight and call.

AFRICAN BROADBILL *Smithornis capensis*

14 cm (5 ½ in). **Identification:** Small insectivore with dumpy appearance and noticeably large head. Black crown and heavily streaked underparts, combined with size and shape, are diagnostic. **Call:** Frog-like *prrruuurr.* **Status:** Visitor; no breeding records from Botswana. **Abundance:** Rare. Only one sighting, in the Okavango Delta in 1988. The type specimen for *S. c. conjunctus* (the subspecies to be found in Botswana) was collected about 50 km west of Victoria Falls, in Zimbabwe, close to the Botswana border. The bird could be a sparsely distributed, overlooked Botswana resident in dense riparian vegetation. **Habitat:** Essentially a forest species, potentially found in riparian woodlands in Botswana. **Habits:** Unobtrusive, but performs a unique circular display flight over its perch, with its white back feathers puffed out, while uttering frog-like call. **Conservation:** Least Concern.

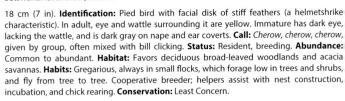

**WHITE-CRESTED
HELMETSHRIKE**

**RETZ'S
HELMETSHRIKE**
P. r. retzii

male

female

**AFRICAN
BROADBILL**
S. c. conjunctus

BUSHSHRIKES Malaconotidae

A family of skulking thicket-dwelling insectivores that resemble true shrikes (p. 250) but are more closely related to batises (p. 238), helmetshrikes (p. 240), and cuckooshrikes (p. 248). Most forage in a manner similar to that of the true shrikes, pouncing on prey on the ground, but some glean insects from foliage. Botswana has 11 species, all sedentary residents. They are found in pairs, and many have distinctive duet calls for maintaining contact in their preferred dense habitat. They are arranged in four groups to assist with identification: The three green-and-yellow bushshrikes (this page), which have olive-green backs and yellow underparts. The two Tchagras (p. 244), which are brownish with striking head markings. The two small, pied, batis-like species (p. 244), which are sexually dimorphic. The four *Laniarius* species (p. 246), which differ in breast color and calls, but occupy similar niches.

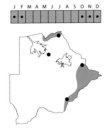

GREY-HEADED BUSHSHRIKE *Malaconotus blanchoti*

Setswana: mmamojêla-rure, mmamaribêla

26 cm (10 ¼ in). **Identification:** Large green and yellow bushshrike. Olive mantle and wing contrast with yellow underparts; breast has pale orange wash. Combination of gray head white lores, massive bill, and pale eye is diagnostic among similar bushshrikes. Only th subspecies *M. b. hypopyrrhus* occurs in Botswana. **Call:** Long, drawn-out, spooky whistle **Status:** Resident, breeding. There are limited egg-laying data from Botswana, but timin conforms with that in the rest of the region. **Abundance:** Common in eastern Botswana but surprisingly scarce in the north, except in Linyanti Swamps and along the Chobe Rive in the vicinity of Kasane (does not occur in the Okavango Delta). **Habitat:** Found in riparia woodlands with tangled undergrowth and in wooded gardens in urban areas. **Habits** Forages for insects and small vertebrates in middle to upper strata of tall trees and henc is easily overlooked; partial to chameleons, reported taking a bat. Regularly caches surplu food under bark or in crevices. **Conservation:** Least Concern.

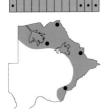

ORANGE-BREASTED BUSHSHRIKE *Chlorophoneus sulfureopectus*

19 cm (7 ½ in). **Identification:** Small green and yellow bushshrike. Predominantly yellow it is much smaller than Grey-headed Bushshrike and has a moderate-size bill; its yellow supercilium, black lores, and dark eye differentiate it further. The orange breast, which i much reduced in female and absent in juvenile, is not a useful field characteristic, since is shared with Grey-headed. Juvenile has short white supercilium. **Call:** Distinctive ringin call comprising five notes, *pee-pee-pee-pee-peeeeee*. **Status:** Resident, breeding. There ar few Botswana egg-laying records. **Abundance:** Common. The Okavango wetland syster is a stronghold for this species. **Habitat:** Prefers dense thickets in riparian and acaci woodlands. **Habits:** Solitary or in pairs. Skulks in mid-stratum of tangled thornbushes; no easy to see. **Conservation:** Least Concern.

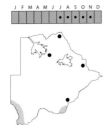

BOKMAKIERIE *Telophorus zeylonus*

23 cm (9 in). **Identification:** Medium-size, mainly yellow bushshrike. It has a bold blac gorget around the yellow throat, and black lores. Juvenile has olive-gray crown an yellowish underparts, and lacks black gorget and lores. The subspecies present in Botswan *T. z. thermophilus*, has slightly paler upperparts than the nominate (not recorded i Botswana). **Call:** Duet, somewhat onomatopoeic, *wik-wik-wik-wik*, followed by *tree-tree tree*, and variations thereof. **Status:** Resident, breeding. Breeds mainly in early summer; th few Botswana egg-laying records conform with those for the region. **Abundance:** Scarce A southern African endemic, the species occurs in Botswana at the limit of its range, i southwestern Kgalagadi District and South-East District. **Habitat:** Favors low bushes an scrub in association with open, broken ground, such as is found in arid scrub savann **Habits:** Occurs in pairs. It is partly terrestrial, and feeds on the ground but calls (in due from a vantage point on low bushes. **Conservation:** Least Concern.

GREY-HEADED
BUSHSHRIKE
M. b. hypopyrrhus

adult

juv.

ORANGE-BREASTED
BUSHSHRIKE

adult

BOKMAKIERIE
T. z. thermophilus

juv.

BLACK-CROWNED TCHAGRA *Tchagra senegalus*

Setswana: phênakgômo, phênêkgômo, rapina, mafurêfurê

21 cm (8 ¼ in). **Identification:** Large brown bushshrike. Combination of black crown, whit supercilium, and black eye stripe is diagnostic. It differs from Brown-crowned Tchagra i larger size, black crown, and distinctive call. **Call:** Long, rambling whistle, *wee-hee, hooy* repeated with some variation. **Status:** Resident, breeding. Limited egg-laying records fror Botswana are similar in timing to those from the rest of the region. **Abundance:** Commo but less so than Brown-crowned Tchagra, except in Zambezi Teak (*Baikiaea plurijug* woodlands, where it is the more common of the two. **Habitat:** Found in mixed woodland both moist broad-leaved woodlands and arid acacia woodlands. **Habits:** Solitary or in pair forages in lower stratum of thickets. When disturbed, flies out "back" of bush to next bus and immediately hops into its interior and flies out the back again, which makes it difficu to see clearly. **Conservation:** Least Concern.

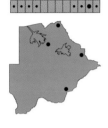

BROWN-CROWNED TCHAGRA *Tchagra australis*

Setswana: phênakgômo, phênêkgômo, rapina, mafurêfurê

18 cm (7 in). **Identification:** Brown bushshrike. Its brown crown, white supercilium, an black eye stripe are diagnostic in combination. Distinctive call and display flight aid i identification. It may be mistaken for Black-crowned Tchagra, which has a black crown an is slightly larger. Two subspecies occur in Botswana: *T. a. rhodesiensis* has paler upperpart than *T. a. australis*. **Call:** Distinctive descending whistle, *tshi-tshi-tshi-tshee-tsheeyu-tsheeyu* given in display flight. **Status:** Resident, breeding. **Abundance:** Common. *T. a. australis* widespread throughout Botswana, but *T. a. rhodesiensis* (collected originally in Kabulabu in Chobe National Park) replaces it in the extreme north. **Habitat:** Found in undergrowth c a variety of woodlands. **Habits:** Solitary or in pairs, forages low in thickets and is not easil seen unless displaying, during which it flies steeply up and glides down with quiverin wings and loud descending call. **Conservation:** Least Concern.

BLACK-BACKED PUFFBACK *Dryoscopus cubla*

Setswana: tlêntlêrêhuu, thênthêlêdi

18 cm (7 in). **Identification:** Small, pied bushshrike. Adult (both sexes) is black and whit Male has a black cap that extends down to below the red eye. Female has a black ca interrupted by a white supercilium above the orange eye. Juvenile has similar marking to female but has pale buffy underparts. *D. c. okavangensis* (the type specimen of whic was collected in Maun in Ngamiland District) is the only subspecies found in Botswan **Call:** Distinctive bisyllabic click-whistle, often given in association with display. Juveni has unusually loud, incessant begging call once fledged. **Status:** Resident, breedinc **Abundance:** Common to abundant, even though Botswana is at the southern and wester edge of its continental range. **Habitat:** Dense woodland habitats, such as northeaster Kalahari mixed woodlands and mixed woodlands of the eastern hardveld. **Habits:** Solitar or in pairs; forages by gleaning foliage for insects. Male calls and displays with back an rump feathers puffed out (hence the name "puffback"). **Conservation:** Least Concern.

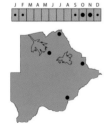

BRUBRU *Nilaus afer*

14 cm (5 ½ in). **Identification:** Small, pied bushshrike with chestnut flanks. Upperpart are black and white in male; browner in female and immature. Two subspecies occur i Botswana: *N. a. brubru* has a broad white eyebrow relative to the narrower eyebrow of *N. c solivagus*. **Call:** Soft but far-carrying ring—*tip-ip-ip, brrrrreeeeee*—that gives away the bird presence. **Status:** Resident, breeding. **Abundance:** Common to abundant. *N. a. brubru* i widespread throughout the country; *N. a. solivagus* may extend into the Tuli Block in easter Botswana. **Habitat:** Found in acacia and mixed woodlands. **Habits:** May be solitary or i pairs. Arboreal; it is a canopy feeder. **Conservation:** Least Concern. **General:** To indicate thi bushshrike's affinity with the true shrikes, it was given a generic name that is an anagram c *Lanius*, the shrike genus.

BLACK-CROWNED TCHAGRA

BROWN-CROWNED TCHAGRA
T. a. australis

crown detail

BLACK-BACKED PUFFBACK
D. c. okavangensis

male puffed display

male

female

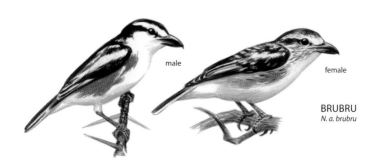

male

female

BRUBRU
N. a. brubru

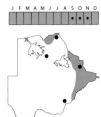

TROPICAL BOUBOU *Laniarius major*

23 cm (9 in). **Identification:** Large boubou with faint buffy-pink wash on the flanks. differs from Southern and Swamp Boubous in color of underparts and in call; see also note about ranges below. Botswana's two subspecies are virtually indistinguishable in the field **Call:** Variable duet; the male calls first, female quickly responds, and then male calls again making a trisyllabic call between them—for example, *haw, chikaarr, haw,* or *kaaa, hoo, kaa* **Status:** Resident, breeding. **Abundance:** Common to abundant. *L. m. limpopoensis,* which occurs in eastern Botswana, is abundant, while *L. m. mossambicus* is common in northern Botswana. Tropical Boubou may hybridize with Swamp Boubou where their ranges overlap (e.g., Savute in Chobe National Park). Tropical Boubou is not found in the Okavango Delta although there are a few accepted records from the Okavango Panhandle at Shakawe. In the eastern part of its range, Tropical Boubou is found along the Limpopo River catchment while Southern Boubou is restricted to the catchments of the Marico and Notwane Rivers in southeastern Botswana. **Habitat:** Found in thickets along watercourses, particularly those in the catchment of the Limpopo River. **Habits:** Territorial; occurs in pairs. Forages in lower stratum of thickets. **Conservation:** Least Concern.

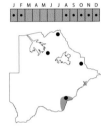

SOUTHERN BOUBOU *Laniarius ferrugineus*

22 cm (8 ¾ in). **Identification:** Large boubou with buffy-cinnamon underparts. In the subspecies that occurs in Botswana, *L. f. transvaalensis,* this coloring is richer on the flanks belly, and vent than in other subspecies. **Call:** Variable whistled duet, such as *weet-wee* (male), *kok-kok-kok* (female); or *whooo* (male), *weeee* (female). **Status:** Resident; no breeding records from Botswana. **Abundance:** Uncommon. A southern African endemic; its range just extends into southeastern Botswana along the catchments of the Marico and Notwane Rivers. **Habitat:** Found in dense, tangled undergrowth and thickets on rock outcrops and along watercourses in a variety of woodland types; also in gardens near Gaborone. **Habits:** Territorial; occurs in pairs. Forages low, often on the ground. **Conservation:** Least Concern

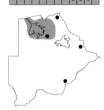

SWAMP BOUBOU *Laniarius bicolor*

Setswana: sasoo, šašoo, šašiô, sasiô

25 cm (9 ¾ in). **Identification:** Large boubou. It differs from other boubous in having pure white underparts; however, some individuals have a faint buffy wash on flanks, and may be misidentified as Tropical Boubou. The call is the best way of separating the three similar boubous. By the time the juvenile fledges, its plumage is indistinguishable from that of the adult. **Call:** Duet consisting of whistle by male and harsh rattle response by female is diagnostic: male whistles *wahooou,* female replies *kak-kak-kak.* Also, harsh *kow-kow-kow* ca **Status:** Resident, breeding. **Abundance:** Common to abundant. **Habitat:** Found in riparian woodlands and thickets fringing rivers, preferably adjacent to permanent swamps. **Habits:** Occurs in pairs. Found in mid- to lower-stratum of riparian woodlands and thickets; hops on the ground. Birds maintain contact with duet call, which is also a territorial advertisement This species may hybridize with Tropical Boubou where their ranges overlap (e.g., Savute in Chobe National Park). Recorded being parasitized by the Black Cuckoo (p. 186) in Botswana **Conservation:** Least Concern.

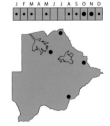

CRIMSON-BREASTED SHRIKE *Laniarius atrococcineus*

Setswana: kgaragoba, kgorogoba, kgoroba, kgorogobê, kgorogoro, nônyane yanama, le.tlhôlanama

22 cm (8 ¾ in). **Identification:** Unmistakable boubou; differs from the other three in its bright crimson breast (*atrococcineus* means "black and scarlet"). Juvenile is initially barred dark brown, but upperparts turn uniformly black and underparts become progressively blotched with crimson patches until adult plumage is attained. There is a rare yellow-breasted form. **Call:** Duet: *quipquip, tzui, quipquip.* **Status:** Resident, breeding. **Abundance:** Common. **Habitat:** An acacia specialist, found in thickets (especially of Black Thorn, *Acacia mellifera*) in Kalahari tree and bush savanna. **Habits:** Pairs call in duet from top of low tree or shrub in territorial advertisement, but spend most time low in vegetation or on the ground where the bird is difficult to see. The species is a host for the brood parasite Black Cuckoo in Botswana. **Conservation:** Least Concern. **General:** Yellow-breasted birds, which have been seen around Maun on a number of occasions, have a pigment deficiency known as schizochroism. The Setswana Bible, which traditionally has a black cover and white pages with red outer margins, is often referred to as *Bukana ya mmala wa Kgorogoba,* "the book with the colors of the Crimson-breasted Shrike."

TROPICAL
BOUBOU
L. m. mossambicus

SOUTHERN
BOUBOU
L. f. transvaalensis

SWAMP
BOUBOU

adult

adult
yellow-breasted
form

juv.

CRIMSON-BREASTED
SHRIKE

247

DRONGOS Dicruridae

Most members of this family worldwide share common behaviors: they perch hunt for insects, often in association with herbivores that act as "beaters"; they mimic calls of raptors and other birds; and they regularly mob large raptors. One species occurs in Botswana; it is a uniform black, rapacious passerine with a deeply forked tail.

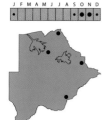

FORK-TAILED DRONGO Dicrurus adsimilis

Setswana: se.rothê, seruthê, thêko, kuamesi, kuamosi, kwiamesi

25 cm (9 ¾ in). **Identification:** Bold, all-black bird with deeply forked tail. Adult has deep red eye. Juvenile has gray tips to black feathers on underparts, which give it a scalloped appearance; eye brown. Two subspecies occur in Botswana; D. a. fugax is slightly smaller than D. a. apivorus. **Call:** Variety of twanging, melodious whistles and creaking sounds; also mimics other birds, particularly raptors. **Status:** Resident, breeding. **Abundance:** Abundant. One of Botswana's most abundant and widespread species. D. a. apivorus is widespread throughout Botswana; D. a. fugax is restricted to northeastern Botswana. **Habitat:** Occurs in wide range of habitat types, notably Kalahari tree and bush savanna. **Habits:** Usually solitary, seen sitting on a low perch from which it hawks insects in the air, on vegetation or on the ground, often returning to its original perch. It has commensal relationship with grazing herbivores, and hawks insects they disturb, sometimes from the back of a mammalian beater. It uses mimicry of their alarm calls to cause Suricates to drop food, which it then pirates. A bold bird, it is often seen chasing raptors. It is one of the first birds to call every morning, before it is light. This is the only recorded host species for the brood parasite African Cuckoo. **Conservation:** Least Concern.

CUCKOOSHRIKES Campephagidae

These arboreal birds are caterpillar eaters (as the family name indicates) and in this respect are similar to cuckoos (p. 180), but the family is more closely related to shrikes (p. 250). Cuckooshrikes have relatively long incubation and fledging periods for birds of their size. Two genera and two species occur in Botswana. Both are sexually dimorphic, the Black Cuckooshrike radically so.

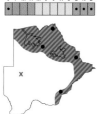

BLACK CUCKOOSHRIKE Campephaga flava

21 cm (8 ¼ in). **Identification:** Male is black and has a yellow-orange gape, and occurs in two color morphs: one is all black (more common in Botswana); the other has a variable amount of yellow on the shoulder. Female is cuckoo-like and has distinct brown barring below, yellow edges to upperwing feathers, and a bright yellow underwing, conspicuous in flight. **Call:** Quiet, trilling trrrrrr; it often gives away the bird's presence. **Status:** Resident, breeding. The resident population is supplemented by breeding intra-African migrants between October and April, and most sightings occur then. The few Botswana egg-laying records for this species conform with those for the rest of southern Africa. **Abundance:** Uncommon to common. **Habitat:** Found in riparian vegetation and mixed woodlands. **Habits:** Unobtrusive. **Conservation:** Least Concern.

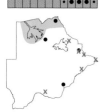

WHITE-BREASTED CUCKOOSHRIKE Coracina pectoralis

27 cm (10 ¾ in). **Identification:** Gray-and-white cuckooshrike. Male has gray head and throat. Female has white breast and throat extending up to base of bill. **Call:** Not very vocal; soft tchee-ree-ree. **Status:** Resident; no breeding records from Botswana. **Abundance:** Uncommon. **Habitat:** Occurs in mature tall woodlands, such as riparian and Mopane (Colophospermum mopane) woodlands. **Habits:** An unobtrusive canopy dweller, it is easily overlooked. **Conservation:** Least Concern.

adult

juv.

**FORK-TAILED
DRONGO**

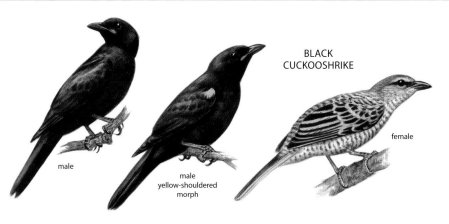

**BLACK
CUCKOOSHRIKE**

male

male
yellow-shouldered
morph

female

male

female

**WHITE-BREASTED
CUCKOOSHRIKE**

MONARCHS Monarchidae

Monarchids are arboreal crested flycatchers that catch insects in tree canopies. They are unrelated to the muscicapid flycatchers (p. 320), according to DNA evidence. A single representative of this family occurs in Botswana, African Paradise Flycatcher, a sexually dimorphic breeding migrant to Botswana.

J F M A M J J A S O N D

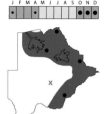

AFRICAN PARADISE FLYCATCHER *Terpsiphone viridis*

Setswana: kgôsi yadinônyane

M: 37 cm (14 ½ in), incl. tail streamers; F: 17 cm (6 ¾ in). **Identification:** Unmistakable orange-brown upperparts, blue-gray crested head and underparts, pale blue bill and eye-ring. Breeding male has bright blue bill and eye wattle and usually, but not always greatly elongate central tail feathers. Breeding female has a less conspicuous blue eye wattle, blue lower mandible and short tail. The nominate, *T. v. viridis*, is the only subspecies found in Botswana. **Call:** Musical, rippling call. Also a harsh, monosyllabic *zeek*. **Status:** Intra-African migrant, breeding. First arrivals are almost invariably recorded on or close to Botswana Independence Day, September 30. There is one unusual egg-laying record from April, just before most birds depart. Some birds overwinter. **Abundance:** Common. **Habitat:** Associated with riparian vegetation around the Okavango Delta, and riparian strips elsewhere. **Habits:** Solitary or in pairs. Perches within tree canopy and catches insects after short, fast flight. Highly vocal and active. The small, cup-shaped nest, bound with spiderwebs and decorated with lichens, is built by the female alone. **Conservation:** Least Concern. **General:** The Setswana name *kgôsi yadinônyane* means "chief of the birds."

SHRIKES Laniidae

True shrikes, the birds of this family have hooked bills, and there is usually a tooth-like projection behind the hook. The name of the principal genus, *Lanius*, means "butcher," in reference to shrikes' habit of dismembering prey items with the hooked beak and sometimes impaling them on thorns. All are perch hunters, taking insects and small vertebrates, which are usually caught on the ground. Botswana has six species; two are Palearctic migrants, and the others are sedentary species, including one that is a vagrant.

J F M A M J J A S O N D

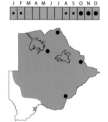

MAGPIE SHRIKE *Urolestes melanoleucus*

Setswana: tilodi, tolodi, mo.tsilodi, tsilodi, mo.tsulodi, tlhômêdi

45 cm (17 ¾ in), incl. tail. **Identification:** Unmistakable, large black shrike with white shoulder bars and very long tail. Female (illustrated) has white flanks (absent in male). Recently fledged juvenile has shorter tail and is dark brown with a white saddle on the back, usually covered by wings but conspicuous when chick is soliciting food. **Call:** Ringing *tilodi* call. The Setswana name is onomatopoeic. **Status:** Resident, breeding. **Abundance:** Common to locally abundant. The dry floodplains on the periphery of the Okavango Delta are a stronghold for this species. **Habitat:** Occurs in open acacia savannas with short grass. **Habits:** Gregarious, in small flocks. Individuals perch hunt from edge of tree or shrub, overlooking open ground, making frequent forays to the ground to catch insects and small vertebrates. **Conservation:** Least Concern.

J F M A M J J A S O N D

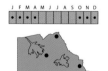

SOUTHERN WHITE-CROWNED SHRIKE *Eurocephalus anguitimens*

Setswana: le.nkutshwêu

24 cm (9 ½ in). **Identification:** Large, white-headed shrike with dark line through eye that extends onto cheeks and terminates in black nape. Juvenile has off-white crown, brown on face only, and white nape. **Call:** Loud, nasal *pepep, pepep*. **Status:** Resident, breeding. **Abundance:** Common. This species's stronghold is in Botswana. **Habitat:** Found in woodlands with open areas and short grass cover and woodlands with Baobab (*Adansonia digitata*) trees. **Habits:** Gregarious; occurs in small parties. Perch hunts from top or outer branches of tree, flying down to the ground to capture invertebrate prey. Often seen perched on roadside wires. **Conservation:** Least Concern.

breeding
male

breeding
female

**AFRICAN PARADISE
FLYCATCHER**
T. v. viridis

juv.

adult

**MAGPIE
SHRIKE**

adult

juv.

**SOUTHERN
WHITE-CROWNED
SHRIKE**

251

SOUZA'S SHRIKE *Lanius souzae*

17 cm (6 ¾ in). **Identification:** Brown and white shrike. It has a white wing bar, which is diagnostic in combination with the long tail with all-white outer feathers. The wing bar distinguishes it from Red-backed Shrike, but makes it similar to immature Southern Fiscal. However, in all plumages, Souza's Shrike has a brown tail with white outer feathers, and the tail is not particularly graduated, as the fiscal's tail is. Male Souza's Shrike has a black face mask and pale gray head; the immature fiscal is overall brownish. Female Souza's Shrike has duller black face mask and buffy flanks. Immature has rich rufous upperparts. **Call:** Not very vocal; ringing *cheeeer*; also harsh alarm, *tzzzick*. **Status:** Visitor at edge of range, or possible resident; no breeding records from Botswana. It breeds in the nearby Zambezi Region of Namibia, so it may be recorded breeding in Botswana in the future. **Abundance:** Rare. The range of this species extends southward marginally into extreme northern Botswana. **Habitat:** Prefers Zambezi Teak (*Baikiaea plurijuga*) woodlands. **Habits:** Solitary; perch hunts in manner similar to that of Southern Fiscal. **Conservation:** Least Concern.

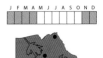

RED-BACKED SHRIKE *Lanius collurio*

18 cm (7 in). **Identification:** Small brown shrike. Male has gray crown, thick black eye stripe, reddish-brown mantle and wings, and buffy breast. Female has white lores and supercilium, a dark brown patch behind the eye, and, most distinctively, scallop-edged feathers on the breast and flanks. Immature resembles female but has more rufous-toned crown and more heavily scalloped, buffy breast and flanks. **Call:** Mostly silent; harsh, squeaky song. **Status:** Palearctic migrant; nonbreeding. **Abundance:** Common to abundant. Botswana provides significant habitat for this species, most of the global population of which spends the boreal winter in southern Africa. **Habitat:** An acacia specialist found in a variety of Kalahari savanna types, it prefers semiarid, acacia-dominated habitats. **Habits:** Solitary; it perch hunts from low bushes, pouncing on insect prey on the ground. Returns to same area in successive years. **Conservation:** Least Concern.

LESSER GREY SHRIKE *Lanius minor*

21 cm (8 ¼ in). **Identification:** Distinctive, chunky shrike, with gray and black upperparts and white underparts (with variable amount of pinkish wash). Adult has a thick black mask that extends onto the forehead; this is reduced to a black eye stripe in younger birds. **Call:** Mostly silent. **Status:** Palearctic migrant, nonbreeding. **Abundance:** Common. Botswana provides significant habitat for this species, most of the global population of which spends the boreal winter in southern Africa. **Habitat:** An acacia specialist found in a variety of Kalahari savanna types, it prefers semiarid, acacia-dominated habitats. **Habits:** Hunts by perching motionless on top of low tree or shrub, periodically making swooping flight to new perch or pouncing on insect on ground. **Conservation:** Least Concern.

SOUTHERN FISCAL *Lanius collaris*

Setswana: tlhômêdi, se.tômêlamitlwa

22 cm (8 ¾ in). **Identification:** Stocky black-and-white shrike with white wing bar that extends to the shoulder. Female is paler than male, but still distinctly black (or charcoal) with white underparts, and has pale chestnut on flanks. Juvenile is browner and has white wing bar, so is sometimes confused with Souza's Shrike; however, juvenile fiscal has shorter, heavily graduated tail with black tips to white outer feathers. The subspecies that occurs in Botswana, *L. c. subcoronatus*, has a white supercilium. **Call:** Harsh grating mixed with musical whistles; often incorporates mimicry. **Status:** Resident, breeding. **Abundance:** Uncommon. Numbers are increased during winter by birds moving up from the south. In the area marked in light green on the map, this species is very sparse and unpredictable. Farther north there have been irregular sightings (Maun, Boteti River). It does not occur in the Okavango Delta. **Habitat:** Found in grasslands with scattered trees or shrubs. **Habits:** Solitary; perches conspicuously on bushes or outer branches of trees, flying to the ground to catch insects and small reptiles. Caches food by impaling it on thorns, as indicated by the Setswana name *se.tômêlamitlwa* ("impaler on thorns"). **Conservation:** Least Concern.

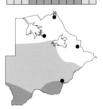

SOUZA'S
SHRIKE

male

male

RED-BACKED
SHRIKE

female

adult

imm.

LESSER GREY
SHRIKE

adult
male

SOUTHERN
FISCAL
L. c. subcoronatus

adult
female

imm.

253

ORIOLES Oriolidae

A family of canopy dwellers that have bright golden or yellow plumage, with variable amounts of black on the wings, and coral-pink bills. They are omnivorous and glean foliage for invertebrates and fruit. All have liquid-sounding calls. Of the three members of the genus *Oriolus* in Botswana, one is a sedentary resident, one has a resident population supplemented by intra-African migrants, and the third is a Palearctic migrant.

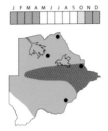

EURASIAN GOLDEN ORIOLE *Oriolus oriolus*

23 cm (9 in). **Identification:** Male easily identified by golden-yellow head and body, black lores, and black wings and tail. In flight, the whole wing appears black (primaries, secondaries, and their coverts) on the upperside, except for a narrow, pale yellowish-white wing bar. On the underside black flight feathers contrast with yellow underwing coverts. These features are useful for separating it from African Golden Oriole. Female is more olive-toned than male and has lightly streaked, whitish underparts and olive-green wings. Both sexes have reddish bill. Immature has dark, gray-green head and off-white underparts with fine streaking. **Call:** Liquid whistle, *weela-weeloo* or variation thereof. Alarm note is single *squeaar*. **Status:** Palearctic migrant, nonbreeding. **Abundance:** Uncommon to locally common, as in bushwillows along Marico River. **Habitat:** Found in a variety of habitats as it migrates across Botswana but prefers broad-leaved and riparian woodlands. **Habits:** Feeds in canopy of tall fruit-bearing trees on insects and fruit. May be seen in small flocks of up to eight birds. Rapid, undulating flight. **Conservation:** Least Concern.

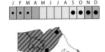

AFRICAN GOLDEN ORIOLE *Oriolus auratus*

24 cm (9 ½ in). **Identification:** Male easily identified by golden-yellow head and body, black eye stripe extending well beyond eye, and yellow and black wings (visible in perched and flying bird). Underwing pattern is similar to that of Eurasian Golden Oriole, but African appears much yellower in flight due to yellow secondaries and yellow secondary coverts on upperwing as well as underwing. Female is more yellowish-green-toned than male, particularly on mantle and upperwing coverts, and has lightly streaked, yellowish underparts, and a dark eye stripe (compare female Eurasian). Immature is similar to female but more heavily streaked on breast. **Call:** Liquid, whistled *fee-yoo*, repeated with permutations. **Status:** Resident and intra-African migrant populations, both breeding. Most sightings occur in summer, but some individuals overwinter. Limited Botswana records indicate that egg-laying may continue until March, as most birds depart by end of April. **Abundance:** Common. **Habitat:** Found in mature broad-leaved woodlands and riparian woodlands. **Habits:** Solitary, but also occurs in small groups when migrating. Forages in canopy of tall trees; its presence is divulged by its call. **Conservation:** Least Concern.

BLACK-HEADED ORIOLE *Oriolus larvatus*

25 cm (9 ¾ in). **Identification:** Adult easily identified by black head and chest contrasting with golden-yellow body plumage. Bill red. Immature has dark head and bill and dull yellow body plumage. The subspecies found in Botswana, *O. l. angolensis*, is much greener on the back than the nominate. **Call:** Liquid *poodleyoo*. **Status:** Resident, breeding. **Abundance:** Common. **Habitat:** Found in moist woodlands, such as riparian, preferably with evergreen or semideciduous vegetation. **Habits:** Solitary or in pairs; forages high up in tree canopy for insects and fruit. Calls in early morning from treetops. **Conservation:** Least Concern.

male

female

**EURASIAN
GOLDEN ORIOLE**

male

adult
male

adult
female

adult
male

imm.

**AFRICAN
GOLDEN ORIOLE**

adult
male

imm.

**BLACK-HEADED
ORIOLE**
O. l. angolensis

adult

PITTAS Pittidae

This family is represented by only one genus in Africa. Members have short wings and tail, and brightly colored plumage. They inhabit dense vegetation, where they forage among leaf litter for small animal prey. They build relatively large, domed nests close to the ground. One species occurs in Botswana, where it is rare.

AFRICAN PITTA *Pitta angolensis*

20 cm (7 ¾ in). **Identification:** Unmistakable bird with short wings and tail and colorful plumage. Its luminous blue wing spots and red belly are diagnostic. Immature, duller than adult, has brown back and pale red belly. **Call:** *Prrrriit*, given in early summer before breeding by displaying bird while it jumps vertically upward from branch with its wings buzzing. **Status:** Vagrant; no breeding records from Botswana. **Abundance:** Rare. Only one accepted record in Botswana, from Maun in Ngamiland District in December 2012. The species is an intra-African migrant that regularly strays outside its normal range in Zimbabwe and Mozambique. **Habitat:** Inhabits tangled undergrowth of riparian woodlands. **Habits:** This bird spends most of its time on the ground, scratching among leaf litter, where it is easily overlooked despite bright colors; it will fly up to perch on a branch if disturbed. **Conservation:** Least Concern.

CROWS Corvidae

The largest passerines, corvids are black or black-and-white birds that forage on the ground but roost and nest in trees. All three species in Botswana belong to the crow or raven genus, *Corvus*. All have harsh, guttural calls. They are apparently the most intelligent of birds. The Setswana name *le.gakabê* is generic for crow.

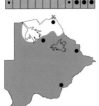

CAPE CROW *Corvus capensis*

Setswana: le.gakabê, le.gakabe, le.hukubu

50 cm (19 ¾ in). **Identification:** The only all-black corvid in Botswana. **Call:** Common call is a harsh *kwaaa*; it also regularly makes a liquid *gollop* call. **Status:** Resident, breeding. **Abundance:** Common to abundant. **Habitat:** Found in open semiarid habitats such as Kalahari tree and bush savanna. **Habits:** Mated pairs stay together; flocks comprise unpaired birds. This species calls and displays from treetops but forages by walking on the ground, digging with beak to extract a variety of foods (it is omnivorous). Nests on telegraph poles where no tall trees exist. The species is a host for the brood parasite Great Spotted Cuckoo. **Conservation:** Least Concern.

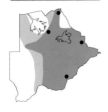

PIED CROW *Corvus albus*

Setswana: le.gakabê, le.gakabe, kgôsi yamanông

49 cm (19 ¼ in). **Identification:** Smallest corvid in Botswana. It has a white collar that extends down onto breast, giving it a distinctly pied appearance. **Call:** Harsh, garrulous cawing. **Status:** Resident, breeding; often nests on utility poles. **Abundance:** Common to abundant in most of the eastern half of the country. Absent from the Okavango Delta. **Habitat:** Found in a wide variety of habitat types, including built environments. **Habits:** Occurs in pairs and small flocks; forages on the ground. Thrives in towns, attracted by human refuse. It is often the first bird at a carcass, hence the Setswana name *kgôsi yamanông*, "chief of the vultures." **Conservation:** Least Concern. **General:** The bird is often affectionately referred to as *Moruti* (pastor, priest), in reference to its white collar.

WHITE-NECKED RAVEN *Corvus albicollis*

Setswana: le.gakabê, mo.kgômilô

52 cm (20 ½ in). Identification: Large black corvid with stout bill and white on neck only. **Call:** Nasal *kraak*. **Status:** Visitor from Zimbabwe and South Africa; no breeding records from Botswana. **Abundance:** Rare; only one accepted sighting to date, from Francistown in September 1999. Its range in Botswana is limited by lack of suitable habitat. **Habitat:** Found in hilly and mountainous areas. **Habits:** Adaptable; it scavenges carrion and at garbage dumps but also takes small live prey on the ground. **Conservation:** Least Concern.

AFRICAN
PITTA

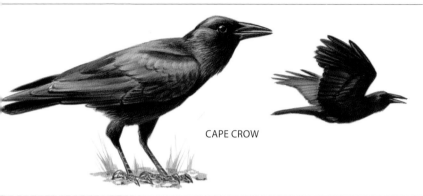

CAPE CROW

PIED CROW

WHITE-NECKED
RAVEN

FAIRY FLYCATCHERS Stenostiridae

This family is allied to the warblers, but its members are flycatcher-like in their behavior and traditionally referred to as flycatchers. One species endemic to southern Africa occurs in Botswana, the diminutive Fairy Flycatcher. It is one of the country's smallest birds.

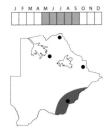

FAIRY FLYCATCHER *Stenostira scita*

12 cm (4 ¾ in). **Identification:** Resembles a small, long-tailed batis (p. 238) but is in a different family. It has a striking black-and-white facial mask, white wing bar, and white outer tail feathers. **Call:** Mostly silent. **Status:** Intra-African migrant, nonbreeding. It is a winter visitor from South Africa. **Abundance:** Scarce, but in some winters (e.g., 1999) more common than in others. The species is a southern African endemic that breeds in South Africa; its range just extends into southern and southeastern Botswana. **Habitat:** Found in acacia savanna, riparian vegetation, and scrubby slopes of hills. **Habits:** Behaves like a warbler, frequently fanning its tail. It forages in bushes, hopping continually from twig to twig. **Conservation:** Least Concern.

TITS Paridae

Small, mainly arboreal, perching birds. Many species hold a food item in the foot in the manner of parrots (an unusual practice) and hammer it with the short, pointed bill. Botswana has three small, sparrow-size species, all belonging to the genus *Melaniparus*. They occur in pairs or small family parties. Arboreal birds, they forage acrobatically among tree foliage for invertebrates, sometimes hanging upside down. All are sedentary, breeding residents; they nest in holes (usually in trees), and some species use helpers in raising young.

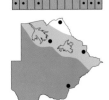

ASHY TIT *Melaniparus cinerascens*

Setswana: se.bataledi

15 cm (6 in). **Identification:** Small passerine with striking black-and-white head and black throat. The gray underparts, however, are its key identification feature. **Call:** Varied; *sikur kurr-kur* or ringing *t'wit-t'wit-t'wit*. **Status:** Resident, breeding. **Abundance:** Common to abundant. Botswana is an important stronghold for the species. **Habitat:** An acacia specialist, prefers Kalahari tree and bush savanna. **Habits:** Occurs in pairs or small groups, often in mixed bird parties; territorial. It forages in low bushes, creeping along branches. It is closely associated with acacias. **Conservation:** Least Concern.

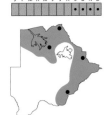

SOUTHERN BLACK TIT *Melaniparus niger*

16 cm (6 ¼ in). **Identification:** Small black passerine with white edges to the wing feathers. Two subspecies occur in Botswana: female and immature of *M. n. xanthostomus* have brownish underparts; those of *M. n. ravidus* have grayish underparts. **Call:** Harsh, varied song—*zeet-zeet-zeet* or *chrr-chrr-chrr*—mixed with more musical, whistled *weerit-weerit* notes. **Status:** Resident, breeding. **Abundance:** Common. *M. n. xanthostomus* is found north of Makgadikgadi Pans; *M. n. ravidus* is found in the east and south of the country. **Habitat:** Occurs in broad-leaved and acacia woodlands. **Habits:** Solitary or in pairs, or often in mixed species bird parties. Mainly insectivorous, it forages from ground level to treetops. **Conservation:** Least Concern.

RUFOUS-BELLIED TIT *Melaniparus rufiventris*

15 cm (6 in). **Identification:** Small passerine with black head, pale yellow eye, and rich rufous belly and underparts. **Call:** Harsh *chweerr-chweerr-chweerr*. **Status:** Visitor or possibly resident; no breeding records from Botswana. **Abundance:** Rare. A Zambezian near endemic, it occurs in the northwestern corner of Botswana at the western and southern limit of its range. **Habitat:** Favors mature broad-leaved Mopane (*Colophospermum mopane*) and Zambezi Teak (*Baikiaea plurijuga*) woodlands. **Habits:** Occurs in pairs or small groups. It feeds in middle to upper strata of canopy. **Conservation:** Least Concern.

FAIRY
FLYCATCHER

ASHY TIT

SOUTHERN
BLACK TIT
M. n. ravidus

male

female

RUFOUS-BELLIED TIT

259

PENDULINE TITS   Remizidae

Diminutive, warbler-like birds; among the smallest birds in Botswana. A key feature of this family is the durable felted nest made from animal and plant down, which has a false entrance concealing the real entrance. It is used for roosting and breeding, and sets these birds apart from their close relatives in the Paridae (p. 258). Botswana has two species.

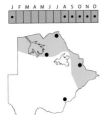

GREY PENDULINE TIT *Anthoscopus caroli*

Setswana: se.setlo

8 cm (3 ¼ in). **Identification:** Diminutive, warbler-like passerine; smallest bird found in Botswana (weighing only 6 g). It is gray above and has pale underparts. Buffy flanks and plain buffy forehead distinguish it from Cape Penduline Tit. There are two subspecies in Botswana: *A. c. hellmayri* has slightly darker, grayish-white throat and chest than *A. c. caroli*. **Call:** Soft, rasping *chichizee, chichizee*, repeated. **Status:** Resident, breeding. **Abundance:** Uncommon. *A. c. caroli* occurs in the northern part of Central District, and in North-East, Chobe, and Ngamiland Districts; *A. c. hellmayri* occurs in the east. **Habitat:** Found in mature broad-leaved woodlands. **Habits:** Occurs in pairs or small family groups, often in mixed bird parties. It is a canopy dweller. It makes a felted, purse-shaped woolen nest, with a false entrance to confuse predators. **Conservation:** Least Concern.

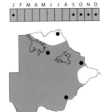

CAPE PENDULINE TIT *Anthoscopus minutus*

Setswana: se.setlo

9 cm (3 ½ in). **Identification:** Diminutive, warbler-like passerine. Yellow flanks and belly combined with black-and-white-patterned forehead are diagnostic. Two subspecies occur in Botswana: *A. m. damarensis* has distinctly yellow underparts, while *A. m. minutus* is generally a drabber bird. **Call:** Soft *tirit, tirit, tirit*. **Status:** Resident, breeding. **Abundance:** Common. *A. m. damarensis* occurs throughout most of Botswana, except the southwest where it is replaced by *A. m. minutus*. **Habitat:** An acacia specialist, found in Kalahari tree and bush savanna and arid scrub savanna. **Habits:** Occurs in small family parties; members maintain contact with one another with soft calls. The felted, pouch-like nests, made of plant fiber, are unique and relatively conspicuous in areas where the bird occurs. **Conservation:** Least Concern.

NICATORS   Nicatoridae

Previously thought to be related to bushshrikes (p. 242) and greenbuls (p. 272), the *Nicator* genus now has its own family. The birds have a shrike-like hooked bill, but the call is more like that of a greenbul. One species occurs in Botswana. The male is significantly larger than the female, although the sexes are alike in terms of plumage coloration. The saucer-shaped platform nest, similar to a dove nest, differs from the cup-shaped nests of shrikes and greenbuls (although it resembles some bushshrike nests).

EASTERN NICATOR *Nicator gularis*

M: 23 cm (9 in), F: 20 cm (7 ¾ in). **Identification:** Similar to a greenbul or bushshrike. It is olive green above with a buffy-olive breast and pale yellow belly. Yellow spots on the wings and its distinctive call are the key identification features. Resembles Grey-headed Bushshrike (p. 242) but is smaller, and its bill is less robust. Yellow-bellied Greenbul (p. 272) has a plain olive back with no yellow spots. **Call:** Liquid *chi-chi-chi-rrupp-chi-chi-woa*, interspersed with whistles and some mimicry. **Status:** Visitor or possibly resident; no breeding records from Botswana. **Abundance:** Rare. The westernmost extent of its southern African range extends marginally into northern Chobe District. There is only one (accepted) sighting, from the Kasane area from December 2012 to January 2013. **Habitat:** Found in riparian woodland and thickets. **Habits:** It is a solitary skulker in dense thickets, where it clambers along upper branches. Best located by call. **Conservation:** Least Concern.

nest

GREY
PENDULINE TIT
A. c. caroli

CAPE
PENDULINE TIT
A. m. damarensis

EASTERN
NICATOR

LARKS Alaudidae

A large family of cryptically colored terrestrial birds that forage, roost, and nest on the ground. Often plumage varies to match substrate color. Sexes look alike (except in sparrow-larks), but males sing from conspicuous posts or in flight; the calls are often the easiest means of identification. There are 16 species in Botswana, including three sparrow-larks, which differ from the others in some respects. Most are sedentary residents, but the granivorous species are highly nomadic. One species is a migrant and one is near endemic to Botswana. For identification purposes, Botswana larks subdivide along taxonomic or ecological lines into several useful groupings (modified from Peacock, 2012), listed below. The Setswana name *se.bota* (*se.botê, se.botha, se.bothê*) is generic for lark; *tshilwane* and *ramokwakwadi* are generic for sparrow-lark.

Sparrow-Larks: Three species belonging to the genus *Eremopterix*. Sexually dimorphic: males have black on face, most females have a black belly patch. They occur in small to large flocks. Their songs are not distinctive. One species is a southern African endemic.

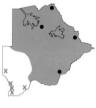

CHESTNUT-BACKED SPARROW-LARK *Eremopterix leucotis*

Setswana: tshilwane, ramokwakwadi

13 cm (5 in). **Identification:** Small lark with superficial resemblance to a sparrow or finch. Male has black crown, white ear coverts, and rich chestnut mantle and back. Female has chestnut mantle and narrow white collar (which differentiates it from female Grey-backed Sparrow-Lark) and a black belly and pale rump (unlike female Black-eared Sparrow-Lark). **Call:** Soft and infrequently heard *cheep-chee* and variations thereof. **Status:** Resident, breeding. May breed opportunistically during any month of the year, though egg-laying peaks in summer. **Abundance:** Common. It is a mobile species often found outside its normal range. Irruptions are observed during dry years. **Habitat:** Favors open savanna woodlands with bare areas, including dry pans; also occurs at reservoir edges and in road verges. **Habits:** Terrestrial seedeater; occurs in small flocks. When disturbed, flies off with irregular flight and then suddenly resettles. **Conservation:** Least Concern.

GREY-BACKED SPARROW-LARK *Eremopterix verticalis*

Setswana: tshilwane, ramokwakwadi

13 cm (5 in). **Identification:** Small lark with superficial resemblance to a sparrow or finch. Male is the only sparrow-lark in Botswana with the combination of gray back and black-and-white head pattern. Female has grayish back and black belly patch, lacks small white collar on hind neck shown by female Chestnut-backed Sparrow-Lark. All three southern African subspecies occur in Botswana: Male of the nominate has dark upperparts and black underparts, while female has brown, slightly rufous upperparts and distinctive black belly; *E. v. khama* is the grayest subspecies (both sexes); *E. v. damarensis* is the palest. Adults of *E. v. khama* and *E. v. damarensis* might be mistaken for pale juveniles. **Call:** Series of high-pitched whistled notes. **Status:** Resident, breeding. May breed opportunistically during any month outside of the summer egg-laying peak. **Abundance:** Common to abundant. It is a mobile species subject to influxes. *E. v. verticalis* is found in South-East, Southern, and Kgatleng Districts and eastern Central District; *E. v. khama* (named after the Botswana royal family) is found in central Botswana and Makgadikgadi Pans; *E. v. damarensis* is found in the western part of the country from Kgalagadi District through Ghanzi into Ngamiland District. **Habitat:** Inhabits wide variety of semiarid Kalahari vegetation types. **Habits:** Gregarious seedeater; feeds in open areas on the ground in large flocks. Often seen in association with Stark's Lark (p. 268). **Conservation:** Least Concern.

BLACK-EARED SPARROW-LARK *Eremopterix australis*

Setswana: tshilwane, ramokwakwadi

13 cm (5 in). **Identification:** Small lark with superficial resemblance to a sparrow or finch. Male is black with chestnut margins to wing feathers and a brown rump, lacking any white in plumage; shows rounded black wings in flight. Female is more lark-like and has chestnut margins to wing feathers and black streaking on breast; lacks black belly patch of the other two sparrow-lark females. Both sexes are rich brown above (to match substrate). **Call:** Single notes or longer, soft twittering. **Status:** Visitor, breeding. Breeds opportunistically, at any time of year, in response to rain. **Abundance:** Rare. A southern African endemic; its range just extends into the extreme southwest of Botswana. **Habitat:** Found in arid scrub savanna on red Kalahari sands. **Habits:** Gregarious and nomadic, moves to areas where rain has fallen, where it feeds on seeds and breeds opportunistically. **Conservation:** Least Concern.

adult male

juv.

adult male

**CHESTNUT-BACKED
SPARROW-LARK**

adult female

adult female

**GREY-BACKED
SPARROW-LARK**

E. v. khama

adult male

juv.

adult male

adult female

adult female

adult male

juv.

adult male

adult female

**BLACK-EARED
SPARROW-LARK**

adult female

Mirafra **larks:** Five species. All have rufous wing panels and streaking on mantle and breast. They feed on insects an[...] seeds and accordingly have bills ranging from conical to longish and strong. All have characteristic songs or engag[...] in wing clapping. Birds are solitary or occur in pairs. One species is endemic to southern Africa and is Near Threatene[...]

MONOTONOUS LARK *Mirafra passerina*

Setswana: se.bota, se.botê, se.botha, se.bothê

14 cm (5 ½ in). **Identification:** Like other *Mirafra* larks, has a rufous wing panel and streakin[...] on mantle and breast. Its distinguishing features are its short conical bill, white belly, an[...] white throat (conspicuous when bird is calling). **Call:** Distinctive, repetitive monotonou[...] call (rendered as *purple jeep*), given throughout day and most of night when breedin[...] **Status:** Resident, breeding. Recorded during summer months, it is possibly also present i[...] winter but overlooked, due to observer reliance on its call (it is silent during winter). Egg[...] laying peaks during rains, when insects are abundant for feeding the chicks. **Abundance[...]** Uncommon to common; highly nomadic, prone to irruptions in years of substantial rain[...] Botswana is an important stronghold; however, it is important to note that although it ca[...] be locally common anywhere in Botswana at certain times, it is not common everywhere[...] all the time—indeed it is usually absent from most areas. **Habitat:** Occurs in semiarid, ope[...] habitats such as Kalahari tree and bush savanna. **Habits:** Terrestrial, but males have callin[...] posts on low vantage points such as bushes. Male also sings during its fluttering displa[...] flights. The species has a complex mating system, unique among larks, characterized initiall[...] by promiscuity, but later in the breeding cycle by monogamy. **Conservation:** Least Concer[...]

MELODIOUS LARK *Mirafra cheniana*

Setswana: se.bota, se.botê, se.botha, se.bothê

13 cm (5 in). **Identification:** Like other *Mirafra* larks, has a rufous wing panel and streakin[...] on mantle and breast. Its distinguishing features are its short conical bill, white eyebrow, an[...] a patch of rufous on the wing at the shoulder (visible in flight). Pale buffy belly and flank[...] differentiate it from Monotonous Lark, in which the belly and flanks are white. **Call:** Chatterin[...] *chi-chi-chi, chew-chew-chew, churr,* repeated with extensive mimicry added. The species is on[...] of the finest mimics in terms of the number and variety of birdcalls incorporated into its son[...] Male sings during characteristic flight, which can last for more than 40 minutes. **Status:** Visito[...] no breeding records from Botswana. Elsewhere in the region egg-laying takes place durin[...] rains, when insects are abundant for feeding the chicks. **Abundance:** Rare. A southern Africa[...] endemic. The northern part of the species's range just extends into southern Botswan[...] A relict population may persist on the Patlana Flats near Sehithwa (shown by a red squar[...] on the map), where a specimen was collected in 1961. **Habitat:** Found in dry grasslands o[...] southeastern Botswana. **Habits:** Terrestrial, but male sings from a perch or more commonl[...] in flight. **Conservation:** Near Threatened. **General:** Now housed in the Ditsong Museum i[...] South Africa, the Patlana specimen (collected by O.P.M. Prozesky) was at one stage regarde[...] as having been misidentified (Penry, 1994). It has subsequently been shown to be *M. chenian[...]* (Davies, 2011).

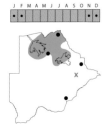

FLAPPET LARK *Mirafra rufocinnamomea*

Setswana: se.bota, se.botê, se.botha, se.bothê

15 cm (6 in). **Identification:** *Mirafra* lark best identified by wing-clapping display flight[...] It has rufous wing panel typical of the genus. Two subspecies occur in Botswana: *M. r[...] mababiensis* is very pale and has grayish upperparts; *M. r. smithersi* is more rufous-toned an[...] has a white belly. **Call:** Quiet whistled calls, given during display flight but less audible tha[...] wing clapping. **Status:** Resident; no breeding records from Botswana. Around the regio[...] egg-laying takes place during rains, when insects are abundant for feeding the chick[...] **Abundance:** Common. *M. r. mababiensis* (the type specimen of which was collected a[...] Tsotsoroga Pan in the Mababe Depression in Chobe National Park) is found in the Ngamilan[...] and Chobe Districts; *M. r. smithersi* is found in the northern part of Central District and th[...] eastern part of Chobe District. **Habitat:** Found in woodlands with clearings, and often alon[...] drainage lines. **Habits:** In common with other larks, this species is terrestrial; howeve[...] it is most conspicuous and easily identified when in flight display. It makes a distinctiv[...] high (50 m [164 ft] or higher), dipping flight, clapping its wings together on every descen[...] **Conservation:** Least Concern.

MONOTONOUS
LARK

MELODIOUS
LARK

FLAPPET
LARK
M. r. mababiensis

EASTERN CLAPPER LARK *Mirafra fasciolata*

Setswana: nônyane yapula; also se.bota, se.botê, se.botha, se.bothê

14 cm (5 ½ in). **Identification:** Wing-clapping *Mirafra* lark with rufous wing panel typical of the genus. Four subspecies in Botswana vary from rufous to pale gray in plumage color. The nominate, *M. f. fasciolata*, is the most rufous-toned, including the dark back; *M. f. deserti* is also quite rufous, including the back; *M. f. kalaharica* and *M. f. nata* are pale. **Call:** Drawn-out, descending *foooeeeee*, uttered toward end of display flight. **Status:** Resident, breeding. Main displaying and egg-laying period is during rains, when insects are abundant for feeding chicks, after which breeding tails off through the end of March. **Abundance:** Common to abundant. *M. f. fasciolata* occurs in the extreme south of Botswana; *M. f. deserti* is found in the extreme southwest; *M. f. kalaharica* is the most widespread subspecies (its type specimen came from Gemsbok Pan near Ghanzi), occurring throughout central Botswana; *M. f. nata* is found around Makgadikgadi Pans (its type specimen was collected from the Nata area). **Habitat:** Found in grasslands. **Habits:** Terrestrial. Easily identified by its display, in which it flies up a few meters from the ground, clapping the wings together loudly before descending with a whistle. **Conservation:** Least Concern. **General:** The Setswane name *nônyane yapula* means "rainbird."

RUFOUS-NAPED LARK *Mirafra africana*

Setswana: se.botêkgômo; also se.bota, se.botê, se.botha, se.bothê

17 cm (6 ¾ in). **Identification:** Large, stocky, heavy-billed lark. It has an erectile, rufous crown/ crest and rufous edges to flight feathers, forming a rufous wing panel clearly visible in flight. Three subspecies occur in Botswana: the rufous coloring is deeper in *M. a. transvaalensis* than in *M. a. grisescens* or *M. a. ghansiensis*, which are paler and similar to one another. **Call:** Distinctive *tseep-tseeoo*, issued from low bush or termite mound and accompanied by vigorous wing clapping (which sometimes causes the bird to be momentarily airborne). **Status:** Resident, breeding. Egg-laying takes place during rains, when insects are abundant for feeding the chicks. **Abundance:** Common to abundant. *M. a. transvaalensis* is found in eastern and southern Botswana; *M. a. grisescens* occurs in the north; *M. a. ghansiensis* (the type specimen of which was collected from Ghanzi District) extends from Ghanzi into Central Kalahari Game Reserve and Kgalagadi District. **Habitat:** Found in open grasslands with scattered shrubs, woodland, and fallow fields. **Habits:** Solitary terrestrial species, found mostly on the ground. **Conservation:** Least Concern.

Savanna larks: Two species belonging to the genus *Calendulauda*. Both are habitat specialists, with the Fawn-colored Lark (p. 268) being more widespread due to its preference for Kalahari tree and bush savanna. They both have small sharp beaks. Birds are solitary or occur in pairs. They have attractive, canary-like songs; Sabota Lark's includes mimicry.

SABOTA LARK *Calendulauda sabota*

Setswana: se.bota, se.botê, se.botha, se.bothê

15 cm (6 in). **Identification:** A distinctive savanna lark. It lacks rufous wing panel found in *Mirafra* larks (pp. 264-266) and Fawn-colored Lark (p. 268). It has an obvious white supercilium, like Fawn-colored, but is more heavily streaked on the breast and has buff outer tail feathers. Raises crest when singing. Four subspecies are found in Botswana: *C. s. sabota* is the most rufous-toned; *C. s. herero* is slightly paler and browner; grayer races *C. s. sabotoides* and *C. s. waibeli* are separated by degree of breast streaking. With the exception of *C. s. herero*, they are all slender billed. **Call:** Includes mimicry, which is interspersed with high-pitched *seee* notes. Male sings during display flight. **Status:** Resident, breeding. **Abundance:** Uncommon to abundant. The precise ranges of the subspecies are not well defined, but *C. s. sabotoides* (type specimen collected in Ghanzi District) extends from Ghanzi eastward to the eastern hardveld, where it is abundant and probably sympatric with *C. s. sabota*. *C. s. herero* is uncommon in the extreme southwest along the Nossob and Molopo Valleys, and *C. s waibeli* is common in northwestern Ngamiland District. **Habitat:** Found primarily in eastern hardveld, but also in northwestern Kalahari tree and bush savanna and in arid scrub savanna. **Habits:** Forages on the ground for seeds and insects. As with many lark species, it only occasionally drinks water. **Conservation:** Least Concern. **General:** The English name is taken directly from the Setswana; this is one of only two birds in which this is the case.

**EASTERN
CLAPPER LARK**
M. f. nata

**RUFOUS-NAPED
LARK**
M. a. grisescens

C. s. sabotoides

C. s. waibeli

SABOTA LARK

267

FAWN-COLORED LARK *Calendulauda africanoides*

Setswana: se.bota, se.botê, se.botha, se.bothê

15 cm (6 in). **Identification:** Savanna lark, of varying coloration, best told by call and its white underparts. Although it has a rufous wing panel like *Mirafra* larks (pp. 264-266), it is most similar to Sabota Lark (p. 266) but has less strongly marked face and less streaking on breast. There are four subspecies in Botswana; ranging from the most reddish brown to the palest gray they are *C. a. harei*, *C. a. sarwensis*, *C. a. africanoides*, and *C. a. makarikari*. **Call:** Elaborate song comprising canary-like trills, increasing in volume and then fading, with a whistle at end. **Status:** Resident breeding. **Abundance:** Abundant; the most frequently seen lark on the sandy Kalahari soil covering most of Botswana. *C. a. africanoides* occurs in the east along the eastern hardveld; *C. a. harei* in the west in Ghanzi and Kgalagadi Districts; *C. a. sarwensis* in Central, Kweneng, and Southern Districts; and *C. a. makarikari* from Makgadikgadi Pans northward into Ngamiland and Chobe Districts. **Habitat:** Inhabits Kalahari savannas with sandy soils. **Habits:** Terrestrial. Often perches on low bushes, singing. **Conservation:** Least Concern.

Nomadic seedeaters: Two species belonging to the genus *Spizocorys*. They are gregarious, finch-like birds with short conical bills. Their songs are not distinctive.

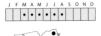

STARK'S LARK *Spizocorys starki*

Setswana: se.bota, se.botê, se.botha, se.bothê

14 cm (5 ½ in). **Identification:** Small desert lark. Generally very pale, it has mostly white underparts and a pale bill and lacks bold facial markings (compare Pink-billed Lark). **Call:** Variable chirps and trills. **Status:** Resident; no breeding records from Botswana. Breeds over winter in most parts of southern Africa. **Abundance:** Scarce. Usually seen in the extreme southwest of Botswana, but recorded sporadically in other parts of the country (sometimes in large flocks). The species has a more extensive range than previously documented. **Habitat:** Favors arid scrub savanna and short grasslands with calcrete or stony areas, such as are found on dry pans. **Habits:** Small flocks forage for seeds on open ground. This lark may congregate in flocks of more than 1,000 birds when conditions are favorable. **Conservation:** Least Concern.

PINK-BILLED LARK *Spizocorys conirostris*

Setswana: se.bota, se.botê, se.botha, se.bothê

13 cm (5 in). **Identification:** Small grassland lark with a conical pink bill. Outer tail feathers are white. The most useful field characteristic is the distinctive facial pattern of a white supercilium, and narrow black eye stripe, moustachial stripe, and malar stripe. Four subspecies occur in Botswana: *S. c. conirostris* is the darkest; *S. c. barlowi* is pale rufous overall; and *S. c. crypta* and *S. c. damarensis* are grayer. **Call:** Not very vocal. **Status:** Resident breeding. Breeds opportunistically, but there is a slight peak in egg-laying in early winter. **Abundance:** Uncommon to common; it is irruptive and nomadic. First sightings of the species in Botswana were in the late 1980s, but under favorable conditions large numbers are now seen, in central Botswana especially. *S. c. barlowi* occurs in Kgalagadi, Southern and South-East Districts; *S. c. crypta* (type specimen from Mampswe in Central District) is found around Makgadikgadi Pans, where it is common; *S. c. damarensis* occurs in Ngamiland District, where it is uncommon; and the nominate extends marginally into South-East District. As with other irruptive and nomadic species, the map may give a false impression of how widespread and abundant it is, since the species can be locally common virtually anywhere, though it usually isn't. **Habitat:** Prefers semiarid, open grasslands, such as those around Rakops, Mopipi Dam, Nata Sanctuary, and Lake Xau in Central District. **Habits:** Terrestrial. Occurs in mobile flocks. **Conservation:** Least Concern.

268

C. a. africanoides

C. a. makarikari

FAWN-COLORED
LARK

STARK'S
LARK

S. c. crypta

PINK-BILLED
LARK

Other larks: Four unrelated but distinctive species. Each is the only representative of its genus in Botswana.

DUSKY LARK *Pinarocorys nigricans*

Setswana: se.bota, se.botê, se.botha, se.bothê

19 cm (17 ½ in). **Identification:** Large, distinctive lark. Superficially resembling Groundscrape Thrush (p. 318), it has a bold black-and-white facial pattern and heavily spotted breast like Groundscraper, but does not share that species's upright posture, yellow lower mandible, or spotting extending down to the flanks. Wing coverts appear scalloped due to buffy margins to feathers. Two subspecies occur in Botswana: *P. n. occidentis* has a plain white belly; *P. n. nigricans* has streaking extending from the breast down onto the belly. **Call:** Usually silent in Botswana. **Status:** Intra-African migrant, nonbreeding. A bird was observed carrying nesting material and displaying in the Tuli Block during April 2010 following heavy late rains; this may represent a change in the breeding status of this species in southern Africa. Most sightings in April are of birds on migration passage. **Abundance:** Uncommon. *P. n. occidentis* occurs throughout Botswana; *P. n. nigricans* overlaps with it in the eastern third of the country. **Habitat:** Found in savannas with short-grass areas among broad-leaved trees and shrubs. **Habits:** Solitary and terrestrial. **Conservation:** Least Concern.

SHORT-CLAWED LARK *Certhilauda chuana*

Setswana: se.bota, se.botê, se.botha, se.bothê

19 cm (7 ½ in). **Identification:** Large, slender lark with relatively long bill. It has a long, off-white supercilium, and the back has a scalloped appearance due to buffy margins to dark brown feathers; lacks rufous wing panel. Short claw on hind toe from which name is derived is not a useful identification feature. **Call:** Thin, drawn-out *si-tseeoou*; also a descending whistle during display flight. **Status:** Resident, breeding. **Abundance:** Uncommon. The species is near endemic to Botswana; the bulk of the population is found in the southeastern part of the country. **Habitat:** Prefers short grasslands with scattered bushes, especially fallow fields. **Habits:** Terrestrial, usually solitary. It has a spectacular display flight during rainy season: it flies vertically into the air, whistling at the peak of its climb (at about 10 m [33 ft]), and then drops down headfirst with wings closed. **Conservation:** Least Concern.

SPIKE-HEELED LARK *Chersomanes albofasciata*

Setswana: se.bota, se.botê, se.botha, se.bothê

14 cm (5 ½ in). **Identification:** Lark with a long, decurved bill (visibly shorter in female), plump shape, upright stance, and white throat contrasting with pale grayish-buff belly. Key field feature is the short, white-tipped tail. The long claw on the hind toe, from which the common name is presumably derived, is not a useful identification feature. The two subspecies found in Botswana—*C. a. kalahariae*, *C. a. barlowi*—are both very pale; the latter is the palest of the subspecies in southern Africa. **Call:** Ringing, chattering call, often given by more than one bird. **Status:** Resident, breeding. Egg-laying is opportunistic and can take place during any month if conditions are suitable. **Abundance:** Common. *C. a. kalahariae* (type specimen collected at Lehututu in Kgalagadi District), occurs in southwestern Botswana; *C. a. barlowi* (type specimen from Lake Xau in Central District), occurs around Makgadikgadi Pans. **Habitat:** Occurs in arid scrub savanna and Kalahari tree and bush savanna, favors open areas with short grass. **Habits:** Terrestrial; pairs or small groups forage on the ground. It is unique among larks in Botswana in being a cooperative breeder. **Conservation:** Least Concern.

RED-CAPPED LARK *Calandrella cinerea*

Setswana: se.bota, se.botê, se.botha, se.bothê

16 cm (6 ¼ in). **Identification:** Lark with rufous breast patches, a red crown (often raised as a short crest), and plain underparts. All three southern African subspecies, which vary in color, occur in Botswana: *C. c. spleniata* is palest, *C. c. cinerea* is darker, and *C. c. alluvia* is the darkest and most rufous-toned. **Call:** Varied, but always includes whistled *treee*. **Status:** Resident, breeding. Breeds opportunistically in any month of the year. The population is supplemented by local intra-African migrants, also breeding, throughout the summer; sightings peak late in the season, from February to April. **Abundance:** Common. *C. c. spleniata* is widespread throughout Kgalagadi, Ghanzi, Ngamiland, and Central Districts; the nominate is found in Southern and South-East Districts; and *C. c. alluvia* is found in the northern part of Ngamiland and Chobe Districts. **Habitat:** Favors short grasslands, especially on dry pans but also on dry floodplains and at drying edges of dams and lakes. **Habits:** Flocks forage in areas of short grass, all the birds hunched and moving in the same direction while individuals pause to peck at seeds or dig with bill. Large flocks of hundreds of birds are occasionally seen. **Conservation:** Least Concern.

DUSKY LARK
P. n. nigricans

SHORT-CLAWED
LARK

SPIKE-HEELED
LARK
C. a. barlowi

RED-CAPPED
LARK
C. c. alluvia

271

BULBULS, GREENBULS, BROWNBULS Pycnonotidae

A multi-generic collection of mainly frugivorous woodland, forest, and thicket dwellers. Botswana has four species. The two bulbuls have dark brown plumage, crests, and striking yellow undertail coverts. The greenbul and brownbul are characterized by their greenish and brownish plumage, respectively, but are more easily identified by their calls, habitat, and foraging behavior. The Setswana name *moritinkolê*, and variations thereof, is used generically for the bulbuls and the brownbul.

AFRICAN RED-EYED BULBUL *Pycnonotus nigricans*

Setswana: maritinkolê, moritinkolê, ramorutiakolê, rankolokotša, mo.ririntlhofê, satope

19 cm (7 ½ in). **Identification:** Medium-size, brown passerine with yellow undertail coverts. Conspicuous red wattle surrounds eye (very occasionally wattle may be yellow). Slightly smaller than Dark-capped Bulbul, which occupies moist woodlands. The nominate, *P. n. nigricans*, which has a whitish belly, is the subspecies found throughout Botswana. **Call:** Setswana name *moritinkolê* is onomatopoeic; in English the call is rendered as *wake up, Gregory*. Similar to call of Dark-capped Bulbul. **Status:** Resident, breeding. **Abundance:** Abundant. One of Botswana's most abundant and widespread species. Birds undertake local movements away from very dry areas during winter. **Habitat:** Occurs in a variety of arid Kalahari savannas; moves into moist woodlands during dry season. **Habits:** Occurs in small groups; forages within tree foliage. The species is a host for brood parasite Jacobin Cuckoo. Hybridizes with Dark-capped Bulbul; resulting offspring have orange eye-ring. **Conservation:** Least Concern.

DARK-CAPPED BULBUL *Pycnonotus tricolor*

Setswana: maritinkolê, moritinkolê, ramorutiakolê, rankolokotša, mo.ririntlhofê, satope

21 cm (8 ¼ in). **Identification:** Larger than African Red-eyed Bulbul. Has narrow black eye wattle. Both southern African subspecies occur; *P. t. tricolor* has a dark brown head; *P. t. layardi* has a black face and pointed crest. **Call:** Setswana name *moritinkolê* is onomatopoeic; in English call is rendered as *wake up, Gregory*. Similar to call of African Red-eyed Bulbul. **Status:** Resident, breeding. **Abundance:** Abundant over most of range; uncommon in southeast. *P. t. tricolor* is found in Ngamiland and Chobe Districts; *P. t. layardi* occurs in the eastern part of Central District and in South-East and Kgatleng Districts. **Habitat:** Occurs in mesic woodlands, such as riparian. **Habits:** Pairs and small flocks forage among tree foliage for fruit and insects. The species is sedentary. It is a host for brood parasite Jacobin Cuckoo. Hybridizes with African Red-eyed Bulbul; resulting offspring have orange eye-ring. **Conservation:** Least Concern.

YELLOW-BELLIED GREENBUL *Chlorocichla flaviventris*

22 cm (8 ¾ in). **Identification:** Combination of yellow underparts with olive sides to breast, plain olive wings and mantle, and white crescent above dark red eye is diagnostic. Only one subspecies, *C. f. occidentalis*, with bright yellow underparts, is found in Botswana. **Call:** Querulous, urgent call, aptly rendered as *do you hear, do you hear, I'm here, here, here, here*. **Status:** Resident, breeding. **Abundance:** Common over its main range; rare resident or occasional visitor in Gaborone and near Kanye. This species may extend its range during years of high rainfall, when its riparian habitat becomes more extensive. **Habitat:** Found in riparian woodlands and thickets, and in forest edges. **Habits:** Small groups of up to 10 birds feed in lower strata of thickets or on the ground. Birds are confiding and easily approachable. **Conservation:** Least Concern.

TERRESTRIAL BROWNBUL *Phyllastrephus terrestris*

Setswana: maritinkolê, moritinkolê, ramorutiakolê, rankolokotša, mo.ririntlhofê, satope

21 cm (8 ¼ in). **Identification:** Nondescript in terms of coloration: brown with white throat. Call, habitat, and habits are more useful for identifying this species. **Call:** Murmuring *wuk, wuk, wukka, wak, wukkle-wukkle*, given by group members. **Status:** Resident, breeding. **Abundance:** Common, especially around the Okavango Delta, along the Chobe River, and along the Limpopo River (as far upriver as Oliphants Drift). **Habitat:** Inhabits dense vegetation such as riparian growth and thickets. **Habits:** Active, busy species; occurs in small flocks of up to five birds. As name suggests, it is largely terrestrial; it hops on the ground, turning leaf litter to find insect food. The genus name *Phyllastrephus* means "leaf tosser," in reference to the characteristic behavior exhibited by this bird. When perched low in undergrowth, frequently flicks wings partly open. **Conservation:** Least Concern.

AFRICAN RED-EYED
BULBUL
P. n. nigricans

DARK-CAPPED
BULBUL
P. t. layardi

YELLOW-BELLIED
GREENBUL
C. f. occidentalis

TERRESTRIAL
BROWNBUL

273

SWALLOWS, MARTINS Hirundinidae

Aerial insectivores with small beaks but large gapes, and angular, pointed wings (quite different from the curved, sickle-shaped wings of swifts, p. 202). They have short legs, perch readily, and frequently alight on the ground—particularly to collect mud and other nest material when breeding. The nesting habits of the Botswana species vary; the martins mainly use tunnels in banks, and the swallows construct mud-pellet nests in a diversity of configurations. Generally the martins are brownish and the swallows blue. Many of the swallows have long tail streamers, which are included in the total length measurement. Most of Botswana's 17 species are migrants, either intra-African or from the Palearctic; only seven species have resident populations. One species is endemic to southern Africa. The Setswana name *pêolane* is generic for swallows and martins as well as swifts.

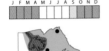

SAND MARTIN *Riparia riparia*

Setswana: pêolane, pêolwane

13 cm (5 in). **Identification:** Small brown martin with forked tail and narrow, pale brown breast band separating white throat from white belly. Larger Banded Martin differs in having a white supercilium and white underwing coverts (visible in flight), while coverts of Sand Martin are brown. Smaller Brown-throated Martin has a brown rather than white throat. **Call:** Not very vocal; quiet churring. **Status:** Palearctic migrant, nonbreeding. **Abundance:** Uncommon. The highest reporting rates for this species in southern Africa are in the Okavango Delta. **Habitat:** Prefers grasslands and woodlands adjacent to water. **Habits:** Aerial insectivore, often seen with Brown-throated Martins and Barn Swallows. Flies actively; does not glide often. **Conservation:** Least Concern.

BANDED MARTIN *Riparia cincta*

Setswana: pêolane, pêolwane

18 cm (7 in). **Identification:** Large brown martin with square tail, white supercilium, and brown breast band separating white throat from white lower breast and belly. In flight, shows white underwing coverts. Two similar subspecies, *R. c. xerica* and *R. c. cincta*, occur in Botswana. **Call:** Not very vocal; squeezed-out *chee-chee-chee*. **Status:** Resident, breeding. The population is supplemented by breeding intra-African migrants, which arrive in the southeast in midsummer. **Abundance:** Uncommon. *R. c. xerica* occurs in northern Botswana, the nominate in southeastern Botswana. **Habitat:** Prefers natural grasslands and floodplains. **Habits:** Aerial insectivore. Digs tunnel nest in vertical sandbank. **Conservation:** Least Concern.

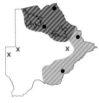

BROWN-THROATED MARTIN *Riparia paludicola*

Setswana: pêolane, pêolwane

12 cm (4 ¾ in). **Identification:** Small brown martin. It usually has a white belly, but an all-brown morph with a brown belly has been recorded in southeastern Botswana. This martin has dark underwing coverts and a forked tail with no white spots (compare Rock Martin). **Call:** Not very vocal. **Status:** Resident, breeding. **Abundance:** Uncommon. **Habitat:** Prefers wetlands in open habitats. **Habits:** Aerial insectivore, usually seen foraging near water. Roosts communally in reeds. May occur in flocks of many dozens over water in the northern wetlands; also in the southeast in flocks of 50-plus. Breeds in tunnel nests in riverbank during winter (until as late as November). Due to local movements, the species is most easily seen between April and November. **Conservation:** Least Concern.

ROCK MARTIN *Ptyonoprogne fuligula*

Setswana: pêolane, pêolwane

13 cm (5 in). **Identification:** Small brown martin with dark upperparts and cinnamon-brown underparts. It has square tail with white spots on most tail feathers. Can be confused only with all-brown morph of Brown-throated Martin, which is smaller, lacks white tail spots, and occupies wetland habitats. Two subspecies occur in Botswana: *P. f. fuligula* is cinnamon brown while *P. f. fusciventris* is smaller and darker brown. **Call:** Not very vocal. **Status:** Resident, breeding. **Abundance:** Uncommon. *P. f. fuligula* occurs in southern and eastern Botswana; *P. f. fusciventris* is a visitor found around the Okavango Delta, Linyanti Swamps, and along the Chobe River. The species is not found regularly in Ngamiland and Chobe Districts, as shown in some books. **Habitat:** Prefers hilly and mountainous areas but frequents towns and cities where it nests on tall buildings, as in Gaborone. **Habits:** Aerial insectivore; flies relatively slowly, with much gliding; in winter, flocks visits wetlands to drink or feed on insects over the water. Builds mud-pellet nest under overhang. **Conservation:** Least Concern.

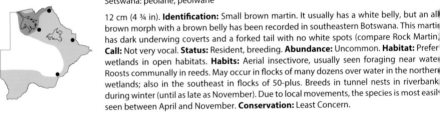

SAND
MARTIN

BANDED
MARTIN

all-brown
morph

BROWN-THROATED
MARTIN

ROCK
MARTIN
P. f. fuligula

COMMON HOUSE MARTIN *Delichon urbicum*

Setswana: pêolane, pêolwane

15 cm (6 in). **Identification:** Small, mostly blue-and-white martin. It differs from Pearl breasted and Grey-rumped Swallows in having a shallowly forked tail, white rump, and plain blue cap. Flight feathers are dark gray. Immature has gray rump and can be confused with Grey-rumped Swallow, which has deeply forked tail. **Call:** Mostly silent. **Status:** Palearctic migrant, nonbreeding (but occasionally breeds elsewhere in southern Africa). **Abundance:** Uncommon to common. **Habitat:** Found over a wide range of habitats from grasslands to savannas while on migration. **Habits:** Migrates in flocks, sometimes together with Barn Swallow. Hawks insects in flight, and roosts in trees or sleeps on the wing. **Conservation:** Least Concern.

PEARL-BREASTED SWALLOW *Hirundo dimidiata*

Setswana: pêolane, pêolwane

14 cm (5 ½ in). **Identification:** Swallow with uniformly dark blue upperparts (including rump and crown) and completely white underparts. Differing from congeners, it lacks chestnut or forehead or throat, lacks a breast band, and lacks any white in tail. **Call:** Soft, squeaky *che, che* **Status:** Resident, population supplemented by Intra-African migrants, nonbreeding. There is a passage through Botswana in winter (mainly from June to November). **Abundance:** Uncommon. **Habitat:** Primarily associated with wetland habitats. **Habits:** Aerial insectivore occurs in pairs or small groups. **Conservation:** Least Concern.

GREY-RUMPED SWALLOW *Pseudhirundo griseopyga*

Setswana: pêolane, pêolwane

14 cm (5 ½ in). **Identification:** Small swallow with deeply forked tail. Pale gray rump and brownish-gray crown distinguish it from similar swallows and martins. **Call:** Not very vocal. Harsh, grating *chaa*, repeated. **Status:** Resident, breeding. Birds are present year round, but increased numbers between April and November indicate that the population is supplemented by intra-African migrants. **Abundance:** Common. **Habitat:** Prefers a mosaic habitat of tall woodlands interspersed with open dry grasslands and floodplains. **Habits:** Forages in small groups over open floodplains catching insects on the wing. Nests underground, usually in disused rodent burrows, which makes it difficult to verify egg laying records. It is most easily seen during the dry months. **Conservation:** Least Concern.

SOUTH AFRICAN CLIFF SWALLOW *Petrochelidon spilodera*

Setswana: pêolane, pêolwane

14 cm (5 ½ in). **Identification:** Small swallow with brownish head and wings, blue mantle, and breast mottled with dark brown. Square tail in flight separates it from the striped swallows (p. 280). **Call:** Soft twittering. **Status:** Intra-African migrant, breeding. Breeds in southeastern Botswana; seen elsewhere on passage. **Abundance:** Scarce. A southern African endemic, entire population breeds in southern Africa. There are breeding colonies in South-East District at Ramatlabama village on a small building; under the bridge over the Moselebe River north of Ramatlabama; at Makokwe village near Papatlo; and at Hildavale village. May occur anywhere in lightly shaded area on map when on passage. **Habitat:** Prefers grasslands and open areas with scattered shrubs; can be seen over a variety of habitats when on passage. **Habits:** Unusual among swallows, most of which are solitary nesters, this species breeds colonially. It builds mud-pellet nests. **Conservation:** Least Concern.

COMMON HOUSE
MARTIN

PEARL-BREASTED
SWALLOW

GREY-RUMPED
SWALLOW

SOUTH AFRICAN
CLIFF SWALLOW

BARN SWALLOW *Hirundo rustica*

Setswana: pêolane, pêolwane

20 cm (7 ¾ in), incl. tail streamers. **Identification:** Well-known swallow with metallic-blue upperparts, chestnut-red forehead and chin, and black gorget; rest of underparts white. Immature has pale throat patch and is brownish above. Long tail streamers are not always present. The subspecies found in Botswana is *H. r. rustica*. **Call:** Soft musical twittering. **Status:** Palearctic migrant, nonbreeding. **Abundance:** Abundant. An estimated three million birds roosted at Chanoga in Ngamiland District in 1994, up to 800,000 roosted at Ngotwane Dam near Gaborone in 2003, and millions roosted in eucalypts in Jwaneng (Southern District) in 2007. **Habitat:** Ranges over a variety of habitats during migration, but prefers reedbeds for roosting. **Habits:** Aerial insectivore. Migrants arrive singly or in small flocks but congregate in huge flocks in autumn before departure. Roosts communally in reedbeds or trees (they have used acacias at Jwaneng in some years and eucalypts in others). **Conservation:** Least Concern.

ANGOLAN SWALLOW *Hirundo angolensis*

15 cm (6 in), incl. tail streamers. **Identification:** Similar to Barn Swallow, it has chestnut-red on forehead and throat, but chestnut extends further down chest to a narrow dark breast band; Barn Swallow has limited chestnut on throat and a broad black breast band (gorget). Remainder of underparts brownish gray (not white as in Barn Swallow). Outer tail streamers are shorter than those of Barn Swallow. **Call:** Soft twittering. **Status:** Vagrant from south-central Africa to northern Botswana; no breeding records from Botswana. **Abundance:** Rare. **Habitat:** Prefers grasslands and floodplains close to large rivers. **Habits:** Aerial insectivore. **Conservation:** Least Concern.

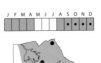

WHITE-THROATED SWALLOW *Hirundo albigularis*

Setswana: pêolane, pêolwane

15 cm (6 in), incl. tail streamers. **Identification:** Similar to congeners; it has metallic-blue back and wings, white underparts, chestnut-red forehead, and black breast band, but a white throat. **Call:** Soft twittering. **Status:** Intra-African migrant, breeding. **Abundance:** Uncommon. Present in Botswana mainly on migration passage. **Habitat:** Prefers riparian forests and adjacent woodlands but may occur in different habitats when on passage. **Habits:** Aerial insectivore. Pairs are seen during breeding, usually perched near nest under rock overhang. **Conservation:** Least Concern.

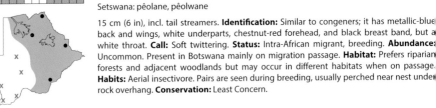

WIRE-TAILED SWALLOW *Hirundo smithii*

Setswana: pêolane, pêolwane

15 cm (6 in), incl. tail streamers. **Identification:** Similar to congeners; it has metallic-blue upperparts and white underparts, but rufous crown and absence of black bar across upper breast distinguish it. Has long, wire-like tail streamers. Immature has a partial breast band and is very similar to immature White-throated Swallow. **Call:** Soft twittering. **Status:** Resident, breeding. **Abundance:** Common. **Habitat:** Associated with large rivers and floodplains. **Habits:** Aerial insectivore; forages over water. Seen in pairs or small family parties. Confiding, often follows and lands on boats on the Chobe River. Makes cup-shaped nest of mud pellets under protective overhang. **Conservation:** Least Concern. **General:** Nests on ferry that crosses the Okavango River at Mohembo; can be seen following the ferry back and forth.

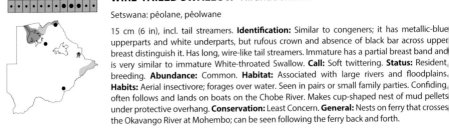

BLACK SAW-WING *Psalidoprocne pristoptera*

17 cm (6 ¾ in). **Identification:** Small, all-black swallow with deeply forked tail. All saw-wings recorded in Botswana have black (not white) underwing coverts. This bird has shorter wings than swifts (p. 202), and flies with slower wingbeats and much gliding. **Call:** Not very vocal. **Status:** Visitor; no breeding records from Botswana. **Abundance:** Rare. The range of this species extends only marginally into extreme eastern Botswana. **Habitat:** Prefers riparian woodlands and wooded gorges, especially those with water. **Habits:** Aerial insectivore; forages at low altitude in pairs or small groups. **Conservation:** Least Concern.

BARN
SWALLOW
H. r. rustica

nonbreeding
adult

imm.

breeding
adult

ANGOLAN
SWALLOW

adult

juv.

WHITE-THROATED
SWALLOW

WIRE-TAILED
SWALLOW

breeding
adult

juv.

BLACK
SAW-WING

279

GREATER STRIPED SWALLOW *Cecropis cucullata*

Setswana: pêolane, pêolwane

19 cm (7 ½ in), incl. tail streamers. **Identification:** Large swallow with chestnut cap, pale chestnut rump, and lightly streaked breast. It is larger and paler than Lesser Striped Swallow. **Call:** Soft *chissik* in flight. **Status:** Intra-African migrant, breeding. **Abundance:** Common in southeastern Botswana (more so than Lesser Striped Swallow), which is the species's main summer range, where it breeds. Sightings of this species in northern, central, and eastern Botswana are of birds on passage (see light blue area on map, where the species may be seen but is scarce). **Habitat:** Traverses a wide range of habitats when migrating. **Habits:** Migrates and forages on the wing with other swallows. Flies relatively slowly, with rapid wingbeats interspersed with gliding. Often nests under bridges or under eaves of houses; this species has high nest-site fidelity, and birds return to the same areas annually. Birds that depart late (during May) are those that raised late broods (they can have multiple broods in a season). **Conservation:** Least Concern.

LESSER STRIPED SWALLOW *Cecropis abyssinica*

Setswana: pêolane, pêolwane

17 cm (6 ¾ in), incl. tail streamers. **Identification:** Swallow with chestnut-red cap and rump, and heavily streaked breast. Male has longer tail streamers than female. It is smaller than Greater Striped Swallow and in the field appears much darker. Two subspecies occur in Botswana: *C. a. ampliformis*, the larger of the two, has longer tail streamers and coarser, darker streaking on breast; *C. a. unitatis* is smaller and has shorter tail streamers and finer, lighter streaking on breast. **Call:** Squeezed-out, descending series of notes, *tzwee, tzwee, tzwee*. **Status:** Resident and intra-African migrant populations, both breeding. The bird is present year-round in the north of the country; it breeds throughout the year. **Abundance:** Common, but less so than Greater Striped Swallow. *C. a. ampliformis* is a breeding resident in northern Botswana, where it is common around the Okavango Delta, Linyanti Swamps, and along the Chobe River; *C. a. unitatis* is a migrant to eastern and southeastern Botswana where it breeds mainly in the summer. **Habitat:** Found in woodlands, including riparian. Frequently seen near human habitation. **Habits:** Aerial insectivore. Builds mud-pellet nests under eaves of buildings, under bridges, or on undersides of large branches of riparian trees. The nests are usurped by White-rumped Swifts and Woodland Kingfishers. **Conservation:** Least Concern.

RED-BREASTED SWALLOW *Cecropis semirufa*

Setswana: pêolane, pêolwane

24 cm (9 ½ in), incl. tail streamers. **Identification:** Large swallow with blue upperparts and chestnut underparts and rump; dark buffy underwing coverts. Slightly smaller than Mosque Swallow, which has white throat and white underwing coverts. **Call:** Soft twittering. **Status:** Intra-African migrant, breeding. **Abundance:** Common; may be seen virtually anywhere in the country while on migration passage. **Habitat:** Found in open savannas and grasslands. **Habits:** Pairs are usually seen on wires along roads or flying near their nest site under bridges or culverts; uses mud-pellet nest. **Conservation:** Least Concern.

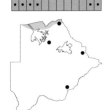

MOSQUE SWALLOW *Cecropis senegalensis*

Setswana: pêolane, pêolwane

24 cm (9 ½ in), incl. tail streamers. **Identification:** Similar to Red-breasted Swallow, but white throat and white underwing coverts differentiate this species. **Call:** Mostly silent. **Status:** Resident, breeding. **Abundance:** Scarce, locally common. Its occurrence in Botswana is at the southern extremity of its continental range. It can be common in northern Botswana during summer, especially in the Linyanti area and along the Namibian border east of Mohembo. **Habitat:** Shows a preference for Mopane (*Colophospermum mopane*) woodlands, often near water. **Habits:** Solitary or in pairs. Aerial insectivore; takes termite alates and other flying insects. Builds mud-pellet nest inside tree cavity. **Conservation:** Least Concern.

adult

juv.

**GREATER STRIPED
SWALLOW**

**LESSER STRIPED
SWALLOW**

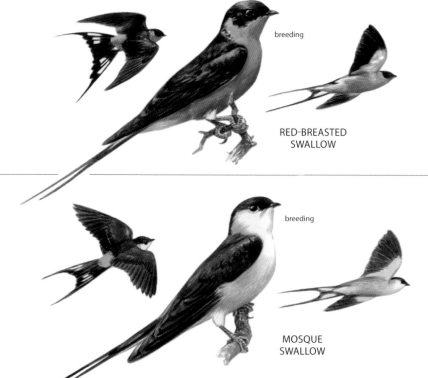

breeding

**RED-BREASTED
SWALLOW**

breeding

**MOSQUE
SWALLOW**

CROMBECS Macrosphenidae

This is a relatively new family, formed during the restructuring of the Sylviidae (p. 306) after the advent of genetic analysis. One species occurs in Botswana, a diminutive, long-billed, short-tailed warbler. It gleans branches for insects and has a distinctive noisy call.

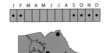

LONG-BILLED CROMBEC *Sylvietta rufescens*

Setswana: poponaka, se.pônê, se.tlhako, se.tôfôi

11 cm (4 ¼ in). **Identification:** Small, long-billed, brownish-gray warbler. Easily recognized by its tailless appearance. Four subspecies occur in Botswana: *S.r. pallida* has pale cinnamon breast and upper belly, prominent pale supercilium, and white throat. *S. r. rufescens* has a dark gray back and a rich rufous belly that contrasts with the white throat; it has the longest bill of the Botswana subspecies. *S. r. fleckii* has paler upperparts than the nominate, and the throat and breast are pale cinnamon. *S. r. ochrocara* has paler gray upperparts than the nominate, the underparts are rich rufous but the throat is buffy, not white. **Call:** Whistled, repeated *tree-cheer, tree-cheer*. **Status:** Resident, breeding. *S. r. flecki*, originally collected from south of Lake Ngami, is widespread throughout the north and east of the country; *S. r. ochrocara* is found around Ghanzi; *S. r. rufescens* occurs in southwestern Botswana. *S.r. pallida* occurs in the extreme north around Kasane and northern Chobe National Park. **Abundance:** Common to abundant. **Habitat:** Found in a variety of woodland types, including Kalahari tree and bush savanna. **Habits:** Forages actively along branches and twigs in lower strata of bushes gleaning insects (mainly ants and ant eggs). It makes a purse-shaped hanging nest with a top entrance. It is a host for the brood parasite Klaas's Cuckoo. **Conservation:** Least Concern.

LEAF WARBLERS, ALLIES Phylloscopidae

This family is centered in the Palearctic; only one species occurs in Botswana, a Palearctic-breeding summer visitor. It has a slender bill, is insectivorous, and gleans prey from leaves and foliage. It has a distinctive melodious song. The Setswana name *kgwarakgwêtlhane* (*kgwêrêkgwêtlhane*) is generic for warbler and applied to birds of various families.

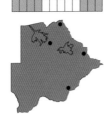

WILLOW WARBLER *Phylloscopus trochilus*

Setswana: kgwarakgwêtlhane, kgwêrêkgwêtlhane

12 cm (4 ¾ in). **Identification:** Small leaf warbler with slender bill, pale supercilium, and flat forehead and usually, pale legs. Two subspecies occur in Botswana: *P. t. trochilus* is olive brown with yellowish underparts, and *P. t. acredula* is light brown with whitish underparts, sometimes tinged yellow. **Call:** Short melodious song with descending notes. Two-note contact call is much more often heard. **Status:** Palearctic migrant, nonbreeding. **Abundance:** Common. The subspecies are sympatric and occur throughout the country. **Habitat:** Found in a variety of habitats with trees and shrubs, including Kalahari tree and bush savanna. **Habits:** Solitary leaf gleaner; flits actively about the foliage in middle and upper strata searching for insects. **Conservation:** Least Concern.

S. r. ochrocara

LONG-BILLED
CROMBEC

S. r. pallida

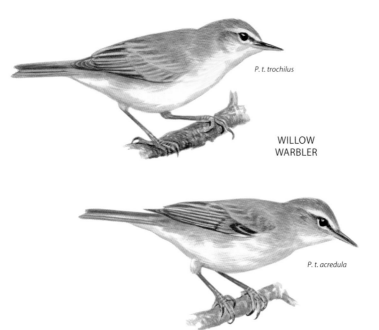

P. t. trochilus

WILLOW
WARBLER

P. t. acredula

REED WARBLERS, ALLIES   Acrocephalidae

This family is a relatively new construct following the disintegration of the large, diverse Sylviidae (p. 306) based on recent genetic analysis. In Botswana it accommodates eight *Acrocephalus* warblers and three close relatives. All have a long, pointed bill and flat forehead. To identify members of this family, note habitat ("Acros" usually in reeds or nearby trees where they feed, *Hippolais* in trees), season (migrants are present only during summer), size, call (often distinctive; breeding residents are more vocal), and sociality (breeding residents in pairs, migrants solitary or in small groups). Wing shape and length are also important: migrants have longer wings, manifest in a long primary projection, in which the primaries extend well beyond the tertials in the folded wing; resident birds have relatively shorter wings. The two *Hippolais* warblers are identified by their migratory nature, preference for woodland habitat, and distinctive calls. Two of the Acros, *A. griseldis* and *A. scirpaceus*, are rare (although the latter may be locally common), and they and *Iduna natalensis* are not regularly encountered. The remaining Acros are identified by their preferences for specific types of reedbeds, migratory versus sedentary nature, distinctive calls, and also their relative size. The Setswana name *kgwarakgwêtlhane* (*kgwêrêkgwêtlhane*) is generic for warbler and applied to birds of various families.

OLIVE-TREE WARBLER   *Hippolais olivetorum*

Setswana: kgwarakgwêtlhane, kgwêrêkgwêtlhane

17 cm (6 ¾ in). **Identification:** Large *Hippolais* warbler. It has a long pinkish-yellow bill with a black ridge, gray upperparts with whitish panels in the wings, a white eye-ring, and a short supercilium that does not reach behind the eye. Underparts whitish. Long primary projection (primaries extend well beyond tertials). Habitat is also useful to confirm identity. **Call:** Pleasant, jumbled warble. **Status:** Palearctic migrant, nonbreeding. Botswana is the most important area for this species during the boreal winter. **Abundance:** Uncommon, although the nonbreeding range of this species is centered on Botswana. It is found primarily in Southern and South-East Districts, the eastern part of Central District, and throughout Ngamiland and Chobe Districts. **Habitat:** Prefers acacia woodlands and thickets, especially *Acacia mellifera*. **Habits:** Solitary. Arboreal; feeds on insects and fruit in middle stratum of densely foliaged thickets. **Conservation:** Least Concern.

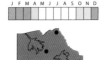

ICTERINE WARBLER   *Hippolais icterina*

Setswana: kgwarakgwêtlhane, kgwêrêkgwêtlhane

13 cm (5 in). **Identification:** *Hippolais* warbler with variable plumage. Gray morph, which has almost white underparts and grayish upperparts lacking yellowish tones, is more common. Yellow morph has yellow-washed plumage above and below. Blue-gray legs aid in identification of both. **Call:** Pleasant, loud, jumbled warble including many squeaks. **Status:** Palearctic migrant, nonbreeding. Botswana is an important area for this species during the boreal winter. **Abundance:** Common. **Habitat:** Found in a variety of wooded habitats, where it forages in middle stratum and canopy. **Habits:** Solitary. Arboreal; does not forage on the ground. **Conservation:** Least Concern.

AFRICAN YELLOW WARBLER   *Iduna natalensis*

Setswana: kgwarakgwêtlhane, kgwêrêkgwêtlhane

15 cm (6 in). **Identification:** Large, unmistakable warbler with rich yellow underparts and olive back and wings. The single Botswana record was of the nominate subspecies, *I. n. natalensis*. **Call:** Rich warble; similar to call of Lesser Swamp Warbler (p. 286). **Status:** Visitor; no breeding records from Botswana. **Abundance:** Rare. The range of this species in southern Africa extends marginally into southeastern Botswana. There is one record, from Phakalane Sewage Lagoons in South-East District in July 1995. **Habitat:** Found in wetlands and adjacent rank vegetation. **Habits:** Solitary or in pairs. **Conservation:** Least Concern.

OLIVE-TREE
WARBLER

yellow
morph

gray
morph

ICTERINE
WARBLER

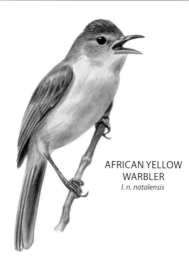

AFRICAN YELLOW
WARBLER
I. n. natalensis

BASRA REED WARBLER *Acrocephalus griseldis*

Setswana: kgwarakgwêtlhane, kgwêrêkgwêtlhane

17 cm (6 ¾ in). **Identification:** Large reed warbler. It has brownish-gray upperparts, a long slender bill, and a long white supercilium. Intermediate in size between Great Reed and Eurasian Reed Warblers. **Call:** Harsh, jumbled warble. **Status:** Vagrant from the Palearctic nonbreeding. **Abundance:** Rare. The single Botswana specimen, identified in the hand, was recorded at Phakalane Sewage Lagoons in South-East District in January 1997. H**abitat:** Favors reedbeds of *Typha*, thickets associated with water. **Habits:** Skulking behavior and inaccessible habitat mean it is easily overlooked. **Conservation:** Endangered.

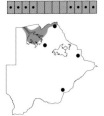

GREATER SWAMP WARBLER *Acrocephalus rufescens*

Setswana: kgwarakgwêtlhane, kgwêrêkgwêtlhane

18 cm (7 in). **Identification:** Large reed warbler. Has dark gray-brown upperparts and pale off-white underparts. It has no supercilium or other striking plumage features; best identified by habitat and call. **Call:** Gurgling, whistled warble (difficult to express in words), *churrup, chree-chree-chree*. **Status:** Resident, breeding. **Abundance:** Common. In Botswana found only in the Okavango Panhandle and Delta, Linyanti Swamps, and along the Chobe River; this is the southernmost extremity of its continental range. **Habitat:** A Papyrus (*Cyperus papyrus*) specialist, found in permanent, freshwater wetlands. **Habits:** Territorial, often heard calling in Papyrus; creeps along stems and Papyrus mats catching insects. Responds well to playback of its call. Weaves open-cup nest into Papyrus inflorescence. **Conservation:** Least Concern.

LESSER SWAMP WARBLER *Acrocephalus gracilirostris*

Setswana: kgwarakgwêtlhane, kgwêrêkgwêtlhane

17 cm (6 ¾ in). **Identification:** Large reed warbler. Has brown upperparts and mainly white underparts with rufous wash on flanks. Usually has fairly distinct supercilium. Short primary projection (the species is not migratory, and hence the primary flight feathers are not much longer than the tertials). **Call:** Liquid warbling notes, *cheroo, chee-chee-chee*, without any harsh grating notes. **Status:** Resident, breeding. **Abundance:** Common to locally abundant. Range extends from the Okavango Delta to Lake Ngami and along the Boteti River during years of high water flows. Also common at wetlands in the east and southeast from Shashe Dam to Phakalane Sewage Lagoons near Gaborone. When the area of the Okavango wetland system contracts during dry periods, so too does the range of this species. **Habitat:** Found in *Phragmites* reedbeds and *Typha* bulrushes in standing water. **Habits:** Hops around within reedbed catching insects. Calls frequently give away its presence. **Conservation:** Least Concern.

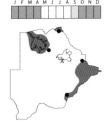

GREAT REED WARBLER *Acrocephalus arundinaceus*

Setswana: kgwarakgwêtlhane, kgwêrêkgwêtlhane

20 cm (7 ¾ in). **Identification:** Largest *Acrocephalus* warbler. Brown upperparts, contrasting white underparts, rufous tinge to flanks, and clearly marked supercilium make it look like a large Lesser Swamp Warbler. However, it is larger and has a heavy bill, more rufous on flanks, and longer primary projection (it is migratory, and hence has long primary feathers, extending well beyond tertials). **Call:** Very vocal; slow guttural warble with harsh grating and squeaky notes (difficult to put in words), *grackle, grackle, che-che-che, grackle*, repeated. **Status:** Palearctic migrant, nonbreeding. **Abundance:** Uncommon. **Habitat:** Found in tall swamp vegetation, such as *Phragmites* reeds; also in thickets in river valleys. **Habits:** Usually solitary. Loud call is first indication of its presence. **Conservation:** Least Concern.

BASRA REED
WARBLER

GREATER SWAMP
WARBLER

LESSER SWAMP
WARBLER

GREAT REED
WARBLER

287

SEDGE WARBLER *Acrocephalus schoenobaenus*

Setswana: kgwarakgwêtlhane, kgwêrêkgwêtlhane

13 cm (5 in). **Identification:** Small reed warbler. Has streaked crown and broad white supercilium. Brown back and mantle are also streaked; rump is plain buffy brown. **Call:** Song is high-pitched, scratchy warble, with harsh notes alternating with trills; includes mimicry. Alarm call a harsh churr and scolding *tucc.* **Status:** Palearctic migrant, nonbreeding. Occasionally birds are recorded as early as November. **Abundance:** Uncommon to locally abundant. **Habitat:** Found in sedges (*Cyperus* spp.) and inundated grasslands, such as seasonal floodplains and reeds around sewage ponds; occasionally in thickets away from water. **Habits:** Solitary or in small groups; creeps about in dense vegetation. Call is usually the first indication of its presence. **Conservation:** Least Concern.

EURASIAN REED WARBLER *Acrocephalus scirpaceus*

Setswana: kgwarakgwêtlhane, kgwêrêkgwêtlhane

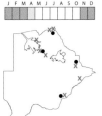

13 cm (5 in). **Identification:** Small, migratory reed warbler. It is gray-brown above (nominate race more rufous) and whitish below. Slightly larger than African Reed Warbler; but eastern *fuscus* race indistinguishable from Marsh Warbler unless heard or bird is in hand and the wing formula can be taken. **Call:** Monotonous soft song comprising different stanzas, repeated randomly. Similar to call of African Reed Warbler. **Status:** Palearctic migrant to extreme northern, eastern, and southeastern Botswana; occasionally occurs at isolated localities elsewhere in Botswana. Nonbreeding. Some individuals may overwinter. **Abundance:** Common in northern wetlands and eastern and southeastern Botswana; scarce elsewhere. Possibly overlooked. **Habitat:** Found in *Phragmites* and *Typha* reedbeds or dense cover away from water; forages in acacias nearby. **Habits:** May occur in large numbers in reedbeds (100-plus birds were recorded at Phakalane Sewage Lagoons in South-East District in 1997). Demonstrates ortstreue–fidelity to a nonbreeding site. **Conservation:** Least Concern.

AFRICAN REED WARBLER *Acrocephalus baeticatus*

Setswana: kgwarakgwêtlhane, kgwêrêkgwêtlhane

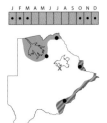

13 cm (5 in). **Identification:** Small resident reed warbler. It is gray-brown above and whitish below. Indistinguishable from Eurasian Reed Warbler unless bird is in hand (when shorter wings and differences in configuration of remiges are apparent). It is smaller and more rufous than Marsh Warbler. Two subspecies occur: *A. b. baeticatus* has a pale buff breast; *A. b. hallae* has a white breast. **Call:** Song is soft, harsh churring stanzas, repeated regularly; sometimes includes mimicry. Similar to song of Eurasian Reed Warbler. **Status:** Resident, breeding. The population in eastern and southern Botswana is supplemented by breeding intra-African migrants during summer. **Abundance:** Uncommon to locally abundant. Higher numbers of birds are consistently present during summer in the eastern and southern part of the country; they are subspecies *A. b. baeticatus. A. b. hallae,* found in the north in Ngamiland and Chobe Districts, is resident. **Habitat:** Occurs in *Phragmites* and *Typha* reedbeds in freshwater wetlands or fringing man-made dams (especially in the southeast). **Habits:** Creeps about in thick cover, foraging solitarily or in pairs. Builds a cup-shaped nest attached to reeds. **Conservation:** Least Concern.

MARSH WARBLER *Acrocephalus palustris*

Setswana: kgwarakgwêtlhane, kgwêrêkgwêtlhane

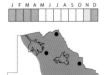

13 cm (5 in). **Identification:** Small reed warbler; similar to Eurasian and African Reed Warblers. Has warm olive-brown upperparts, paler buffy-white underparts, and faint short supercilium. Best identified by song or in the hand by differences in wing formula. **Call:** Varied; includes numerous imitations of local birds. The five African species it most often imitates are Dark-capped Bulbul, Grey-backed Camaroptera, Black-backed Puffback, Tawny-flanked Prinia, and Red-faced Cisticola. **Status:** Palearctic migrant, nonbreeding. **Abundance:** Uncommon; locally common (as in the Tuli Block, where 10 were recorded in a 100 m [330 ft] transect). **Habitat:** Prefers dense, lush thickets in woodlands; occasionally found in reedbeds in water as at Phakalane Sewage Lagoons. **Habits:** Solitary; remains within dense vegetation. **Conservation:** Least Concern.

SEDGE
WARBLER

EURASIAN REED
WARBLER

AFRICAN REED
WARBLER
A.b. hallae

MARSH
WARBLER

GRASSBIRDS, ALLIES Locustellidae

This is a relatively new family established following the disintegration of the Sylviidae (p. 306) based on genetic evidence. Only two species occur in Botswana; both are thickset and have long, broad, graduated tails. One is resident, the other a Palearctic migrant. Characteristic calls aid in their detection and identification. The Setswana name *kgwarakgwêtlhane* (*kgwêrêkgwêtlhane*) is generic for warbler and applied to birds of various families.

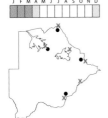

RIVER WARBLER *Locustella fluviatilis*

Setswana: kgwarakgwêtlhane, kgwêrêkgwêtlhane

13 cm (5 in). **Identification:** This warbler has uniform, dark gray-brown upperparts, a small, pale supercilium, and a slender bill that is brownish with a paler, yellowish base. It has a pale throat and the upper breast is faintly streaked. **Call:** Song with locust-like quality, *krt-krit, tzee-zee-zee zee*, the latter part sounding like harsh, fast stridulation. **Status:** Palearctic migrant, nonbreeding. All Botswana records are from between December 27 and April 7. **Abundance:** Scarce (easily overlooked, probably more common). First located by the Tati River in Francistown in March 1985; regular along Thamalakane River in Maun and in Kasane Forest Reserve. **Habitat:** Prefers shrubs and thickets that are mixed with long grasses. **Habits:** Skulks low in thickets, near the ground (but does not forage on the ground). **Conservation:** Least Concern.

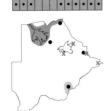

LITTLE RUSH WARBLER *Bradypterus baboecala*

Setswana: kgwarakgwêtlhane, kgwêrêkgwêtlhane

14 cm (5 ½ in). **Identification:** Plump warbler with long and rounded tail, dark brown upperparts, pale rufous vent, and faint streaking on breast. The two subspecies found in Botswana are very similar. **Call:** Unique series of accelerating notes, *krak, krak, krak, krak kruk-kruk-kruk-kruk*. **Status:** Resident, breeding. **Abundance:** *B. b. msiri* occurs in the Okavango wetland system, the Linyanti Swamps, and along the Chobe River, where it is common. *B. b. transvaalensis* occurs in southeastern Botswana, where it is uncommon; also an occasional visitor to Makgadikgadi Pans. **Habitat:** Prefers *Cyperus* sedges and *Typha* bulrushes in freshwater wetlands. Also found at sewage ponds. **Habits:** Solitary or in pairs. Skulks in dense reedbeds, usually low (but not on the ground). Best detected and identified by its call. **Conservation:** Least Concern.

CISTICOLAS, ALLIES Cisticolidae

A family of small warblers with cryptic plumage; sexes are alike. Cisticolas are drabber in breeding (summer) plumage, and more richly colored in nonbreeding (winter) plumage. They are monogamous; nests are purse-like with a side-top entrance, and chicks are altricial. Some species are sedentary while others are more mobile or nomadic, and they are mainly insectivorous. Botswana has 24 species. The 13 cisticolas, which make up the bulk of the family in Botswana, are small, brownish insectivores with thin, straight bills; their overall similarity can make identification a challenge. Fortunately, they occupy varied habitats and have different calls and behaviors; some perform aerial courtship displays accompanied by songs and wing snapping. The other family members include two prinia species, two apalises, two wren-warblers, three eremomelas, a camaroptera, and the prinia-like Rufous-eared Warbler. The Setswana name *tôntôsi* is generic for cisticola.

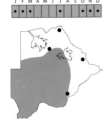

RUFOUS-EARED WARBLER *Malcorus pectoralis*

15 cm (6 in). **Identification:** Long-tailed warbler similar to prinias (p. 298). It has a streaked mantle, obvious rufous ear patch, and black chest band of variable width; band is absent in adult in winter and in juvenile. Subspecies *M. p. ocularius* is found in Botswana. **Call:** Rapid squeaky *reet-reet-reet....* **Status:** Resident, breeding. The July egg-laying record indicates that the species breeds opportunistically outside its usual breeding period. **Abundance:** Scarce to common. A southern African endemic; range extends northward into southern Ngamiland and northwestern Central District (much farther north than other books indicate). **Habitat:** Found in low arid scrub and scattered, stunted bushes, especially Trumpet-thorn (*Catophractes alexandri*). **Habits:** Forages on the ground, running quickly, often with tail cocked. Shy, hides deep in bushes. Calls from top of low bush. **Conservation:** Least Concern.

RIVER
WARBLER

LITTLE RUSH
WARBLER
B. b. msiri

adult

RUFOUS-EARED
WARBLER
M. p. ocularius

juv.

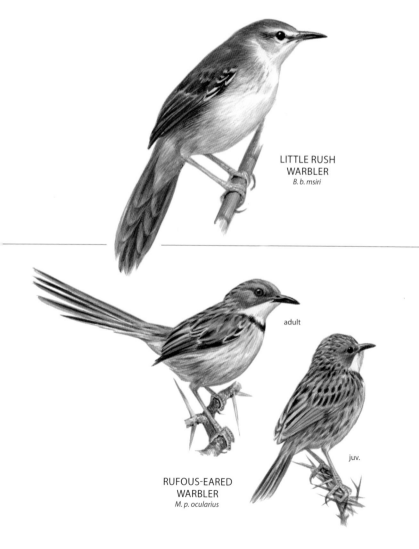

ZITTING CISTICOLA *Cisticola juncidis*

Setswana: tôntôsi

11 cm (4 ¼ in). **Identification:** Diminutive short-tailed cisticola. Its streaked crown, black streaks on back, rufous flanks, and subterminal black tail band are diagnostic in combination. Similar to Desert Cisticola, but display flights and habitat preferences help separate the two. **Call:** Distinctive *zit … zit … zit*, or *klink … klink … klink*, given in undulating flight by displaying male. **Status:** Resident, breeding. **Abundance:** Common. **Habitat:** Found in moist, open, tall grasslands usually (but not always) by wetlands. **Habits:** Nomadic, moving between suitable habitats. Male undertakes dipping display flight about 20 m (66 ft) above the ground, calling on every dip. **Conservation:** Least Concern.

DESERT CISTICOLA *Cisticola aridulus*

Setswana: tôntôsi

11 cm (4 ¼ in). **Identification:** Small, short-tailed cisticola, similar to Zitting Cisticola but paler in color. Display flights, accompanied by distinctive call, help separate the two; habitat preferences also differ. Two subspecies are found in Botswana, both pale overall. **Call:** Rapid, repeated *ting-ting-ting*, or *zik-zik-zik*, given by male in display flight. In alarm gives *tuk … tuk … tuk* call, accompanied by wing snaps. **Status:** Resident, breeding. The species probably breeds opportunistically when conditions are right. **Abundance:** Common; it is the typical cisticola of the Kalahari. Nomadic, it moves widely and irregularly in response to rain. *C. a. kalahari* occurs over most of Botswana; *C. a. eremicus* replaces it in Ngamiland and Chobe Districts. **Habitat:** Found in open, short grasslands in dry areas. **Habits:** When breeding, male displays with low flight, between 5 and 10 m (16 and 33 ft) above the ground, calling as described above. This species is a host of the brood parasite Cuckoo-finch in Botswana. **Conservation:** Least Concern.

PALE-CROWNED CISTICOLA *Cisticola cinnamomeus*

Setswana: tôntôsi

11 cm (4 ¼ in). **Identification:** Small, short-tailed cisticola. Difficult to identify. Breeding male has pale creamy crown, rufous flanks, and blackish lores. Nonbreeding adult of both sexes has pale lores and streaked crown and back. **Call:** Male during display flight gives thin *tee, tee, tee …*, while ascending and in high-level flight, followed by shrill *tree, tree, tree*, while diving down at end. **Status:** Vagrant; no breeding records from Botswana. **Abundance:** Rare. Botswana is outside the species's normal range (eastern Zimbabwe and eastern South Africa). However, there are records from Xugana in the Okavango Delta, which are substantiated by museum specimens. **Habitat:** Occurs in moist grasslands. **Habits:** Unobtrusive and overlooked outside breeding season. **Conservation:** Least Concern.

CLOUD CISTICOLA *Cisticola textrix*

Setswana: tôntôsi

10 cm (4 in). **Identification:** Small, short-tailed cisticola. It is similar to Zitting and Desert Cisticolas, but note its plain brown crown and long legs. *C. t. major*, which has brown plumage overall except for a white breast, is the subspecies that occurs in Botswana; it has light streaking to the sides of the breast. **Call:** Displaying male issues whistled notes, *chu-che-che-che*, before characteristic *chik-chik-chik* as he dives downward. Display involves no wing snapping. **Status:** Visitor or possibly resident; no breeding records from Botswana. Elsewhere in southern Africa it breeds during summer rains. **Abundance:** Rare. The species's southern African range just extends to southeastern Botswana. **Habitat:** Occurs in grasslands with short grass and bare patches. **Habits:** Male, conspicuous when breeding, conducts high, cruising display flight, above 50 m, followed by vertical downward dive, calling as described above. **Conservation:** Least Concern.

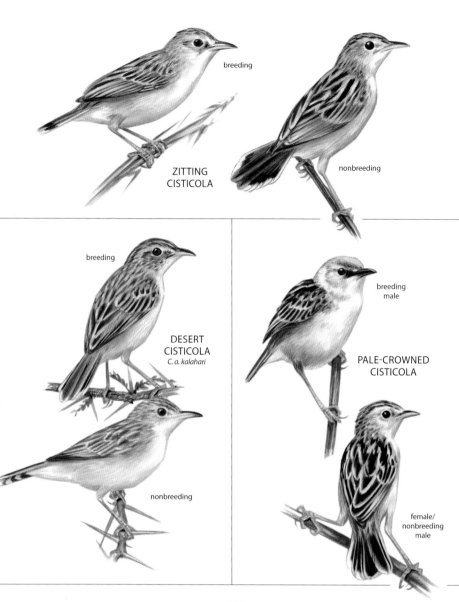

breeding

nonbreeding

ZITTING
CISTICOLA

breeding

DESERT
CISTICOLA
C. a. kalahari

nonbreeding

breeding
male

PALE-CROWNED
CISTICOLA

female/
nonbreeding
male

CLOUD
CISTICOLA
C. t. major

LUAPULA CISTICOLA *Cisticola luapula*

Setswana: tôntôsi

13 cm (5 in). **Identification:** Large, long-tailed wetland cisticola with dark-streaked back. It is identified by the rufous wing panel, bold black back feathers with buff edges, a rufous crown, and overall whitish underparts. It is found alongside similar Chirping Cisticola, from which it is best separated by call and by the white tips to the tail feathers (Chirping has buffy tips). It is also noticeably whiter below than Chirping. **Call:** Loud *tik, tik* or *tidick tik tik tik tik tik* . **Status:** Resident, breeding. **Abundance:** Common. Occurs in Botswana at the southwestern edge of its continental range. **Habitat:** Occurs in permanent swamps with emergent vegetation such as *Phragmites* reeds and *Miscanthus* grasses. **Habits:** Calls from prominent reeds or *Miscanthus* grass; does not venture far from cover. **Conservation:** Least Concern.

CHIRPING CISTICOLA *Cisticola pipiens*

Setswana: tôntôsi

14 cm (5 ½ in). **Identification:** Large, long-tailed, slender wetland cisticola with streaked back. It has a brownish crown and dull brown wing panel and is distinctly buffy below (compare Luapula Cisticola). **Call:** Four cricket-like notes, *chit chit chit chreeee*, given by breeding male. **Status:** Resident, breeding. **Abundance:** Common. A Zambezian species, it occurs in Botswana at the southern limit of its continental range. **Habitat:** Prefers tall *Miscanthus* grasses and Papyrus (*Cyperus papyrus*) standing in water. **Habits:** A noisy species; male sometimes snaps its wings while calling. **Conservation:** Least Concern.

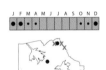

LEVAILLANT'S CISTICOLA *Cisticola tinniens*

Setswana: tôntôsi

14 cm (5 ½ in). **Identification:** Large, long-tailed wetland cisticola with bold black streaking on back, rufous crown, and rufous wing panel. Only the nominate subspecies occurs in Botswana. **Call:** Musical song, *cheep, cheer-ooeee*, repeated, given by male. **Status:** Visitor in wet years; no breeding records from Botswana. **Abundance:** Rare. Occurs in Botswana at the western limit of its South African range. **Habitat:** Found in rank grasses, sedges, and weeds in wetlands. **Habits:** Perches on low vegetation when not foraging among reeds. Does not venture far from cover. **Conservation:** Least Concern.

CROAKING CISTICOLA *Cisticola natalensis*

Setswana: tôntôsi

15 cm (6 in). **Identification:** Large cisticola (largest in Botswana) with streaked back. It has a robust bill, which is diagnostic in concert with the warm brown plumage worn in winter, when the bill is pale gray with pale yellow or pink base in both sexes. When breeding, male becomes grayer, and its bill is black. **Call:** Diagnostic; series of staccato croaking notes uttered in flight, *kweet-kweet-kweet*, repeated, given by displaying male. **Status:** Resident; no breeding records from Botswana. **Abundance:** Rare. Range extends into northern Botswana from Zimbabwe; the species is recorded more regularly on the Zimbabwean side of Kazuma Pan. Also occurs in Nogotsaa/Tchinga area of Chobe National Park. The type specimen for *C. n. holubii* is from Pandamatenga, but it's not clear whether it came from Botswana or Zimbabwe. **Habitat:** Found in open, rank, moist grasslands. **Habits:** Frequents rank grasses, often feeding on the ground. Male makes low display flight, while calling. **Conservation:** Least Concern.

breeding

CHIRPING
CISTICOLA

breeding

LUAPULA
CISTICOLA

nonbreeding

nonbreeding

breeding
adult

worn
plumage
(late summer)

nonbreeding
adult

LEVAILLANT'S
CISTICOLA
C. t. tinniens

imm.

breeding
female

CROAKING
CISTICOLA
C. n. holubii

nonbreeding
adult

breeding
male

295

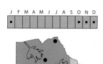

RATTLING CISTICOLA *Cisticola chiniana*

Setswana: tôntôsi

M: 16 cm (6 ¼ in), F: 14 cm (5 ½ in). **Identification:** Large, long-tailed cisticola with streaked back and a rufous-brown crown. The three subspecies found in Botswana are difficult to separate in the field. **Call:** Distinctive harsh, rattling call, *chee chee chee churrrrrr*, given mainly by male during breeding season. **Status:** Resident, breeding. **Abundance:** Common to abundant; by far the most common cisticola within its range. *C. c. chiniana* occurs in eastern Botswana; *C. c. smithersi* (type specimen collected in Pandamatenga, Chobe District) is found around Makgadikgadi Pans and northeastward into Chobe District; *C. c. frater* occurs throughout Ngamiland District. **Habitat:** Prefers dry acacia scrub interspersed with grasslands. **Habits:** Forages low among tangled grasses and thornbushes. Sings and calls from top of low bushes; when it does so, black interior of mouth is often clearly visible. Never ventures far from cover. **Conservation:** Least Concern.

TINKLING CISTICOLA *Cisticola rufilatus*

Setswana: tôntôsi

14 cm (5 ½ in). **Identification:** Large, long-tailed cisticola with streaked back. It is identified by rufous crown and ear coverts separated by distinct white supercilium. Two subspecies occur in Botswana: *C. r. venustula* has a darker reddish crown and more heavily streaked back than *C. r. rufilatus*. **Call:** Plaintive whistles, usually but not always followed by soft, tinkling trill, *weeet-weeet-weeet, trrrrrrrrr*, given by breeding male. Similar in structure to call of Rattling Cisticola but not in tone. **Status:** Resident, breeding. **Abundance:** Common. Its center of abundance in southern Africa is the Kalahari in Botswana. *C. r. rufilatus* is widespread throughout the country; *C. r. venustula* is restricted to northwestern Ngamiland District. **Habitat:** Found in scrub in open, arid, deciduous woodlands. **Habits:** Shy and retiring, best located by call. Breeding male calls from top of small bush. **Conservation:** Least Concern.

RED-FACED CISTICOLA *Cisticola erythrops*

Setswana: tôntôsi

14 cm (5 ½ in). **Identification:** Large, long-tailed cisticola with unstreaked back and slight rufous tinge to cheeks. Upperparts are plain olive gray from crown to tail. **Call:** Highly vocal; territorial call is a ringing *tik-tik-tik-TEE-TEE-TEE*, rising to crescendo. **Status:** Resident, breeding. There are few egg-laying records from Botswana, but they do not differ in their timing from those recorded elsewhere in southern Africa. **Abundance:** Common along the Chobe River between Kasane and Kazungula where suitable habitat exists, but its presence does not extend farther westward into Chobe National Park. Scarce elsewhere in its range in Botswana. Does not occur in the Okavango Delta. **Habitat:** Found in riparian vegetation, rank growth in drainage lines and on hillside slopes. **Habits:** Remains concealed in rank vegetation but calls frequently. **Conservation:** Least Concern.

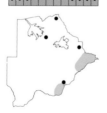

LAZY CISTICOLA *Cisticola aberrans*

Setswana: tôntôsi

14 cm (5 ½ in). **Identification:** Large, long-tailed cisticola with unstreaked back, dull rufous cap, and pale supercilium. Only the nominate, *C. a. aberrans*, which is relatively dark, is found in Botswana. **Call:** Long, plaintive *tweee*, given by members in a group. **Status:** Resident, breeding. The few egg-laying records from Botswana are similar in timing to those from elsewhere in southern Africa. **Abundance:** Scarce. **Habitat:** Inhabits grassy slopes and rocky outcrops with scattered trees in eastern hardveld. **Habits:** Hops around in dense cover or on rocks; never ventures far from cover. Often cocks the long tail in a prinia-like fashion. **Conservation:** Least Concern.

RATTLING
CISTICOLA

breeding

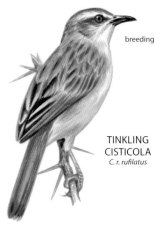

breeding

TINKLING
CISTICOLA
C. r. rufilatus

breeding

RED-FACED
CISTICOLA

nonbreeding

LAZY
CISTICOLA
C. a. aberrans

nonbreeding

297

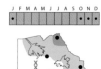

NEDDICKY   *Cisticola fulvicapilla*

Setswana: tôntôsi

11 cm (4 ¼ in). **Identification:** Small, short-tailed cisticola with unstreaked back, rufous cap, and variably colored underparts, depending on subspecies. The two subspecies found in Botswana, *C. f. hallae* and *C. f. dexter*, are both very pale and have grayish-buff underparts. **Call:** Monotonous *tjiek-tjiek-tjiek*, given by breeding male. **Status:** Resident, breeding. **Abundance:** Common. *C. f. hallae* (described from a specimen collected in Tsotsoroga Pan in Chobe National Park) is found in Ngamiland and Chobe Districts; *C. f. dexter* (type specimen from Kanye in Southern District) occurs in the eastern part of Central District and throughout Southern and South-East Districts. **Habitat:** Found in understory of woodlands, including the Zambezi Teak (*Baikiaea plurijuga*) woodlands in Chobe District and wooded, rocky hills in eastern and southeastern Botswana. **Habits:** Male sings from exposed perch during breeding; otherwise unobtrusive. **Conservation:** Least Concern.

GREY-BACKED CAMAROPTERA   *Camaroptera brevicaudata*

13 cm (5 in). **Identification:** Small, rotund warbler with olive-green wings and gray head, back, and rump. The combination of the gray back and yellow "socks" at the tops of the (relatively long) legs is diagnostic. The chin is almost white, and the eye is dark orange. **Call:** Distinctive soft bleating; also a loud, ongoing *krak-krak-krak-krak…*, like the sound of two stones being knocked together. **Status:** Resident, breeding. **Abundance:** Abundant. The Okavango Delta is a stronghold for this species in southern Africa. **Habitat:** Prefers thickets and tangled undergrowth in a variety of moist woodlands; often in cover on rocky hills in the southeast, avoiding dry open bush. **Habits:** Solitary or in pairs; hops about in low bushes and undergrowth, its short tail cocked. It makes a ball-shaped nest with a covering of living leaves stitched in place with spiderwebs. **Conservation:** Least Concern.

TAWNY-FLANKED PRINIA   *Prinia subflava*

Setswana: tôntôbane, tôntôsi, rantwêêsane, mmantwêêsane, rantwêêtwêê

13 cm (5 in). **Identification:** Long-tailed warbler with brown upperparts and whitish underparts. Combination of long, broad supercilium, rufous flanks, warm brown flight feathers, and long expressive tail is diagnostic. Juvenile is yellowish below and has yellow base to bill. Two subspecies occur in Botswana: *P. s. bechuanae* is much paler than *P. s. affinis*. **Call:** *Blip-blip-blip-blip*, made by both sexes; sounds like two stones being hit together. **Status:** Resident, breeding. **Abundance:** Common to abundant. *P. s. bechuanae* (type specimen collected in Mababe, Ngamiland District) occurs in northern Botswana ; *P. s. affinis* occurs in the eastern part of Central District as well as Kgatleng, Southern, and South-East Districts. **Habitat:** Found in scrubby undergrowth and rank grasses in a wide range of moist vegetation types. **Habits:** Solitary or in pairs or small groups. Forages low, its tail held vertically much of the time. The species is a host for the brood parasite Cuckoo-finch in Botswana. Prinias probably lay the most variable eggs of any bird; this is likely an outcome of their long coevolutionary struggle with Cuckoo-finch. **Conservation:** Least Concern.

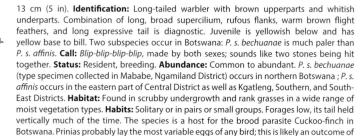

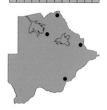

BLACK-CHESTED PRINIA   *Prinia flavicans*

Setswana: tôntôbane, tôntôsi, rantwêêsane, mmantwêêsane, rantwêêtwêê, kgôsi yadinônyane

14 cm (5 ½ in). **Identification:** Long-tailed warbler easily identified when breeding by well-defined, broad black chest band. The band is absent in nonbreeding birds, and may appear as streaks in transitional plumage. Two subspecies occur in Botswana: *P. f. flavicans* has pale yellow underparts; *P. f. nubilosa* has bright yellow breast and belly. **Call:** *Chip, chip, chip*, made by both sexes. Similar to call of Tawny-flanked Prinia but harsher. **Status:** Resident, breeding. **Abundance:** Abundant. One of Botswana's most abundant and widespread species. *P. f. flavicans* occurs in the central, southern, and western part of the country; *P. f. nubilosa* is found in the north and east. **Habitat:** Occurs in scrub and rank grasses in open semiarid Kalahari woodlands. **Habits:** Hops about low in bushes and thorny thickets, with its tail exaggeratedly cocked (to beyond 90°). **Conservation:** Least Concern. **General:** The name *kgôsi yadinônyane*, "chief of the birds," is from a traditional Setswana story about the birds' competition to choose a chief by seeing who could fly the highest. Tôntôbane was the winner.

NEDDICKY
C. f. dexter

breeding

GREY-BACKED
CAMAROPTERA

TAWNY-FLANKED
PRINIA
P. s. bechuanae

breeding
adult

BLACK-CHESTED
PRINIA
P. f. nubilosa

nonbreeding
adult

juv.

299

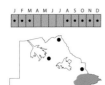

BAR-THROATED APALIS *Apalis thoracica*

13 cm (5 in). **Identification:** Long-tailed warbler. Male has black bar separating white throat from yellow underparts. In female, throat bar may be reduced or absent. Pale eye in both sexes. Two subspecies occur in Botswana: *A. t. flaviventris* has pale yellow belly and gray crown and back; *A. t. rhodesiae* also has yellow belly, but its crown is brown. **Call:** Duet; male makes harsh *blip-blip-blip-blip*, female responds with soft *ti-ti-ti-ti-ti*. **Status:** Resident, breeding. The few Botswana egg-laying records conform with those from the rest of southern Africa in terms of timing. **Abundance:** Uncommon; Botswana is on the western extremity of the species's range. *A. t. flaviventris* occurs in eastern and southern Botswana; *A. t. rhodesiae* may extend into northeastern Botswana from neighboring Zimbabwe. **Habitat:** Found in thickets and woodlands associated with drainage lines and hills; also undergrowth at base of cliffs and kopjes. **Habits:** Forages actively in low thickets, often in small groups or mixed bird parties, gleaning for insects. **Conservation:** Least Concern.

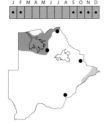

YELLOW-BREASTED APALIS *Apalis flavida*

12 cm (4 ¾ in). **Identification:** Long-tailed warbler with bright yellow breast, white belly, and red eye. Male has black breast spot, which sometimes forms incomplete band. Two subspecies occur in Botswana: *A. f. flavida* is more yellowish (including throat) than *A. f. neglecta*, which has a white throat. **Call:** Duet; male makes loud *chizzik-chizzik-chizzik*, female gives quieter *krik-krik-krik*. **Status:** Resident; no breeding records from Botswana. **Abundance:** Common. *A. f. flavida* is found in Ngamiland and Chobe; *A. f. neglecta* occurs sparsely in eastern Botswana. **Habitat:** Favors riparian woodlands. **Habits:** Active leaf gleaner, forages in pairs in tree canopy. **Conservation:** Least Concern.

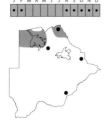

GREEN-CAPPED EREMOMELA *Eremomela scotops*

12 cm (4 ¾ in). **Identification:** Small, short-tailed warbler with olive-green upperparts (including crown), pale eye, yellow wash to throat and breast, and a whitish belly. Legs are pale red. Two subspecies occur in Botswana: *E. s. pulchra* has a grayer mantle and white belly than *E. s. scotops*. **Call:** Monotonous *twip-twip-twip*. **Status:** Resident; no breeding records from Botswana. **Abundance:** Uncommon. Mboma Island and Xakanaxa in Moremi Game Reserve are good places to see this species. *E. s. pulchra* is found in Ngamiland and Chobe Districts; *E. s. scotops* may extend marginally into eastern Botswana from neighboring Zimbabwe. **Habitat:** Occurs in canopy of Zambezi Teak (*Baikiaea plurijuga*) woodlands, and riparian woodlands of the Okavango Delta. **Habits:** Found in small groups, frequently in mixed bird parties, foraging in tree canopies. **Conservation:** Least Concern.

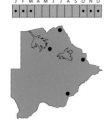

YELLOW-BELLIED EREMOMELA *Eremomela icteropygialis*

11 cm (4 ¼ in). **Identification:** Small, short-tailed warbler, with grayish-brown upperparts and breast, and yellow belly. Three subspecies occur in Botswana: *E. i. helenorae* and *E. i. sharpei* are both generally pale overall and have pale yellow wash to belly; *E. i. polioxantha* has a bright yellow belly and gray chest. All three have reddish-brown eyes and dark gray legs. **Call:** Whistled *chirri-chirri-chirri*. **Status:** Resident, breeding. **Abundance:** Common. *E. i. helenorae* occurs in Ngamiland and Chobe Districts and the northern part of Central District; *E. i. sharpei* is found in Ghanzi and Kgalagadi Districts; *E. i. polioxantha* occurs in the eastern part of Central District and throughout Kgatleng, Southern, and South-East Districts. **Habitat:** Prefers low bushes in savannas and on edges of woodlands; particularly common in arid areas. **Habits:** Occurs in small groups and forages for insects on outer twigs and leaves of low shrubs. **Conservation:** Least Concern.

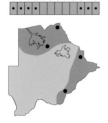

BURNT-NECKED EREMOMELA *Eremomela usticollis*

11 cm (4 ¼ in). **Identification:** Small, short-tailed, pale warbler with gray upperparts, whitish underparts, a pale eye, and pale red legs. It has a brown collar, which is diagnostic during summer (breeding plumage) but may be reduced or absent in nonbreeding season. **Call:** High-pitched *ti-ti-ti-ti-ti*. **Status:** Resident, breeding. The few Botswana egg-laying records conform with those from elsewhere in southern Africa. **Abundance:** Common. The Okavango Delta and Limpopo River valley are strongholds for this species in southern Africa. **Habitat:** An acacia specialist, it occurs in acacia woodlands in mesic areas. **Habits:** Small groups feed in acacia canopies. **Conservation:** Least Concern.

**BAR-THROATED
APALIS**
A. t. flaviventris

male

female

**YELLOW-BREASTED
APALIS**
A. f. flavida

**GREEN-CAPPED
EREMOMELA**
E. s. pulchra

**YELLOW-BELLIED
EREMOMELA**
E. i. polioxantha

nonbreeding

breeding

**BURNT-NECKED
EREMOMELA**

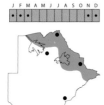

STIERLING'S WREN-WARBLER *Calamonastes stierlingi*

14 cm (5 ½ in). **Identification:** Small warbler with whitish underparts that are finely barred in dark gray from throat to vent. Similar to Barred Wren-Warbler, which has brown underparts, the color in some cases obscuring the barring. Unlike Barred, Stierling's has no breeding or nonbreeding plumage distinction. **Call:** Cricket-like *birririt-birrit-birrit*, repeated incessantly during summer. **Status:** Resident, breeding. **Abundance:** Common, although Botswana is at the southwestern edge of its range. **Habitat:** Found in understory and thickets in Zambezi Teak (*Baikiaea plurijuga*) woodlands. Where its range overlaps with that of Barred Wren-Warbler, it is associated with Mopane (*Colophospermum mopane*) and Zambezi Teak. **Habits:** Pairs forage in woodland understory and canopy. This species is the ecological counterpart of Barred Wren-Warbler in Zambezi Teak woodlands; both species stitch living leaves into their nests. **Conservation:** Least Concern.

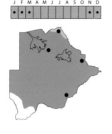

BARRED WREN-WARBLER *Calamonastes fasciolatus*

14 cm (5 ½ in). **Identification:** Small warbler, paler than Stierling's Wren-Warbler. Breeding male has dark brown breast, the color of which obscures barring, and paler buffy belly. Female and nonbreeding male have buffy underparts overlaid with brown barring. *C. f. fasciolatus*, the subspecies found throughout Botswana, has less distinct barring on underparts than other populations and has no barring on the abdomen. **Call:** Diagnostic; distinctive, loud, penetrating *streep-streep-streep....* **Status:** Resident, breeding. **Abundance:** Common. It is a Kalahari "special" (i.e., one of the birds that characterizes the Kalahari). **Habitat:** An acacia specialist; where it occurs in mixed woodlands, it is due to an acacia component. **Habits:** Creeps about in dense thickets and on the ground, often with tail raised. It is the ecological counterpart of Stierling's Wren-Warbler in acacia woodlands; both species stitch living leaves into their nests. **Conservation:** Least Concern.

BABBLERS Leiothrichidae

A family of noisy, thrush-like, terrestrial birds. Members of this family that occur in Botswana are babblers; they live in woodlands in small family groups and forage mainly on the ground. Often, one group member acts as a sentinel, perching on the top of a bush while the other group members forage. They are territorial, and group members use a loud, babbling call in advertising their claim. Groups also "capture" young birds from neighboring groups, which helps avoid inbreeding. They are obligate cooperative breeders, the helpers assisting with nest building, incubation, and chick raising. All Botswana species except Black-faced Babbler are hosts for the brood parasite Levaillant's Cuckoo. Four species, all of the genus *Turdoides*, are found in Botswana. One species is endemic to southern Africa. The Setswana generic name for babbler, *le.tshêganôga* ("laugher at snakes"), is a reference to the chattering call often given in alarm.

SOUTHERN PIED BABBLER *Turdoides bicolor*

Setswana: le.tshêganôga, le.tshoganôga, le.nkutshwêu

26 cm (10 ¼ in). **Identification:** Unmistakable, black-and-white thrush-like bird with ruby-red eye. Juvenile has dark eye and is mostly brown; with age, white blotches emerge progressively on breast and head. **Call:** Typical babble, given by individuals or whole group. **Status:** Resident, breeding. **Abundance:** Common to abundant. A typical Kalahari species, endemic to southern Africa; Botswana is a major stronghold. **Habitat:** An acacia specialist, found in a variety of Kalahari tree and bush savanna types. **Habits:** Gregarious, cohesive flocks maintain territories. The species forages low in shrubs or on the ground. **Conservation:** Least Concern.

STIERLING'S
WREN-WARBLER

breeding
male

female/
nonbreeding male

BARRED
WREN-WARBLER
C. f. fasciolatus

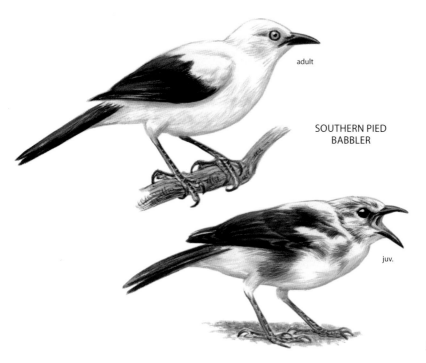

adult

SOUTHERN PIED
BABBLER

juv.

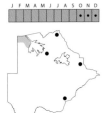

BLACK-FACED BABBLER *Turdoides melanops*

Setswana: le.tshêganôga, le.tshoganôga

28 cm (11 in). **Identification:** Brown, thrush-like passerine with pale iris, which distinguishes it from all other brown babblers. Scalloped breast feathers, due to white edges, differentiate it from Arrow-marked Babbler. Brown (not white) rump separates it from Hartlaub's Babbler. The subspecies found in Botswana, *T. m. querula*, has noticeable black lores. **Call:** Typical babbler churring call, given individually or in chorus. **Status:** Resident; no breeding records from Botswana. **Abundance:** Uncommon. Highly localized, nowhere common within its range in northwestern Ngamiland District. **Habitat:** Found in stands of tall, mature Camel Thorn (*Acacia erioloba*) in northwestern Kalahari tree and bush savanna. **Habits:** Gregarious flocks are territorial and have fixed ranges. This species typically occurs in smaller flocks and is more discreet than other babbler species. It feeds by hopping on the ground or in lower stratum of canopy. **Conservation:** Least Concern.

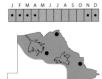

ARROW-MARKED BABBLER *Turdoides jardineii*

Setswana: le.tshêganôga, le.tshoganôga

24 cm (9 ½ in). **Identification:** Brown, thrush-like bird with orange-red eye and arrow-shaped white feather tips on throat and breast. Juvenile has dark eye, whitish gape, and dirty white flecks on breast. Three subspecies occur in Botswana: *T. j. tamalakanei* and *T. j. convergens* both have buff-tinged underparts and are very similar in appearance; *T. j. jardineii* is grayer and has no buffy tinge to underparts. **Call:** Loud babble, given by individuals or whole group. **Status:** Resident, breeding. **Abundance:** Common to abundant. *T. j. tamalakanei* (type specimen collected from the vicinity of the Thamalakane River) is found throughout Ngamiland and Chobe Districts; it is replaced by *T. j. convergens* in the eastern part of Central District and throughout North-East District; *T. j. jardineii* is found in the extreme east in the Tuli Block and Southern, South-East, and Kweneng Districts. **Habitat:** Inhabits a variety of woodland types, including arid Kalahari tree and bush savanna, in which it prefers thickets and riparian strips. **Habits:** Gregarious; family parties hop about on the ground turning leaf litter in a thrush-like manner. **Conservation:** Least Concern.

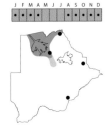

HARTLAUB'S BABBLER *Turdoides hartlaubii*

Setswana: le.tshêganôga, le.tshoganôga

26 cm (10 ¼ in). **Identification:** Brown, thrush-like bird with deep red eye and white rump—that latter a useful field feature, visible even in side view but most conspicuous in flight. The subspecies found in Botswana, *T. h. griseosquamata*, has distinct white edges to the feathers on the head, neck, and mantle, which give it a gray-scaled appearance (the subspecific name means "gray scales"). The nominate subspecies is browner and lacks the scaled appearance. **Call:** Typical loud babble, by individuals or group in chorus. **Status:** Resident, breeding. **Abundance:** Common to abundant. The range of *T. h. griseosquamata* (type specimen from the Boteti River) extends along the Boteti River to Lake Xau during years of high water flow from the Okavango Delta; *T. h. hartlaubii* may extend into Botswana's extreme north from the adjacent Zambezi Region of Namibia. **Habitat:** Found in riparian woodlands. **Habits:** Occurs in groups, which are territorial year-round. Semiterrestrial; small flocks can be seen hopping on the ground or foraging low in the undergrowth. **Conservation:** Least Concern.

BLACK-FACED BABBLER
T. m. querula

ARROW-MARKED BABBLER
T. j. convergens

adult

juv.

HARTLAUB'S BABBLER
T. h. griseosquamata

SYLVIID BABBLERS Sylviidae

The previously large and diverse family Sylviidae (once called Old World warblers and which included all warblers and cisticolas) has been split, giving several groups their own families. The much reduced family is left with a group of species more closely related to babblers and therefore now called sylviid babblers. There are only three species in Botswana, small leaf gleaners all belonging to the genus *Sylvia*; one of these is the former Chestnut-vented Titbabbler, now Chestnut-vented Warbler. Based on its morphology, behavior, vocalizations and mitochondrial DNA sequences, it clearly belongs in the genus Sylvia. The Setswana *kgwarakgwêtlhane* is a generic name for warblers and is used for birds of various families.

GARDEN WARBLER *Sylvia borin*

Setswana: kgwarakgwêtlhane, kgwêrêkgwêtlhane

14 cm (5 ½ in). **Identification:** Warbler with plain plumage that lacks any distinctive markings. It has a short bill, with both upper and lower mandibles mostly dark brown, and a pinkish base. It has a large dark eye and an eye-ring made up of a single band of white feathers. In the nominate subspecies, found throughout Botswana, the overall color is grayish brown. **Call:** Jumbled warble with whistled notes; often heard from foliage while bird remains unseen. **Status:** Palearctic migrant, nonbreeding. **Abundance:** Uncommon to common. **Habitat:** Found in thickets, mainly in acacia woodlands. **Habits:** Usually located and identified by song, as it calls from dense thickets. Known to be insectivorous, but prior to migration it visits fruiting shrubs and trees, such as fig trees, where it may be seen eating the fruits to obtain vegetable fats; these contribute toward the buildup of fat reserves needed to fuel migration. **Conservation:** Least Concern.

COMMON WHITETHROAT *Sylvia communis*

Setswana: kgwarakgwêtlhane, kgwêrêkgwêtlhane

14 cm (5 ½ in). **Identification:** Warbler with white throat, plain gray (male) or brown (female) head, and brown mantle. Tertials have broad rusty-brown edges, forming a rufous wing panel visible in both adult and immature birds. **Call:** Sustained warbling interspersed with mainly chattering notes. **Status:** Palearctic migrant, nonbreeding. **Abundance:** Uncommon to common. **Habitat:** Prefers acacia and Zambezi Teak (*Baikiaea plurijuga*) woodlands where it is found in the understory. Often found among *Grewia* bushes and in these and other bushes around pans in the Makgadikgadi Pans area. **Habits:** Solitary; frequents lower strata of dense thickets. **Conservation:** Least Concern.

CHESTNUT-VENTED WARBLER *Sylvia subcaerulea*

Setswana: para-lanku, para-lwanku, mmabolumara, ma.tlhô-aleburu

14 cm (5 ½ in). **Identification:** Warbler with obvious pale eye. The combination of gray plumage and chestnut vent is diagnostic. The subspecies found throughout Botswana, *S. s. cinerascens*, is pale gray overall. **Call:** *Tjeriktik, tik, tik, tik,* or variation thereof. **Status:** Resident, breeding. **Abundance:** Abundant. One of Botswana's most abundant and widespread species. The center of its abundance is in the Kalahari. **Habitat:** Found in scrub and thickets, particularly acacia. **Habits:** Forages by hopping along branches within the canopy of shrubs and bushes. **Conservation:** Least Concern.

GARDEN
WARBLER
S. b. borin

male

COMMON
WHITETHROAT

CHESTNUT-VENTED
WARBLER
S. s. cinerascens

WHITE-EYES Zosteropidae

A family of small warbler-like birds that have prominent white feathery eye-rings and greenish or yellowish plumage; however, plumage color is unreliable as an aid to differentiating species. Arboreal birds seen in small flocks, white-eyes feed on insects and fruit. Their tongues are brush-tipped, adapted to sucking up liquids. Sexes alike; species are monogamous. Three species occur in Botswana.

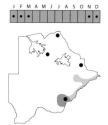

CAPE WHITE-EYE *Zosterops capensis*

12 cm (4 ¾ in). **Identification:** Typical white-eye: greenish-yellow warbler-like bird with a distinct white eye-ring. The yellowest subspecies, *Z. c. caniviridis*, is found in Botswana; it has yellow underparts, washed with olive on the flanks, and a bright yellow throat and upper breast. The upperparts are a consistent olive color. Flocks of Cape White-eyes normally include a variety of color forms. **Call:** Weak *phee* contact call; also a quiet rambling warble. **Status:** Resident, breeding. **Abundance:** Uncommon to locally common. The species is a southern African endemic; it occurs in Botswana at the northern limit of its range. **Habitat:** Frequents many different woodland habitats, including suburban gardens. **Habits:** Pairs or small groups forage among leaf foliage for fruits and insects. **Conservation:** Least Concern.

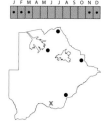

ORANGE RIVER WHITE-EYE *Zosterops pallidus*

12 cm (4 ¾ in). **Identification:** Cinnamon tinge to underparts helps differentiate this species from the other white-eyes, although color is an unreliable aid to identification in this family. **Call:** Similar to that of Cape White-eye. **Status:** Visitor or resident; no breeding records from Botswana. Egg-laying dates are probably similar to those for Cape White-eye. **Abundance:** Uncommon. Only one accepted record, from Oxford farm, Molopo Block, Kgalagadi District. **Habitat:** Found in riparian and other woodlands. **Habits:** Similar to Cape White-eye, from which the species has recently been split. **Conservation:** Least Concern.

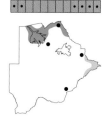

AFRICAN YELLOW WHITE-EYE *Zosterops senegalensis*

12 cm (4 ¾ in). **Identification:** Slightly smaller and yellower than Cape White-eye; underparts are uniformly yellow. The yellowest of the three subspecies is found in Botswana, *Z. s. anderssoni*, which has rich yellow underparts and a yellow wash over the upperparts. However, care should be taken when using color as an aid to identification in the Zosteropidae. **Call:** Soft, whistled warble. **Status:** Resident, breeding. **Abundance:** Common around the Okavango wetland system, Linyanti Swamps, and along the Chobe River; uncommon elsewhere in its range in Botswana. **Habitat:** Occurs in riparian forests and thickets. **Habits:** Small groups maintain contact while foraging among foliage for fruit and insects. This species is a host for the brood parasite Green-backed Honeybird. **Conservation:** Least Concern.

TREECREEPERS Certhiidae

A family of cryptically colored, small passerines with slender bills, which are decurved in the creepers. They are arboreal and characteristically forage for invertebrates on vertical tree trunks and large branches. Creepers have unusually long hind toe and claw, the combined length of which is longer than the tarsus. They have a cup-shaped nest, well camouflaged with lichens, in a fork of a tree. Only one species occurs in Botswana, a visitor.

AFRICAN SPOTTED CREEPER *Salpornis salvadori*

14 cm (5 ½ in). **Identification:** Unmistakable: long decurved bill and white spots on dark upperparts are distinctive. **Call:** Soft sibilant call; not very vocal. **Status:** Visitor; no breeding records from Botswana. **Abundance:** Rare. It is a typical species of Zambezi Teak (*Baikiaea plurijuga*) woodlands found only in the extreme north of the country (the bulk of the population occurs beyond the borders of Botswana). Only one accepted sighting to date, in Kasane in Chobe District in June 1994. **Habitat:** A Zambezi Teak specialist, seldom found in other broad-leaved woodland types. **Habits:** Creeps along trunk and branches in upper strata of tall trees, often with a jerky action, gleaning insects from bark. **Conservation:** Least Concern.

CAPE
WHITE-EYE
Z. c. caniviridis

ORANGE RIVER
WHITE-EYE

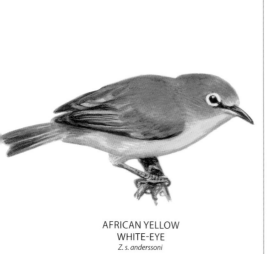

AFRICAN YELLOW
WHITE-EYE
Z. s. anderssoni

AFRICAN SPOTTED
CREEPER

309

STARLINGS Sturnidae

A large, diverse family, its members united by their shape and generalized short beaks, and stout legs; many have glossy plumage due to structural colors not pigments (dark greenish blue in half of those occurring in Botswana). Most forage on the ground in small groups for insects or fallen fruit. Nearly all are cavity nesters and lay blue eggs; an exception is the Wattled Starling, which makes an untidy, oval twig nest and lays white eggs. Botswana has 12 species; most of these are sedentary residents, but one is an introduced species, one is a vagrant, and three are visitors from populations just beyond Botswana's borders. The "glossy" starlings are called *le.gôdi* in Setswana.

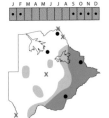

COMMON MYNA *Acridotheres tristis*

23 cm (9 in). **Identification:** Dark brown starling with black head and rich yellow bill and eye-ring. In flight, shows conspicuous white patches in the wings. **Call:** Noisy varied song with chattering, whistled trills, and warbles. **Status:** Resident; no breeding records from Botswana. **Abundance:** Common. An alien species (native to Asia), rapidly extending its range northward and westward in Botswana. First sighting was in Gaborone in March 1991. **Habitat:** Occurs in urban areas and increasingly in other habitats. **Habits:** Gregarious, noisy, adaptable. Forages on the ground; roosts communally in trees. **Conservation:** Least Concern.

ROSY STARLING *Pastor roseus*

21 cm (8 ¼ in). **Identification:** Adult in breeding plumage is unmistakable: pink underparts and mantle contrast with black head, wings, and tail. Nonbreeding birds are brown with buffy underparts. **Call:** Not very vocal. **Status:** Vagrant (from Palearctic); no breeding records from Botswana. **Abundance:** Rare. Only one accepted record, from Kasane in Chobe District in September 2007, of an adult in breeding plumage. Considered a genuine vagrant rather than an escaped captive bird. There is another record from arid scrub in neighboring Kalahari Gemsbok National Park in South Africa. **Habitat:** As a vagrant, it can occur in a variety of habitats. **Habits:** Solitary. Forages on the ground. **Conservation:** Least Concern.

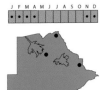

WATTLED STARLING *Creatophora cinerea*

Setswana: pônyane

21 cm (8 ¼ in). **Identification:** Nonbreeding adult has nondescript gray, white, and black/brown plumage and a small patch of bare yellow skin behind the eye; in flight, the white rump is a useful field feature. Flight feathers are dark brown in female, black in male. Breeding male is striking, with variable bare black and yellow skin on head, and pendent black wattles. **Call:** In flight, loud *chack, chack*. **Status:** Resident, breeding. **Abundance:** Common. Subject to irruptions and local movements. Birds from the arid Kalahari move to the fringes of the Okavango Delta during the dry season. **Habitat:** Occurs in dry, open Kalahari tree and bush savanna and grasslands; in winter, there are influxes into riparian woodlands in the northern part of the country, and into Gaborone, where it feeds on flowers of exotic trees. **Habits:** Gregarious; forages on the ground in small flocks, often following mammalian herbivores to get flushed insects. Small tight flocks fly fast and direct when moving to water or feeding area. Breeds colonially in large "cities" in trees. **Conservation:** Least Concern.

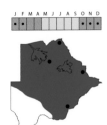

VIOLET-BACKED STARLING *Cinnyricinclus leucogaster*

Setswana: reole

18 cm (7 in). **Identification:** Small starling, sexually dimorphic in plumage. Both sexes have yellow eyes. Male, unmistakable, has iridescent violet (or plum) upperparts and white underparts. Thrush-like female is brown above and has white breast heavily streaked in brown. Juvenile resembles female but has brown eye. **Call:** Squeaky, nasal whistle, *chee-cheeoo*, and variations thereof. **Status:** Intra-African migrant, breeding. Seen mainly between October and April, but some birds overwinter. **Abundance:** Common. **Habitat:** Found in Kalahari tree and bush savanna and open, mixed broad-leaved woodlands. **Habits:** Occurs in pairs when breeding, in small flocks during nonbreeding season. An arboreal species, it forages in the tree canopy, mainly for fruits and insects. It is a cavity nester. **Conservation:** Least Concern.

COMMON
MYNA

breeding

nonbreeding

ROSY
STARLING

WATTLED
STARLING

nonbreeding
male

female

breeding
male

adult
male

imm.
male

adult
female

VIOLET-BACKED
STARLING

CAPE STARLING *Lamprotornis nitens*

Setswana: le.gôdi, le.gwêdi, le.gôdilo, le.sôlôpila

23 cm (9 in). **Identification:** Short-tailed, glossy starling with greenish-blue plumage and orange eye. Similar in size (though noticeably stockier) to Greater Blue-eared Starling, but Cape has darker (orange) iris and less glossy plumage lacking purple wash on thighs, and lacks dark eye stripe extending to ear coverts. Only subspecies *L. n. phoenicopterus* occurs in Botswana. **Call:** Musical *trrr-reeu, treer, treer*, and variations thereof. **Status:** Resident, breeding. **Abundance:** Abundant. One of Botswana's most abundant and widespread species. **Habitat:** Found in a variety of habitats, including semiarid Kalahari tree and bush savanna. **Habits:** Pairs or small flocks congregate at fruiting trees, where they can be found high up in the canopy. It also forages on the ground for insects and fallen fruit. The species has multiple broods. It is a host for the brood parasites Greater Honeyguide and Great Spotted Cuckoo. **Conservation:** Least Concern.

GREATER BLUE-EARED STARLING *Lamprotornis chalybaeus*

Setswana: le.gôdi, le.gwêdi, le.gôdilo, le.sôlôpila

22 cm (8 ¾ in). **Identification:** Short-tailed, glossy starling with broad, dark eye stripe and obvious dark ear coverts and a yellow iris (variable in tone). It has very iridescent greenish plumage with a purple wash on the thighs. Differs from similar Cape Starling in these features and in being noticeably more slender. **Call:** Song comprises nasal *squee-eear, sque-eear-eear*. **Status:** Resident, breeding. **Abundance:** Common. **Habitat:** Found in tall, lush woodlands associated with major rivers. **Habits:** Occurs in pairs; gregarious when not breeding. Forages on the ground and in tree canopy. It is a tree-hole nester. **Conservation:** Least Concern.

MIOMBO BLUE-EARED STARLING *Lamprotornis elisabeth*

Setswana: le.gôdi, le.gwêdi, le.gôdilo, le.sôlôpila

18 cm (7 in). **Identification:** Short-tailed glossy starling with yellow eye. Similar to Greater Blue-eared Starling but slightly smaller, and its dark blue mask is narrower and appears as a black eye stripe. Juvenile is distinctive, with chestnut underparts (in other greenish-blue starlings, juveniles are duller than adults). **Call:** Chirpier than call of Greater Blue-eared, *chirp, chirrup, choo, chirp*. **Status:** Visitor from Zambia and Zimbabwe; no breeding records from Botswana. **Abundance:** Rare to scarce; an irruptive species, it is occasionally seen in groups of several dozen. Occurs in Botswana at the southwestern limit of its range in southern Africa. First record was of two female specimens, collected in Serondela, Chobe National Park, in 1967. **Habitat:** Essentially a bird of miombo woodlands, it is found in Zambezi Teak (*Baikiaea plurijuga*) and riparian woodlands in northern Chobe District. **Habits:** Frugivorous; feeds on the ground. Forms flocks after breeding, when presence of juveniles aids identification. **Conservation:** Least Concern. **General:** Previously considered a subspecies of Lesser Blue-eared Starling.

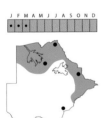

MEVES'S STARLING *Lamprotornis mevesii*

34 cm (13 ½ in). **Identification:** Slender, long-tailed, glossy starling with dark eye. Tail appears graduated and is almost as long as body. Only subspecies *L. m. mevesii*, which has a blue sheen to the plumage, is found in Botswana. **Call:** Chattering song with harsh *treear, treear* notes. **Status:** Resident, breeding. **Abundance:** Common to abundant. *L. m. mevesii* was originally described from a specimen collected at the Okavango River. **Habitat:** Found in tall woodlands with an open understory and bare ground, especially Mopane (*Colophospermum mopane*) and riparian woodlands. A Zambezian species; its range in Botswana coincides with the Mopane belt. **Habits:** Small family groups forage within the tree canopy and on the ground. A tree-hole nester, it is a host for brood parasite Great Spotted Cuckoo. **Conservation:** Least Concern.

CAPE STARLING
L. n. phoenicopterus

GREATER BLUE-EARED
STARLING

MEVES'S
STARLING
L. m. mevesii

adult

juv.

MIOMBO BLUE-EARED
STARLING

313

BURCHELL'S STARLING *Lamprotornis australis*

Setswana: le.gôdi, le.gwêdi, le.gôdilê, le.gwêdile, le.gwêditshane

32 cm (12 ½ in). **Identification:** Large, robust, long-tailed starling with dark eye. Tail much shorter than body length; wings project halfway down tail (compare Meves's Starling) **Call:** Harsh *kreek-chirow, kraa-chirr*, and variations thereof. **Status:** Resident, breeding. **Abundance:** Common to abundant. Its southern African stronghold is in Botswana. **Habitat:** Prefers Kalahari tree and bush savanna with large trees, particularly Mopane (*Colophospermum mopane*) and Camel Thorn (*Acacia erioloba*), and stretches of bare ground. **Habits:** Pairs and small flocks feed on the ground and in the tree canopy. Large numbers roost communally in reedbeds in wetlands. A tree-hole nester, it is a host for brood parasite Great Spotted Cuckoo. **Conservation:** Least Concern. **General:** Partially leucistic individuals regularly seen.

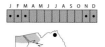

SHARP-TAILED STARLING *Lamprotornis acuticaudus*

22 cm (8 ¾ in). **Identification:** Glossy starling with golden-green wash to plumage and crimson (male, when breeding) or orange-yellow (female) eye. Wedge-shaped, pointed tail is diagnostic among starlings, although it may vary from square to rounded to forked and is definitive only when bird is in flight. **Call:** Soft, warbled *chree, chree*, completely unlike calls of other starlings in the region. **Status:** Visitor or sparse resident; no breeding records from Botswana. Breeding data shown are from egg-laying records in the adjacent Kavango Region of Namibia. **Abundance:** Scarce. It is a Zambezian species that occurs in Botswana at the southern limit of its range. **Habitat:** Prefers deciduous broad-leaved woodlands, especially Zambezi Teak (*Baikiaea plurijuga*) and Mopane (*Colophospermum mopane*). Often found in partially cleared fields in woodlands during summer. **Habits:** Occurs in pairs or small family groups, but flocks of up to 45 birds may be seen during nonbreeding season. Forages mainly on the ground, often with other glossy starlings. It is a cavity nester. **Conservation:** Least Concern.

RED-WINGED STARLING *Onychognathus morio*

Setswana: le.tsôpi

30 cm (11 ¾ in). **Identification:** Large starling, sexually dimorphic in plumage, with dark eye. It has dark bluish-black plumage, with contrasting rufous primaries that are especially visible in flight. Male is uniformly dark. Female has gray head and gray streaking extending down onto breast and mantle. Juvenile resembles male. **Call:** Plaintive but liquid whistle, *woop-cheeoo-lacheee*. **Status:** Resident, breeding. **Abundance:** Common, although Botswana is on the western edge of its range in southern Africa. Its range has recently extended up the Zambezi River to Kasane, where it is now resident and regularly seen. **Habitat:** Found in rocky hills and wooded gorges, a habitat type restricted to eastern Botswana, but also occurs in Gaborone, where it nests on tall buildings. **Habits:** Pairs or flocks forage in fruit trees; sometimes flock into Gaborone in winter. The species is host to brood parasite Great Spotted Cuckoo. **Conservation:** Least Concern.

PALE-WINGED STARLING *Onychognathus nabouroup*

27 cm (10 ¾ in). **Identification:** Large, bluish-black starling with orange eye and off-white primaries conspicuous in flight. At rest, rufous edges to primaries are visible, which could lead to confusion with Red-winged Starling. However, Pale-winged is slightly smaller, has a shorter tail, and occurs in a different part of Botswana. **Call:** Nasal, squeaky, jumbled song. **Status:** Visitor; no breeding records from Botswana. **Abundance:** Rare. Occurs in southwestern Botswana at the eastern extremity of its range. There have been no accepted records since 1985. **Habitat:** Prefers rocky outcrops in arid scrub savanna. **Habits:** Small flocks forage for fruits and insects. Undertakes local movements in response to food availability. **Conservation:** Least Concern.

314

SHARP-TAILED
STARLING

BURCHELL'S
STARLING

male

female

RED-WINGED
STARLING

PALE-WINGED
STARLING

OXPECKERS Buphagidae

An endemic African family of highly specialized passerines, adapted to feed on ectoparasites on mammalian hosts. Species have flattened bills for scissoring off ticks, sharp claws for clinging to host, and stiff, woodpecker-like tails for support. They are cooperative breeders and construct grass nests lined with mammal hair in natural cavities. The family contains two closely related species, which sometimes hybridize in the wild. Both are present in Botswana, where they are referred to by the name *kalatshômi*. The oxpeckers were previously placed in the Sturnidae but, based on genetic evidence, have been elevated to their own family.

YELLOW-BILLED OXPECKER *Buphagus africanus*

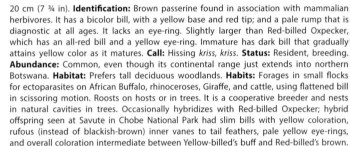

Setswana: kala, kalatshômi, kalatshôni, le.kalatshômi

20 cm (7 ¾ in). **Identification:** Brown passerine found in association with mammalian herbivores. It has a bicolor bill, with a yellow base and red tip; and a pale rump that is diagnostic at all ages. It lacks an eye-ring. Slightly larger than Red-billed Oxpecker, which has an all-red bill and a yellow eye-ring. Immature has dark bill that gradually attains yellow color as it matures. **Call:** Hissing *kriss, kriss.* **Status:** Resident, breeding. **Abundance:** Common, even though its continental range just extends into northern Botswana. **Habitat:** Prefers tall deciduous woodlands. **Habits:** Forages in small flocks for ectoparasites on African Buffalo, rhinoceroses, Giraffe, and cattle, using flattened bill in scissoring motion. Roosts on hosts or in trees. It is a cooperative breeder and nests in natural cavities in trees. Occasionally hybridizes with Red-billed Oxpecker; hybrid offspring seen at Savute in Chobe National Park had slim bills with yellow coloration, rufous (instead of blackish-brown) inner vanes to tail feathers, pale yellow eye-rings, and overall coloration intermediate between Yellow-billed's buff and Red-billed's brown. **Conservation:** Least Concern.

RED-BILLED OXPECKER *Buphagus erythrorhynchus*

Setswana: kala, kalatshômi, kalatshôni, le.kalatshômi

19 cm (7 ½ in). **Identification:** Brown passerine found feeding on ectoparasites on mammalian hosts. The combination of all-red bill and conspicuous yellow eye-ring is diagnostic for adult. Juvenile has brown bill and gray eye-ring; as it matures, the bill starts to become orange along the gape and the eye-ring to become paler. Lack of pale rump distinguishes all ages from larger Yellow-billed Oxpecker. **Call:** Hissing *churrr;* flight call is *tzik-tzik.* **Status:** Resident, breeding. **Abundance:** Common, even though Botswana is at the western edge of the species's southern African range. **Habitat:** Catholic in its choice of woodland types. **Habits:** Occurs in small flocks. Gleans ticks from mammalian herbivores; primary hosts are antelopes, donkeys, and cattle. A tree-cavity nester, it occasionally hybridizes with Yellow-billed; hybrid offspring seen at Savute in Chobe National Park had slim bills with yellow coloration, rufous (instead of blackish-brown) inner vanes to tail feathers, pale yellow eye-rings, and overall coloration intermediate between Yellow-billed's buff and Red-billed's brown. **Conservation:** Least Concern.

juv.

imm.

adult

YELLOW-BILLED
OXPECKER

imm.

juv.

adult

RED-BILLED
OXPECKER

THRUSHES Turdidae

This family is a relatively recent split from the Muscicapidae (p. 320); following restructuring based on genetic analysis, the old subfamily Turdinae is now elevated to family status. Thrushes are terrestrial birds that engage in run-stop-search foraging behavior, often turning leaf litter in search of food. Birds are solitary or occur in pairs, and sexes are alike. The nest is an open cup in a tree fork. All species have similarly structured melodious songs. Three species occur in Botswana: all are so-called typical thrushes of genus *Turdus*.

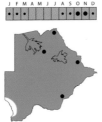

GROUNDSCRAPER THRUSH *Turdus litsitsirupa*

Setswana: le.tsutsurôpu, le.tsotsorôpu, le.tsetseropa

21 cm (8 ¼ in). **Identification:** Woodland thrush. Heavily spotted underparts and plain gray wings without wing bars makes this species distinctive. It has a bold black-and-white facial pattern; bicolor bill has yellow lower and black upper mandible. In flight, pale chestnut patches are visible in the wings. Sometimes confused with Dusky Lark (p. 270), which has scalloped pattern on wings and white, unspotted flanks, while spotting extends onto flanks in Groundscraper. **Call:** The Setswana names and the specific part of the scientific name are all onomatopoeic and derived from the call. **Status:** Resident, breeding. **Abundance:** Common. **Habitat:** Occurs in open woodlands, both broad-leaved and acacia. **Habits:** Apart from territorial males, which sing from treetops, this species is terrestrial and forages on the ground, solitarily or in pairs. Has upright stance. Runs quickly for a short distance, pauses, flips over leaves, picks up invertebrate food, runs forward, and repeats the pattern. Frequently flicks wings, like a chat. **Conservation:** Least Concern.

KURRICHANE THRUSH *Turdus libonyana*

Setswana: tsintsiru

22 cm (8 ¾ in). **Identification:** Woodland thrush. Combination of orange bill, black malar stripe, and orange-buff flanks is diagnostic. Two subspecies occur in Botswana: coloring of *T. l. libonyana* is darker than that of *T. l. chobiensis*. **Call:** Short, deliberate whistle, repeated several times but with a minor variation each time. Also sharp *chit-cheeo*, mainly at dusk. **Status:** Resident, breeding. **Abundance:** Common to abundant. *T. l. libonyana* (described from a type specimen collected in Kurrichane, which is now Zeerust, South Africa) is found in South-East District; *T. l. chobiensis* is more widespread and found in the east and north of the country. **Habitat:** Prefers moist broad-leaved woodlands and thickets. **Habits:** Terrestrial, runs along the ground with body horizontal but adopts upright posture when static. Turns over leaf litter in search of invertebrate food. **Conservation:** Least Concern.

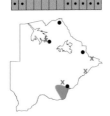

KAROO THRUSH *Turdus smithi*

24 cm (9 ½ in). **Identification:** Woodland thrush with dark gray upperparts and paler gray breast and flanks, extending to vent; orange confined to belly. Both upper and lower mandibles of bill are orange. When the bird is seen close-up, a golden eye-ring is discernible. Could be confused with closely related Olive Thrush (*T. olivaceus*), which, however, does not occur in Botswana; Olive has orange bill with dark dorsal ridge on upper mandible, orange belly and flanks, and white vent. **Call:** Melodic whistle, *cheeoo-cheeoo-cheucheet*, and variations thereof, repeated. **Status:** Resident, breeding. The few egg-laying records from Botswana conform, in terms of timing, with those from elsewhere in southern Africa. **Abundance:** Common, even though the species's range just extends into southeastern Botswana. First recorded in Gaborone in 1985 but has extended its range since then. A vagrant was seen in Maun, Ngamiland District, in 2012. The species is a southern African endemic. **Habitat:** Prefers riparian woodlands; also frequently seen in suburban gardens. **Habits:** Solitary or in pairs. Terrestrial; runs in horizontal posture, stands upright when it pauses, turns over leaves in search of food. **Conservation:** Least Concern.

GROUNDSCRAPER
THRUSH

wing-flick

KURRICHANE
THRUSH
T. l. chobiensis

adult

imm.

juv.

KAROO
THRUSH

CHATS, OLD WORLD FLYCATCHERS Muscicapidae

This heterogeneous group is a reconstructed family based on DNA evidence; previously it included every kind of "flycatcher," including tit-babblers and batises. Some species, such as those that made up the old subfamily Turdinae, are now placed in different families, and new related genera have been added to the Muscicapidae. At present, this remains a morphologically, behaviorally, and ecologically diverse family. Members are small to medium-size passerines that vary according to foraging strategy. Some are aerial insectivores, others glean insects from leaves or the ground. Juveniles usually have spotted plumage while they are dependent on parents. Botswana has 30 species, including robin-chats (*Cossypha*), scrub robins (*Cercotrichas*), wheatears (*Oenanthe*, *Myrmecocichla*), chats (a variety of genera), stonechats (*Saxicola*), rock thrushes (*Monticola*), palm thrushes (*Cichladusa*), and flycatchers (several genera including *Melaenornis* and *Muscicapa*). The sequence of species has a taxonomic underpinning but is modified to facilitate identification by grouping species that look similar.

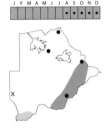

SHORT-TOED ROCK THRUSH *Monticola brevipes*

18 cm (7 in). **Identification:** Thrush-like species of rocky areas. Male of *M. b. pretoriae* (the subspecies that occurs in Botswana) has uniformly slate-gray head, throat, mantle, back, and wings; and orange underparts. (Male of the other subspecies has white on crown.) Female is brown above and has white throat speckled with brown, and pale orange underparts. Male's blue-gray mantle and back differentiate it from Cape Rock Thrush, which has blue-gray head only (and is no longer recognized as occurring in Botswana). **Call:** Whistled notes, including some mimicry. **Status:** Resident, breeding. **Abundance:** Common. Its range enters Botswana in the southeastern part of the country. A nomadic species, it makes irregular seasonal movements. **Habitat:** Occurs in rocky hillsides with trees in eastern hardveld. **Habits:** Solitary or in pairs. **Conservation:** Least Concern.

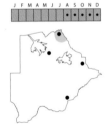

MIOMBO ROCK THRUSH *Monticola angolensis*

18 cm (7 in). **Identification:** The only rock thrush not associated with rocks. Similar to Short-toed Rock Thrush, but ranges do not overlap. Male and female have black speckles on hind crown, mantle, and wings. Female has dark malar stripe. **Call:** Repetitive whistled phrases. **Status:** Resident, breeding. There is only one Botswana egg-laying record, from November, which falls within the August to December breeding range for this species in southern Africa. **Abundance:** Rare. **Habitat:** The species is habitat specific, found in Zambezi Teak (*Baikiaea plurijuga*) woodlands. **Habits:** Occurs in pairs; forages for insects, mostly on the ground. **Conservation:** Least Concern.

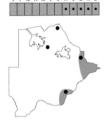

MOCKING CLIFF CHAT *Thamnolaea cinnamomeiventris*

22 cm (8 ¾ in). **Identification:** Large chat. Adult of both sexes has rich chestnut belly, vent, and rump. Male is glossy black above and has white shoulder patch. Female is slate gray above. Female of the subspecies found in Botswana, *T. c. odica*, is paler than other subspecies. **Call:** Loud, whistled call; mainly comprises mimicry of other species. **Status:** Resident, breeding. **Abundance:** Uncommon. Occurs in eastern Botswana at the western limit of its southern African range. **Habitat:** Found in rocky hills and outcrops of eastern hardveld. **Habits:** The species is confiding around human dwellings. Forages in pairs or small family parties, on the ground or among rocks. On alighting, raises and lowers tail slowly. Uses nests of Little Swift or striped swallows. Usually has two broods per season; lays three clutches only if there is an early failure of the first clutch. **Conservation:** Least Concern.

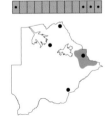

BOULDER CHAT *Pinarornis plumosus*

23 cm (9 in). **Identification:** Large blackish-brown chat with few distinctive plumage features. In flight, shows white outer tips to tail and row of white spots along center of each wing. **Call:** Monotonous squeaking, likened to the sound of a bicycle tire being pumped. **Status:** Resident, breeding. There are few egg-laying records from Botswana. **Abundance:** Common. Occurs in eastern Botswana at the southwestern edge of its range. **Habitat:** Prefers isolated, lightly wooded rock outcrops and granite boulders in eastern hardveld. **Habits:** Occurs in pairs or family parties. Hops and flies over boulders, raising and lowering tail conspicuously on alighting. Cooperative breeder. **Conservation:** Least Concern.

**SHORT-TOED
ROCK THRUSH**
M. b. pretoriae

male

female

**MIOMBO
ROCK THRUSH**

male

female

male

male

**MOCKING CLIFF
CHAT**
T. c. odica

female

**BOULDER
CHAT**

CAPE ROBIN-CHAT *Cossypha caffra*

17 cm (6 ¾ in). **Identification:** This robin-chat has orange throat and chest, gray bel
and flanks, rufous and black tail, and white supercilium. The nominate, *C. c. caffra*, whic
has a narrow supercilium, is the only subspecies in Botswana. Juvenile is sooty brow
with buffy mottling overall. **Call:** Whistled phrases containing limited mimicry. **Statu**
Visitor; no breeding records from Botswana. **Abundance:** Rare. The bulk of the populatio
occurs beyond the country's borders, and the species undertakes latitudinal movement
into southeastern Botswana from South Africa during winter. **Habitat:** Prefers thickets i
riparian woodlands; seen in suburban gardens. **Habits:** Calls mainly at dawn and dus
Conservation: Least Concern.

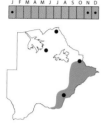

WHITE-THROATED ROBIN-CHAT *Cossypha humeralis*

16 cm (6 ¼ in). **Identification:** Predominantly black-and-white robin-chat. White throat an
breast, white wing bar, and white supercilium are distinctive field features. The tail is rufou
and black. Juvenile has buff-and-black-mottled head and mantle, and buff-and-brown
mottled underparts, but this plumage is short-lived. **Call:** Warbles mixed with mimicr
Status: Resident, breeding. The few egg-laying records from Botswana conform with thos
from the rest of southern Africa in terms of timing. **Abundance:** Common. A souther
African endemic, it occurs in Botswana at the western edge of its range. **Habitat:** Prefer
thickets along dry watercourses. **Habits:** Forages on the ground for invertebrates. Bathe
regularly in rainwater puddles. **Conservation:** Least Concern.

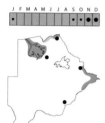

WHITE-BROWED ROBIN-CHAT *Cossypha heuglini*

Setswana: rabogale, mmalesêka, qwetwa

19 cm (7 ½ in). **Identification:** Large robin-chat. Slate-gray wings, broad white supercilium
separating black crown from black facial mask, and bright orange underparts are diagnostic ir
combination. **Call:** Rich, melodious duet, which rises to a crescendo and then suddenly stops
male issues repeated *trickle-choc-twee* (or similar) and female joins near end with *tlee, tlee*. Ver
little mimicry. **Status:** Resident, breeding. **Abundance:** Abundant throughout mapped range
except along edge of Linyanti Swamps, where its habitat has been modified by elephants
Habitat: Prefers riparian forest, where it occurs in tangled undergrowth. **Habits:** Pairs are founc
low in riparian thickets, where they duet, especially in early morning and late afternoon. Birds
forage among plant litter on the ground, turning and checking under leaves for termites anc
other invertebrates. **Conservation:** Least Concern. **General:** An individual with most of the face
and ear coverts white instead of black has been recorded from Tuli Block in eastern Botswana.

RED-CAPPED ROBIN-CHAT *Cossypha natalensis*

17 cm (6 ¾ in). **Identification:** Robin-chat with orange underparts and head, darker rufous
crown, and slate-blue wings. Juvenile is mottled overall. **Call:** Loud medley of whistles
incorporating many other birdcalls and local sounds; a fine mimic. **Status:** Visitor; no breeding
records from Botswana. **Abundance:** Rare. Range extends along the Zambezi Valley as far as
the confluence of the Chobe River; to date, there is only one accepted record, from Kasane in
November 1996. The deciduous thickets the bird favors along the Zambezi River are suitable
only from November to March, so this is the time to look out for this species in Chobe. **Habitat:**
Found in undergrowth of riparian forest; also deciduous thickets along rivers and drainage lines
(e.g., along Zambezi Valley in Zimbabwe). **Habits:** Forages mainly on the ground but calls from
concealed position low in thicket. Has distinctive habit of jerking tail up into vertical position
and then letting it slowly return to horizontal. **Conservation:** Least Concern.

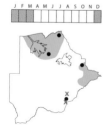

THRUSH NIGHTINGALE *Luscinia luscinia*

17 cm (6 ¾ in). **Identification:** Olive-brown, warbler-like relative of thrushes, robins, and
chats. It has a russet-colored tail and slightly reddish tinge to upperparts, large dark brown
eyes surrounded by a pale eye-ring, brown mottling on the breast and a dull white belly.
Call: Rich melody interspersed with variable notes, including gurgling and harsh grating
sounds. **Status:** Palearctic migrant, nonbreeding. Birds arrive after the first summer rains.
Abundance: Uncommon, though easily overlooked. **Habitat:** Found in dense riparian
thickets; favors Woolly Caper-bush (*Capparis tomentosa*) thickets. **Habits:** Solitary, skulking
denizen of dense thickets, best located and identified by its song. **Conservation:** Least
Concern.

CAPE ROBIN-CHAT
C. c. caffra

adult

juv.

WHITE-THROATED ROBIN-CHAT

WHITE-BROWED ROBIN-CHAT

adult

RED-CAPPED ROBIN-CHAT

juv.

THRUSH NIGHTINGALE

323

COLLARED PALM THRUSH *Cichladusa arquata*

20 cm (7 ¾ in). **Identification:** Robin-like bird with russet wings and back, a pale yellow throat bordered by narrow black necklace, and pale gray face with pale eye. **Call:** Robin-like warble that includes mimicry. **Status:** Resident, breeding. **Abundance:** Uncommon. First recorded in Botswana in Kasane in northern Chobe District in 1994, where it now breeds regularly. This species seems to be extending its range, as it has been seen as far south as Nata village, and is occasionally seen in the Okavango Delta, Chobe Enclave, Linyanti Swamps, and Selinda Spillway (where also recorded breeding). **Habitat:** Occurs in thickets in *Hyphaene* palm savannas. **Habits:** Small groups forage in trees or sometimes on the ground, where they hop like thrushes. **Conservation:** Least Concern.

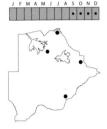

BEARDED SCRUB ROBIN *Cercotrichas quadrivirgata*

17 cm (6 ¾ in). **Identification:** Medium-size robin with white supercilium, white crescent beneath eye, white moustachial stripe, and black malar stripe—the specific name *quadrivirgata* refers to these four facial markings, which are diagnostic. The short, stiff feathers at the wrist that form the alula are white-tipped and in combination with the white patch at the base of the primaries are diagnostic. Can be confused with northern subspecies of White-browed Scrub Robin (*C. l. ovamboensis*), but unmarked rufous breast and flanks, darker brown upperparts, and lack of two white wing bars distinguish it. **Call:** Loud, melodious whistle. **Status:** Resident; no breeding records from Botswana. **Abundance:** Rare, except in vicinity of Kasane, where it is regarded as uncommon. It is a lowland species, and its range extends along the Zambezi Valley to the Chobe River, where it is regularly seen. Rare in the Okavango Delta, but there are confirmed sightings (most records of Bearded Scrub Robin from the Okavango are misidentifications and are actually the *ovamboensis* subspecies of White-browed Scrub Robin). **Habitat:** Occurs in riparian woodlands and scrub. **Habits:** Mainly terrestrial, feeds on insects among leaf litter on the ground. **Conservation:** Least Concern.

KALAHARI SCRUB ROBIN *Cercotrichas paena*

Setswana: phênê, phêna, pêne, tswetlha

16 cm (6 ¼ in). **Identification:** Medium-size robin with distinctive creamy, unstreaked breast. Tail has rufous base and broad blackish-brown band extending to the graduated white tip; tail pattern is usually conspicuous in flight. **Call:** Song comprises sharp whistles and includes imitations of other birds' calls—up to 32 have been recorded in the song of a single individual. **Status:** Resident, breeding. **Abundance:** Abundant. One of Botswana's most abundant and widespread species. A typical Kalahari species, it has its stronghold in Botswana. **Habitat:** Found in a variety of habitats, especially Kalahari tree and bush savanna. A favored habitat within this savanna is Black Thorn (*Acacia mellifera*) bushes lining pan margins. **Habits:** After alighting, this bird jerks the tail up and flicks the wings away from and above the body a few times. On the ground, it assumes a characteristic posture with tail raised and wings drooping. It walks and/or runs on the ground when foraging. When flushed, it flies only as far as the nearest cover. **Conservation:** Least Concern. **General:** The specific epithet in the scientific name is probably taken from the Setswana name *phêna*.

WHITE-BROWED SCRUB ROBIN *Cercotrichas leucophrys*

Setswana: phênê, phêna, pêne, tswetlha

15 cm (6 in). **Identification:** Medium-size robin with blackish-brown streaking on breast that is diagnostic among scrub robins. This streaking is prominent in one of Botswana's two subspecies, *C. l. pectoralis*. The pale subspecies, *C. l. ovamboensis*, has indistinct streaking on breast, a rufous rump, and faint malar stripes; it can be confused with Bearded Scrub Robin. Two white bars on the wing coverts and exaggerated raising and lowering of the tail are reliable field characteristics in both subspecies. **Call:** Whistled medley at dawn and dusk, often ending with distinctive *churrr* in the evening. Call includes little mimicry. **Status:** Resident, breeding. **Abundance:** Common to abundant. *C. l. pectoralis* is found in eastern Botswana, from North-East District southward to South-East District. *C. l. ovamboensis* occurs in Ngamiland and Chobe Districts and in the northern part of Central District. **Habitat:** Occurs in dense undergrowth in dry acacia and broad-leaved woodlands. **Habits:** Solitary or in pairs. Regularly fans tail and cocks it vertically, almost touching back of head. Forages on the ground (where it hops and/or runs) or lower stratum of thickets. Male sings from prominent perch. The species is an occasional host for brood parasite Klaas's Cuckoo. **Conservation:** Least Concern.

adult

juv.

COLLARED PALM
THRUSH

BEARDED SCRUB
ROBIN

KALAHARI SCRUB
ROBIN

WHITE-BROWED
SCRUB ROBIN

C. l. pectoralis

C. l. ovamboensis

MOUNTAIN WHEATEAR *Myrmecocichla monticola*

19 cm (7 ½ in). **Identification:** Polymorphic species; male can occur in one of two main color morphs, gray or black, both with variable white shoulder patches (sometimes absent). Female is sooty brown. All forms invariably have white rump and undertail coverts and white outer tail feathers, which aid identification. In the subspecies found in Botswana, *M. m. monticola*, the black morph male lacks white stripe above eye (occasionally shown in the other subspecies). **Call:** Canary-like whistled trills interspersed with harsh churrs. **Status:** Visitor or sparse resident; no breeding records from Botswana. **Abundance:** Rare. The range of this species extends only marginally to southwestern Botswana. **Habitat:** Inhabits rocky slopes and ridges in arid scrub savanna. **Habits:** Perch hunts for insects from low bushes, termite mounds or on walls and buildings. **Conservation:** Least Concern.

J F M A M J J A S O N D

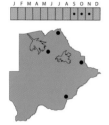

CAPPED WHEATEAR *Oenanthe pileata*

Setswana: ntidi

17 cm (6 ¾ in). **Identification:** Black crown, face mask, and breast band make adult unmistakable. Botswana's two subspecies, *O. p. neseri* and *O. p. livingstonii*, differ primarily in the width of the black breast band, which is wider in the latter. Juvenile may be mistaken for Isabelline Wheatear but has dark buff upperparts (darker than those of the other wheatears). **Call:** Series of scratchy whistles and short mimicked sequences. **Status:** Resident, breeding. The few Botswana breeding records, from between September and November, are probably a subset of the southern African egg-laying dates, July to January. **Abundance:** Common to abundant. Botswana is a stronghold for this species in southern Africa. *O. p. livingstonii* occurs in North-East District, the eastern part of Central District, and southward through Kgatleng to South-East and Southern Districts; *O. p. neseri* occurs in the remainder of the country. The Botswana population of this species is nomadic, its movements unclear. Thousands were seen on Pitsane grasslands in South-East District in May and June 1981; all had left by August, indicating a through passage. **Habitat:** Found in a variety of habitats, including Kalahari tree and bush savanna, where it favors open areas with bare ground. **Habits:** Terrestrial; has very erect stance. When foraging, runs short distance with body near horizontal, stops in upright posture, raises and lowers tail, occasionally flicks wings, runs forward again. Also perches on low bushes and termitaria. Nests underground in rodent burrow; egg-laying is therefore difficult to confirm. **Conservation:** Least Concern.

ISABELLINE WHEATEAR *Oenanthe isabellina*

16 cm (6 ¼ in). **Identification:** Similar to juvenile Capped Wheatear but has pale yellow-gray upperparts; whitish supercilium; short, stiff, black feathers on the wrist (alula); and a broad black tail band. **Call:** Mostly silent; occasional high-pitched whistle. **Status:** Vagrant (from north of equator), nonbreeding. **Abundance:** Rare. Only one accepted record, from Lesoma in Chobe District in January 2013. A published claim of two individuals photographed in Chobe National Park in December 1972 was subsequently rejected. **Habitat:** As a vagrant, may occur in a variety of woodland types. **Habits:** Forages on the ground in manner like that of Capped Wheatear. **Conservation:** Least Concern.

J F M A M J J A S O N D

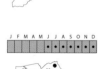

FAMILIAR CHAT *Oenanthe familiaris*

Setswana: kgatatswê, tlhwalamatlôtla, samathudi

15 cm (6 in). **Identification:** Uniformly brown chat with nondescript plumage, except for the rufous tail and rump. Rufous tail has central black bar and black terminal band forming a T. Juvenile is similar to juvenile Sickle-winged Chat (p. 328) but distinguished from it by this tail pattern (Sickle-winged Chat has dark triangle at end of tail on upperside). Botswana has three subspecies of Familiar Chat: *O. f. galtoni* is paler than the more common *O. f. hellmayri*; *O. f. falkensteini* has whitish belly. **Call:** Unmelodious *tee, chack-chack*, often heard at dawn. **Status:** Resident, breeding. **Abundance:** Common to abundant. The pale western subspecies, *O. f. galtoni*, occurs in the extreme southwest of Botswana, in the Nossob Valley. The range of *O. f. hellmayri* includes the southeastern part of Kgalagadi District, Southern and South-East Districts, Kweneng, Kgatleng, the eastern part of Central District, and North-East District. *O. f. falkensteini* may occur sparsely and irregularly in Ngamiland and Chobe Districts, at scattered localities where suitable habitat exists (e.g., Tsodilo and Goha Hills). This species occupies isolated pockets of suitable habitat outside its normal range; recorded sightings are indicated on the map with red Xs. **Habitat:** Prefers broken ground and rocky habitats (e.g., eastern hardveld). **Habits:** Confiding; perches conspicuously and frequently flicks its wings, a useful field characteristic. **Conservation:** Least Concern.

MOUNTAIN
WHEATEAR
M. m. monticola

female

male
black morph

male
gray morph

CAPPED
WHEATEAR
O. p. neseri

adult

juv.

ISABELLINE
WHEATEAR

adult

juv.

wing-flick

FAMILIAR CHAT
O. f. hellmayri

SICKLE-WINGED CHAT *Emarginata sinuata*

15 cm (6 in). **Identification:** Pale buffy chat with pale rufous rump. Differs from Familiar Chat (p. 326) by dark triangle on dorsal side of buffy tail, visible in flight. "Sickle-winged" (as well as scientific name) refers to wavy margin of second primary, visible only when bird is in hand. **Call:** Not very vocal; harsh chirps and churrs. **Status:** Visitor; no breeding records from Botswana. **Abundance:** Rare. A southern African endemic and scarce local visitor to Botswana, which lies at the northern extremity of its range. **Habitat:** Occurs on bare ground with sparse short growth and scattered bushes. **Habits:** Flies from one low perch to another when searching for insects. Flicks wings frequently when stationary. **Conservation:** Least Concern.

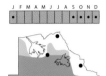

ANT-EATING CHAT *Myrmecocichla formicivora*

Setswana: le.ping, ping

18 cm (7 in). **Identification:** Uniformly dark brown chat that reveals distinct white patches in wing (formed by white bases to primaries) in flight. Male is very dark brown and has white shoulder patch. Female and juvenile are paler and lack white on shoulder. **Call:** Plaintive whistle; also a pleasant, canary-like song. **Status:** Resident, breeding. Egg-laying occurs within mammal burrows, therefore difficult to confirm. The Botswana records may be only a subset of the records for southern Africa, which generally indicate that egg-laying can continue until April. **Abundance:** Common. A southern African endemic. **Habitat:** Occurs in open grassy habitats with patches of scrub. **Habits:** Perches on low bush to scan surroundings for insects. Makes tunnel nest in roof of Aardvark or Hyena burrow; and is often seen on the ground on sandy area next to burrow opening. Adult has fluttering hovering display flight. **Conservation:** Least Concern.

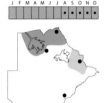

ARNOT'S CHAT *Myrmecocichla arnotti*

18 cm (7 in). **Identification:** Pied coloration distinguishes this chat from other sympatric species. Adult of both sexes is mostly black and has white shoulder patch. Male has white cap. Female has brown cap and white throat. Immature male has reduced white on crown. **Call:** Territorial call is series of whistles and trills. Group responds immediately to playback of call. **Status:** Resident, breeding. **Abundance:** Uncommon to common. **Habitat:** Mopane (*Colophospermum mopane*) specialist, virtually confined to mature Mopane woodland with open understory. It also occurs in Zambezi Teak (*Baikiaea plurijuga*) woodlands in Chobe District. **Habits:** Small territorial flocks forage together by flying from tree to tree and looking into cracks and crevices in the trunk and major branches. Birds also hop on the ground and forage among leaf litter. The species, a cooperative breeder, nests in tree cavities. **Conservation:** Least Concern.

WHINCHAT *Saxicola rubetra*

14 cm (5 ½ in). **Identification:** This chat looks similar to female African Stonechat, but it has brown (not white) rump and uppertail coverts, which are visible in flight. Male has dark streaked crown and conspicuous supercilium. Female has pale supercilium and lacks the white wing bar of female stonechat. **Call:** Not very vocal. **Status:** Vagrant (from Palearctic), nonbreeding. **Abundance:** Rare. There are only two accepted records of this species in Botswana. **Habitat:** Prefers grasslands, but as a vagrant it can occur in a variety of habitats. **Habits:** Hunts insects from low perch. **Conservation:** Least Concern.

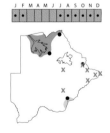

AFRICAN STONECHAT *Saxicola torquatus*

14 cm (5 ½ in). **Identification:** Sexually dimorphic chat. Male has black head and throat, white wing bar, and white rump. Female is buffy overall, and has faint eyebrow, white wing bar, and white rump. Only one subspecies, *S. t. stonei*, is found in Botswana. **Call:** Indistinct scratchy whistles. **Status:** Resident, breeding, in the north; winter visitor to the east and southeast. The few Botswana egg-laying records fall within the dates for southern Africa. **Abundance:** Common. **Habitat:** Occurs in permanent freshwater wetlands with wet floodplains and areas of rank grass growth. **Habits:** Solitary or in pairs. Perches low on reed or grass stems, from which it detects insect prey. **Conservation:** Least Concern

SICKLE-WINGED
CHAT

ANT-EATING
CHAT

adult

juv.

adult male

adult female

ARNOT'S
CHAT

male

female

breeding
male

nonbreeding
male

WHINCHAT

female

AFRICAN
STONECHAT
S. t. stonei

breeding
adult male

adult male
fresh plumage
(post breeding)

adult female

juv.

329

PALE FLYCATCHER *Melaenornis pallidus*

16 cm (6 ¼ in). **Identification:** Mouse-colored flycatcher with gray-brown upperparts, paler (but not white) underparts, a faint pale eye-ring, and dark lores. Margins of the wing feathers are pale, as are the outer tail feathers. Juvenile is heavily streaked above and spotted below. **Call:** Fast, scratchy warble. **Status:** Resident, breeding. **Abundance:** Uncommon to common. **Habitat:** Occurs in broad-leaved woodlands. It is the ecological counterpart of its congener Marico Flycatcher, which occupies acacia savannas. **Habits:** Solitary or in pairs; perch hunts from low vantage point for invertebrates on the ground. Makes cup-shaped nest on outer twigs of tree. **Conservation:** Least Concern.

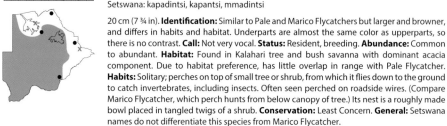

CHAT FLYCATCHER *Melaenornis infuscatus*

Setswana: kapadintsi, kapantsi, mmadintsi

20 cm (7 ¾ in). **Identification:** Similar to Pale and Marico Flycatchers but larger and browner, and differs in habits and habitat. Underparts are almost the same color as upperparts, so there is no contrast. **Call:** Not very vocal. **Status:** Resident, breeding. **Abundance:** Common to abundant. **Habitat:** Found in Kalahari tree and bush savanna with dominant acacia component. Due to habitat preference, has little overlap in range with Pale Flycatcher. **Habits:** Solitary; perches on top of small tree or shrub, from which it flies down to the ground to catch invertebrates, including insects. Often seen perched on roadside wires. (Compare Marico Flycatcher, which perch hunts from below canopy of tree.) Its nest is a roughly made bowl placed in tangled twigs of a shrub. **Conservation:** Least Concern. **General:** Setswana names do not differentiate this species from Marico Flycatcher.

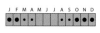

MARICO FLYCATCHER *Melaenornis mariquensis*

Setswana: kapadintsi, kapantsi, mmadintsi

18 cm (7 in). **Identification:** This flycatcher has brown upperparts and white underparts, the contrast between them easily seen in the field (compare Pale and Chat Flycatchers). *M. m. acaciae* is the palest of the three subspecies in Botswana; *M. m. mariquensis* has pale upperparts and probably is not separable in the field from *acaciae*; *M. m. territinctus* has dark brown upperparts. **Call:** Harsh, sparrow-like cheeps and churrs strung together to form unmelodious song. **Status:** Resident, breeding. **Abundance:** Abundant. One of Botswana's most abundant and widespread species. A typical Kalahari species, it is the most common flycatcher in the central and southern Kalahari. *M. m. acaciae* occurs in central and western Botswana; *M. m. mariquensis* occurs in southern and eastern Botswana; *M. m. territinctus* is found in the extreme north. **Habitat:** An acacia specialist, especially *M. m. acaciae*, which is found in Kalahari tree and bush savanna. The nominate is found in mixed savanna of the eastern hardveld. *M. m. territinctus* occurs in northwestern Kalahari tree and bush savanna and northeastern Kalahari mixed woodland and scrub, where it prefers open scrubby areas. The species is the ecological counterpart of its congener Pale Flycatcher, which occupies broad-leaved woodlands. **Habits:** Solitary or in pairs. Usually seen perched on lower outer edge of small tree or bush, from which it makes short sally to the ground to capture invertebrate prey. On returning to perch, raises and lowers tail. Makes cup-shaped nest. **Conservation:** Least Concern.

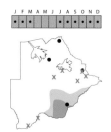

FISCAL FLYCATCHER *Melaenornis silens*

18 cm (7 in). **Identification:** Pied flycatcher. Male is black and white; female is brown where male is black. White panels on either side of the tail are visible in flight. Bears marked resemblance to Southern Fiscal (p. 252); however, it is more slender, it has a less robust bill, its white wing bars extend only halfway along the wing, not to the shoulders, and the Southern Fiscal lacks white panels in the tail. **Call:** High-pitched sibilant whistle. **Status:** Resident, no breeding records from Botswana. Resident population in southeastern Botswana is supplemented by nonbreeding migrants from the South African breeding population from May to September. Egg-laying in southern Africa takes place between July and March and is probably the same in Botswana. **Abundance:** Uncommon to common. A southern African endemic, it occurs in southeastern Botswana at the northern extremity of its range. There was an influx of Fiscal Flycatchers into Bobirwa area of eastern Botswana in 2002, farther north than they usually occur. **Habitat:** Occurs in open vegetation with scattered trees and shrubs. **Habits:** Solitary; hawks insects from a perch, capturing them on the ground. **Conservation:** Least Concern.

PALE
FLYCATCHER

CHAT
FLYCATCHER

adult

juv.

adult

juv.

MARICO
FLYCATCHER
M. m. acaciae

FISCAL
FLYCATCHER

adult
male

adult
female

juv.

SOUTHERN BLACK FLYCATCHER *Melaenornis pammelaina*

Setswana: se.rothê, se.ruthê

20 cm (7 ¾ in). **Identification:** All-black flycatcher with brown eye and slightly notched tail. Juvenile is also black but heavily spotted with buff. Slender shape and eye color distinguish adult from Fork-tailed Drongo (p. 248). The black base to the bill distinguishes it from all-black morph of male Black Cuckooshrike (p. 248). **Call:** Loud whistles interspersed with thin *tseep-tsoo-tsoo*. **Status:** Resident, breeding. **Abundance:** Uncommon to common. The bulk of this species's population occurs beyond the borders of Botswana; its range extends only marginally into the country. **Habitat:** Found in tall, moist woodlands with open spaces. **Habits:** Solitary or in small groups. Perch hunts in manner of a flycatcher, making short aerial sallies to catch insects on the ground. Builds simple cup nest in a natural hollow in a tree. **Conservation:** Least Concern. **General:** This species is not usually differentiated from Fork-tailed Drongo by Batswana, and the two species share a common Setswana name, *se.rothê*.

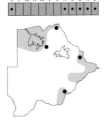

GREY TIT-FLYCATCHER *Myioparus plumbeus*

14 cm (5 ½ in). **Identification:** Small gray flycatcher. White outer tail feathers are clearly visible as bird constantly fans and flicks tail (a characteristic behavior for which it is given the alternative name Fan-tailed Flycatcher). Face plain; lacks bolder facial markings of Ashy Flycatcher. It is paler below (on belly) than Ashy. **Call:** Unmusical, soft, repeated *trreee … trreee….* **Status:** Resident, breeding. Breeding data shown are from the few Botswana egg-laying records. **Abundance:** Uncommon. **Habitat:** Found in riparian woodlands. **Habits:** Solitary, in pairs, or occasionally in small groups. The tail is fanned constantly as the bird forages actively in the tree canopy. Places nest in tree cavity. **Conservation:** Least Concern.

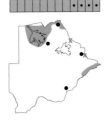

ASHY FLYCATCHER *Muscicapa caerulescens*

15 cm (6 in). **Identification:** Small flycatcher with blue-gray plumage. A white loral stripe extends above eye, a white crescent curves below eye, and a dark loral stripe between the two continues slightly behind eye. Tail is plain gray (compare Grey Tit-Flycatcher). The pale subspecies, *M. c. impavida*, occurs in Botswana. **Call:** Soft *pit PIT pit-pit*, often heard at dusk. **Status:** Resident, breeding. **Abundance:** Common to abundant. Occurs in Botswana at the western limit of its southern African range. **Habitat:** Found in riparian vegetation and dense thickets, where it occupies middle and upper strata. **Habits:** Solitary or in pairs. Hawks insects from perch, catching them in the air. A static perch hunter, it remains motionless for extended periods (compare Grey Tit-Flycatcher). Often nests in human habitation. **Conservation:** Least Concern.

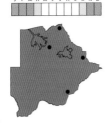

SPOTTED FLYCATCHER *Muscicapa striata*

14 cm (5 ½ in). **Identification:** Small, slender, long-winged flycatcher. It has relatively large head and slender lower body and a noticeably large, dark eye. Faint streaking on head and breast aid in separating it from other brown flycatchers. "Spotted" in the common name refers to juvenile plumage, which is replaced before the birds arrive in Botswana. **Call:** Quiet, unobtrusive sibilant whistle. **Status:** Palearctic migrant, nonbreeding. **Abundance:** Common to abundant. This species has declined significantly in the past few decades. **Habitat:** Occurs in a variety of open woodlands, where it is found along edges of the tree line. **Habits:** Hawks insects in the air or on the ground from a low perch (including fences, and on the outer side of trees and bushes. Returns frequently to same perch, almost always flicks wings on alighting; also flicks tail rapidly. **Conservation:** Least Concern.

adult

juv.

SOUTHERN BLACK
FLYCATCHER

GREY
TIT-FLYCATCHER

ASHY
FLYCATCHER
M. c. impavida

SPOTTED
FLYCATCHER

333

SUNBIRDS Nectariniidae

Small nectarivorous birds, members of this family have decurved bills for probing flowers and long, tubular tongues for sucking up nectar. They occasionally hover to feed, but usually perch. Males of Botswana's seven species have iridescent, colorful plumage (although some have drab eclipse plumage). Females (except female Collared Sunbird) are drab gray or brown and pose identification challenges. All build a similar nest: an oval ball of plant material bound with cobwebs, with the entrance at the top of one side. All sunbirds are given the same generic Setswana names.

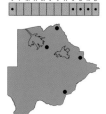

MARICO SUNBIRD *Cinnyris mariquensis*

Setswana: se.gôkgô, se.monamonê, mmalepana-leôme, mmabobi, talatala, talêtalê, rabogôma

13 cm (5 in). **Identification:** Male appears dark but in the right light shows metallic-green head and purple and maroon breast bands. Similar to slightly smaller male Purple-banded Sunbird, which has narrower breast bands and slightly shorter bill. No eclipse plumage. Female is gray-brown with gray-streaked yellow underparts. **Call:** *Chip-chip-chip* notes leading to fast, warbled song. **Status:** Resident, breeding. **Abundance:** Common to abundant; it is the most frequently seen sunbird throughout the Kalahari. **Habitat:** An acacia specialist, it inhabits dry Kalahari tree and bush savanna. **Habits:** Probes flowers of mistletoe plants (*Tapinanthus* spp.) growing on acacias; gathers when acacias flower to catch insects. Several males may gather on treetops and sing together. Builds a pear-shaped nest, covered on the outside with spiderwebs and with a side entrance near the top. It is a host for the brood parasite Klaas's Cuckoo. **Conservation:** Least Concern. **General:** There is a record of an individual living for eight years.

SHELLEY'S SUNBIRD *Cinnyris shelleyi*

Setswana: se.gôkgô, se.monamonê, mmalepana-leôme, mmabobi, talatala, talêtalê, rabogôma

11 cm (4 ¼ in). **Identification:** Male is iridescent dark green above (including head and throat) and has narrow blue upper breast band separated from black belly by broad scarlet band. Male in eclipse plumage has drab brown upperparts, with limited iridescence on rump and crown. Female is typically gray-brown with gray-streaked yellow underparts. **Call:** Fast, high-pitched twitter. **Status:** Visitor from Zambia and Zimbabwe; no breeding records from Botswana. **Abundance:** Rare. A Zambezian endemic; Botswana is just outside its range along the Zambezi River drainage in western Zimbabwe and the Zambezi Region of Namibia. **Habitat:** Occurs in broad-leaved woodlands such as Zambezi Teak (*Baikiaea plurijuga*). **Habits:** This species is overlooked, due to its small size and superficial similarity to Marico Sunbird. **Conservation:** Least Concern.

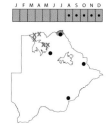

PURPLE-BANDED SUNBIRD *Cinnyris bifasciatus*

Setswana: se.gôkgô, se.monamonê, mmalepana-leôme, mmabobi, talatala, talêtalê, rabogôma

11 cm (4 ¼ in). **Identification:** Similar to Marico Sunbird, but breast bands are narrower in male, and breast is only lightly streaked in female. Both sexes have slightly shorter bills than Marico. Male in eclipse plumage resembles immature male (illustrated) but does not have gape flange. **Call:** Fast, warbled song similar to that of Marico Sunbird (and not useful for differentiating between the two species). **Status:** Resident; no breeding records from Botswana. **Abundance:** Rare, except in vicinity of Kasane in northern Chobe District, where it is uncommon. **Habitat:** Occurs in moist, broad-leaved woodlands, riparian growth, and gardens. **Habits:** Feeds on nectar and insects at flowering trees. Builds an oval nest with side entrance, using plant fibers and pieces of lichens. **Conservation:** Least Concern.

adult
male

imm.
male

MARICO
SUNBIRD

adult
female

SHELLEY'S
SUNBIRD

breeding
male

female

male
eclipse
plumage

PURPLE-BANDED
SUNBIRD

breeding
male

female

male immature
(without gape = male
nonbreeding/eclipse)

335

COLLARED SUNBIRD   *Hedydipna collaris*

Setswana: se.gôkgô, se.monamonê, mmalepana-leôme, mmabobi, talatala, talêtalê, rabogôma

10 cm (4 in). **Identification:** Small, short-billed forest species. Both sexes have emerald-green upperparts and yellow belly (no eclipse plumage in male). The subspecies found in Botswana, *H. c. zambesiana*, has bright yellow underparts, and the male has a purple breast band below a blue one. **Call:** High-pitched *cheee-cheee-cheee*, and short chirpy song similar to song of Willow Warbler (p. 282). **Status:** Resident, breeding. There is an egg-laying record from May, outside the usual breeding season. **Abundance:** Common. **Habitat:** Found in undergrowth of riparian woodlands. **Habits:** Pairs feed on nectar and insects in lower stratum of shrubs. The species makes an untidy oval-shaped nest with side entrance. **Conservation:** Least Concern.

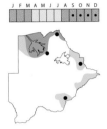

AMETHYST SUNBIRD   *Chalcomitra amethystina*

Setswana: se.gôkgô, se.monamonê, mmalepana-leôme, mmabobi, talatala, talêtalê, rabogôma

14 cm (5 ½ in). **Identification:** Male is black overall, except amethyst throat and metallic-green forehead (it has no eclipse plumage). Female is olive gray above and has variable, dirty-yellow underparts. Two subspecies occur, males of which differ subtly, while females are more distinguishable: *C. a. amethystina* female has a black throat, while *C. a. kirkii* has a pale gray throat. **Call:** High-pitched, fast twittering. **Status:** Resident, breeding. Birds undertake seasonal movements, and most sightings are between August and March. **Abundance:** Uncommon, though it can be common in Zambezi Teak (*Baikiaea plurijuga*) woodlands during summer, attracted by the tree's flowers. *C. a. amethystina* occurs in the eastern part of Central District and throughout Kgatleng, South-East, and Southern Districts; *C. a. kirkii* is found in Ngamiland, Chobe, and North-East Districts. **Habitat:** Found mainly in broad-leaved woodlands but also in gardens, farmlands, and along roadsides. **Habits:** It is an active feeder at flowering trees and plants, probing for nectar and catching insects; particularly fond of Wild Dagga (*Leonotis nepetifolia*) in the southeast. May form small groups at food source. Builds untidy oval nest with side entrance. **Conservation:** Least Concern.

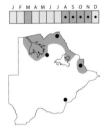

SCARLET-CHESTED SUNBIRD   *Chalcomitra senegalensis*

Setswana: se.gôkgô, se.monamonê, mmalepana-leôme, mmabobi, talatala, talêtalê, rabogôma

14 cm (5 ½ in). **Identification:** Male easily identified: black with iridescent scarlet chest (no eclipse plumage). Female is dark olive gray above and has a darker and more mottled breast than female Amethyst Sunbird. Botswana's two subspecies, the more widespread *C. s. saturatior*, are virtually indistinguishable in the field. **Call:** Loud *chip, cheeuw* notes, repeated. **Status:** Resident, breeding. The population is subject to local movements; most sightings occur between August and November and again in March. **Abundance:** Uncommon. *C. s. gutturalis* is found only in North-East District; *C. s. saturatior* occurs throughout Ngamiland and Chobe Districts. **Habitat:** Occurs in a variety of woodlands, including riparian woodlands. **Habits:** Noisy and conspicuous at food source. Builds untidy oval nest with side entrance. **Conservation:** Least Concern.

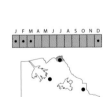

COPPER SUNBIRD   *Cinnyris cupreus*

Setswana: se.gôkgô, se.monamonê, mmalepana-leôme, mmabobi, talatala, talêtalê, rabogôma

12 cm (4 ¾ in). **Identification:** Breeding male is dark overall, almost blackish, but copper sheen shows in good light. Female is olive gray above and has off-white underparts tinged with yellow. Male in eclipse plumage is similar to female but has variable areas of dark feathers showing through. **Call:** High-pitched twittering interspersed with occasional loud *che-che-che* notes. **Status:** Resident, breeding. The few egg-laying records from Botswana conform to the timing of those in the rest of southern Africa. **Abundance:** Rare, except in the area around Kasane in northern Chobe District, where it is uncommon. **Habitat:** Found in Zambezi Teak (*Baikiaea plurijuga*) woodlands, edges of riparian woodlands, and gardens (especially in Kasane and Kazungula). **Habits:** Pairs frequent flowering plants, where they feed on nectar and insects. Builds untidy oval nest with side entrance. The species is a host for the brood parasite Klaas's Cuckoo. **Conservation:** Least Concern.

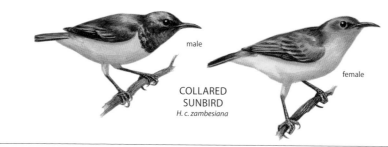

COLLARED SUNBIRD
H. c. zambesiana

male

female

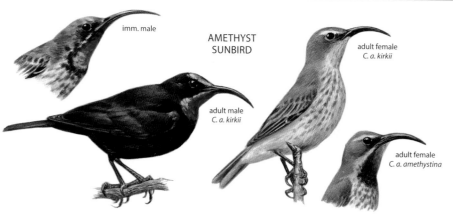

AMETHYST SUNBIRD

imm. male

adult male
C. a. kirkii

adult female
C. a. kirkii

adult female
C. a. amethystina

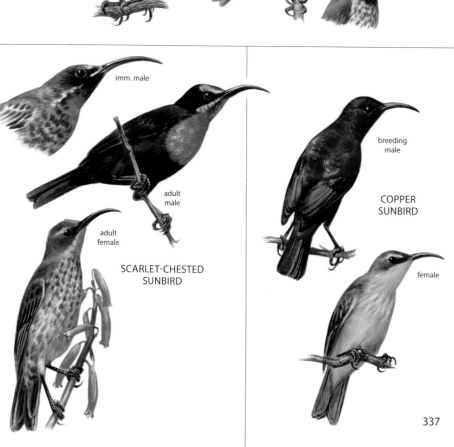

imm. male

adult male

adult female

SCARLET-CHESTED SUNBIRD

breeding male

COPPER SUNBIRD

female

337

WHITE-BELLIED SUNBIRD *Cinnyris talatala*

Setswana: se.gôkgô, se.monamonê, mmalepana-leôme, mmabobi, talatala, talêtalê, rabogôma

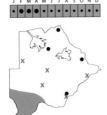

11 cm (4 ¼ in). **Identification:** Small sunbird. Male has white belly and iridescent green head, throat, mantle, and back. Female also has white underparts and is uniformly brown above. Subadult male has dull brown feathers interspersed among iridescent green feathers. **Call:** High-pitched *chewi-cheewi-cheewi*, interspersed with short, sharp *chit* notes and twittering. **Status:** Resident, breeding. The population is supplemented by irregular seasonal influx of birds from wetter areas in the southern African region. **Abundance:** Common to abundant. This is a Zambezian species that extends well into northern and eastern Botswana. **Habitat:** Prefers mesic woodlands; common in Mopane (*Colophospermum mopane*) and acacia. **Habits:** A noisy species often heard before it is seen. Builds oval nest with side entrance; outside is covered with spiderwebs and incorporates dried leaves, giving nest appearance of leaves caught in cobwebs. **Conservation:** Least Concern.

DUSKY SUNBIRD *Cinnyris fuscus*

Setswana: se.gôkgô, se.monamonê, mmalepana-leôme, mmabobi, talatala, talêtalê, rabogôma

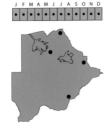

12 cm (4 ¾ in). **Identification:** Breeding male unmistakable, with orange tufts at sides of breast, and striking contrast between black head and throat/breast and white belly. Female has whitish underparts, making it very similar to female White-bellied Sunbird, but the species' ranges do not normally overlap. Male in eclipse plumage is similar to female but has black feathers remaining on throat. **Call:** Distinctive, soft *tchiff-tchiff*, and a warbled, whistled song. **Status:** Resident; no breeding records from Botswana. Egg-laying is opportunistic but appears to peak between February and April in southern Africa. **Abundance:** Scarce. The bulk of the population occurs elsewhere in the region, and its range just extends into southwestern Botswana. **Habitat:** Occurs in arid scrub savanna with scattered trees and shrubs associated with broken ground. **Habits:** Solitary or in pairs, but concentrations may form at flowering plants along dry watercourses. Builds untidy oval nest with side entrance. **Conservation:** Least Concern.

SPARROWS Passeridae

The quintessential passerines, sparrows are small seedeaters with stout conical bills and plumage in shades of brown and gray. Bill color changes in the breeding season in some species. Although related to ploceid weavers (p. 344), nests vary: some are cavity nesters, while others construct ball-shaped, untidy nests of grass (which, however, are not woven). The sparrow-weavers, as the name implies, are intermediate in terms of nest design. Botswana has five species belonging to the genus *Passer* and three other closely related species. The Setswana *tswere* is a generic name for sparrow.

WHITE-BROWED SPARROW-WEAVER *Plocepasser mahali*

Setswana: mo.gale, mo.galê

17 cm (6 ¾ in). **Identification:** Chunky weaver-like sparrow that has a broad white eyebrow and shows a conspicuous white rump in flight. Male has black bill, while that of female (and juvenile) is pale. Only the nominate subspecies is found in Botswana. **Call:** Lively chattering interspersed with whistles. The call is known by every Motswana, as it is played on Radio Botswana every hour to herald the news. **Status:** Resident, breeding. Egg-laying is opportunistic, recorded in all months. **Abundance:** Abundant. One of Botswana's most abundant and widespread species. **Habitat:** Occurs in dry Kalahari tree and bush savanna (particularly where acacias are prevalent) with a mixture of bare and well-grassed areas. **Habits:** A noisy and gregarious species, found in small flocks. It forages by walking on the ground. It is a monogamous, cooperative breeder. The untidy straw nests (always located on the western sides of trees) are conspicuous. Nests with two entrances are used for roosting so are occupied year-round. **Conservation:** Least Concern.

breeding
male

subadult
male

female

**WHITE-BELLIED
SUNBIRD**

breeding
male

male eclipse
plumage

female

**DUSKY
SUNBIRD**

adult
male

adult
female/juv.

**WHITE-BROWED
SPARROW-WEAVER**
P. m. mahali

339

SOCIABLE WEAVER *Philetairus socius*

Setswana: kgwêrêrê, kwane, phôrôgôtlhô

14 cm (5 ½ in). **Identification:** Brown, weaver-like sparrow with pale beak, brown cap, black face and bib, and dark scallop-edged feathers on mantle and flanks. Juvenile lacks the black bib. **Call:** Noisy, excited, high-pitched chattering at nest. **Status:** Resident, breeding. Breeds opportunistically after rains, during any month. In summer, egg-laying takes place within six days of rain falling. **Abundance:** Common to abundant. Endemic to the arid west of southern Africa; the eastern edge of its range just extends into southwestern Botswana. **Habitat:** Found in arid scrub savanna and Kalahari tree and bush savanna. **Habits:** Birds forage by hopping on the ground, searching for seeds and insects, particularly harvester termites. Highly gregarious in nature (the generic name means "loving companions"), the species is known for its unique, huge, colonial nest, used for breeding and roosting. It is the largest nest of any bird species in the world. Pygmy Falcons, Acacia Pied Barbets, Red-headed Finches, and Rosy-faced Lovebirds also use the nest as a relatively safe site to roost and breed. However, the nest is not immune to attacks by the Honey Badger, which breaks in from the top to get to the weaver chicks. **Conservation:** Least Concern.

GREAT SPARROW *Passer motitensis*

Setswana: tswere

16 cm (6 ¼ in). **Identification:** Large, chunky sparrow. Male has rufous back and rump, black eye stripe, heavy black bill, and distinctive bib. Female is drab but more rufous than female House Sparrow, and has a black bill. Two subspecies occur: the nominate is pale, while *P. m. subsolanus* has a darker crown and mantle. **Call:** Slow-paced, unmusical chirps. **Status:** Resident, breeding. Egg-laying peaks after rains, since the young are fed on insects (which emerge after rain), not seeds. **Abundance:** Common. The Kalahari in Botswana is the stronghold for this species in southern Africa. *P. m. subsolanus* is found in the eastern part of Central District, North-East District, and Kgatleng and South-East Districts. *P. m. motitensis* occurs throughout the remainder of the country, except for Ngamiland and Chobe Districts. **Habitat:** Occurs in open, arid Kalahari tree and bush savanna, especially where acacias are prevalent. **Habits:** Monogamous, with long term pair-bond and both sexes defending territory. Pairs forage for seeds on the ground; they also capture insects to feed young. Seldom found in association with humans. Builds untidy grass nest in thorny shrub. **Conservation:** Least Concern.

HOUSE SPARROW *Passer domesticus*

Setswana: tswere

14 cm (5 ½ in). **Identification:** Introduced sparrow with a heavily black-streaked brownish back. Male has chestnut upperparts, a gray rump, black face and bill, and distinctive black bib. Female is grayish brown and has a pale bill. Similar species are Great Sparrow, which has a rufous rump, and Yellow-throated Petronia (p. 342), which has prominent buffy eye stripe. **Call:** Unmusical chirps and cheeps, and harsher churrs. **Status:** Resident, breeding. There is one unusual egg-laying record from May, outside the normal timing. **Abundance:** Common to abundant in urban areas, especially in the eastern hardveld. Scarce elsewhere in its range in Botswana. An alien species, it has become naturalized in southern Africa. **Habitat:** Occurs in man-made environments. **Habits:** A human-commensal species, it feeds and nests in association with urban and rural settlements. **Conservation:** Least Concern.

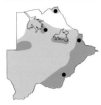

CAPE SPARROW *Passer melanurus*

Setswana: thorobê, tswere

15 cm (6 in). **Identification:** Male easily identified by striking black-and-white head; white supercilium extends backward and down to neck, forming a distinct crescent. Female has gray head with distinct white supercilium, also forming a crescent (which distinguishes it from Southern Grey-headed Sparrow, p. 342, with which its range overlaps). **Call:** Unmusical chirps. **Status:** Resident, breeding. **Abundance:** Common. **Habitat:** Found in Kalahari tree and bush savanna, especially in acacias along drainage lines. **Habits:** Pairs and small flocks forage by hopping on the ground, searching for seeds and insects (the latter are the principal food for young). The nest is a scruffy ball of plant material placed in a tree. The species is one of the hosts for the brood parasite Diederik Cuckoo. **Conservation:** Least Concern.

adult

juv.

SOCIABLE
WEAVER

male

GREAT SPARROW
P. m. motitensis

female

HOUSE
SPARROW

female

male

CAPE
SPARROW

male

female

NORTHERN GREY-HEADED SPARROW *Passer griseus*

Setswana: mmamojêla-rure, tswere

16 cm (6 ¼ in). **Identification:** Small gray passerine with rufous-brown wings, clearly defined white rectangle on center of throat, and black, conical bill. Slightly larger and chunkier than its sister species, Southern Grey-headed Sparrow, from which it can also be distinguished by its darker head, heavier bill, and less prominent white shoulder stripe. The bill is black year-round. **Call:** Unmusical series of chirps. **Status:** Resident; no breeding records from Botswana. Egg-laying dates are probably similar to those of Southern Grey-headed. **Abundance:** Rare, except in area around Kasane in northern Chobe District, where it is common. This species is extending its range southward and has only recently been recorded in Botswana; it may prove to be more widespread in northern Botswana than currently thought. **Habitat:** Found in association with human habitation; also occurs in woodlands. **Habits:** Pairs or small groups forage by walking or hopping on open ground, searching for seeds. Often seen on or around buildings. **Conservation:** Least Concern.

SOUTHERN GREY-HEADED SPARROW *Passer diffusus*

Setswana: mmamojêla-rure, tswere

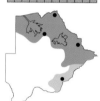

15 cm (6 in). **Identification:** The plain gray head of this species separates it from most other sparrows, except closely related Northern Grey-headed. It is slightly smaller than its sibling species, has a smaller bill, and shows less contrast under throat; however, these features are very variable. Bill is black in breeding birds and pinkish-brown in nonbreeding. **Call:** Unmusical chirps and churrs. **Status:** Resident, breeding. The distinct peak in egg-laying from January to March occurs during the rains, when insects are available for feeding chicks. **Abundance:** Abundant. One of Botswana's most abundant and widespread species. **Habitat:** Occurs in a variety of habitats, including broad-leaved and acacia woodlands. **Habits:** Found in pairs and small flocks; not as human-commensal as Northern Grey-headed Sparrow. Walks (rather than hops) on the ground when foraging for seeds. May be nomadic in arid parts of its range, where it forms large nonbreeding flocks at the end of the dry season. It is a cavity nester but also uses nests of the striped swallows. **Conservation:** Least Concern.

YELLOW-THROATED PETRONIA *Gymnoris superciliaris*

Setswana: mmamojêla-rure, tswere

16 cm (6 ¼ in). **Identification:** Sparrow with broad off-white supercilium and white wing bars. Pale yellow spot at base of white throat is not a reliable field characteristic; juvenile lacks yellow throat spot. Similar Streaky-headed Seedeater (p. 378) has well-streaked crown and lacks white wing bars. **Call:** Very distinctive trisyllabic whistle, *tree-tree-tree*. Also a longer *chew-chew-chew-chew*.**Status:** Resident, breeding. **Abundance:** Common. **Habitat:** Found in mesic broad-leaved woodlands and savannas. **Habits:** Arboreal; usually seen in tree canopy, where it is easily located and identified by its call. Walks along branches; frequently flicks wings and tail. It is a tree-hole nester. **Conservation:** Least Concern.

**NORTHERN
GREY-HEADED
SPARROW**

adult

**SOUTHERN
GREY-HEADED
SPARROW**

breeding
adult

nonbreeding
adult

juv.

**YELLOW-THROATED
PETRONIA**

yellow spot
usually difficult
to see

343

WEAVERS, QUELEAS, BISHOPS, WIDOWBIRDS Ploceidae

A diverse family, somewhat unified in form (shape, size), and by the standardized woven nests they make. The family divides comfortably into three groups, outlined below. The Setswana *thaga* is the commonly used generic name for weavers, queleas, and bishops; *talane*, *tale*, and *talanyana* are also used generically, particularly for the yellow weavers. The widowbirds that have long tails, and bear a superficial resemblance to the paradise whydahs (p. 368), share the Setswana name *mo.lope* with that species.

Weavers: Eleven species. Six of the seven *Ploceus* species are yellow (all but Chestnut Weaver), and all are sexually dimorphic, polygynous birds. Males usually acquire bright breeding plumage seasonally. Most species construct a woven, ball-shaped nest, with a ventral entrance, attached to reeds or a pendent twig of a tree. Red-billed Buffalo, Scaly-feathered, Thick-billed, and Red-headed Weavers are anomalous with regard to nests and/or plumage coloration, and are placed in different genera.

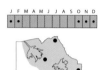

LESSER MASKED WEAVER *Ploceus intermedius*

Setswana: thaga, talane, tale, talanyana

14 cm (5 ½ in). **Identification:** Small yellow weaver with slender bill. Breeding male is easily recognized by combination of pale eye, black facial mask extending on head to mid-crown, black bib rounded ventrally, and gray legs (compare Southern Masked Weaver). The pale eye and gray legs also distinguish female and nonbreeding male from Southern Masked. *P. i. cabanisii* is the only subspecies found in Botswana. **Call:** Excited swizzling. **Status:** Resident, breeding. **Abundance:** Uncommon to common. **Habitat:** Occurs in open woodlands and acacia savannas, preferring those near water. **Habits:** Gregarious; flocks forage on the ground, primarily for insects but also for seeds. Colonial breeder; nests are often very close together (they may even be suspended from other nests). Polygynous; males have two or three females at any one time. Male constructs nests with short, narrow entrance tunnels; females line the nests. The narrow tunnels restrict entrance by parasitizing Diederik Cuckoos. **Conservation:** Least Concern.

SOUTHERN MASKED WEAVER *Ploceus velatus*

Setswana: thaga, talane, tale, talanyana

M: 15 cm (6 in), F: 14 cm (5 ½ in). **Identification:** Small yellow weaver. Breeding male recognized by the combination of dark red eye, black facial mask extending only to forehead, black bib pointed ventrally, and pale pinkish-gray legs (compare Lesser Masked Weaver). Nonbreeding male retains dark red eye. Female has pale pinkish-gray legs and usually has dark brown eye, but a small percentage have red eye when breeding. Eye and leg color differentiate this species from Lesser Masked in all plumages. **Call:** Swizzling and churring notes. **Status:** Resident, breeding. **Abundance:** Common to abundant; the commonest weaver in Botswana. **Habitat:** Catholic in its choice of habitats; prefers Kalahari tree and bush savanna with acacias. Not necessarily associated with water, unlike other yellow weavers in Botswana. **Habits:** Gregarious; flocks forage on the ground for seeds and insects. Roosts communally, often in groups of thousands, in winter months as in reeds at Phakalane Sewage Lagoons. Breeds in single-male colonies consisting of one male and several females (although there may be up to four males). Males are successively polygynous. Claims that females destroy substandard nests made by the male are not true; the male may remove an old unused nest in order to construct a new one in its place. The species is host to the brood parasite Diederik Cuckoo. **Conservation:** Least Concern.

VILLAGE WEAVER *Ploceus cucullatus*

Setswana: thaga, talane, tale, talanyana

M: 17 cm (6 ¾ in), F: 15 cm (6 in). **Identification:** Yellow weaver distinguished from related species by the spotted back in both sexes. Adult of both sexes has red eye and heavy black bill. Two subspecies occur in Botswana: breeding male of *P. c. nigriceps* has completely black head; *P. c. spilonotus* breeding male has black facial mask but yellow crown. **Call:** Swizzling, chattering notes. **Status:** Resident, breeding. **Abundance:** Uncommon. Birds in northern Botswana belong to subspecies *P. c. nigriceps*, those in the east to *P. c. spilonotus*; there is no overlap in their ranges. **Habitat:** Occurs in woodlands near water. **Habits:** Colonial nester; males are successively polygynous. It has been calculated that a male will travel a total of about 20 km (12 mi) to gather materials when constructing one nest. Gregarious; occurs in large flocks and roosts communally outside the breeding season. **Conservation:** Least Concern.

LESSER MASKED WEAVER
P. i. cabanisii

nonbreeding male

breeding male

female

SOUTHERN MASKED WEAVER

nonbreeding male

breeding male

female

nonbreeding male

breeding male
P. c. nigriceps

breeding male

female

VILLAGE WEAVER
P. c. spilonotus

345

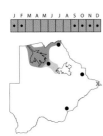

SPECTACLED WEAVER *Ploceus ocularis*

15 cm (6 in). **Identification:** Yellow weaver, with plain olive back and wings, that has a pale eye accentuated by black eye stripe (forming "spectacles"). Male has black throat and orange wash to breast and face; female lacks black bib. Both sexes have thin black bill, the color of which does not change seasonally. Unusual among weavers in Botswana in male lacking nonbreeding plumage. Juvenile can be told from other weavers by slender bill. Two subspecies occur: birds of *P. o. tenuirostris* have a more slender bill than those of *P. o. suahelicus*. **Call:** Descending whistle, *deee-deee-deee-deee*, more like call of Diederik Cuckoo (p. 184) than the swizzling call of most weavers. **Status:** Resident, breeding. **Abundance:** Uncommon. *P. o. tenuirostris* (described from a specimen collected in Sepopa in Ngamiland District) is found along the Okavango Panhandle, in the Okavango Delta, and along the Chobe River; *P. o. suahelicus* occurs in extreme eastern Botswana. **Habitat:** Found in freshwater wetlands, riparian woodlands and thickets. **Habits:** Mainly insectivorous, forages solitarily or in pairs. Monogamous, solitary nester. The male builds a substantial nest with a long, narrow entrance tunnel; it is sometimes located within *Phoenix* palm islands. **Conservation:** Least Concern.

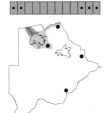

HOLUB'S GOLDEN WEAVER *Ploceus xanthops*

Setswana: talê

M: 18 cm (7 in), F: 16 cm (6 ¼ in). **Identification:** Largest yellow weaver in Botswana. Male is golden yellow overall. Female is greenish yellow. Both sexes have pale iris and black bill. Unusual among weavers in Botswana in male lacking nonbreeding plumage. Juvenile has brown iris and bicolor bill (upper mandible is black, lower is pale pinkish gray). Two subspecies occur in Botswana: *P. x. xanthops* breeding male has distinctive orange wash to throat; *P. x. jamesoni* lacks orange on throat. **Call:** Multisyllabic call ending in short swizzle; regularly heard in vicinity of nest. **Status:** Resident, breeding. **Abundance:** Common to abundant. *P. x. xanthops* is found around the Okavango wetland system and along the Chobe River; it extends its range down the Boteti River and toward Lake Ngami during years of high floods in the Okavango Delta. *P. x. jamesoni* should be looked for in the extreme east. **Habitat:** Found in riparian woodlands and thickets. **Habits:** Monogamous, solitary nester. Pairs stay together year-round; unpaired birds form small flocks. **Conservation:** Least Concern.

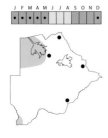

SOUTHERN BROWN-THROATED WEAVER *Ploceus xanthopterus*

15 cm (6 in). **Identification:** Yellow weaver. Breeding male is the only weaver in its range to have chestnut-brown throat and face (but not forecrown) and black bill. The specific epithet *xanthopterus* refers to bright yellow panels in the breeding male's wings. Breeding female has yellow underparts but lacks brown throat and has a pale bill. Nonbreeding birds of both sexes are dull olive brown above and have buffy chin and throat, white belly, and pinkish-brown bill. Botswana birds belong to subspecies *P. x. castaneigula*, in which breeding male has an expansive chestnut-brown throat. **Call:** Squeezed-out swizzling interspersed with harsh *chack* notes. **Status:** Resident, breeding. **Abundance:** Common. The species occurs in Botswana at the southern limit of its central African range. Its range has contracted in recent decades, coinciding with low water flows in the Okavango wetland system. During the 1960s, it was recorded along the Boteti River to Makalamabedi, 60 km (37 mi) downstream of Maun, by Reay Smithers. During the 19th century, specimens were collected at Lake Ngami. **Habitat:** Occurs in permanent swamps with Papyrus (*Cyperus papyrus*) and *Phragmites* reedbeds, and adjacent riparian woodlands. **Habits:** Occurs in pairs, and in small flocks when not breeding. Polygynous, breeds colonially; males weave small nests with no entrance tunnel in reedbeds over water. **Conservation:** Least Concern.

CHESTNUT WEAVER *Ploceus rubiginosus*

M: 15 cm (6 in), F: 13 cm (5 in). **Identification:** Breeding male distinctive; it has black head and throat, reddish eye, rich chestnut underparts and upperparts, and black wings with noticeably pale edging to the feathers. Female and nonbreeding male both have reddish eye but are duller; they have grayish-brown head with faint supercilium, gray-brown upperparts with white-edged feathers, and off-white underparts, but nonbreeding male has brown wash to upper breast. **Call:** Swizzling; also a loud *tchup* call in flight. **Status:** Resident, breeding. The few Botswana breeding records conform to the pattern in the region. **Abundance:** Scarce; can be locally common. The range of this species just extends into northwestern Botswana from Namibia; also recorded from extreme southwest. Nomadic, it breeds opportunistically in Ngamiland District during years of good rains. **Habitat:** Occurs in open, semiarid northwestern Kalahari tree and bush savanna. **Habits:** In years of substantial rain, there is an influx, first of males, which construct nests, and then of females. After courtship, mating, and egg-laying have occurred, the males leave, while the females remain to rear the chicks. **Conservation:** Least Concern.

male

SPECTACLED WEAVER
P. o. tenuirostris

female

male

female

HOLUB'S GOLDEN WEAVER
P. x. xanthops

nonbreeding male

female

breeding male

SOUTHERN BROWN-THROATED WEAVER
P. x. castaneigula

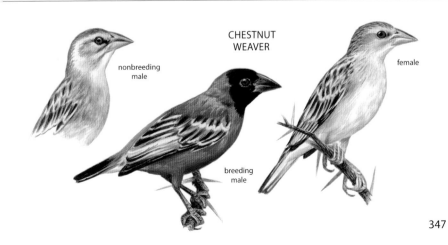

CHESTNUT WEAVER

nonbreeding male

female

breeding male

347

RED-BILLED BUFFALO WEAVER *Bubalornis niger*

Setswana: poênyane, kgwêrêrê, le.sêla-mitlwa, le.sêlammitlwa, le.sêlamebitlwa, ghwênê

23 cm (9 in). **Identification:** Large, dark weaver. Male is black, with red bill, and has white wing patches that are conspicuous when perched and in flight. Variable amount of white on sides of breast sometimes visible in perched bird. Female and immature are slate gray, with pale red bill, and their breast feathers are edged in white, creating scalloped appearance. **Call:** Noisy chattering at nest. **Status:** Resident, breeding. **Abundance:** Common to abundant. **Habitat:** Found in dry Kalahari tree and bush savanna; shows a preference for Mopane (*Colophospermum mopane*) and Camel Thorn (*Acacia erioloba*). **Habits:** Gregarious; occurs in small flocks, noisy near nests. Forages for seeds and insects on the ground in tight groups. Prefers to build its large, conspicuous, communal stick nests in acacias and Baobabs (*Adansonia digitata*). Polygynous; one male and several females occupy a nest. The birds are closely associated with their nests year-round. Their egg-laying peaks late, after grasses have seeded and insects are available for the chicks. **Conservation:** Least Concern.

SCALY-FEATHERED WEAVER *Sporopipes squamifrons*

Setswana: le.tsetsenkana, le.ntsetsekhwane, le.tsintsitlhwane, tsintsitlhwane, le.tsêtsênkane tswiitswii

10 cm (4 in). **Identification:** Small, finch-like weaver. Adult has conspicuous black wing coverts with white edges, which give the feathers a scaled appearance. These combined with the pink bill and a distinct black malar stripe (that gives the bird a moustached look) make this species unmistakable. **Call:** High-pitched chattering. **Status:** Resident, breeding. Breeds opportunistically year-round, though egg-laying peaks in summer. **Abundance:** Abundant. One of Botswana's most abundant and widespread species. It is a characteristic Kalahari species, and Botswana is its stronghold in southern Africa. **Habitat:** An acacia specialist of the Kalahari Basin, prefers low, open acacia shrubs interspersed with grassy patches. **Habits:** Occurs in pairs and small family groups; forages on the ground for seeds. Large nonbreeding flocks are seen in the Central Kalahari Game Reserve at the end of the dry season. The species doesn't need to drink water. Nests semi-colonially; makes a small ball-shaped nest of fine grass in the interior of a thornbush. **Conservation:** Least Concern.

THICK-BILLED WEAVER *Amblyospiza albifrons*

M: 20 cm (7 ¾ in), F: 16 cm (6 ¼ in). **Identification:** Massive bill and dark brown plumage make this weaver unmistakable. Male has white forehead and white patches in wings. The smaller female is lighter brown and heavily streaked, but huge bill is diagnostic. Botswana birds are of the dark brown subspecies, *A. a. maxima*, which has white scalloping to its underparts. **Call:** When displaying near nest, has a chattering, swizzling call; otherwise mostly silent. **Status:** Resident, breeding. Egg-laying data shown are for subspecies *A. a. maxima*. **Abundance:** Uncommon, local, found along the Okavango Panhandle and at isolated places around the Okavango Delta; also occurs in Linyanti Swamps and along the Chobe River. The type specimen for *A. a. maxima* was collected by Austin Roberts in 1932 on the Chobe River near Kasane town. **Habitat:** Occurs in freshwater wetlands and riparian forests adjacent to reeds (*Phragmites* spp.), bulrushes (*Typha capensis*), or Papyrus (*Cyperus papyrus*). **Habits:** Polygynous; male weaves several nests between vertical reed stems. The finely woven, very neat, ball-shaped nests have a side entrance; nests with spout-like projections at entrance are used for egg laying, while those without spouts are used for roosting. **Conservation:** Least Concern.

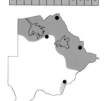

RED-HEADED WEAVER *Anaplectes rubriceps*

Setswana: thaga, talane, tale, talanyana

14 cm (5 ½ in). **Identification:** Distinctively marked weaver; both sexes have a gray mantle and wing feathers edged with yellow. The orange bill, which becomes reddish in breeding male, is diagnostic in both sexes. The head is bright scarlet in breeding male; in nonbreeding male and female it is yellow. **Call:** Swizzling, interspersed with cheeping and churring notes. **Status:** Resident, breeding. **Abundance:** Common throughout its range in Botswana, except in South-East District, where it is uncommon. **Habitat:** Favors mesic, deciduous broad-leaved woodlands, particularly Mopane (*Colophospermum mopane*). **Habits:** Inconspicuous outside breeding season. Feeds on the ground on seeds and insects, but also gleans tree foliage. Usually a solitary nester (monogamous), but may be polygynous and colonial. Male builds distinctive nest of fine twigs and leaf petioles with elongate tunnel entrance. Often associated with Baobabs (*Adansonia digitata*). Abandoned nests are occasionally used by Blue Waxbill and Cut-throat Finch for breeding. **Conservation:** Least Concern.

RED-BILLED
BUFFALO WEAVER

male

female

SCALY-FEATHERED
WEAVER

THICK-BILLED
WEAVER
A. a. maxima

male

female

RED-HEADED
WEAVER

nonbreeding
male

breeding
male

female

Queleas: Two species of mainly brown, weaver-like birds. Sexually dimorphic; bill color may change seasonally, in both sexes. Monogamous or polygynous, they breed colonially. The males construct finely woven nests with a side entrance at the top.

RED-HEADED QUELEA *Quelea erythrops*

Setswana: thaga, bo.raga, bo.ragane

11 cm (4 ¼ in). **Identification:** Small weaver. Breeding male has a red head; red color does not extend onto breast or mantle. There is a broad black line extending from the base of the bill down onto the breast. Female and nonbreeding male are nondescript; they are similar to Red-billed Quelea but do not have red bill at any stage. Red-headed Quelea could be confused with Cardinal Quelea (*Q. cardinalis*), which has not yet been positively recorded in Botswana but is illustrated for comparison; Cardinal breeding male has more extensive red on head and throat than Red-headed. **Call:** Twittering chorus. **Status:** Visitor or intra-African migrant. No breeding records from Botswana, but it is suspected to have bred in the Kwando area in northern Ngamiland (during January). **Abundance:** Rare, except on Chobe River floodplain near Kasane, where it is scarce. The species is nomadic and irruptive in response to rain and food availability. **Habitat:** Occurs in rank, moist grasslands. **Habits:** It is a highly mobile, gregarious species that can temporarily be locally common. **Conservation:** Least Concern.

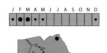

RED-BILLED QUELEA *Quelea quelea*

Setswana: thaga, bo.raga, bo.ragane

12 cm (4 ¾ in). **Identification:** Small, short-tailed brown weaver with red legs and red bill in breeding male, and nonbreeding male and female (breeding female's bill is yellow). The species is polymorphic, showing a variety of male breeding plumages, some of which are illustrated. Breeding plumage is short-lived, and most of the time male and female are similar, red-billed birds. They differ from nonbreeding bishops (p. 352) in bill and leg color and in having yellow (instead of buff) edges to the primaries. *Q. q. lathamii* is the subspecies found in Botswana. **Call:** Chattering chorus; in large flocks, can be very loud. **Status:** Resident, breeding. Breeds opportunistically in response to rainfall. Main egg-laying period is in the second half of the wet season. **Abundance:** Common to abundant. One of the most numerous bird species on earth, and one of Botswana's most abundant and widespread species. A flock of an estimated 100 million birds occurred in Moremi Game Reserve in 1988! Highly nomadic; birds travel as far as 3,000 km (1,860 mi) in response to rain. **Habitat:** Occurs in a wide variety of woodlands and grasslands; prefers acacia savannas for breeding. **Habits:** Highly gregarious and roosts communally, the roosts attracting many raptors. Flocks move ahead of the early summer rains so they can feed on the dry, ungerminated seeds, and follow the later rains so that they can get the new crop when the grasses have set seed and insects (mainly caterpillars and grasshopper nymphs) are available for the chicks. Interestingly, the species is monogamous but breeds colonially (most monogamous weavers breed in pairs), often in very large colonies in Black Thorn (*Acacia mellifera*) and other acacia species. It has one of the shortest breeding cycles of any bird. Birds may breed again in the same season by undertaking further long-distance "breeding migrations." **Conservation:** Least Concern.

breeding
adult male

Cardinal
Quelea
(for comparison
only)

breeding
adult male

adult
female

RED-HEADED
QUELEA

nonbreeding
adult male

nonbreeding
adult male

juv.

RED-BILLED QUELEA
Q. q. lathamii

swarms

nonbreeding
male

breeding
male

a. to f. = breeding male
plumage varieties

nonbreeding
female

a.

b.

c.

d.

breeding
female

e.

f.

351

Widowbirds: Six species belonging to the genus *Euplectes*. Sexually dimorphic, weaver-like birds, mainly brown when not breeding, but males have striking breeding plumage. The males construct partially woven nests with side entrance and domed roof.

YELLOW-CROWNED BISHOP *Euplectes afer*

Setswana: thaga

11 cm (4 ¼ in). **Identification:** Small, weaver-like species. Male in black and yellow breeding or transitional plumage is unmistakable. Female and nonbreeding male are nondescript small brown birds with streaked plumage and a buffy supercilium. Male has dark gray legs at all stages, whereas Southern Red Bishop has pale pinkish-gray legs at all stages. The subspecies found in Botswana is *E. a. taha*. **Call:** High-pitched buzzing and swizzling during display flight. **Status:** Resident, breeding. Breeds in response to rain and has a relatively short egg-laying peak when grassy ephemeral pans are available. **Abundance:** Uncommon. Nomadic; moves around widely in response to rain and can temporarily be locally common. **Habitat:** Occurs in grasslands; favors tall grasses standing in water for breeding. **Habits:** Displaying males, with puffed-out feathers and slow flight, look like giant bumblebees as they fly over ephemeral bodies of water; also found in permanent wetlands such as sewage lagoons. Polygynous; each male builds nests for and mates with several females; females line the nests. Forms flocks outside breeding season and moves widely. **Conservation:** Least Concern.

SOUTHERN RED BISHOP *Euplectes orix*

Setswana: thaga, mo.hubê, thagamohubê

M: 13 cm (5 in), F: 12 cm (4 ¾ in). **Identification:** Small, weaver-like species. Red-orange and black breeding male is unmistakable. Nonbreeding male and female are nondescript small brown birds with heavily streaked plumage; the breast is buffy with darker streaking. Male has pale pinkish-gray legs at all stages. The species is more heavily streaked than Yellow-crowned Bishop. **Call:** High-pitched swizzling mixed with chattering and whistling. **Status:** Resident, breeding. Egg-laying peaks during the main rains. **Abundance:** Common. **Habitat:** Found in grasslands near water; breeds in reedbeds or in rank vegetation flanking wetlands. **Habits:** Polygynous colonial breeder; male weaves oval nest with hooded side entrance, in reeds or occasionally herbaceous plants (e.g., Donkey-burr [*Xanthium strumarium*]). The species forms nomadic flocks and moves irregularly when not breeding. **Conservation:** Least Concern.

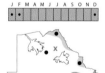

WHITE-WINGED WIDOWBIRD *Euplectes albonotatus*

Setswana: mo.lope, mo.nope, mo.lepe, mmamonopê

M: 17 cm (6 ¾ in), F:13 cm (5 in). **Identification:** Similar to Fan-tailed Widowbird (p. 354), but male has yellow shoulder and white wing bar (formed by white bases of flight feathers in combination with white edges to wing coverts). Breeding male is mainly black; nonbreeding male is predominantly buffy brown, retaining yellow shoulder and white wing bar. Female is also buffy brown but has less distinctive wing markings, with a small mustard-yellow area on the shoulder and no white wing bar; underparts are white and less streaked than those of the other female widowbirds. **Call:** Squeezed-out *squee-squee-squeezzz*. **Status:** Resident, breeding. **Abundance:** Uncommon to locally common, as at sewage lagoons in the southeast. **Habitat:** Occurs in seasonally inundated floodplains and in rank grasses near water. **Habits:** Polygynous; breeding male displays to and consorts with flocks of females. Male fans tail in similar manner to Fan-tailed Windowbird. Male builds partially woven nest with side entrance. Roosts communally in winter months, such as in reeds at Phakalane and Gaborone Game Reserve. **Conservation:** Least Concern.

YELLOW-CROWNED
BISHOP
E. a. taha

male
transitional

female/
nonbreeding
male

breeding
male

SOUTHERN RED
BISHOP

female/
nonbreeding
male

breeding
male

male
transitional

breeding
male

WHITE-WINGED
WIDOWBIRD

nonbreeding
male

female

353

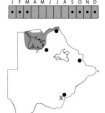

FAN-TAILED WIDOWBIRD *Euplectes axillaris*

Setswana: mo.lope, mo.nope, mo.lepe, mmamonopê

M: 17 cm (6 ¾ in), F: 13 cm (5 in). **Identification:** Breeding male distinctive; mainly black it has medium-length black tail, red shoulder (hence alternative name Red-shouldered Widowbird), and buffy margins to the black wing feathers; it has no white bar in wing, a in Long-tailed Widowbird. Nonbreeding male is buffy overall and has black wing feathers edged with buff and a clearly visible red shoulder. Female is similar but shoulder is reddish brown. The subspecies found in Botswana is *E. a. bocagei*; the shoulder patch can be quite orange-yellow. **Call:** High-pitched twittering during display; otherwise, not very vocal. **Status:** Resident, breeding. **Abundance:** Common. *E. a. bocagei* occurs in northern Botswana at the southern limit of its continental range, and the Okavango wetland system is the best place in southern Africa to see this subspecies. **Habitat:** Found in freshwater wetlands in *Phragmites* reedbeds and stands of Papyrus (*Cyperus papyrus*). **Habits:** Displaying male is conspicuous, perched on reeds with the broad, rounded tail fanned (hence common name) issuing a noisy call. Male builds partially woven nest with side entrance and projecting hood the nest is sometimes woven into a Papyrus umbel. The species has a fairly long breeding season over summer, as it breeds in relatively permanent wetlands. During nonbreeding season it forms flocks. **Conservation:** Least Concern.

RED-COLLARED WIDOWBIRD *Euplectes ardens*

Setswana: mo.lope, mo.nope, mo.lepe, mmamonopê

M: 35 cm (13 ¾ in), incl. long tail; F: 12 cm (4 ¾ in). **Identification:** Breeding male distinctive it has black plumage, long narrow tail, and red collar across throat (earning it the nickname "Cut-throat"). Nonbreeding male and female are nondescript little brown birds with a bold buff supercilium, yellow wash on head and breast, and heavily streaked upperparts However, nonbreeding male has diagnostic black chevron pattern on undertail coverts and has blackish legs (compare Long-tailed Widowbird). **Call:** Buzzing, tinkling song during display. **Status:** Visitor; no breeding records from Botswana. **Abundance:** Rare. Only one record to date, a displaying male in February 1986. The bulk of the population of this species occurs outside Botswana, and the range extends marginally into South-East District only **Habitat:** Occurs in grasslands with scattered trees. **Habits:** Polygynous; male attracts females during display flights with long tail spread vertically, so it appears broadly fanned in sideview. **Conservation:** Least Concern.

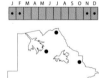

LONG-TAILED WIDOWBIRD *Euplectes progne*

Setswana: mo.lope, mo.nope, mo.lepe, mmamonopê

M: 60 cm (23 ½ in), incl. tail; F: 17 cm (6 ¾ in). **Identification:** Large, spectacular widowbird breeding male is unmistakable. Nonbreeding male retains red and buffy white in the wings (although much reduced) and is larger than female and other widowbirds. Legs of nonbreeding male are pale pinkish gray. Female is tawny overall, with light streaking on breast and flanks. **Call:** Not very vocal; during display male has subdued swizzling song **Status:** Resident; no breeding records from Botswana. **Abundance:** Uncommon to locally common. The bulk of the population occurs beyond the borders of Botswana, and the South African population just reaches the southeastern part of the country. Expands toward Gaborone in years of high rainfall. **Habitat:** Occurs in open grasslands. **Habits:** Polygynous, male performs spectacular flapping display flight with drooping tail flared to attract females Male builds several nests, which are subsequently lined by incubating females. When not breeding, the species forms nomadic flocks of up to 50 individuals that wander irregularly **Conservation:** Least Concern.

breeding male

male transitional

female/nonbreeding male

male transitional

FAN-TAILED WIDOWBIRD
E. a. bocagei

breeding male

male transitional

RED-COLLARED WIDOWBIRD

nonbreeding male

breeding male

breeding male

nonbreeding male

female

female

LONG-TAILED WIDOWBIRD

WAXBILLS, ALLIES Estrildidae

A large group of diminutive granivores with stout, conical bills. Monogamous and solitary nesters, they construct closed, ball-shaped nests in small trees or appropriate disused weaver and sparrow nests. Nests are not cleaned by adults and become fouled with the chicks' droppings. Not very vocal, these birds issue soft songs during courtship; males often display with nesting material. All species lay white eggs. The chicks of most have distinctively patterned mouths, with spots on tongue, palate, and floor of mouth. This is probably a strategy to reduce the risk of brood parasitism; nevertheless, many species are parasitized by members of the family Viduidae, whose chicks have closely matching mouth spots. Sixteen species occur in Botswana, comprising waxbills, finches and firefinches, pytilias, and mannikins. The Setswana *ralebiibii* is a generic name for firefinches.

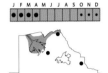

BROWN FIREFINCH *Lagonosticta nitidula*

Setswana: ntsetse, le.biibii, ralebiibii

10 cm (4 in). **Identification:** Dark gray-brown firefinch with red tinge to face and throat (more prominent in male) and small white spots on sides of breast (generic name means "spotted flanks"). The gray-brown rump is a reliable field characteristic; the bill is dark with pinkish sides, but color isn't always obvious. **Call:** Soft *tseet*. **Status:** Resident, breeding. **Abundance:** Common. Confined to the Okavango wetland system, Linyanti Swamps, and Chobe River, at the southern limit of its continental range. **Habitat:** Occurs in dense vegetation of thickets and riparian areas. **Habits:** Pairs feed on the ground, pecking at small seeds. The species nests in disused weaver nests; it is apparently a host for brood parasite Village Indigobird (subspecies *okavangoensis*). **Conservation:** Least Concern.

RED-BILLED FIREFINCH *Lagonosticta senegala*

Setswana: ntsetse, le.biibii, ralebiibii

M: 10 cm (4 in), F: 9 cm (3 ½ in). **Identification:** Male predominantly pink and slightly larger than female, which is brown. Both sexes have red bill; red rump and uppertail coverts (a useful field feature for separating this species from Brown Firefinch); and buffy undertail (not black as in Jameson's Firefinch). Faint white spots on underparts and a narrow yellow eye-ring are visible close-up (in both sexes). **Call:** Soft call, not easily audible to humans but distinct enough to be mimicked by Village Indigobird (p. 364). **Status:** Resident, breeding. **Abundance:** Common. **Habitat:** Prefers woodlands and savannas near water, particularly riparian thicket vegetation. Occurs in gardens. **Habits:** Pairs forage together on the ground for small seeds; small flocks form where seeds are abundant. Nest is a small round ball of plant material, profusely lined with feathers (from other birds); nest often associated with human habitations. The species is a host for brood parasite Village Indigobird (subspecies *amauropteryx*, which has a red bill, and *okavangoensis*, whitish bill). **Conservation:** Least Concern.

JAMESON'S FIREFINCH *Lagonosticta rhodopareia*

Setswana: ntsetse, le.biibii, ralebiibii

11 cm (4 ¼ in). **Identification:** Male is pink overall. Female is pinkish-buff. Both sexes have a blue bill, a few faint white spots on flanks, and black undertail coverts (compare Red-billed Firefinch, which has buffy undertail). In common with Red-billed but in contrast to Brown Firefinch, this species has a red rump, visible in flight. Botswana birds all belong to subspecies *L. r. jamesoni*. **Call:** Soft trill followed by high-pitched *wink-wink-wink-wink*. Mimicked by its brood parasite, Purple Indigobird (p. 364). **Status:** Resident, breeding. **Abundance:** Common. **Habitat:** Occurs in broad-leaved woodlands, where it occupies open grassy areas edged with thickets. **Habits:** Pairs and small flocks forage for seeds on the ground, often in tall, tangled grasses. The species is a host for brood parasite Purple Indigobird. **Conservation:** Least Concern.

BROWN
FIREFINCH

male

female

RED-BILLED
FIREFINCH

adult
male

adult
female

imm. male

JAMESON'S
FIREFINCH
L. r. jamesoni

male

female

ORANGE-WINGED PYTILIA *Pytilia afra*

Setswana: kgakanagae, kgakana-yagae, ramotwiisana

12 cm (4 ¾ in). **Identification:** Small seed-eating finch with golden-orange flight feathers forming distinctive wing panel. Both sexes have golden mantle, olive-mottled underparts, and red bill. Male has red from forehead to throat and extending behind eye onto ear coverts. Female has plain gray head; differs from female Green-winged Pytilia in its orange wing panel and olive underparts (compared to olive wing panel and black-barred flanks and belly in Green-winged). **Call:** Not very vocal. **Status:** Resident; no breeding records from Botswana. **Abundance:** Scarce. A Zambezian species, it occurs in Botswana at the extreme southwestern edge of its range. **Habitat:** Favors Zambezi Teak (*Baikiaea plurijuga*) woodlands. **Habits:** Feeds in pairs or small groups on the ground in woodland understory. It is a known host for brood parasite Broad-tailed Paradise Whydah, but there are no records of such in Botswana. **Conservation:** Least Concern.

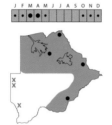

GREEN-WINGED PYTILIA *Pytilia melba*

13 cm (5 in). **Identification:** Small seed-eating finch with olive-green wing panel, olive mantle, black-barred underparts, and red bill. Male has red forehead and throat, but red does not extend behind eye as it does in Orange-winged Pytilia. Female has gray head and differs from female Orange-winged Pytilia in its olive-green wing panel and barred underparts. **Call:** Soft but beautiful canary-like trill. **Status:** Resident, breeding. **Abundance:** Common to abundant. **Habitat:** Occurs in acacia and riparian thickets with sources of drinking water. **Habits:** Pairs feed on seeds on the ground, fly up into low bushes when disturbed. This species places its grass-ball nest in interior of shrub. It is a host for brood parasite Long-tailed Paradise Whydah. **Conservation:** Least Concern.

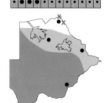

RED-HEADED FINCH *Amadina erythrocephala*

Setswana: ntsetse, rantsipitsipi

14 cm (5 ½ in). **Identification:** Finch with large, conical white bill. Male has dull red head and resembles Red-headed Quelea (p. 350) but differs in having white blotching on chest and flanks. Female is similar to male but has plain gray-brown head and is more scalloped below; these features differentiate it from female Cut-throat Finch, which has barred crown and nape, and sparse barring on underparts. The subspecies found throughout Botswana is *A. e. dissita*. **Call:** Soft, ringing *chuck, chuck*, frequently repeated. **Status:** Resident, breeding. **Abundance:** Common. This species has its stronghold in Botswana. Nomadic and irruptive, it moves widely and irregularly and can temporarily be locally abundant. **Habitat:** Occurs in dry Kalahari tree and bush savanna with open grasslands. **Habits:** Small flocks forage for seeds on the ground and are seen regularly at water holes. Since the species is irruptive, it is sometimes seen in large flocks (up to 400 birds), especially in the Central Kalahari Game Reserve and Kgalagadi Transfrontier Park at the end of the dry season. It uses old weaver nests (of Southern Masked, Lesser Masked, and Sociable) and nests of House Sparrows for breeding. **Conservation:** Least Concern. **General:** Cut-throat and Red-headed Finches crossbreed under natural conditions, and these hybrids may occur in Botswana. They have a heavy bill and white spots on breast and flanks like Red-headed, and a broad red throat (red sometimes extends to forehead) and distinctive chestnut belly like Cut-throat.

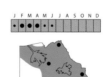

CUT-THROAT FINCH *Amadina fasciata*

Setswana: ntsetse, rantsipitsipi

12 cm (4 ¾ in). **Identification:** Male has red band on throat (thus the name "Cut-throat") that makes it unmistakable. Female has barred head and underparts, which differentiate it from larger female Red-headed Finch. Two subspecies occur: *A. f. meridionalis* has whiter throat and pale underparts; *A. f. contigua* is darker, with ocher-buff underparts. **Call:** Warbling song, infrequently heard; high-pitched *ee-eet* flight call. **Status:** Resident, breeding. **Abundance:** Uncommon to common. *A. f. meridionalis* is found in the north; *A. f. contigua* occurs in the east and south. **Habitat:** Prefers dry broad-leaved woodlands and savannas. **Habits:** Forages on the ground for seeds; drinks regularly. Uses old weaver nests (Red-headed Weaver, Lesser Masked Weaver) for roosting and breeding. **Conservation:** Least Concern. **General:** Cut-throat and Red-headed Finches crossbreed under natural conditions, and these hybrids may occur in Botswana. They have a heavy bill and white spots on breast and flanks like Red-headed, and a broad red throat (red sometimes extends to forehead) and distinctive chestnut belly like Cut-throat.

ORANGE-WINGED
PYTILIA

female

male

GREEN-WINGED
PYTILIA

female

male

male

female

RED-HEADED
FINCH
A. e. dissita

Red-headed x Cut-throat
hybrid male

male

female

CUT-THROAT
FINCH
A. f. meridionalis

BLUE WAXBILL   *Uraeginthus angolensis*

Setswana: le.biibii

12 cm (4 ¾ in). **Identification:** Powder-blue face, underparts, and rump are diagnostic in both sexes; female is paler than male. Juvenile has powder-blue coloration confined to face and breast. **Call:** Piercing *seeep-seeep-seeep*, clearly audible despite small size of bird. **Status:** Resident, breeding. **Abundance:** Common to abundant. **Habitat:** Favors semiarid and mesic savannas and woodlands, particularly where Umbrella Thorn (*Acacia tortilis*) is prevalent. **Habits:** Pairs and small flocks forage for seeds on the ground among tangled grasses. The species almost invariably builds nest close to active wasp nest, for the protection offered by the wasps. Lays first egg while nest is flimsy grass shell, still under construction. Recorded nesting in abandoned Red-headed Weaver nest. **Conservation:** Least Concern.

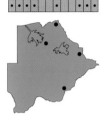

VIOLET-EARED WAXBILL   *Uraeginthus granatinus*

Setswana: raletsôku, le.biibii

14 cm (5 ½ in). **Identification:** Large, colorful waxbill with distinctive violet ear coverts in both sexes. Bright blue rump is a conspicuous field feature, clearly visible as the bird flies. Male has rich chestnut breast; paler female has warm buffy underparts. **Call:** Whistled *tiu-woo-wee*, repeated. **Status:** Resident, breeding. Occasionally lays eggs outside the normal range of months; there is one record from July. **Abundance:** Common to abundant. Botswana is the center of its range in southern Africa. **Habitat:** Prefers arid shrublands (acacias, *Grewia* spp., *Catophractes alexandri*) in open Kalahari tree and bush savanna. **Habits:** Pairs feed on seeds on the ground, often with other small seedeaters. The species builds ball-shaped grass nest with side entrance. It is the sole host of brood parasite Shaft-tailed Whydah. **Conservation:** Least Concern.

COMMON WAXBILL   *Estrilda astrild*

Setswana: ramotsiisanêng

12 cm (4 ¾ in). **Identification:** Predominantly brown waxbill; both sexes have bright red bill and eye stripe. Male has bright red belly patch; female has paler belly patch. Juvenile has black bill and tinge of red on belly. **Call:** Shrill *chewi-chee, chewi-chee*, or *chip, chip* series, repeated. **Status:** Resident, breeding. **Abundance:** Common. **Habitat:** Occurs in moist, rank vegetation near water and on fallow fields. **Habits:** Small flocks feed on seeds on the ground or perch on grass inflorescences and peck seeds off. The species is the primary host of brood parasite Pin-tailed Whydah. Juvenile Pin-tailed Whydahs recorded with Common Waxbills at Phakalane Sewage Lagoons in February 1997 and January 1998. **Conservation:** Least Concern.

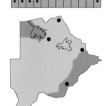

BLACK-FACED WAXBILL   *Estrilda erythronotos*

Setswana: le.biibii, se.ntsipitsipi

12 cm (4 ¾ in). **Identification:** Grayish-red waxbill, female slightly paler than male. The black face and cheek is a key identification feature of both sexes, as is the red rump, which shows clearly in flight. **Call:** Soft *foo-weee* repeated. **Status:** Resident, breeding. **Abundance:** Common. Botswana is a major stronghold for this species in southern Africa. **Habitat:** Found in dry Kalahari tree and bush savanna, particularly where acacias are prevalent and where a source of drinking water is available. **Habits:** Pairs and family parties feed on seeds on the ground, often under thickets, and drink regularly at water holes. The species builds an untidy grass nest with entrance tube and sometimes a "cock's nest" on top, apparently to distract predators away from the real entrance. Roosts in unused weaver nests at night. **Conservation:** Least Concern.

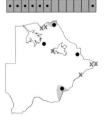

ORANGE-BREASTED WAXBILL   *Amandava subflava*

9 cm (3 ½ in). **Identification:** Distinctive, short-tailed waxbill that has yellow underparts with olive-barred flanks, and orange-red rump and undertail coverts. Both sexes have red bill and black lores; male has red supercilium. **Call:** Soft, slow *tink tink tink* in flight. **Status:** Resident, breeding. **Abundance:** Rare, except in Kasane (Chobe District) and Gaborone (South-East District) areas, where it is uncommon; locally common at Phakalane. Recorded in the Okavango Delta twice before 1990 but not since. **Habitat:** Found in moist grasslands. **Habits:** Occurs in flocks, usually up to 20 birds, occasionally as many as 50 birds. Feeds on seeds on the ground or pecks them from grass seed-heads. It is not easily visible in grass cover. It is a regular brood host of Pin-tailed Whydah. **Conservation:** Least Concern.

male

female

BLUE
WAXBILL

female

VIOLET-EARED
WAXBILL

male

COMMON
WAXBILL

adult

juv.

BLACK-FACED
WAXBILL

male

ORANGE-BREASTED
WAXBILL

female

361

QUAILFINCH *Ortygospiza atricollis*

10 cm (4 in). **Identification:** Short-tailed finch with brown upperparts and barred breast and flanks. The center of the male's belly is rufous, whereas the female's is buffy. Breeding male has red bill; in nonbreeding male and female, the upper mandible is brown. White eye-ring, visible close-up, gives the bird a "spectacled" appearance. **Call:** Metallic *djink-djink* or *klink-klink*, given as it flies off; diagnostic. **Status:** Resident, breeding. **Abundance:** Common. Nomadic; moves widely in search of suitable conditions. **Habitat:** Occurs in short grasslands, damp areas by pans and dams, and in dry floodplains with open ground between tufts. **Habits:** Highly terrestrial; does not even perch on grass stems. Usually in small flocks. The characteristic call the bird gives as it flies off is often the first clue to its presence. Sits tight when approached while feeding in grassland; flushes reluctantly and gains height and flies some distance. Nests on the ground, laying eggs in thin-walled grass ball. **Conservation:** Least Concern.

LOCUST FINCH *Paludipasser locustella*

9 cm (3 ½ in). **Identification:** Male unmistakable; small dark finch with red bill, face, throat, and breast. Female is similar to female Quailfinch but darker below and has a spotted back and orange-red in wings (the latter clearly visible in flight in both sexes). **Call:** Squeaking *chip, chip* in flight. **Status:** Visitor (from elsewhere in southern Africa); no breeding records from Botswana. **Abundance:** Rare. Four specimens were collected in Xugana in December 1975, and one sight record was reported in Shindi in December 1991, both in the Okavango Delta. **Habitat:** Occurs in wet, poorly vegetated patches among long grasses. **Habits:** Terrestrial, easily overlooked; feeds on bare ground in damp grasslands. Flushes reluctantly, and calls softly on take-off. **Conservation:** Least Concern.

MAGPIE MANNIKIN *Lonchura fringilloides*

11 cm (4 ¼ in). **Identification:** Large mannikin with black head (black covers the nape), gray-brown wings, black patches on flanks, and black rump. Easily distinguished from Bronze Mannikin by these features and its larger size. **Call:** Piping *pee-oo, pee-oo.* **Status:** Visitor; no breeding records from Botswana. **Abundance:** Rare. Only one accepted record, from Kabulabula in Chobe National Park (March 1994). The bulk of the species's population occurs beyond the borders of the country, and its range extends only marginally into Botswana. **Habitat:** Found in riparian woodlands and on floodplains. **Habits:** Usually seen in flocks; feeds on seeds. **Conservation:** Least Concern.

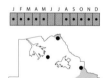

BRONZE MANNIKIN *Lonchura cucullata*

9 cm (3 ½ in). **Identification:** Small seedeater with black face and throat, dark brown crown and nape, and white underparts. Upperparts are grayish brown, flanks and rump finely barred. Key field features are black head extending to dark brown breast; contrasting white underparts; and bronzy-green shoulder patches. Adult has black upper mandible and white lower. Immature has uniformly brown plumage and all-dark bill, lacking white on lower mandible. This species differs from Magpie Mannikin in its smaller size, two-tone bill, brown nape, and barred rump. **Call:** Soft, ringing, repeated *tjie, tjie, tjie*, given by flock members. **Status:** Resident, breeding. **Abundance:** Locally common in northern Chobe District around Kasane, and in and around Gaborone in the southeast; rare elsewhere. Its range just extends into northern, eastern, and southern Botswana. **Habitat:** Found in moist, wooded habitat with access to drinking water. **Habits:** Flocks feed on grass seeds on inflorescences and on the ground, and fly to cover when disturbed. Members construct a nest-like structure, termed a dormitory, for group roosting at night. Pair builds a grass nest in interior of tree canopy for breeding; they often nest close to wasp nests. The species is occasionally a host for brood parasite Pin-tailed Whydah. **Conservation:** Least Concern.

QUAILFINCH

male

female

LOCUST
FINCH

male

female

adult

juv.

MAGPIE
MANNIKIN

BRONZE
MANNIKIN

adult

juv.

INDIGOBIRDS, WHYDAHS Viduidae

An African endemic family of small, obligate brood parasites that target estrildids or, in the case of the Cuckoo-finch, cisticolas and prinias. Viduines (genus *Vidua*) are sexually dimorphic; males assume breeding plumage during summer and display and/or call from song posts (often mimicking their brood host's song) to attract females. Indigobird males become glossy black, and whydah males acquire long tail feathers. They are all polygynous and promiscuous. Viduines lay white eggs similar to those of their hosts, and when the chicks hatch in the host's nest, they imitate the begging calls of their foster-siblings. The viduine chicks have a pattern of spots in the mouth that match those of their host's chicks, so the host is unable to discern any difference between its own and the parasite chicks. The Cuckoo-finch has a similar breeding strategy, differing only in detail. Botswana has six viduines and one *Anomalospiza*, which means "unusual finch." The whydahs are known by the generic Setswana name *mo.lope*, which also applies to the long-tailed widowbirds (p. 352).

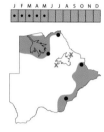

J F M A M J J A S O N D

VILLAGE INDIGOBIRD *Vidua chalybeata*

11 cm (4 ¼ in). **Identification:** Bill and leg color are key to identifying indigobirds. In this species, birds of subspecies *V. c. amauropteryx* have red legs and red bill, while those of *V. c. okavangoensis* have red legs and a pale white bill. Breeding males are black (with a steel-blue sheen) and have a dusky wing panel and tail. Nonbreeding males and females are pale below and have brown wing feathers edged in white, brown-streaked upperparts with white-edged feathers, and a bold, off-white supercilium. The short, squat bill is particularly noticeable in the female. Males are in transitional plumage in December and May, either acquiring black feathers at the start of breeding, or having the black plumage mottled with brown at the end. **Call:** Male calls from fixed song post, a soft song mimicking brood hosts. **Status:** Resident, breeding. For the breeding bar data, the few Botswana egg-laying records from March and April have been supplemented by observations of displaying males between January and May. **Abundance:** Common. *V. c. amauropteryx* occurs mainly in eastern and southern Botswana. *V. c. okavangoensis* (its type specimen collected in Maun, in Ngamiland) is found around the Okavango wetland system, Linyanti Swamps, and the Chobe River. The precise ranges of these subspecies are yet to be elucidated, since individuals with red bills and red legs have been recorded in Maun, and males with red legs and white bills have been netted in Francistown (North-East District). **Habitat:** Occurs in a variety of open woodlands with permanent water. **Habits:** Males in breeding plumage perch conspicuously (and sing) for long periods on their favored song posts (dead twigs on tops of shrubs and low trees) and are easily observed between December and May. Indigobirds mimic the songs of their hosts and of neighboring indigobirds, creating distinct "song neighborhoods." During breeding, the male, with his feathers puffed out, performs short bouncy, dipping display flight over female. The species parasitizes Red-billed Firefinch, with which it is sympatric. Apparently, *V. c. okavangoensis* also parasitizes Brown Firefinch. Both sexes have shuffling gait (neither walking nor hopping) when foraging for seeds on bare ground or short-grass areas. **Conservation:** Least Concern.

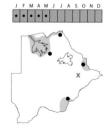

J F M A M J J A S O N D

PURPLE INDIGOBIRD *Vidua purpurascens*

11 cm (4 ¼ in). **Identification:** This indigobird has a white bill and whitish legs (compare Village Indigobird). Breeding male is black, with purple sheen, and has a dusky wing panel and tail; some breeding males have a pinkish tinge to their legs and could be mistaken for Dusky Indigobird in southern Botswana where there is potential for overlap (Dusky occurs on the South African side of the Limpopo River). Nonbreeding male and female are pale below, with variable brown wash on breast, and have brown-streaked upperparts with white-edged feathers and a bold off-white supercilium. Males are in transitional plumage in December and May. **Call:** Male calls from fixed song post, a soft song mimicking that of brood host, Jameson's Firefinch. **Status:** Resident, breeding. There are few records of egg-laying in Botswana; it probably takes place between January and May, as in other parts of southern Africa. **Abundance:** Uncommon. **Habitat:** Occurs in broad-leaved and acacia woodlands with tall grass. **Habits:** Males are conspicuous on their prominent song posts from January to May; during the remainder of the year they form part of small flocks, which may be seen foraging for seeds on the ground. The species parasitizes Jameson's Firefinch in Botswana. **Conservation:** Least Concern.

breeding
male
V. c. okavangoensis

VILLAGE
INDIGOBIRD

male
transitional

breeding
male
V. c. amauropteryx

female/
nonbreeding male

breeding
male

PURPLE
INDIGOBIRD

female/
nonbreeding male

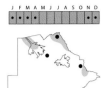

CUCKOO-FINCH *Anomalospiza imberbis*

13 cm (5 in). **Identification:** Weaver-like brood parasite ("cuckoo" in name refers to this behavior) related more to indigobirds than finches. Adult male has mustard-yellow plumage and a stout, conical black bill. Female is similar to Southern Red Bishop (p. 352): off-white below with variable streaking on flanks, streaked tawny above, legs and bill soft pink. Juvenile has variable pale yellowish plumage, streaked tawny on upperparts, and black upper mandible and yellowish lower mandible. **Call:** Canary-like twittering; no mimicry of brood hosts. **Status:** Resident, breeding. The few Botswana egg-laying records are from February to April, which is the latter half of the egg-laying period for southern Africa. **Abundance:** Scarce **Habitat:** Occurs in open grasslands and/or floodplains and heavily vegetated marshes. **Habits:** Pairs and flocks of up to 16 may be observed in reeds, sometimes in association with Fan-tailed Widowbirds. In Botswana the species parasitizes Tawny-flanked Prinia and Desert Cisticola. **Conservation:** Least Concern.

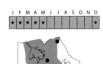

PIN-TAILED WHYDAH *Vidua macroura*

Setswana: mo.lope

M: 30 cm (11 ¾ in), incl. long tail; F: 11 cm (4 ¼ in). **Identification:** Breeding male is black and white, with red bill and long tail feathers. In nonbreeding plumage, both male and female are buffy overall, with bold streaking on mantle; flight feathers are buffy white and black-edged; and bill is red. Black stripes on crown and through eye aid identification. Female bill changes to black in breeding plumage. Both sexes have gray legs. **Call:** Displaying male has lively *peetsy peetsy eet eet eet* call. Does not mimic calls of brood hosts. **Status:** Resident; breeding. Parasitizes the Common Waxbill. Juveniles recorded with Common Waxbills at Phakalane Sewage Lagoons in February 1997 and January 1998. Egg-laying data are based on records from the region and behavioral observations. **Abundance:** Common, especially in Ngamiland, Chobe, and part of Central District. **Habitat:** Prefers open, mesic habitats. **Habits:** Males are seen with small harems of females feeding on seeds on the ground. Breeding male has spectacular display flight, hovering over females with tail flapping up and down, and aggressively chases other birds away from its display arena. (Male is in breeding plumage between January and May.) The species primarily parasitizes Common Waxbill, but this pairing differs from other viduid-estrildid relationships in that Pin-tailed Whydah does not mimic the waxbill's call or the palate markings of the chick. **Conservation:** Least Concern.

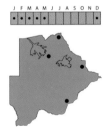

SHAFT-TAILED WHYDAH *Vidua regia*

Setswana: mo.lope

M: 28 cm (11 in), incl. long tail; F: 11 cm (4 ¼ in). **Identification:** Breeding male is distinctive; it has buff and black plumage, red bill and legs, and long tail feathers with broad distal ends. Female and nonbreeding male have buffy underparts, black and brown wings, and red bills and legs. **Call:** Male mimics call of its brood host, Violet-eared Waxbill. **Status:** Resident, breeding. Parasitizes the Violet-eared Waxbill. Egg-laying is known to take place from December to May, but possibly continues into winter, as males are seen in breeding plumage through August in some years (see egg-laying period for its host, p. 360). **Abundance:** Common to abundant. Botswana is a stronghold for this species in southern Africa. Its range and abundance closely match those of its breeding host, Violet-eared Waxbill. **Habitat:** Occurs in dry grassy acacia and broad-leaved woodlands, especially where Umbrella Thorn (*Acacia tortilis*) and Camel Thorn (*Acacia erioloba*) are prevalent. Also favors pan margins with Trumpet-thorn (*Catophractes alexandri*) shrubs. **Habits:** During breeding season, single male in breeding plumage is seen with harem of nondescript brown females. Male flies over female, intermittently flapping wings in hovering display and waving long tail. The species congregates in flocks at water in arid areas of Botswana. It forages on the ground, using shuffling motion of the feet to uncover seeds. **Conservation:** Least Concern.

breeding
adult male

breeding
adult female

juv.

CUCKOO-FINCH

breeding
adult female

breeding
adult male

male
display

PIN-TAILED
WHYDAH

female/
nonbreeding
adult male

imm.

juv.

breeding
adult male

male
transitional

SHAFT-TAILED
WHYDAH

female/
nonbreeding
male

367

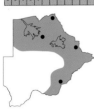

LONG-TAILED PARADISE WHYDAH *Vidua paradisaea*

Setswana: mo.lope, mo.lopê

M: 36 cm (14 ¼ in), incl. long tail; F: 15 cm (6 in). **Identification:** Breeding male is easily recognizable; it has a golden-yellow nape patch and tapering long tail, both of which distinguish it from Broad-tailed Paradise Whydah. In Botswana, male comes into breeding plumage in January (later than elsewhere in southern Africa) and birds in transitional plumage can be seen at this time. By April, males are usually changing back to nonbreeding plumage, although if rains have been substantial, some males retain full nuptial dress until August. Female and nonbreeding male are streaked gray-brown above and have black-and-white-striped heads; the dark eye stripe extends back around the ear coverts, making a dark C shape on the cheek. Head markings along with blackish bill separate it from nonbreeding indigobirds (p. 364). **Call:** Male mimics song of its brood parasite, Green-winged Pytilia (p. 358). **Status:** Resident, breeding. **Abundance:** Common. **Habitat:** Prefers open acacia woodlands. **Habits:** Small flocks feed on seeds on ground. During its conspicuous aerial display, breeding male flies with the two shorter, broad tail feathers flared, which gives the bird a conspicuous humpbacked appearance, before it dives back down. Male also hovers, with slow wingbeats, over female. The species parasitizes Green-winged Pytilia, with which it is sympatric, and its egg-laying period coincides with the main breeding period of its host. **Conservation:** Least Concern.

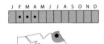

BROAD-TAILED PARADISE WHYDAH *Vidua obtusa*

Setswana: mo.lope, mo.lopê

M: 27 cm (10 ¾ in), incl. long tail; F: 15 cm (6 in). **Identification:** Breeding male is unmistakable; it has broad, rounded tail feathers (its tail is distinctly shorter than that of Long-tailed Paradise Whydah) and a chestnut-orange nape patch (compare Long-tailed's corn-colored nape). Female and nonbreeding male are similar; they have buffy underparts, streaked gray-brown upperparts, and black-and-white-striped heads. **Call:** Male mimics call of its brood host, Orange-winged Pytilia (p. 358). **Status:** Resident; no breeding records from Botswana. It most likely bred in Kasane (Chobe District) in 1994 following local irruption. **Abundance:** Scarce, but highly irruptive and sometimes locally abundant. There was an invasion, reportedly of thousands, of Broad-tailed Paradise Whydahs in Kasane in 1994. It is a Zambezian species that occurs in Botswana at the extreme southwestern limit of its range. **Habitat:** Occurs in Zambezi Teak (*Baikiaea plurijuga*) woodlands. **Habits:** Polygynous; males are seen with small flocks of females foraging for seeds on the ground or stripping seeds from grass inflorescences. Occasionally flocks of more than 50 may be seen. Egg-laying coincides with that for Orange-winged Pytilia, which it parasitizes. **Conservation:** Least Concern.

LONG-TAILED PARADISE
WHYDAH

adult male
transitional

breeding
adult male

nonbreeding
adult male

adult
female

juv.

BROAD-TAILED
PARADISE WHYDAH

breeding
adult male

juv.

adult female/
nonbreeding male

369

WAGTAILS, LONGCLAWS, PIPITS Motacillidae

Members of this family are slender, elongate terrestrial insectivores with relatively long legs and tails. Some have white (or buffy) outer tail feathers; wagtails and pipits frequently wag their tails. Sixteen motacillids in three genera occur in Botswana. All are monogamous, and most are breeding residents. The wagtails nest near water, usually above ground level; the longclaws and pipits nest at ground level.

Pipits: *Anthus*, nine species. Predominantly brown birds with plain or streaked backs and plain or streaked underparts. Genetic analysis shows that they fall into three groups of the following size classes: large, small, and diminutive. In addition to size, habitat and behavior are important keys to identification. Seven are resident, one is an intra-African migrant, and one is a Palearctic migrant.

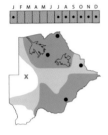

BUFFY PIPIT *Anthus vaalensis*

18 cm (7 in). **Identification:** Large pipit with plain back, which differentiates it from most congeners except Plain-backed Pipit. Buffy Pipit has paler, buffier upperparts than that species, an indistinct, pale supercilium, little streaking below, and a pinkish base to lower mandible (Plain-backed has yellow lower mandible). Two subspecies occur in Botswana: A. v. chobiensis is very pale and has faint streaking on breast; A. v. exasperatus is slightly darker above. **Call:** Sparrow-like chirping. **Status:** Resident, breeding. **Abundance:** Uncommon; more widespread, but less common, than Plain-backed Pipit. A. v. chobiensis occurs in the northern half of the country, A. v. exasperatus in the south. **Habitat:** Occurs in semiarid savannas with open grassy plains and bare ground. **Habits:** Performs frequent, exaggerated tail wagging, making its hindquarters bob up and down, more than other pipits. Builds open cup nest on ground next to grass tuft. **Conservation:** Least Concern.

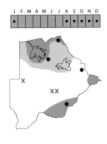

PLAIN-BACKED PIPIT *Anthus leucophrys*

17 cm (6 ¾ in). **Identification:** Large pipit with brownish-gray unmarked back and plain, unmarked mantle, which differentiate it from other congeners, except Buffy Pipit (compare that species's description and habitat preferences). Lower mandible is yellowish (Buffy Pipit has pinkish base to lower mandible). Two subspecies are found in Botswana: A. l. leucophrys is warm brown above and has buffy underparts; A. l. tephridorsus has ash-gray upperparts and pale brown underparts. **Call:** Monotonous, repeated *cheert-cheroo*. **Status:** Resident, breeding. The few egg-laying records for Botswana fall between August and January, as recorded in the rest of southern Africa. **Abundance:** Common (both subspecies). In the Okavango, Plain-backed Pipit is more common than Buffy Pipit. The subspecies are allopatric: A. l. leucophrys is found in southeastern Botswana; A. l. tephridorsus occurs in Ngamiland and Chobe Districts. **Habitat:** Occurs in mesic grasslands with bare ground; the northern subspecies is found on such habitat in Okavango Delta floodplains. **Habits:** Forages and nests on the ground. Occurs solitarily or in small flocks. Male calls in aerial display or from low bush. Builds cup-shaped nest on the ground. **Conservation:** Least Concern.

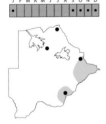

STRIPED PIPIT *Anthus lineiventris*

18 cm (7 in). **Identification:** Large pipit, easily identified by the clear yellow edges to the wing feathers. Underparts are extensively streaked. It has specific habitat requirements (rocky slopes, see below). **Call:** Loud song, comprising a series of musical whistled notes, unlike songs of all other pipits. **Status:** Resident; no breeding records from Botswana. **Abundance:** Scarce. **Habitat:** Found in eastern hardveld, on wooded, rocky slopes or on or near rocky outcrops. **Habits:** Solitary birds are usually seen on rocky ground. Male calls from prominent rock. This species has a more musical song than other pipits. **Conservation:** Least Concern.

BUFFY
PIPIT

PLAIN-BACKED
PIPIT
A. l. tephridorsus

STRIPED
PIPIT

371

AFRICAN PIPIT *Anthus cinnamomeus*

Setswana: kelema-kele-nôsi

17 cm (6 ¾ in). **Identification:** Large pipit with white (not buffy) outer tail feathers and a mottled back. Adult has yellowish base to lower mandible (can be pinkish in juvenile), well-streaked breast, face, and throat, and broad buff supercilium. Four species occur in Botswana: *A. c. grotei* is the palest, followed by the slightly less pale *A. c. bocagii*; *A. c. spurius* is the darkest and most richly marked; *A. c. rufuloides* has buffy underparts and gray-brown upperparts. This geographic variation in plumage makes identification of the species challenging. **Call:** Male calls *chree-chree-chree-chree-chree, chree-chree-chree-chree-chree* during display flight. **Status:** Resident, breeding. The population is supplemented by migrants from South Africa during winter (nonbreeding season). **Abundance:** Common. By far the most numerous and widespread pipit in Botswana. *A. c. bocagii* occurs in most of the southern half of the country; *A. c. spurius* extends from the north into Ngamiland and Chobe Districts; *A. c. grotei* is found around the Makgadikgadi Pans. Apparently *A. c. rufuloides*, which occurs over much of South Africa, is partially migratory and moves into large parts of Botswana during winter. **Habitat:** Occurs in moist grasslands, open areas adjacent to pans and lakes, and dry floodplains. *A. c. grotei* favors margins of salt pans. **Habits:** Solitary or in pairs. Ground dweller with erect "leggy" stance, it runs a short distance and then stops and dips its tail two or three times. Male sings during aerial display, rising in stepped flight between each song and the next, and then sings while circling, and finally dives earthward. The species places its cup-shaped nest on the ground in a grass tuft. **Conservation:** Least Concern.

MOUNTAIN PIPIT *Anthus hoeschi*

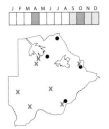

19 cm (7 ½ in). **Identification:** Large pipit with heavily streaked breast, dark mottled back, no white in tail (outer tail feathers buffy), and base of lower mandible pinkish. These features separate it from the similar African Pipit. (Note, however, that juvenile African Pipit can have pinkish on lower mandible.) Like African Pipit, it has broad buff supercilium. **Call:** Not vocal when in Botswana. **Status:** Intra-African migrant, nonbreeding. **Abundance:** Rare. Passage migrant from wintering grounds in Central Africa; regularly seen at Lake Ngami in Botswana during early and late summer as birds transit to and from their only breeding grounds, the Drakensberg Mountains in Lesotho and South Africa. **Habitat:** Found in areas along pan margins with shrubs and low bushes. **Habits:** Occurs in small flocks of up to 16 birds. **Conservation:** Least Concern.

LONG-BILLED PIPIT *Anthus similis*

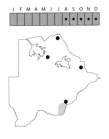

19 cm (7 ½ in). **Identification:** Large pipit with faintly marked mantle (can appear plain from a distance) and lightly streaked breast. Buffy outer tail feathers. Length of bill is not a good identification feature, despite species's name; base of lower mandible is yellow or pinkish. The subspecies found in Botswana is *A. s. nicholsoni*. **Call:** Slow, repetitive *chreep, chreep, chroop.* **Status:** Resident; no breeding records from Botswana. **Abundance:** Scarce to uncommon. The bulk of the population of this species occurs beyond the borders of the country, and it extends only marginally into southeastern Botswana where it is regularly seen in rocky wooded hills near Lobatse. **Habitat:** Found in rocky grasslands and slopes. **Habits:** Occurs in pairs, or in small nonbreeding groups during winter. Forages by walking on the ground to find invertebrate prey; when disturbed, flies off with dipping flight. **Conservation:** Least Concern.

WOOD PIPIT *Anthus nyassae*

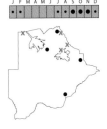

18 cm (7 in). **Identification:** Large pipit found only in woodlands; it is one of the few pipits that will fly up into trees. Similar in appearance to related Long-billed Pipit, which occurs in grasslands rather than woodlands. It has a boldly marked head pattern, including a whitish supercilium, and buffy outer tail feathers. Wood Pipits found in Botswana, which are of subspecies *A. n. chersophilus*, are generally paler than those found in Zimbabwe. **Call:** Slow, high-pitched *tseep, tsip, treep,* and variations thereof. **Status:** Resident; no breeding records from Botswana. **Abundance:** Rare. **Habitat:** Prefers broad-leaved woodlands, especially Zambezi Teak (*Baikiaea plurijuga*), with short grass beneath the trees. **Habits:** Forages among leaf litter on woodland floor but readily flies up into trees if disturbed. **Conservation:** Least Concern.

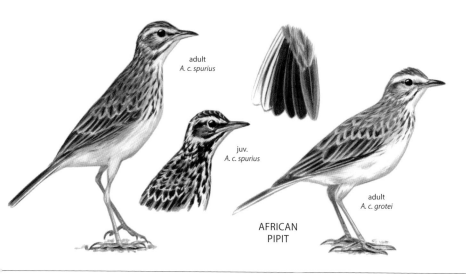

adult
A. c. spurius

juv.
A. c. spurius

adult
A. c. grotei

AFRICAN
PIPIT

MOUNTAIN
PIPIT

LONG-BILLED
PIPIT
A. s. nicholsoni

WOOD
PIPIT
A. n. chersophilus

373

TREE PIPIT   *Anthus trivialis*

14 cm (5 ½ in). **Identification:** Small pipit that is markedly streaked on breast (almost blotched). It is one of the few pipits that will fly up into and perch in a tree. Buffy background color to breast contrasts with plain white belly; flanks are finely streaked. Wing coverts are edged in white (compare Striped Pipit, p. 370), forming two short, white wing bars. Similar Bushveld Pipit is smaller, has a shorter tail, and is less boldly streaked on breast. **Call:** Not vocal when in Botswana. **Status:** Palearctic migrant; nonbreeding. **Abundance:** Rare. **Habitat:** Occurs in broad-leaved woodlands, including hillside slopes with scattered trees. **Habits:** Feeds on the ground solitarily or in loose parties, but will readily perch in trees when flushed, or even walk along branches. Regularly wags tail. **Conservation:** Least Concern.

BUSHVELD PIPIT   *Anthus caffer*

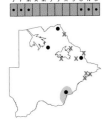

13 cm (5 in). **Identification:** Diminutive pipit with short tail. It has heavily streaked, tawny upperparts, warm rufous wash on lower flanks, and a conspicuous white eye-ring. Underparts are less streaky than those of the larger Tree Pipit, which may share its woodland habitat. However, Bushveld Pipit mainly occurs in southeastern Botswana, while the Tree Pipit is found mainly in the north, so they rarely overlap. Bushveld is one of the few pipits that will fly up into trees. **Call:** Repeated *skee-trup*, given in display flight by male. **Status:** Resident; no breeding records from Botswana. **Abundance:** Scarce. **Habitat:** Occurs in broad-leaved woodlands with open, bare ground. **Habits:** Semiarboreal; feeds on the ground but flies into trees when flushed. Male calls from dead branch or while in display flight. This pipit seldom wags its tail. **Conservation:** Least Concern.

Longclaws: *Macronyx*, two species. These birds are cryptically colored above, but have bright throats and bold black breast bands. They take off in jerky, flapping flight with stiff wings when flushed. Both species are resident, although Cape Longclaw, a southern African endemic, just enters southeastern Botswana.

CAPE LONGCLAW   *Macronyx capensis*

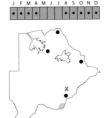

20 cm (7 ¾ in). **Identification:** Pipit-like bird with cryptically colored upperparts and orange underparts. Its orange throat fringed with a black necklace is diagnostic. Juvenile has buffy throat with indistinct black necklace. *M. c. colletti*, the subspecies found in Botswana, has a clean orange breast without any gray streaking, and lacks gray wash to flanks. White-tipped tail feathers are visible during stiff-winged, flap-and-glide flight. **Call:** Plaintive *meeew*. **Status:** Resident; no breeding records from Botswana. In southern Africa, egg-laying takes place between August and April in areas with summer rainfall, and this is probably the pattern in Botswana too. **Abundance:** Uncommon. A southern African endemic, its range just extends into southeastern Botswana; probably more common in years of high rainfall. **Habitat:** Occurs in moist grasslands. **Habits:** Forages solitarily or in pairs on the ground; occasionally sings from termite mound or low bush. **Conservation:** Least Concern.

ROSY-THROATED LONGCLAW   *Macronyx ameliae*

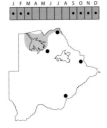

19 cm (7 ½ in). **Identification:** Pipit-like bird with cryptically colored upperparts and underparts suffused with rosy wash, which is paler in female. The rosy throat is diagnostic. Nonbreeding male has narrower or broken breast band (sometimes absent). In both sexes, white outer tail feathers and dark back are visible during stiff-winged, flap-and-glide flight. Botswana birds belong to subspecies *M. a. altanus*, distinguished by boldly streaked upperparts. **Call:** Repetitive *pee-chu, pee-chu, pee-chu*. **Status:** Resident, breeding. The few Botswana egg-laying records fall between September and March, the egg-laying period for southern Africa. **Abundance:** Uncommon, even though the Okavango wetland system, Linyanti Swamps, and Chobe River are a stronghold in southern Africa. **Habitat:** Found in moist grasslands and seasonally inundated floodplains. **Habits:** Forages on the ground in short or medium-length grass, eating mainly invertebrates. **Conservation:** Least Concern.

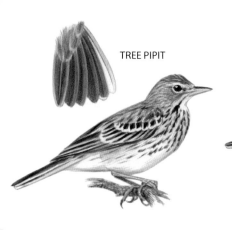

TREE PIPIT

BUSHVELD
PIPIT

breeding
adult

juv.

CAPE
LONGCLAW
M. c. colletti

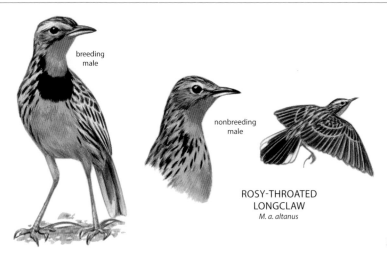

breeding
male

nonbreeding
male

ROSY-THROATED
LONGCLAW
M. a. altanus

Wagtails: *Motacilla*, five species. Long-tailed, boldly marked birds that nod the head back and forth and wag the tail while they walk. They also have a characteristic undulating flight. Two species are resident, one is a Palearctic migrant, and two are vagrants.

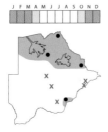

WESTERN YELLOW WAGTAIL *Motacilla flava*

17 cm (6 ¾ in). **Identification:** This migrant wagtail is highly variable in plumage. Adult has a greenish back, unpatterned mantle, and yellow underparts, although the shade of yellow can vary from pale to rich and bright. It differs from the Grey Wagtail by its much shorter tail and its olive-green upperparts. Juvenile shows very little yellow (restricted to vent) and is overall pale olive brown. Birds seen in Botswana, during summer, are nonbreeding and are difficult to separate to subspecies level. Those occurring in Botswana are *M. f. flava*, *M. f. lutea*, *M. f. thunbergi*, *M. f. feldegg*, and *M. f. beema* (the last two are rare visitors). At the end of summer, some individuals attain partial breeding plumage before departing, and it is at this time that it is possible to identify the subspecies. **Call:** Mostly silent in Botswana. **Status:** Palearctic migrant; nonbreeding. **Abundance:** Uncommon, but may be locally common. Most numerous in February and March, when flocks of up to 100 birds may be seen prior to their northward passage. **Habitat:** Found in dry floodplains and short grasslands along edge of water. **Habits:** Frequently bobs hindquarters and nods head back and forth while walking, in typical wagtail fashion. **Conservation:** Least Concern.

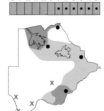

CAPE WAGTAIL *Motacilla capensis*

Setswana: mo.salakatane, mo.selekatane, mo.kgôrônyane, mo.kgwêrênyane

20 cm (7 ¾ in). **Identification:** Dull-plumaged wagtail. It is gray-brown above and has a dark breast band separating white throat from off-white underparts. Two subspecies occur in Botswana: *M. c. capensis* has a prominent breast band, while in *M. c. simplissima* this feature is reduced to a single breast spot. The white outer tail feathers are a feature of all our wagtails. Note that juvenile African Pied Wagtail (p. 378), although also grayish, can be distinguished by extensive areas of white on its wings. **Call:** Plaintive *tsee-eep*. **Status:** Resident, breeding. **Abundance:** Common; more widespread than African Pied Wagtail. *M. c. simplissima* occurs in the Okavango Delta (including Lake Ngami) and along the edge of the Linyanti Swamps and Chobe River. *M. c. capensis* occurs in southern and eastern Botswana, including Makgadikgadi Pans. **Habitat:** Found along edges of bodies of water; suburban gardens. Subspecies *M. c. simplissima* is a swamp dweller, specializing in aquatic environments. **Habits:** Solitary or in pairs; runs along the ground or at water's edge catching insects. Builds an open cup nest near the ground or on ledges of buildings. **Conservation:** Least Concern.

GREY WAGTAIL *Motacilla cinerea*

19 cm (7 ½ in). **Identification:** Wagtail with blue-gray head, cheeks, mantle, and shoulders. It has a distinct white supercilium and a dark wing patch with a narrow white bar; bright yellow rump, uppertail coverts, and lower flanks. Nonbreeding bird is whitish to pale yellowish below (whitest on throat), but by March or April, shows bright canary yellow underparts, and the throat becomes black in breeding male. It has relatively short legs and a very long, white-edged tail, pumped up and down constantly. **Call:** Alarm call a thin metallic *tsit*. **Status:** Vagrant (from the Palearctic); nonbreeding. **Abundance:** Rare. **Habitat:** Found along waterways, notably fast-flowing rocky streams and rivers, but vagrants can occupy a variety of habitats. **Habits:** Displays exaggerated tail wagging. Walks rapidly, chasing insects on the ground, but will fly into a tree if disturbed; also catches insects in flight. **Conservation:** Least Concern.

MOUNTAIN WAGTAIL *Motacilla clara*

19 cm (7 ½ in). **Identification:** Predominantly gray and white wagtail with a long tail and distinctive dark breast band on otherwise clean white underparts. Upperparts blue-gray, rather than gray-brown as in Cape Wagtail; it also has longer tail than Cape. **Call:** *Chissik* call, almost invariably given when bird takes flight. **Status:** Visitor or resident; no breeding records from Botswana. It is not clear whether the few birds recorded in Botswana are visitors from the South African population or a small resident population. **Abundance:** Rare. **Habitat:** Found along streams in hilly, wooded country, as in the Moremi Gorge in the Tswapong Hills in eastern Botswana. **Habits:** Solitary birds or pairs forage along stream edges for insects. Birds perch on favored rocks in river. **Conservation:** Least Concern.

WESTERN YELLOW WAGTAIL

breeding
M. f. feldegg

nonbreeding
M. f. flava

breeding
M. f. thunbergi

breeding
M. f. lutea

CAPE WAGTAIL

adult
M. c. simplissima

adult
M. c. capensis

juv.

nonbreeding

breeding
male

GREY WAGTAIL

MOUNTAIN WAGTAIL

377

AFRICAN PIED WAGTAIL   *Motacilla aguimp*

Setswana: mo.salakatane, mo.kôtatsiê

20 cm (7 ¾ in). **Identification:** Pied coloration distinguishes this wagtail from all others in Botswana. The nominate subspecies, which has black on the flanks and a broad black breast band, occurs in Botswana. **Call:** Plaintive *too-weee*. **Status:** Resident, breeding. **Abundance:** Locally common, but generally uncommon in the Okavango Delta, where it is replaced by Cape Wagtail (p. 376). Engages in local movements during nonbreeding season (winter). **Habitat:** Found on sandbanks and margins of large rivers, including the Limpopo, Okavango, and Chobe. Also occurs at edges of large dams, notably Shashe Dam, and at sewage ponds in the southeast. **Habits:** Feeds solitarily or in pairs along edge of river. Builds an open cup nest, usually above water, in flood debris, clump of reeds, or tree stump. **Conservation:** Least Concern.

FINCHES, CANARIES, SEEDEATERS   Fringillidae

Small, granivorous passerines with conical bills. Females have duller plumage than males. Monogamous; both sexes care for chicks. Botswana has six species in two genera, *Crithagra* (five species) and *Serinus* (one species). The single *Serinus* differs from the others in its black, chestnut, and white color pattern. All are sedentary but may undertake irregular local movements in response to rain. Yellow canaries are called *mo.ragane* in Setswana.

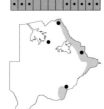

STREAKY-HEADED SEEDEATER   *Crithagra gularis*

15 cm (6 in). **Identification:** The streaked crown, in combination with pale brown ear coverts, is diagnostic. It has prominent long, white eyebrow. Superficially resembles Yellow-throated Petronia (p. 342), which has plain breast, buffy-white supercilium, and stout seedeater bill; however, Streaky-headed Seedeater has streaked crown and lacks white wing bars. Two subspecies occur in Botswana: the nominate has pale brown plumage; *C. g. mendosa* has darker upperparts and flanks. **Call:** Series of high-pitched trills and whistles. **Status:** Resident; no breeding records from Botswana. **Abundance:** Scarce. Occurs in Botswana at the western edge of its range in southern Africa. *C. g. gularis* occurs in the eastern and southeastern part of the country; *C. g. mendosa* is found from North-East District northward along the Botswana-Zimbabwe border. **Habitat:** Found in wide range of woodland habitats. **Habits:** Occurs solitarily or in pairs, or in small flocks of up to a dozen birds during nonbreeding season. Unobtrusive. **Conservation:** Least Concern.

BLACK-EARED SEEDEATER   *Crithagra mennelli*

13 cm (5 in). **Identification:** Small canary identified by streaked crown, black facial mask extending to ear coverts, and streaked underparts. Female paler than male. Can be mistaken for Streaky-headed Seedeater, which, however, has plain grayish-brown underparts. **Call:** Fast, jumbled whistle, including some trills. **Status:** Visitor or resident; no breeding records from Botswana. **Abundance:** Rare, though more common in some years. A Zambezian species, it occurs in Botswana at the western limit of its southern African range. **Habitat:** Occurs in Zambezi Teak (*Baikiaea plurijuga*) woodlands of the Chobe District. **Habits:** Usually solitary or in pairs, it often joins mixed-species groups. **Conservation:** Least Concern.

BLACK-HEADED CANARY   *Serinus alario*

Setswana: tsilwane

13 cm (5 in). **Identification:** Small, slender seedeater. Male has variable amount of black on head and breast, and white belly. Female has gray on head, which extends down onto breast. Both sexes have rufous-chestnut wings. Superficially resembles Cape Sparrow (p. 340). Both subspecies, *S. a. alario* and *S. a. leucolaemus*, could potentially occur in Botswana. Male of the nominate has plain black head and breast, while *leucolaemus* male has a variable amount of white on face, throat, and breast. **Call:** Sustained, jumbled song with trills and whistles. **Status:** Visitor; no breeding records from Botswana. **Abundance:** Rare. A southern African endemic, its range just extends into southwestern Botswana. First and only accepted record, from Kweyane in Kgalagadi District (1982–83), was of a flock of birds of subspecies *S. a. alario*. **Habitat:** Occurs in arid scrub savanna. **Habits:** Small flocks forage on the ground and in low bushes. The species is nomadic in response to rain. **Conservation:** Least Concern.

AFRICAN PIED WAGTAIL
M. a. aguimp

adult

juv.

imm.

STREAKY-HEADED SEEDEATER
C. g. mendosa

adult

juv.

BLACK-EARED SEEDEATER

BLACK-HEADED CANARY
S. a. alario

male

male
S. a. leucolaemus

female

379

BLACK-THROATED CANARY *Crithagra atrogularis*

Setswana: mo.ragane

11 cm (4 ¼ in). **Identification:** The most noticeable feature of this small canary is its yellow rump; the black throat for which it is named is variable and is absent in juvenile. Both sexes are predominantly gray and white, streaked with dark brown above, and have white tips to tail feathers. The pale subspecies, *C. a. semideserti*, is widespread in Botswana; the nominate is darker. **Call:** Rich jumble of whistled notes, including trills. **Status:** Resident, breeding. **Abundance:** Common. *C. a. semideserti* (type specimen from Mochumi Pan, south of Lake Ngami) occurs across most of Botswana; *C. a. atrogularis* is confined to the southern part of the country. **Habitat:** Favors semiarid woodlands where drinking water is available. **Habits:** Found in small parties foraging on the ground; seen at water holes. It makes an open, cup-shaped nest. **Conservation:** Least Concern.

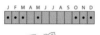

YELLOW-FRONTED CANARY *Crithagra mozambica*

Setswana: mo.ragane

12 cm (4 ¾ in). **Identification:** Small canary with gray crown, yellow supercilium, and black malar stripe; the facial pattern is diagnostic. Bright yellow rump and white-tipped tail feathers are conspicuous in flight. Female is paler than male. This species and similar Yellow Canary have allopatric ranges in Botswana, with little overlap. Two subspecies occur: *C. m. mozambica* is paler than *C. m. vansoni*, which has darker, greener upperparts and rich yellow underparts. **Call:** Series of high-pitched trills and whistles (including mimicry). **Status:** Resident, breeding. **Abundance:** Common, but restricted to moist, well-wooded parts of Botswana. *C. m. mozambica* occurs in the eastern and southern parts of the country; *C. m. vansoni* is found in Ngamiland and Chobe Districts (its type specimen was collected in Zweizwei in Chobe National Park). **Habitat:** Occurs in a variety of woodlands, including broad-leaved and acacia; also in gardens. **Habits:** Seen in small flocks, often with other small seedeaters, foraging on the ground. Frequently seen drinking at water holes. It makes a cup-shaped nest in interior of tree canopy. **Conservation:** Least Concern.

YELLOW CANARY *Crithagra flaviventris*

Setswana: mo.ragane

14 cm (5 ½ in). **Identification:** Robust canary with relatively small bill. Male has bright yellow underparts and olive-yellow upperparts. Female is streaked grayish brown above and buffy yellow below and has a yellow rump. Botswana birds all belong to *C. f. damarensis*, the yellowest of the southern African subspecies. Yellow-fronted Canary, which has bold facial markings, overlaps little in range. Since these birds occur in pairs, the marked plumage coloration difference between the sexes in the Yellow Canary further separates it from Yellow-fronted. **Call:** Series of high-pitched trills and whistles. **Status:** Resident, breeding. **Abundance:** Common to abundant. It is the common canary of the Kalahari. **Habitat:** Found in arid, open Kalahari tree and bush savanna. **Habits:** Occurs in pairs; seen on the ground and in low trees, and regularly at water holes. It builds a cup-shaped nest in shrub foliage. **Conservation:** Least Concern.

BLACK-THROATED
CANARY
C. a. atrogularis

male

female

YELLOW-FRONTED
CANARY

breeding
male

female/
nonbreeding male

adult
female

YELLOW
CANARY
C. f. damarensis

adult
male

juv.

BUNTINGS Emberizidae

Buntings are small seedeaters with short, conical bills. Most have striking head patterns with alternating black and white stripes. They have streaked, cryptically colored upperparts and plain underparts. Botswana has four species of the genus *Emberiza*. Granivorous, they feed on the ground in a horizontal, crouched posture, scratching for seeds with relatively large feet. They are monogamous and are solitary nesters.

LARK-LIKE BUNTING *Emberiza impetuani*

15 cm (6 in). **Identification:** Pale brown bunting, rather nondescript. It lacks the characteristic head pattern of other buntings. From a distance, a rufous wing panel can be discerned. It has a buffy supercilium, and a variable pale patch on the ear coverts, but a close-up view is needed to see the latter. **Call:** Repetitive canary-like song. **Status:** Resident, breeding. Breeds opportunistically year-round, but egg-laying mainly occurs from February to April. **Abundance:** Uncommon to locally abundant. The species is highly nomadic, and large irruptions have been recorded. **Habitat:** Occurs in semiarid Kalahari tree and bush savanna, often on dry, open pans. **Habits:** Gregarious; flocks—sometimes numbering more than 50 birds—feed in hunched position on the ground in bare or short-grass areas. Comes to water to drink. Breeding male sings from low perch. The species makes a cup-shaped nest on the ground. **Conservation:** Least Concern.

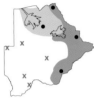

CINNAMON-BREASTED BUNTING *Emberiza tahapisi*

Setswana: kwabebe

15 cm (6 in). **Identification:** Small brown bunting with rich cinnamon underparts and striking black-and-white head markings. Folded wings are dark brown and black, with white edges to feathers creating scalloped appearance. Male has more contrastingly marked head than female. **Call:** Almost cricket-like *tee-trrr, chirri-chee*, repeated. **Status:** Resident, breeding. Numbers are supplemented during summer by intra-African migrants, also breeding. **Abundance:** Common. **Habitat:** Occurs on rocky outcrops and stony areas on lightly wooded hillsides, mainly in eastern hardveld. **Habits:** Pairs or small flocks occur on rocky substrate, foraging on the ground. Alternative name "Rock Bunting" is indicative of its habitat preference. It builds a cup-shaped nest on the ground. **Conservation:** Least Concern.

CAPE BUNTING *Emberiza capensis*

16 cm (6 ¼ in). **Identification:** Brown bunting with a black bill, white throat, and pale gray underparts, the combination of which is diagnostic among buntings. Rufous wings contrast with grayish back. The head is striped but less boldly than that of Cinnamon-breasted Bunting. The subspecies *E. c. limpopoensis* occurs in Botswana. **Call:** Loud *chip-chip-chip-CHE-chip*, rising in volume and dropping at end. **Status:** Resident; no breeding records from Botswana. **Abundance:** Rare. The bulk of the population occurs beyond the borders of the country; its range just reaches southeastern Botswana but there are very few records. **Habitat:** Occurs in shrublands on rocky slopes. **Habits:** A confiding species, usually seen in pairs feeding on the ground. **Conservation:** Least Concern.

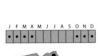

GOLDEN-BREASTED BUNTING *Emberiza flaviventris*

Setswana: thagapitse

16 cm (6 ¼ in). **Identification:** Yellow throat, golden-orange breast, and striking black-and-white head make this species unmistakable. Bicolor bill (gray upper mandible, yellow lower) apparent at close quarters. Female is paler than male. Botswana birds belong to the pale subspecies, *E. f. kalaharica* (described from a type specimen collected at Tsotsoroga Pan in Chobe National Park). **Call:** Variety of whistles, such as *weechee-weechee-weechee* and *sweecher-sweecher-sweecher*. Also a characteristic *zzhrrr*. **Status:** Resident, breeding. **Abundance:** Common to abundant. **Habitat:** Occurs in open broad-leaved and mixed woodlands. **Habits:** Pairs and small flocks forage on the ground for seeds. Drinks daily at water holes in arid areas. Nest is an open cup, placed in a small shrub. **Conservation:** Least Concern.

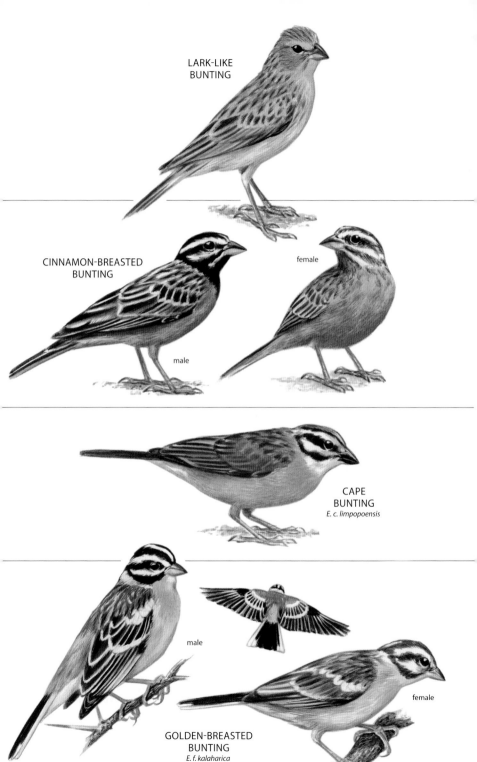

LARK-LIKE
BUNTING

CINNAMON-BREASTED
BUNTING

female

male

CAPE
BUNTING
E. c. limpopoensis

male

GOLDEN-BREASTED
BUNTING
E. f. kalaharica

female

383

Appendix of Additional Species

The following species were added to the Botswana National List while this book was in production:

RED-NECKED BUZZARD *Buteo auguralis*

38 cm (15 in). **Identification:** Small buzzard with rufous head and neck. Adult has rufous chest, white belly with dark spots, and rufous tail. Immature has mostly white underparts with a few dark brown spots on the belly and flanks, and looks similar to immature Forest Buzzard (*Buteo trizonatus*). Could easily be overlooked among the numerous Common Buzzards present in summer, although only superficially similar to that species. **Status:** Visitor from central and western Africa, nonbreeding. It is resident as far south as central Angola, and dispersing immatures are likely to reach Botswana occasionally. **Abundance:** Rare. First recorded in Chobe National Park by Peter McCalmont in July 2014 (record confirmed in late 2014). Second record from Kasana Forest Reserve in January 2015. **Conservation:** Least Concern. **General:** Immatures are more likely to be sighted than adults; sightings should be substantiated by a rarity report and photographs, if possible.

PIED WHEATEAR *Oenanthe pleschanka*

14 cm (5 ½ in). **Identification:** A distinctive species unlike any other wheatear found in Botswana. Male breeding plumage is strikingly pied, but only a nonbreeding bird has been recorded to date. Nonbreeding adult has pale supercilium, dark face, ear coverts, and throat, and white underparts with a trace of buff on the breast. **Status:** Vagrant from the Palearctic. Migrating individuals do not usually reach as far south as southern Africa. **Abundance:** Rare. A single bird was seen and photographed by Richard du Toit in the Kalwezi Valley in Chobe National Park in December 2014. **Conservation:** Least Concern. **General:** Any future sightings should be substantiated by a rarity report and photographs, if possible.

The following species are likely to occur in Botswana in the future:

GREATER SPOTTED EAGLE *Clanga clanga*
CARDINAL QUELEA *Quelea cardinalis*
BLUE QUAIL *Excalfactoria adansonii*
BLACK-RUMPED BUTTONQUAIL *Turnix nanus*
WHITE-THROATED BEE-EATER *Merops albicollis*
RED-CAPPED CROMBEC *Sylvietta ruficapilla*
NORTHERN WHEATEAR *Oenanthe oenanthe*

References

Borello, Wendy D., and Remigio M. Borello. *Birds of Botswana: An Annotated Working Bibliography, 1835 - 1995*. South Africa: Russel Friedman Books CC, 1997.

Chittenden, Hugh, David Allan, and Ingrid Weiersbye. *Roberts Geographic Variation of Southern African Birds*. Cape Town: The John Voelcker Bird Book Fund, 2012.

Cole, Desmond T. *Setswana – Animals and Plants*. Gaborone: The Botswana Society, 1995.

Davies, Greg. "A disputed Botswana specimen of melodious lark *Mirafra cheniana* (Aves: Alaudidae), revisited." *Annals of the Ditsong National Museum of Natural History* 1 (2011): 171-179.

Gill, Frank and David Donsker. 2014. IOC World Bird List (v 4.3). Downloaded from http://www.worldbirdnames.org.

Oake, Ken. "Observations of Birds Breeding in Botswana." Unpublished report, last modified 2014.

Peacock, Faansie. *Chamberlain's LBJs*. Pretoria: Mirafra Publishing, 2012.

Penry, Huw. *Bird Atlas of Botswana*. Pietermaritzburg: University of Natal Press, 1994.

Skinner, Neville J. "The breeding seasons of birds in Botswana I: Passerine families." *Babbler* 29-30 (1995): 9-23.

Skinner, Neville J. "The breeding seasons of birds in Botswana II: Non-passerine families (sandgrouse to woodpeckers)." *Babbler* 31 (1996): 6-16.

Skinner, Neville J. "The breeding seasons of birds in Botswana III: Non-passerine families (ostrich to skimmer)." *Babbler* 32 (1997): 10-23.

Tarboton, Warwick. *Roberts Nests & Eggs of Southern African Birds*. Cape Town: The John Voelcker Bird Book Fund, 2011.

Species Index

About the Author

Peter Hancock is a field biologist with a consuming interest in Botswana's fauna and flora. His work as a conservationist has taken him to virtually every corner of the country over the past 25 years. He is a compulsive collector of information on all aspects of Botswana's natural history and maintains comprehensive databases on a wide range of taxa. In his spare time he enjoys photographing and writing about Botswana's wildlife, and has published books and popular articles on a range of topics for both local and international audiences. He lives in Maun, Botswana.

About the Artist

Ingrid Weiersbye is an artist and naturalist whose lifelong specialty has been the painting and study of birds as a subject matter. *Birds of Botswana* is the latest of several southern African field guides she has illustrated in recent years. Ingrid's interests and enthusiasm extend to all aspects of the natural world—something instilled by her upbringing in the wilder areas of Zimbabwe. She works from her studio in Kwazulu-Natal, South Africa, and travels extensively (particularly in Africa) in pursuit of these Interests.